STO

ACPL ITEM
DISCARDED

Y0-AAI-806

The Cult of the Dead in a Chinese Village

Emily M. Ahern. "The best study of Chinese ancestor worship yet produced. It will mark a new stage in the study of the subject."—*Maurice Freedman.* A complex and pervasive form of ancestor worship, the cult of the dead reveals the basic design of society in the Taiwanese village of Ch'inan, reflecting personal relationships, geographical, social, and political divisions, and the villagers' world view. Illustrated. $10.00

Illness and Shamanistic Curing in Zinacantan

AN ETHNOMEDICAL ANALYSIS. *Horacio Fabrega, Jr. and Daniel B. Silver.* The most comprehensive and detailed work yet accomplished in the new field of medical anthropology, this study focuses on how a Mayan community views illness and how it organizes itself in respect to treatment. Much attention is given to the social and psychological characteristics of the native shamans who control nearly all medical practice in the community as well as a substantial part of religious ritual. $10.95

Japanese Economic Growth

TREND ACCELERATION IN THE TWENTIETH CENTURY. *Kazushi Ohkawa and Henry Rosovsky.* This study, which emphasizes the dramatic growth of the Japanese economy since World War II, attempts to fit Japan's experience into a historical growth model of the type familiar to economists. The authors establish the basic pattern of Japan's 20th-century growth and consider individual aspects of this growth in detail, concluding with a look at Japan's economic future. $15.00

 Stanford University Press

New books on important subjects:

PARTY AND FACTION IN AMERICAN POLITICS: THE HOUSE
OF REPRESENTATIVES, 1789-1801 *by Rudolph M. Bell.*
Vast new strata of information are uncovered, and unsuspected
coalitions revealed. This quantitative analysis of actual voting records will revise simplistic views
of our government's formative years. *$13.95*

BEGINNINGS

AMERICA FOR AMERICANS: ECONOMIC NATIONALISM
AND ANGLOPHOBIA IN THE LATE NINETEENTH CENTURY
by Edward P. Crapol. A strident economic nationalism called for
commercial independence and for trade domination in this hemisphere. It intensified animosity
for England throughout America. "An important contribution. . ."—*Library Journal $12.50*

ANGLOPHOBIA

THE UNBOUNDED FRAME: FREEDOM AND COMMUNITY
IN NINETEENTH CENTURY AMERICAN UTOPIANISM
by Michael Fellman. Intellectuals of many persuasions sought to
invent perfect communities, then disagreed on basic concepts. Analyzes utopian thought from
Brisbane through Howells. "An important contribution to American intellectual history."
—*Merle Curti $10.00*

COMMUNES

ART AND POLITICS: CARTOONISTS OF THE *MASSES* AND
LIBERATOR by Richard Fitzgerald. The period from 1911 to
1924 was an uneasy time. Radical publishing flourished in America.
Fitzgerald examines five cartoonists and their work, for this study-in-depth: art in service of
ideology. 60 illustrations. *$14.50*

RADICALS

ROOTS OF MARYLAND DEMOCRACY, 1753-1776 *by David
Curtis Skaggs.* A widespread poor tenantry, denied vote or office,
surged in democratic revolution against the gentry leadership.
Skaggs' conclusion is clear: many Marylanders fought the War of the Revolution primarily to
change prevailing structures within the colony. *$12.00*

MARYLANDERS

EBONY KINSHIP: AFRICA, AFRICANS, AND THE AFRO-
AMERICAN *by Robert G. Weisbord.* Black nationalism in America
grows out of a 150-year search for black dignity, identity, prosperity.
This book documents that search. Foreword by Floyd B. McKissick. "A skilled survey of black
nationalist movements. . . .Worthwhile reading, especially since material on. . .the topic is so
rare."—*Library Journal $10.95*

RACIAL PRIDE

Available from **GREENWOOD PRESS**

a division of Williamhouse-Regency Inc.

51 Riverside Avenue, Westport, Connecticut 06880

Kindly mention THE ANNALS *when writing to advertisers*

New from Columbia

EUROPEAN SECURITY AND THE ATLANTIC SYSTEM

WILLIAM T. R. FOX AND WARNER R. SCHILLING, EDITORS

A collection of essays prepared for an Institute of War and Peace Studies project on problems of European security, particularly as they relate to the progress made by the North Atlantic countries in the field of arms control.

Institute of War and Peace Studies, Columbia University
$10.00

AMERICAN ARMS AND A CHANGING EUROPE

Dilemmas of Deterrence and Disarmament

WARNER R. SCHILLING, WILLIAM T. R. FOX, CATHERINE M. KELLEHER, AND DONALD J. PUCHALA

A companion volume to *European Security and the Atlantic System*, this book analyzes the problems and choices the United States will face in the decade ahead in the pursuit of three goals: European security, strategic security, and arms control. *Institute of War and Peace Studies, Columbia University*
$12.00 cloth; $3.95 paper

SOVIET-THIRD WORLD RELATIONS

Volume One: Soviet-Middle East Relations

CHARLES B. MCLANE

A comprehensive and detailed survey of the Soviet Union's political, economic, and cultural relations with the countries of the Middle East since 1955. This is the first of a three-volume series sponsored by the Central Asian Research Centre in London.
$15.00

AID TO RUSSIA 1941–1946

Strategy, Diplomacy, the Origins of the Cold War

GEORGE C. HERRING, JR.

A re-examination of the evolution of American policies for lend-lease and aid to Russian reconstruction within the context of the formation, development, and subsequent breakdown of the wartime alliance between the United States and the Soviet Union.

Contemporary American History Series
$15.00

COLUMBIA UNIVERSITY PRESS

Address for orders: 136 South Broadway, Irvington, New York 10533

VOLUME 409 SEPTEMBER 1973

THE ANNALS

of The American Academy *of* Political
and Social Science

RICHARD D. LAMBERT, *Editor*
ALAN W. HESTON, *Assistant Editor*

INCOME INEQUALITY

Special Editor of This Volume
SIDNEY WEINTRAUB
Professor of Economics
Wharton School of Finance and Commerce
University of Pennsylvania
Philadelphia, Pennsylvania

PHILADELPHIA

© 1973, by THE AMERICAN ACADEMY OF POLITICAL AND SOCIAL SCIENCE
All rights reserved

Library of Congress Catalog Card Number 73–78959

The articles appearing in THE ANNALS are indexed in the *Reader's Guide to Periodical Literature,* the *Book Review Index,* the *Public Affairs Information Service Bulletin,* and *Current Contents: Behavioral, Social, and Management Sciences.* They are also abstracted and indexed in *ABC Pol Sci, Historical Abstracts* and/or *America: History and Life.*

International Standard Book Numbers (ISBN)

ISBN 0-87761-168-8, vol. 409, 1973; paper—$3.00
ISBN 0-87761-169-6, vol. 409, 1973; cloth—$4.00

Issued bimonthly by The American Academy of Political and Social Science at Prince and Lemon Sts., Lancaster, Pennsylvania 17604. Cost per year for individuals: $12.00 paperbound; $16.00 clothbound. Institutions: $15.00 paperbound; $20.00 clothbound. Add $1.00 to above rates for membership outside U.S.A. Second-class postage paid at Lancaster and at additional mailing offices.

Editorial and Business Offices, 3937 Chestnut Street, Philadelphia, Pennsylvania 19104.

CONTENTS

1771051

BOOK DEPARTMENT

UNITED STATES

ECONOMICS

SOCIOLOGY

PREFACE

Earnings discrepancies vex our society. The main bout involves income shares. Surfacing in many forms and wearing countless disguises, the elements of the conflict are often obscured. Dissents, defined superficially in other terms, are never far from absolute, and relative, income underpinnings.

A century ago, Karl Marx conjectured that the imbalance between workers and capitalists would usher in the revolution. Poverty of the work force would sound the death knell for private property. While he erred in predicting chronic grief for labor, even in our quasi-affluent age the distributive unevenness remains critical, affecting our politics, economic policy and social structure.

The ubiquity of the income confrontation can be illustrated in a variety of contexts. Unemployment: the jobless want income, work and enjoyment of the fruits of their participation in production; they wish to relieve the frustration of idleness with the dignity of employment. Inflation: the distortion in income status, as various earnings lag behind prices, is a festering sore creating public unrest. Farm and food prices: farmers want higher prices, while consumers insist on lower sums —a classic pocketbook battle. Rent control: tenants and landlords are locked in an adversary contest over income benefits. Racism: jobs, especially better jobs, constitute a vital ingredient in the Black protest; the income dimension is overwhelming. Welfare: recipients clamor for more generous pay-outs; taxpayers usually reject the demands. Women's liberation: income subordination and pay discrimination are prominent factors in the movement. Taxes: the perennial controversy over footing the bill establishes the proposition that the best tax is one on somebody else. Devaluation: irreparable losses have been inflicted on everyone contemplating foreign travel or purchasing imported wares.

The list can be lengthened indefinitely. Alarm at Senator McGovern's intention to alter relative incomes undoubtedly aborted his election chances in 1972. The Nixon victory was interpreted as a mandate to preserve the income status quo. Even "crime in the streets" contains an income aspect; behind the menace to civilized living, the violence entails a wealth transfer from the law-abiding to the lawless.

In opening up their pages to the inequality theme, the editors of THE ANNALS invited a lively intellectual and practical controversy on an emotionally charged subject on which predilections often determine the viewpoint. In subsequent pages, eighteen experienced and distinguished economists have prepared essays that illuminate the complex ramifications of the issue.

With two exceptions, the contributors were entirely free to explore the subject in their own way. Neither topics nor facets of the main theme were assigned. Considering the competence and eminence of the authors, it was surmised that whatever they chose to emphasize would be significant, revealing a consensus or a diversity of opinion in small, or large, respects. Furthermore, it was expected that the aspects to which the authors addressed themselves would yield substantial clues to the ultimate controversial battleground. Validation of this purpose has been abundantly realized.

Rather than box them into groups which would fail to encompass, in many cases, the range and perspective of the contribution, the articles are listed alphabetically by author. A sentence or two may provide an inkling of their content.

Assaying some nebulous dimensions of inequality, Professor Boulding demolishes any illusion that income sharing promises a simple and enduring solution. Conflicts breed inequality; social harmony can mitigate extreme disparities. After some reflections on distributive norms, Professor Bronfenbrenner draws upon the philosopher John Rawls and discusses equity and equality concepts. The equality objective is discerned by Professor Weisskopf as a philosophical quest requiring economic implementation; he surmises that ecological constraints on growth foreshadow more equality in the future.

Professor Johnson perceives inequality as a by-product of the operation of the economic system in providing opportunities for free choice and self-fulfillment. Income dispersion is attributed to the capacity of individuals in exploiting opportunities, rather than to inherited property.

Tracing the recent War on Poverty, Professor Thurow is less than sanguine on public receptivity to equality programs. Professor Smolensky affirms the lack of support by the nonpoor, despite the heavy costs inherent in the flight to the suburbs generated, in large part, by income inequality. Undaunted by the pessimism, Professor Fusfeld advances a legislative package for lifting minimum wages, improving education and providing tax aids for those below the poverty line.

Professor Lampman elaborates the virtues and defects of the usual measures of inequality, stressing the variety of concepts to answer diverse queries. Performance and process indices are contrasted to demarcate the economic game from its outcome. Professor Hamilton, upon request, surveys income by sex in the Chicago region and reports that female incomes in several occupations were 10 to 17 percent below male earnings.

Professor Davidson, in diagnosing the premise that income inequality fosters growth—which the younger Keynes elicited from the classicists—rejects the proposition as anachronistic, although he concedes that greater equality would impose extra strains on monetary management. Coincidentally, a similar idea in the older Keynes has intrigued Professor Minsky. Against the prevailing private investment strategy for full employment related to rentier savings, he advocates a public employment design to avert boom-bust episodes and to iron out inequalities.

Professor Scitovsky emphasizes that the provision of public services has been a modest leveller, so far. A fascinating point is that the statistics understate inequality; for, those with higher earnings derive more pleasure from work. The notion may help decipher the puzzle of widespread unhappiness, despite abundant possessions.

Three of the contributors fastened on the relation of education to income inequality. Nobel prize winner Jan Tinbergen, using Netherlands data, appraises the prospect for income improvement through schooling. His judgment is that a slow, intergenerational process is involved. The joint article by Messrs. Staaf and Tullock develops the striking and disconcerting theme that outlays for higher education actually foster inequality. Professor Stiglitz also ponders the easy optimism on education as the gateway to riches; distributive aspects of alternative financing routes are briefly evaluated.

Professor Nell criticizes the orthodox marginal productivity theory of distribution as implausible, unconvincing and objectionable in its moral and social overtones. Key concepts emanate from the recent "reswitching" controversy in the specialized literature. The argument, though concise and analytic, can repay close study.

Professor Kravis was requested to concentrate on inequality in the world economy. Findings will be enlightening and shocking to anyone looking out beyond our national borders.

Reading the collection might confirm the platitude that economists disagree. It is right that they should do so in a matter as sensitive and complex as income redistribution; understanding and policy must end as composite, and compromise, in a subject so profound and diffuse, wherein objective policy tests are elusive and even inconclusive, when they can be devised. For, what we hope to do is to influence the future on the basis of data that belong to the past. Caution in taking big and irreversible steps may constitute the finer wisdom for the evolutionary society.

The essays sift the crucial issues. Some earlier defenses of inequality have toppled beyond possible revitalization, thus, cannot confuse future discussion. If the productivity thesis supporting inequality is fatally flawed, some bias sustaining the mechanistic income outcome may be permanently obsolete and institutional amelioration may win new adherents. Nevertheless, logic and judgment in forging policy will still be in season.

The debate will move on. The symposium should make it possible to identify the ultimate obstacles in the intermittent proposals for social reform in income allocation.

SIDNEY WEINTRAUB

Equality and Conflict

By Kenneth E. Boulding

ABSTRACT: The pursuit of equality is likely to be frustrated unless there is better knowledge about the processes in society which increase or diminish it. There are severe conceptual difficulties in defining inequality; ultimately, they always involve some sort of evaluation, especially in regard to those social variables which are subject to strong evaluation, such as status, income and virtue. Equality must be defined in dynamic, whole-life terms. Cross-sectional measures at a moment of time are extremely misleading. If all young people were poor and all old people were rich, society would look very unequal; however, everyone might have equal income over their whole life. The major dynamic process which produces inequality is inheritance not only of capital, but of culture and status. Inheritance laws and the grants economy, especially the tax system, are important in the dynamics of equality. Historically, much inequality is created by conquest and revolution. What tends to produce equality is a rise of integrative power—that is, the development of an extended and intense sense of community. This is most visible in the national state. World equality depends on the development of a sense of world community.

Kenneth E. Boulding has been Professor of Economics at the University of Colorado since 1967; and has held teaching appointments at the University of Edinburgh, Colgate University, Fisk University and the University of Michigan. He has been active in the areas of general economic theory, economics and ethics and evolutionary theory. He served as President of the Society for General Systems Research (1957–1959), and President of the American Economic Association (1968). Currently, he is Director of the Program of Research on General Social and Economic Dynamics of the Institute of Behavioral Science, President of the Association for the Study of the Grants Economy and President-elect of the International Studies Association. Professor Boulding is author of about fourteen books, ranging from Economic Analysis (1941) to The Economy of Love and Fear: A Preface to Grants Economics (1973).

EQUALITY is a concept more preached about than it is researched. The preaching is not necessarily useless; it does serve to create images of a gap between the ideal and the real, without which there is no dynamics in society at all. Nevertheless, preaching is not enough. It can even be adverse to human welfare when it sets in motion false images of the real or unrealistic images of the ideal. In fact, unless the general dynamics of a system is well understood, action which is intended to narrow the gap between real and ideal may widen it. This is particularly likely to be the case where dissatisfactions are vague and the sources of dissatisfaction little understood. Under these circumstances, action to diminish dissatisfactions may easily increase them; improved knowledge of the dynamics of the system involved may be extremely rewarding. This is true especially of the pursuit of equality, which, in the absence of adequate understanding of what dynamic processes increase or diminish equality, can be a frustrating and self-defeating quest.

DEFINING EQUALITY

At the outset, one of the problems which must be faced is that any measure of inequality has to be contrived. Equality and inequality are crude perceptions of a rather vague property of sets. Thus, suppose one takes the simplest example, that of sets of numbers. Equality in this case is identity. The set $\{5, 5, 5, 5, 5\}$ is obviously equal. The set $\{3, 4, 5, 6, 7\}$ is clearly more equal than the set $\{1, 3, 5, 7, 9\}$. But is the set $\{2, 2, 2, 2, 17\}$—call it Case I —more or less equal than the set $\{1, 1, 1, 7, 15\}$—call it Case II? It would be interesting to do a series of psychological experiments on people's perceptions of equality; I regret that, if any have been done, I am not familiar with them.

One can order the last two cases, of course, if a statistical measure of inequality is adopted. There are, however, a number of possible competing measures. For each of the following measures perfect equality equals 0; the larger the index, the more unequal the set.

(1) One might simply take the measure E_1 as the difference between the smallest and the largest numbers, divided, perhaps, by the sum of the numbers—which would mean that Case II ($E_1 = 14/25 = .56$) is more equal than Case I ($E_1 = 15/25 = .60$).

(2) One might take the sum of the absolute differences from the mean, regardless of sign, and divide this by the sum of the numbers—both cases are then equally equal, the measure in each case being $E_2 = 24/25 = .96$.

(3) One might take the more familiar standard deviation, which is the square root of the sum of the squares of the deviations from the mean, divided by the sum—in this instance, Case II ($E_3 = .49$) is more equal than Case I ($E_3 = .54$).

(4) One might take a standard measure, the Gini index. By taking the cumulative distribution, subtracting this from the cumulative equal distribution, adding these deviations and dividing by the sum of the cumulative equal distribution, the Gini index would be calculated. (Shown in table 1.) Case I is now the more equal.

The results for all of the four measures are summarized in Table 2. There is an almost indefinite number of possible measures, some which have achieved a

TABLE 1
GINI INDEX

	CASE I					TOTAL	CASE II					TOTAL
Distribution	2	2	2	2	17	25	1	1	1	7	15	25
Cumulative distribution	2	4	6	8	25	45	1	2	3	10	25	41
Cumulative equal distribution	5	10	15	20	25	75	5	10	15	20	25	75
Difference	3	6	9	12	0	30	4	8	12	10	0	34

Gini Index $\qquad E_4 = \dfrac{30}{75} = .40 \qquad\qquad E_4 = \dfrac{34}{75} = .45$

respectable status in statistics and some which have not. Short of a very extensive series of psychological experiments —and it is highly probable that these will be inconclusive—it is hard to pick out any particular measure as clearly superior to all the others.

When sets of real objects or persons are considered, the problem of defining inequality, or even equality, becomes much more difficult. If the objects are not identical, some property of the objects must be singled out which can be represented either by a number or by some qualitative magnitude and which can be arranged on a scale—such as: very small, small, medium, large, very large. For instance, a single human being can be identified according to: height, weight, pulse rate, metabolism, skin color, hair color, eye color and so on, almost indefinitely. Some characteristics, such as height, can be expressed by cardinal numbers; here, if one agrees on a measure of equality, one

can presumably decide how equal in height any particular set of human beings is. The concept of equality, or inequality, becomes more difficult as the characteristics become more qualitative. Skin color, perhaps, can be measured by light reflection and graded on a scale; thus, one group might be equally dark, another equally light and another mixed or unequal. The concept of inequality seems less and less appropriate in terms of these qualitative variables. Is a group consisting half of blue-eyed people and half of brown-eyed people unequal? Here, the concept of similarity seems to have some meaning, but equality does not. Similarity may imply equality, but dissimilarity does not necessarily imply inequality.

QUALITATIVE VALUES AND EQUALITY

This raises the interesting question: does the concept of equality, or inequality, always imply some evaluation of the variable in question? For someone

TABLE 2
FOUR COMPETING MEASURES OF PERFECT EQUALITY

MEASURE	PERFECT EQUALITY	CASE I	CASE II
E_1	0	.60	.56*
E_2	0	.96	.96
E_3	0	.54	.49*
E_4	0	.40*	.45

* More equal.

who regards blue eyes as better than brown eyes, a group with mixed blue and brown eyes would be unequal: the blue-eyed people would be somehow higher and the brown-eyed people, lower. The same would be true, of course, for anyone who valued brown eyes more than blue eyes. The concept of inequality creeps in when differences are evaluated and put on some kind of graded scale. This principle may not apply to simple sets of numbers, although it is clear that when thinking of inequality—not simple heterogeneity or dispersal—one may be assuming, almost unconsciously, that large numbers are better, if one is thinking of "goods," or that small numbers are better, if one is thinking of "bads." Therefore, when a set of people is said to be unequal, there is an almost implicit assumption that they are being ranked according to some quantity being evaluated. The assumption is that they are not simply different. Even in the case of height, there is some implication that being tall may be better than being short—if people are regarded as unequal in height, instead of merely different.

It is not surprising that the property of equality, or inequality, becomes most important in the case of those variables where there are very strong evaluations, such as: status, wealth, income, health, longevity, creativity, productivity, criminality and virtue. The problem of the measurement of equality is not solved even when a number is assigned to each person and a measure of inequality in the set of numbers, which then substitutes for the set of persons, is agreed upon. If the set is expanded to include the whole life of the individuals concerned, cross-sectional measurements, as of a given moment or short period of time, become of very dubious value. Suppose a society existed in which all old people were rich and all young

people were poor, and all had an equal expectation of life. Then the inequality in either wealth or income might be very great on a cross-sectional basis, but each individual in the society might have exactly the same income over his whole life. The same might be true of status, if all young people had low status and all old people, high status.

No society has ever existed which conformed to this rule. Nevertheless, old people do tend to have higher wealth, incomes and status than young people, at least up to a certain point; this means that any cross-sectional measurements tend to overestimate the inequality. How much it is overestimated is extraordinarily hard to say, because it is most difficult to choose the total set over which to make comparisons when genuine inequality exists over time. Should it be all human beings who have ever lived? In such a case, there is very real inequality between those who lived earlier and were poor and those who lived later and were rich. Any kind of development creates inequality over time. It seems absurd to take all human beings who have ever lived as a frame of reference, but if one does not do that, then how does one limit the frame of reference? Should it be all the people who have lived since 1800, since 1700 or since some other century? In any exact form, the concept of equality, or inequality, simply dissolves as we try to take account of these intertemporal differences.

In effect, a great deal of discussion—especially preaching—on this subject assumes that men are angels and that we are discussing a society of immortal beings, in which case these intertemporal problems would not arise. However, the dynamics of the system cannot be discussed realistically without these intertemporal comparisons being made. It is the intertemporal dynamics of the system which determine whether equality of any variable is increasing or decreasing, either in terms of cross-sections at a moment of time or in terms of its temporal comparison over brief periods of time. Preaching about equality means preaching about the whole space-time continuum. This is rather daunting for a sensitive preacher.

DYNAMIC PROCESSES OF SOCIETY

In spite of these difficulties of definition and measurement, the perceptions of equality and inequality and the evaluation of these perceptions are important elements of the dynamic processes of human society, simply because of the pressures for action which are created by a perception of divergence between an actual situation and a supposedly attainable ideal. When inequality is perceived as illegitimate, strong forces are set in motion to change things—even though the resulting change may not always be in the direction of equality. In another paper I have described justice—and equality is a component of justice—as a "Holy Grail:" [1] in spite of the fact that it may never be found, the search for it is the excuse for a great deal of the organization of society. The unmeasurability and indefinability of inequality, therefore, does not prevent it from being an extremely important concept in the dynamics of society. Equality, like justice, is one of those perceptions of social life which is more important at the edges, than it is in the middle. It is almost impossible to define either equality or justice and, I think, quite impossible to come to any agreement on what the optimum of

1. Kenneth E. Boulding, "Social Justice as a Holy Grail: The Endless Quest" (Paper presented at the Contributions to a Just Society Conference, University of Waterloo, Ontario, May 1972). To be published in the conference volume.

either is; yet, we are aware of inequality, as we are of injustice. These extremes are important; indeed, the more extreme, the more important. Perceptions of gross inequality and gross injustice are prime movers in the legitimation or delegitimation of social institutions; hence, they are also prime movers in the dynamics of society. A society by no means always goes to the place for which it thinks it has a ticket. With different tickets—that is, with different perceptions of inequality, injustice and illegitimacy—it will go to different places.

The dynamic processes by which equality—however defined or measured —is increased or decreased in society are very imperfectly understood. No social science has produced a model which even remotely resembles the complex operations of the total dynamics of society in this respect. In any such model there would have to be two major systems: (1) inheritance and (2) life history. The system of inheritance determines the social net worth of a baby at birth in terms of: capital, family, language, cultural relations, status position and chances in life that the baby will inherit. A baby born into a rich family, living in a rich country—that is, well endowed with resources and institutions—and speaking a world language, has a much higher net worth at birth than a baby born into a poor family living in a poor country with a pathological culture and speaking a local language. The second baby has a very poor chance of living a life any better than that of its parents. The distributions of these net worths at birth is perhaps the most significant field over which equality should be measured.

Differences in inheritance, however, are the result of long dynamic processes. They reflect the accumulation of a long succession of life histories and inheritances. Therefore, we must study the second system, or that which happens to individuals in the course of their lives—particularly in regard to changes in net worth. Is the inheritance which an individual receives at birth conserved, dissipated or expanded? A society in which a preponderance of individuals dissipate their inheritance will decline, and total inheritance will shrink from generation to generation. A society in which the bulk of the individuals conserve and expand their inheritances —by saving, learning, improving their environment and accumulating capital, knowledge, skill and healthy cultural patterns—will find that its inheritance grows with each generation. The inequality in the world is primarily a result of its history of inheritance over the significant past.

The distribution of inheritance is also very significant. Inheritance must not simply be thought of as that which a person leaves when he dies; rather, it is that which he distributes to others over the whole course of his life—including, of course, everything he leaves when he dies. In the case of physical capital, it is clear that gifts have much the same kind of status as inheritance. The study of gifts has been neglected in economics until the recent revival of interest in it, under the heading of grants economics.[2] Gifts, again, may not be merely material things. They may be the gift of an idea, a literary work, a form of organization or a creative artwork. Whenever a person gives more to his environment than he takes from it, over the course of a lifetime, he has increased the inheritance of those who receive the gifts. Similarly, there may be negative gifts: a person may

2. See Kenneth E. Boulding, *The Economy of Love and Fear* (Belmont, Cal.: Wadsworth Publishing, 1973).

take more than he gives; an army may devastate a country. All gifts or grants are not equally legitimate; some may be regarded as highly illegitimate. Exploitation has to be defined as the giving of an illegitimate grant, for example, that of a slave to his master.

If total bequests—including the lifetime gifts of an individual—are spread widely over a large number of persons, inheritances will tend to become more equal. If bequests are concentrated on a single person or a few persons, inheritances become more unequal. A simple example of this is the difference between primogeniture and equal distribution of estates. This is what the *egalité* of the French Revolution was mainly about. Primogeniture is a device for preserving, and even for increasing, inequality. If the rich marry only each other, are infertile and leave their wealth to but the eldest child, wealth is concentrated and becomes more unequal. If the rich and poor intermarry, have a lot of children and distribute estates among them equally, this produces a dynamic process tending towards equalization.

The tax system, in the same way, can be an important agent in moving the dynamic process towards either equalization or concentration. Progressive income and inheritance taxes tend towards equality; regressive taxes, tax loopholes for the rich and absence of inheritance taxes tend towards inequality. Without any explicit model of this process, the parameters of society which carry it over the boundary line into increasing equality and those which carry it into increasing inequality are not easily determined. A careful study of these processes would seem a high priority research project for the next generation, if the demand for equality and justice is to produce any supply.

The role of conflict in increasing or diminishing inequality is crucial, although very complex. A simple, but very depressing, model would be one in which conflict creates inequality, especially if one side wins and the other side loses. The resulting inequality would lead to further conflict, and so on. We have here an unfortunate example of destabilizing feedback, which can increase both inequality and conflict until some limit is reached. Historically, conflict emerges as one of the major sources of inequality of inheritance. Virtually all depressed classes and minorities have originated at the time of some sort of conquest. The conquerors were given a superior status and inheritance, which they may have found easy to extend and conserve; the conquered were given a poor inheritance, which was hard to improve. Unfortunately, the principle: "To him that hath shall be given," has a good many examples; it is one of the systems increasing inequality. It is easier for the rich to save, than it is for the poor; it is easier for the powerful to conserve and expand their power, than it is for the powerless to increase what little power they have.

Almost invariably, minority problems in different parts of the world have some kind of past conquest in their history. Slavery is almost always the result of a conquest. The French Canadians in Canada, the Chicanos and Indians in the United States, the Catholics in Northern Ireland, the Bantu and the Asians in South Africa, the rural population in the Soviet Union, the Koreans in Japan, the Arabs in Israel, the caste system in India, the class structure in Britain and many other countries are all relics of past conquests which have created a self-perpetuating class structure. Revolutions seem a poor answer to this problem, because they also create a class structure of the conquerors and the conquered. There may be some replacement of one upper class by another, but revolutions often increase the power of the upper class at the same time that they change its personnel. We see this, for instance, in the Soviet Union where the upper echelons of the Communist Party have power far beyond that of the Czar and his aristocracy. They may be using power for more legitimate purposes, but this does not affect the fundamental fact of the concentration of power itself. It is ironic that even the American Revolution produced an essentially monarchical society in the United States; George III surely would have given his eye-teeth to have the powers of President Nixon and, perhaps, would have engendered a much more republican society in Great Britain, in spite of the titular monarchy.

Whether or not inequality produces conflict depends mainly on the degree to which inequality can be legitimated. There have been very few examples of successful revolutions. On the whole, the historical record is that those in power tend to stay in power; revolutions rarely change the inequality of the distribution of power in society. Whether the Chinese Revolution is an exception to this—which it may well be —only time can tell.

INTEGRATIVE POWER OF COMMUNITY

If conflict creates inequality, what then creates equality? A simple, and therefore no doubt inadequate, answer to this is the rise of, what I have called, integrative power. This takes place through: a rise in the sense of community; the identification of individuals with larger and larger reference groups; the creation of organizations which symbolize larger and larger communities, such as, the church and the national state; and in the development, therefore, of an overall grants economy which can distribute inheritances more and more widely. The tendency for "to him that hath shall be given" is hence offset. If there is any offset to the dismal feedback of conflict producing inequality, producing conflict, producing more inequality, producing more conflict, it is the benign feedback of community producing grants, producing community, producing more grants, producing more community. There are, however, limits to this process.

It is true that community produces grants. The largest grants are made in the most intense community, which is the family; the next largest, in the next most intense community, which is the national state. Some grants do not produce community, but create a sense of illegitimacy which is destructive to community. Grants, furthermore, are not the only things which produce community. Community is produced by poets, rhetoric, preaching and, especially, common experiences. For this reason, a common enemy has been so important in the production of communities, especially the national state. The United States was the creation of George III; Germany, of Napoleon. Because mankind as a whole has few common experiences and no common enemy—except itself—the community of mankind is very hard to achieve. As the immortal Pogo remarks: "We have met the enemy and he is us."

Another factor in the development of grants is the perception of their efficiency—that is, how much does my sacrifice increase your welfare? It is easy to get grants for disaster relief and rehabilitation, hard to get them for long-run development and for permanent redistributions of income. If I perceive that by giving up a dollar I

can benefit you one hundred dollars, I am quite willing to do it; if by giving up one dollar I only benefit you fifty cents, I am less willing to do it. Therefore, improving the perceived efficiency of grants is one of the major elements in the formation of community, and without community, there can be no equality.

The rise of public grants in the United States—from a small amount at the turn of the century to over 7 percent of the gross national product today—is a symbol of the rise of the sense of the national community. This has not been enough, however, to create much change in the relative distribution of income, partly because of the inefficiency of the granting process—a great many grants have gone to the rich, especially agricultural and educational subsidies—but also because there is a sense that the poor are not really part of even the national community. Only by visibly becoming members of the community will the poor gain integrative power, which is necessary for the achievement of redistribution. The very small threat power of the poor is significant only if it produces a trigger to raise integrative power. Non-violence —as in the case of Martin Luther King —is often much more effective than violence which easily destroys integrative power.

We have a long way to go before we achieve a world community and even an approximate world equality. The easy roads all lead the other way. Nevertheless, there is a road towards world community which can be discovered. To discover, and follow, it is a major priority of the next one hundred years.

Equality and Equity

By Martin Bronfenbrenner

Abstract: The terms equality and equity are widely confused. Despite their phonetic similarity and philological connections, they are quite distinct. The equality of a distribution of income or wealth is basically a matter of fact and is, therefore, basically objective. The equity of the same distribution is basically a matter of ethical judgment and is, therefore, basically subjective. The discussion attempts to avoid extraneous issues, such as whether the particular poor—at any time or place—are apt to be morally superior, or inferior, to the particular rich; and whether economic, as distinguished from ethical, maldistribution can cause, or has caused, economic depression. The paper begins with the valiant attempts by the marginal-utility economists of the turn of the century to frame an objective case for income equalization and with A. P. Lerner's later extension of this case. It then moves on to the rebuttals of conservative opponents. Three more recent attempts—under the headings of (1) interdependent utility functions, (2) limiting the domain of inequality and (3) John Rawls' recent theory of justice in generalized ethics—are then summarized. The discussion ends, however, on a skeptical note.

Martin Bronfenbrenner is Kenan Professor of Economics at Duke University and is currently Visiting Professor at Aoyama Gakuin University. He also teaches Japanese History. Prior to assuming his present post, Professor Bronfenbrenner taught at Roosevelt, Wisconsin, Michigan State, Minnesota and Carnegie-Mellon Universities. He is author of a treatise on Income Distribution Theory. *His nonacademic professional experience has been in the United States Treasury, the Federal Reserve System and in the far East.*

IN twenty-five years of teaching income distribution to budding economists, I have been struck both by the prevalence of confusion between the terms "equality" and "equity" among students and by my own inability to remedy this confusion. The confusion, if such it be, carries with it important ideological consequences. For if equality were indeed equity and equity, equality, the major normative issue of distribution theory would be reduced to a matter of definition and would be amenable to an obvious and simple solution.

DEFINITIONAL EXERCISES

Being neither a linguist nor a philologist, I cannot guess intelligently whether—and to what degree—the confusion of equality and equity in the English language is generally prevalent. Since the words have a common Latin root, one might expect confusion in most of the Romance languages, which are more directly and exclusively related to Latin than is English. Nor should anyone be surprised to find some confusion prevailing over a wider range, since ethical philosophers define commutative justice, or equity, precisely as the equal treatment of equal things or persons. On the other hand, in Japanese, the only non-European language with which I am at all acquainted, equality is *byōdō* and equity is *kōhei*.[1] There is active debate about their inter-

1. These words are related in that the same Chinese character forms the *byō* in *byōdō* and the *hei* in *kōhei,* but Japanese attach little significance to such relations—particularly when the character in question is a common one, as in this case. By itself, the character signifies a plain or plateau, and is also one of the most famous family names in early Japanese history. In compounds, it also appears in the words for peace, tranquility, a bargain, an average, and a steppe or prairie.

relations, but it proceeds unencumbered by verbal magic.

The distinction between commutative and distributive equity is at least as old as Aristotle's *Ethics*. We have already defined commutative justice as the equal treatment of equals. Distributive equity, on the other hand, is the appropriate treatment of unequals in view of the differences between them. This concept is not particularly helpful; in fact, it opens the Pandora's box of distributional issues—in American slang, the whole can of worms. At any rate, distributional equity is nonmechanical in principle. It implies that the distribution of income, wealth or whatever is being distributed will be in accordance with principles of justice; therefore, my personal view is that the concept of distributive equity is largely, if not completely, a subjective matter. This implies the impossibility, in principle, of objectively judging whether something called maldistribution exists in a given society and whether one distribution is better than another. Such a view annoys my twentieth century liberal friends and colleagues in both the American and the Japanese institutions where I have taught, because it denies the possibility of proving their views; they find no comfort in the converse proposition that these views cannot be disproved.

Distributional equality—as distinguished from equity—is a mechanical or statistical matter in a first approximation. When one talks about equal income or wealth per unit, problems arise as to the definition of the units considered: in the numerator, should one be interested in the flow of income or the stock of assets—wealth? What allowances should be made for fringe benefits, receipts in kind, social prestige? In the denominator, is the individual, the nuclear family or the ex-

3 1833 04357 5213

tended family the focus of interest?[2] May the number of units be augmented or diminished in such special circumstances as illness, age, handicaps, extraordinarily slow or fast depreciation of human capital? Problems also arise in any regime permitting private property in the means of production, in the weighting of incomes from manual labor, and nonmanual labor, and property involving varying degrees of uncertainty-bearing or managerial responsibility—inasmuch as some forms of income and wealth are more secure than others or involve smaller sacrifices of leisure. In principle, however, equality means what it says.

DODGING ISSUES: CLEARING THE AIR

To limit the scope of the discussion and to minimize entanglement in extraneous issues, I shall avoid—or evade—whole classes of important problems, usually by making special assumptions which I realize will be less than half true.

—I shall not be concerned with the truth or falsehood of Leo Durocher's law, "Nice guys finish last"—in pedantic jargon, that a man's moral worth, x, is correlated negatively with his income or wealth, y. At the same time, I shall avoid the opposite Social Darwinian assumption that x and y are correlated positively, which we might call Herbert Spencer's law.[3] Avoidance of both Durocher's and Spencer's hypotheses is tantamount to an implicit neutral assumption that x and y are independent of each other; thus, the identities of neither the rich nor the poor will affect the analysis.

—I shall be speaking of income and wealth almost interchangeably. This usage implies that wealth is simply income capitalized at a uniform real market rate of interest. In practice, property income is capitalized into physical capital at a systematically lower rate than that at which labor income is capitalized into human capital—for example, for security against a loan. Thus, the wealth position of the representative man with one thousand dollars of property income per unit of time is superior to that of a representative man with one thousand dollars of labor income during the same unit of time.

—I shall attempt no distinctions between the ethical bases of labor and property income. I shall take as given whatever may be the existing institutions of physical property and its inheritance [4] or, what

2. A nuclear family basically consists of one husband, wife and their natural children; in some cases, a small number of other close relatives by blood, marriage or adoption are included. An extended family combines a number of nuclear ones—commonly, the nuclear families of the extended family's head, his adult sons and his retired parents—especially if they live together in a common compound. In the American context, the definition of the family—the spending unit or the consumer unit—takes on practical importance in connection with the division of responsibility among working adult children, state social security agencies and private charity for the support of the aged poor.

3. In America, William Graham Sumner's law. A concise statement of Sumner's position is: "Let it be understood that we cannot go outside of this alternative: liberty, inequality, survival of the fittest, not—liberty, equality, survival of the unfittest. The former carries society forward and favors all its best members; the latter carries society backward and favors all its worst members," as cited in Arthur Schlesinger, Jr., "Ideas and the Economic Process," in *American Economic History,* ed. Seymour E. Harris (New York: McGraw-Hill, 1961), p. 14.

4. However, I shall assume that there are no property rights in other human beings,

amounts to the same thing, as though each unit's income were divided similarly between functional sources—despite all the evidence that, in fact, the relative importance of the property component in income increases with income size, once we pass the lower tail of the distribution.

—I shall not be discussing the validity of economic, as distinct from ethical, maldistributionism. Economic maldistributionism is the combination of two strongly-held beliefs about the operation of the macro-economy: (1) it suffers from constant or periodic tendencies to under-consumption and over-saving; (2) these tendencies are caused by a distributional flaw—too high a proportion of the national income going to the saving, and too little to the consuming, levels of society. They are not caused by any defect in the society's mechanisms of money and credit, by any tendency at all income levels to attempt hoarding of cash or by any undertaking of capital investment without sufficient attention to the demand for any eventual increment of consumption goods. To ignore this broad and important range of issues implies that either the doctrine of economic maldistributionism is wrong or, less restrictively, that its consequences are remediable within reasonably short periods by appropriate combinations of fiscal and monetary policy, without resort to redistribution.

—Finally, I shall not consider the possibility, or desirability, of remedying whatever degree of maldistribution one may believe to exist

that is, the absence of such institutions as slavery, indentured service or peonage.

in any society or the choice between alternative mixes of whatever redistribution methods there may be. In short, this paper will address maldistribution exclusively as a problem distinct from the closely related issue of redistribution within capitalist or socialist institutions and distinct from the choices between the two systems.

NORMS OF INCOME DISTRIBUTION

Economists owe to Jan Pen, of the Netherlands, the following twenty-one norms which dominate much current discussion of distributional equity.[5] Some of them are completely inconsistent with others, and many stress redistribution equally with maldistribution.

1. Distribution is irrelevant, because income is irrelevant. Already, there is too much consumption of the sort which makes people unhappy in the long run. Property is theft, and "income distribution" is an expression which legitimizes it.
2. All should get the same income with slight differentiation by size of family, age or other "elementary differences in wants" (compare with norm 12, below).
3. Incomes should be received only from work. Under this socialist norm, how to divide the total wage bill still remains a problem.
4. The rich are too rich. The top k percent—k equalling 1, 10?—should be stripped of all their surplus above some maximum level.
5. High and even medium incomes

5. Jan Pen, *Income Distribution* (London: Allen Lane Penguin, 1971), pp. 293–315. Our discussion is greatly condensed and omits the bulk of Pen's commentaries on individual norms.

are immoral so long as impermissible poverty exists. By impermissible poverty, Pen refers to incomes below the present fifteenth or twentieth percentile of the country's personal income distribution. A number of American writers prefer poverty lines at approximately 50 percent of the national median income.

6. Inequality is too great so long as some are rich while many workers cannot support their families decently. Pen interprets the papal encyclicals as expressing this position on behalf of the Catholic Church.

7. There should be progressive taxation in accordance with ability to to pay. Pen supports this position on marginal-utility grounds which, as we shall find in the next section, are somewhat shaky.

8. Money easily earned—which refers particularly to income from property and income by bequest—should be taxed more severely than other income.

9. Ill-gotten gains should be eliminated. Pen means those incomes from monopoly, graft and crime. He adds speculation to this list, but probably means only such speculative abuses as cornering markets, spreading false rumors and abusing preferential access to information.

10. Income distribution should be acceptable to all. This Utopian position Pen ascribes to Jan Tinbergen, in particular. For example, assume that income receivers A and B in the same community know each other's work and income. Income is justly distributed if neither A nor B is willing to change places with the other.

11. Nondiscrimination by race, religion, color or sex; equal pay for equal work; and equal access to preferable jobs (closely allied with norm 21, below).

12. To each according to his wants, at least his legitimized wants. When only "primary differences in wants" are recognized, this principle is egalitarian, as is the socialist "to each according to his need." When a sufficiently wide range of wants is legitimized, the same principle becomes antiegalitarian (compare with norm 2 above).

13. Support for the family as an institution, to include stress on family allowances, higher pay for married workers, provision of child care for working women and, also, unhampered inheritance.

14. More even distribution of property. Pen's suggestions involve minimal wealth to the value of a house or apartment of one's own, some multiple of one's annual income or a sum sufficient to finance one job at the going capital-labor ratio. Some American proposals would reserve corporate income tax receipts for equal distribution, to give every citizen a stake in corporate profits.

15. Reward for deserving professions and, also, for unusual merit in any field. This is the first of a series of norms which are antiegalitarian either in principle—as in this case—or in practice.

16. Reward for special effort (which has the same effect as norm 15, immediately above).

17. Leave people as you find them—or minimal interference with distribution, as determined by market forces. This would be

antiegalitarian in practice, at least in capitalist societies.

18. Expropriation of land rent and other forms of economic surplus, which can be taken over without reducing the stock of productive resources.

19. Suppression of wage-price spirals and other manifestations of cost-push inflation, for the particular benefit of pensioners and small renters.

20. Income distribution keyed to maximum production and growth (as with norm 17, probably anti-egalitarian in practice).

21. Equal opportunity for all at starting (once this is achieved, norm 17 and/or 20 should apply; compare also with norm 11, above).

Here, as elsewhere in his treatise, Pen is not adverse to making his own position clear and to indulging in occasional preaching on the side. He believes that norms 5, 7, 8, 10, 11, 14, 15, 16, 19, 20 and 21 are of the greatest practical importance. "With a little give and take," he argues, "these eleven principles can perhaps be combined into a practical policy" of income redistribution.[6] At the same time, Pen is careful to state his conclusions only as subjective preferences, with which he hopes most men of good will can agree, and never as objective or scientific laws of economics. For example, faced with members of the libertarian Mont Pélerin Society, who tend to emphasize norms 17 and 21 to the exclusion of most others, Pen could advance against them, as far as one can gather from his book, no argument more telling than the proportion of ethically nonpariah people whom these doctrines might leave stranded below admittedly arbitrary

poverty lines and amenable to crime and revolution.

UTILITY THEORIES

Economists have been accused of "irrational passion for dispassionate rationality," by John M. Clark, a distinguished member of the profession, himself. Certainly, most of them distrust policy prescriptions impervious to dispassionate rationalization—at least in their own field, which includes distribution theory. Almost equally, they distrust the late unlamented Dr. Josef Goebbels' injunctions "mit Ihrem Blut zu denken" and the currently chic New Left or existentialist nonrational ways of knowing. Kenneth E. Boulding has distinguished economists from business men in a quatrain with a similar moral:

Business men are rather dumb;
Their model is the rule of thumb;
Economists, it must be said,
Would much prefer the rule of head.

The utility revolution of the 1870s—against cost theories of value, of which the labor theory of value is best known—was later to serve two generations of Anglo-Saxon reformist economists as a scientific foundation for doctrines of egalitarianism and as a criticism of the capitalist order's maldistribution of the country's income. Perhaps the single most important group in this tradition were the Fabian-Socialists of England, who intellectually dominated the British Labour Party for much of this period.

I propose to distinguish two stages in the application of utility theory to maldistribution problems. The earlier of these stages culminated in Arthur C. Pigou's *Wealth and Welfare* (1913); in revised editions, the title became *The Economics of Welfare*. The later stage focused on Abba P. Lerner's *Economics of Control* (1944).

6. Ibid., p. 317.

The conventional Fabian of the late-Victorian or Edwardian vintage, insofar as he concerned himself with theoretical economics, attached overweening significance to utility. Albeit somewhat apologetically, he regarded utility as a measurable entity, such as temperature—not quite the same as height or weight because the zero point of utility remained arbitrary. Simultaneously, it measured both actual and anticipated satisfaction; the representative consumer, sufficiently rational and well-informed, would reduce the distinction between satisfaction *ex post* and *ex ante* to a quibble. Furthermore, utility was to be considered uniform by all individuals; thus, A's satisfaction, expressed in utils, could be added to B's, expressed in identical utils, and the sum interpreted as the social utility of—A and B's—society.[7] The supply side of any particular market—or, indeed, the total real income to be distributed—was sometimes taken as given and as largely independent of distribution. More often, the prospect of reduced supply and income—if one went too far with egalitarianism—remained in the background as an imprecise and fuzzy limit to the implications of the utility, or demand, side of theoretical analysis.

The implications of the utility, or demand, side were quite egalitarian and implied maldistribution in the highly nonegalitarian outcomes of free market processes. These egalitarian implications were particularly clear in public finance and taxation. If levying taxes to support general public expenditures were to be based upon any of three desired alternative principles: (1) equal sacrifice of utility by all individuals regardless of pretax income; (2) equiproportional sacrifice of utility by all individuals regardless of pretax income; or (3) minimum total sacrifice, leaving maximum utility "for the contemplation of God," it would follow that taxation should be progressive rather than proportional. Moreover, taxation would be more progressive if based upon principle three, than on principle two, than on principle one. Principle three—minimum sacrifice—implies, in fact, that the entire tax to be paid by the n richest taxpayers—the size of n depending upon only the cost of the expenditures to be financed.[8]

Passing on to the second stage of utility analysis, Lerner's contribution has been to generalize these conclusions. In particular, the interpersonal comparability assumption is replaced by a substantially weaker one. Lerner's assumption is that of any pair of individuals, A and B, the richer and the poorer are equally apt to have the higher utility function for income or wealth as a whole. The other assumptions, plausible and otherwise, are retained. Using his weaker assumption about interpersonal comparability, Lerner shows that, starting from any position other than equality of incomes between A and B, a utility gain from moving towards greater equality can be expected; a move in the opposite direction would result in a loss of utility.[9]

Lerner's probabilistic assumption of equal likelihood is plausible enough, if A and B come from disparate social

7. Alternatively, possible differences between the efficiencies of A and B as "pleasure machines" were ignored deliberately, less because of the difficulty of measurement than because, insofar as they existed, they were so largely consequent on past inequalities of distribution that allowances for them were clearly apologetics for the status quo.

8. If this essay were a textbook chapter, a proof of this proposition would be offered as an exercise.

9. A. P. Lerner, *Economics of Control* (New York: Macmillan, 1944), chap. 3, especially pp. 30–32. Compare Martin Brofenbrenner, *Income Distribution Theory* (Chicago: Aldine, 1971), chap. 5, sec. 5, pp. 99–101.

classes so that at least one of the pair has never had the opportunity for a career choice which might have put him in the other's position. But if A, the poorer of the two, is a chemistry teacher who might have been a physician in private practice and B is a successful physician who rejected a teaching career to enter medical school, it is rather likely that A prefers additional leisure, with a quieter and longer life, to the additional income of B; B has quite consciously made the opposite choice.[10] In such a case, Lerner's method cannot show any presumption of utility gain from equalizing the two incomes. All one can say in such cases is that, with no rule of interpersonal comparison, A gains from equalization at B's expense. Of the net effect upon the society, one can say nothing.

ANTIEGALITARIAN REBUTTALS

In their rebuttals, antiegalitarians have been quick to stress the restrictive nature of utility theory assumptions, especially the assumptions about interpersonal comparison of utilities and the possible—but unproven—production, supply and income effects of equalization. They go further and make a case for distributive laissez-faire, which Richard H. Tawney has called "the religion of inequality." Their case, insofar as it is independent of Social Darwinism and Herbert Spencer's law, concentrates upon criticizing particular

redistribution methods in particular societies. Perhaps the most pervasive of such arguments anticipates the decline of cultural values to the mass level, if income is redistributed. The example quoted below, by Paul Leroy-Beaulieu, the French liberal economist, has an 1880 dateline and transcends laissez-faire in the interests of maintaining or increasing inequality:

The real danger to civilized societies in the future is not that there will be too great an inequality of conditions but that there will be too little, and that in a few decades a dreary uniformity of incomes and ways of life will produce apathy and stagnation.[11]

Such fears were more plausible in homogeneous small country societies—such as nineteenth century Holland rather than nineteenth century France. They seem extreme in terms of America a century later with its regional, racial and, above all, occupational variations. In the American case, the white collar differential between the ordinary clerk and the ordinary manualist has turned negative; the skilled craftsman's income approximates the income of the average professional man; and the typical family farm requires substantial capital investment over and above the value of its land. However, the blue-collar and white-collar cultural differences and

---

10. Among the saddest cases of academia are the once idealistic, young men who chose peace and quiet, and/or interesting lives, at twenty but have changed their tastes at fifty; influenced, perhaps, by materialistic wives and children they find that it is too late to shift to better careers with higher incomes. Private professions and business also have their quota of embittered and dyspeptic rich men who regret the materialism of their youth and wish that they had chosen more meaningful occupations 30 years ago, rather than higher incomes.

11. Paul Leroy-Beaulieu, *Collectivism: A Study of Some of the Leading Social Questions of the Day*, trans. and abridged by Sir Arthur Clay (London: J. Murray, 1908). Unlike most writers in the aristocratic tradition, particularly in France, Leroy-Beaulieu does not in this passage make the unprovable claim that any, and every, mass or middlebrow culture is inherently inferior to the haute couture of contemporary aristocracy. Presumably, a society of Westchester Counties would lead, for Leroy-Beaulieu, to the same "apathy and stagnation" as a society of Harlems.

the rural and urban differences show no signs of disappearing, despite the homogenizing consequences of air transportation and nationwide mass communication.

Similarly, say the antiegalitarians, private charity and philanthropy will vanish if incomes are equalized. The arts, education and scholarships must then be supported by public bodies, governments or governmental corporations. A maldistribution of power over the public mind and taste would result, which would be more deleterious and monopolistic than the maldistribution of income and wealth which it was supposed to remedy. Such a line of argument assumes a highly centralized system of administration—patterned on Bismarck's Germany, Napoleon's France or Meiji Japan; it is less valid in a federal system, such as the American, or an international grouping with free migration, such as the European community. On the American academic scene, there seem to be many differences in intellectual climate among the public universities of different states, rival institutions funded by the same state, private institutions aimed at similar clienteles and private and public institutions with similar ambitions within a given state.

Another of their common claims is that redistributive taxation falls with greater severity upon those who are getting rich rather than upon those who are rich—that is, progressive income tax rates which prevent the accumulation of new fortunes may be but a minor inconvenience to those living on income from fortunes accumulated in the past. This is quite true, so long as major recourse for redistributive purposes is income, rather than wealth, taxes. The moral is not that redistribution be abandoned, but that less emphasis be put on income taxation. Two other

charges are also heard against redistribution by fiscal means—public expenditures, as well as taxes. (1) They cannot be enforced adequately, short of tyranny—maldistribution of power once more. (2) Redistribution by public expenditure, supplementing or subsidizing the expenditures of the poor, may indeed—even with nonprogressive taxation—take from the rich more than it returns to them. But it may give less to the poor than to the middle class, who administer the programs and live on these budgets. In other words, the largest net gainers may not be the poor, but the middle classes.[12] Neither of these charges has yet been quantitatively demonstrated for any sufficiently broad range of fiscal activity as a whole.

THREE RECENT CONTRIBUTIONS

In this subjective limbo, I believe, the discussion of distributive equity stood in 1966, when I wrote the "Maldistribution?" chapter of *Income Distribution Theory*. In the succeeding years, there have appeared, in English, several ambitious attempts to carry the subject further on an objective and rationalistic basis. While the philosopher's stone of scientific distribution theory continues to elude the economic geologists, some new research merits special consideration: (1) the intensive application of interdependent utility functions by economists affiliated mainly with the University of Virginia and the Urban Institute in Washington; (2) the approach called "limiting the

---

12. An alleged tendency of social expenditures to hurt both rich and poor for the benefit of the middle classes is sometimes called Director's law, named for the economist Aaron Director. Supporting evidence for Director's law is drawn largely from public higher education, patronized mainly by children of middle and upper class families and funds supplied mainly from sales taxes on the consumption of the poor.

domain of inequality," by James Tobin of Yale;[13] (3) the distribution-theory implications of the theory of justice, by the Harvard philosopher John Rawls.[14]

Interdependent utility functions

If there are n individuals and m goods in a community, the utility function of individual i may be written:

$$U_i = U_i(x_{1i}, x_{2i}, \ldots, x_{mi}, w_i);$$
$$(i = 1, 2, \ldots, n). \quad (1)$$

where the terms in x—all positive [15]—are quantities of each of the m goods and services demanded or supplied per period by individual i, and where w_i measures his wealth at the end of the period.

Nothing in equation (1) relates to any individual other than i. Each individual's satisfaction depends upon only his own income, wealth and supplies of productive services, with no reference whatsoever to the position of anyone else. The interdependent utility function, as in equation (2), below, complicates our jargon; however, it is nothing more than a realistic generalization of equation (1) to include the income, y_j, and the wealth, w_j, of individuals 1, 2, . . . , n other than i, himself $(i \neq j)$:

$$U_i = U_i(x_{1i}, \ldots, x_{ni}, w_i;$$
$$(y,w)_n)$$

$$(y,w)_1, \ldots, (y,w)_j, \ldots$$
$$(i \neq j) \quad (2)$$

Apostles of income redistribution believe that the representative individual's

utility, U_i, is related positively to the income and wealth position, $(y,w)_j$, of his fellowman, j, if i's original position is substantially higher than j's. Of course, exceptions are recognized in cases of personal, racial, religious or similar enmity. The motivation may be benevolence towards those poorer than oneself, indirect insurance to lessen the probability of violent crime against oneself and one's property at the hands of the poor or, an even less direct motivation, to secure higher incomes all round, if higher incomes for the poor elicit higher quantities or qualities of their labor for the community.[16] In addition, U_i may be related negatively to $(y,w)_j$, if j's original position is higher than i's. Here, again, the motivation may be malevolence or envy towards the rich or the liberation of one's family from pressure of keeping up with the Joneses. A sharp welfare economist can also point out—quite correctly—that in practice, one's attitudes towards both the rich and the poor have an undistinguishable effect upon one's demand for redistribution; either set of attitudes, without the other, can suffice to set off redistribution demands.

The public good is another technical-economic notion involving interdependence effects. A good—or, more usually, a service—falls in this category if the amount most, or all, individuals are willing to spend on the service conforms with utility functions such as (1)

13. James Tobin, "On Limiting the Domain of Inequality," *Journal of Law and Economics* 13 (October 1970).

14. John Rawls, *Theory of Justice* (Cambridge, Mass.: Belknap, 1971), especially chap. 2 and 5.

15. For example, an x term may be defined as the number of bedbugs, lice or roaches exterminated rather than "consumed."

16. On the quantitative side, there is an apparent conflict with the economics of the labor supply and the labor-leisure choice. Economic theory concludes that increased income from nonlabor sources will lower, not raise, an individual's labor supply—by increasing his demand for leisure; compare Bronfenbrenner, *Income Distribution,* chap. 9, sec. 6 and 11. This all assumes, however, a given and constant utility function, U. Redistributionists may plausibly hope that equality may shift utility functions in directions favorable to the labor supply.

or (2); this also depends significantly upon the amount they believe other individuals are spending on the same good or service. Education, charity, highways, defense, sanitation and police and fire protection are all cases for which an individual is willing to spend more as a member of a collectivity than he is willing to spend on his own. His willingness is motivated by the greater probability that his expenditures will help accomplish something of significance and the smaller probability that his neighbor will not obtain a free ride on the basis of these efforts.

The next step has been to combine these ideas and to treat income redistribution as a public good. As a simple model, a three-person society can be postulated. A and B are two brothers, perhaps one with a superior income position and the other with a superior wealth position. C, their aged, widowed mother, has no significant sources of income or wealth. It is easy to envisage A, B and C arranging to transfer income, and/or wealth, from the two brothers to their aged mother—or A and B working out an arrangement for the benefit of C. There are a number of such arrangements possible, all of which would improve the position of C, while subjectively leaving neither A nor B worse off than before—since C's welfare presumably enters significantly into their utility functions. The redistribution is a public good in this three-person society, since it improves the position of at least one member of the society while leaving the others no worse off than they were at starting. From the viewpoint of the welfare economist, the postredistribution position is superior to the preredistribution one. The second position is sometimes called Pareto-superior and the first, Pareto-inferior, in honor of Vilfredo Pareto, the great Italian economist and sociologist.

At the same time, one cannot prove that any such Pareto-superior position will exist; the likelihood of existence decreases as one deals with larger and more diverse societies.

Returning to the simple three-person society, one can imagine the redistributional process continuing further—a step at a time, with each outcome Pareto-superior to all those that preceded it. Eventually, the passage to successively Pareto-superior positions may stop. A particular distribution might be reached from which improvement of the position of any party will involve injury to at least one of the others; such a position is called Pareto-optimal.[17] Even in this simple society, no Pareto-optimal position may exist or there may be a multiplicity of such positions. The unique Pareto-optimal position may be unstable, in the sense that it can be reached only by chance, with any small departure tending to become larger as negotiations proceed. Most importantly, even a unique and stable Pareto-optimal redistribution need not conform to any critic's conception of distributive equity. We cannot even be certain that a stable Pareto-optimal redistribution—assuming that it can exist—will be more equal than the original distribution.

Limiting the domain of inequality

It is fascinating to read Professor Tobin's seminal essay on this subject from the interdependent-utility point of view. Suppose that the middle and working classes sufficiently dislike the poor—both the unemployed poor and those relegated to some secondary or substandard labor market[18]—to block

17. Compare Harold M. Hochman and James D. Rogers, "Pareto-Optimal Redistribution," *American Economic Review* 59 (September 1969).

18. Thomas Vietorisz and Bennett Harrison, among contemporary American writers, have

any Pareto-optimal redistribution of generalized purchasing power in favor of the poor. Can nothing more then be done for them? Professor Tobin is sanguine. There exist certain merit wants, as public finance theorists call them. These include basic food, housing, health care and education. Presumably, the better off—in particular, the third and fourth quintiles of the income distribution—will consent to meet the merit wants of the lowest quintile in higher quantities and on easier terms than they will redistribute generalized purchasing power. At the same time, additional satisfaction of these merit wants will increase, to some extent, the real incomes and, more importantly perhaps, the future incomes of the poor.

Certainly, something of the sort has happened, and is happening, in the United States and elsewhere under circumstances when outright income redistribution is politically unfeasible. Food stamps, public housing, medicare and medicaid programs are cases in point, as is the proliferation of public universities and junior colleges with open-admission and credit-no-entry features. Apparently, society will trust the poor to a greater extent with that which it thinks the poor ought to want—merit wants—than it will trust the poor with that which they may actually want more —generalized purchasing power. Tobin accedes, on the principle that half a loaf is better than either no bread or pie in the sky when you die, and proposes concentrating attention upon increasing the quantity and quality of public services available to the poor rather than upon proposals for income floors or negative income taxes.

Here, again, there are limits. They

been active in defining and measuring such labor markets, particularly in the larger American cities.

are connected, perhaps, to the attitudes of the third and fourth quintiles of the income distribution rather than to those of the top quintile; so, at least, the American election results of 1972 seem to suggest. These limits can become—if only periodically—more stringent than Tobin would prefer to recognize. Public housing, yes; but not if it is too near the rest of us; if it is higher in quality than ours; if "they" do not maintain it; or if their criminal elements take over the housing projects.[19] Medical assistance, yes; but not if it raises taxes or doctors' fees too much or if it seriously impinges upon the medical time and hospital beds available for the rest of us. Educational assistance, yes; but not if Sonny is kept off the state university's main campus and is relegated to the backwoods boondock branch to make room for some slum kid with lower college board scores and higher propensities to riot and make trouble. And so it goes.

Distribution in the Theory of Justice

John Rawls is a social philosopher and political theorist in the great tradition of Locke, Hume, Marx and Mill. Which is to say, *inter alia*, that, at the professional level, he accepts responsibility for thorough knowledge not only of technical philosophy, but also of the several social studies to which his work is related. In economics, Rawls' contribution has an impressive freshness and novelty. Professor Rawls' *Theory*

19. In Tokyo public housing projects have almost none of the crime and drug problems that have plagued, for example, Pruitt-Igoe in St. Louis. Tokyo's public housing has not only a long waiting list but exhaustive investigation of everyone who wishes to live in the project. There is also a minimum—as well as a maximum—income requirement for eligibility; not only the criminal and problem elements, but the poorest of the poor, are effectively excluded.

of Justice springs from both Kantian ethical principles and the seventeenth and eighteenth century theories of social contract. He is explicitly reacting against the individualist ethical tradition of English Utilitarianism, which has dominated conventional economics. It would be fair to view Rawls as a technically modernized reincarnation of the Königsberg sage and his book as one Kant might have written, had technical economics of our day been added to his formidable professional armamentarium. Rawls' message, as a whole, brings good tidings of great joy to the contemporary New Left, not only in terms of economic maldistributionism but also in terms of a number of political overtones: support for civil disobedience and intense minorities, denunciation of private campaign funds as inconsistent with liberty, and so on. His economics applies the complex notion of lexicographic or, as he calls it, lexical utility.

In a simple model of lexical utility, two goods, x and y, are the only claimants for a consumer's expenditure. Furthermore, x has a higher degree of essentiality than y, in a somewhat special sense; this special sense is that the consumer in question cannot possibly be better off consuming x_1 units of x per period than consuming x_2 units—with $x_2 > x_1$—no matter how much of the less essential y he has at his disposal. At the same time, y is also desirable; thus, consumption of (x_1, y_2) is preferable to consumption of (x_1, y_1)—with $y_2 > y_1$. The mathematical implication of this so-called lexical assumption is that no utility function, U, can exist for x and y and that a great number of comforting and convenient results, which economists have derived from utility functions, no longer hold.

Rawls draws these social and economic consequences: (1) Let x be a set of primary social goods, not a single good. Rawls treats these as inherently equal in their distribution between individuals; liberty and moral worth are examples. (2) Let y be a set of goods, the ordinary commodities, "butter and eggs and a pound of cheese," with which economics deals. An individual with (x_2, y_1) in Utopia or Communia is better off than he would be with (x_1, y_2) in America—however small the differential $(x_2 - x_1)$ or however large the differential $(y_2 - y_1)$. In other words, no increment of American style material affluence is worth even an infinitesimal sacrifice of primary social goods. To this extent, the primary social goods of liberty and moral worth take precedence in Rawls' system. These goods are—at least implicitly—ordinal, if not measurable.[20] They are also inherently equal, in the sense that none in society has more than the least endowed. Furthermore—if I interpret Rawls correctly—inequality of conventional economic income and wealth, in practice, can probably reduce the quantity of primary social goods for the poor and, therefore, for society as a whole.

Even if not primary in Rawls' sense, income and wealth are, to some extent, important; some sacrifices may be worth making to secure more of them. Accordingly, certain inequalities are sanctioned as fair in Rawls' system of "justice as fairness," but only to the extent that, within a hypothetical original situation of society, they receive democratic approval. This original situation is one in which no individual

20. The distinction between ordinality—or ordinal measurability—and measurability—or cardinal measurability—is often put in the following way: The entity x is ordinal whenever the statement $x_3 > x_2 > x_1$ is meaningful. In addition, x is measurable if the statement $(x_3 - x_2) > (x_2 - x_1)$ is also meaningful.

knows his position in advance and can cast his vote with complete unselfishness—that is, none knows either his relative standing in such attributes as IQ and physical stamina or what the relative social standing of his particular race, sex, religion or age group [21] may be. Rawls suggests that equity—conceived of as fairness—with whatever degree of inequality individuals in this hypothetical original position and with lexical utility functions would approve, would serve as a means to increase the welfare of the society's least-advantaged members—whose identity, when the vote was taken, would be completely unknown. It seems safe to assume that the degree of inequality sanctioned in the Rawls system would be substantially smaller than that which prevails in American or Western European capitalism—or, for that matter, in any of the "people's democracies."

Rawls believes, then, that only such inequalities are equitable—and that only these would be approved in a democratic vote as both fair and preferable to the original position—as improve the absolute economic welfare of the least advantaged segment in the actual economy as it develops. Should the advantage engendered by inequality to the least favored economic segment raise them above one or more segments previously better off, the rule would be applied again for the benefit of the new lower depths; presumably through convergent series of adjustments, an asymptotic state would be reached from which further shifts toward inequality would

be disallowed. Also, it must be assumed that equalizing processes, which aid the least privileged segment of the economy, will not lower the absolute position of any other underprivileged segment, below the mean or median income of the economy. Rawls' theory makes this assumption straight-forwardly and explicitly. In the light of the last American election returns, I felt considerable uncertainty about its validity.[22] If what Rawls calls "chain connection and close-knitness" do not hold between two underprivileged segments, A and B, some or all forms of inequality which benefit A may injure B. One is left, in economist McCulloch's phrase, "at sea, without rudder or compass."

So original, ingenious, scholarly and articulate is Rawls' ethical-systematic case for "justice as fairness," or "equity as equality," that readers can easily overlook the essentially subjective elements in the impressive and orderly structure. Are our utility functions indeed lexical? Are Rawls' primary goods —despite Socialist sneers at "liberty to starve"—primary? Can anyone really envisage how he might think and feel— in particular, his preferences for, or aversions to, risk and uncertainty—in the Rawls "original situation" or the contractarian "state of nature?" What relevance—beyond the definitional—do,

21. In dynamic economic problems involving the distribution of the formal theory of economic growth, the most important distributive aspect is not only between age groups but between generations which may not overlap in time. Rawls does not attempt to evade this problem; he supposes that none originally is aware of the relative position of his generation, vis-à-vis posterity in the growth process.

22. These results, themselves, apply to a society where every voter knows not only whether he is "poor, young, female, and/or black," but also what being "poor, young, female, and/or black" means; thus, they are irrelevant to Rawls' original position. The results may be interpreted as a protest against a particular set of equalizing methods attributed to Senator McGovern and his supporters—heavy tax increases, accelerated inflation—and not to inequality, as such. They may be interpreted, less favorably to Rawls' theses, as anxiety—on the part of quintiles 2 and 3 of the income distribution—to maintain their differentials above the lowest quintile.

or should, an individual's presumptive thoughts and feelings have to his actual decisions? What if the requisite chain connections and close-knitness are incomplete among the poor, either in the original or the actual situation—or, perhaps, in both? Finally, what can anyone in any existing society say about the degree of inequality justified by Rawls' "loophole"—production for the imaginary poor in an imaginary state of affairs, while retaining consistency with absolute equality of the primary social goods?[23] Would the resulting inequality be as minimal as Rawls and his partisans anticipate? Reflected upon in tranquility, Rawls' rationalization for equality in the name of equity and his subordination of the production and supply of ordinary economic goods and services will maintain its appeal to many of his readers, while appalling a good many others. Still others will regard it as meaningless *gainen no yūgi*

23. The Marxist-humanist arguments for "moral incentives" and educational conditioning of "new Socialist man" are aimed at securing maximum production independent of economic reward; they are off limits in the Rawls system, as I understand it. They are based on a party-line monopoly of propaganda and public enlightenment to an extent incompatible with Rawls' concern for liberty, however sincere their rejection of forced labor.

and *kijō no kūron*,[24] for the reasons of the hypothetical elements in his system and his neglect of operational, intermediate steps for getting "from here to there" and for ascertaining where "there" may be.

Conclusion

There may be some objective connection, positive or negative, between equity and equality in the distribution of income and wealth. It may transcend both Alexander Pope's, "One truth is clear: Whatever is, is right" and Henry Simons' disdain for the existing distribution as esthetically "unlovely." Unfortunately, we still do not know what that connection is or how, if at all, it relates to the economists' Pareto-optimality. We can confirm neither the humanistic instincts of the egalitarians nor the skeptical instincts of the practical men. One or another philosopher's' stone, which would confirm one or another set of instincts—or possibly amalgamate them—still awaits some venturesome economic geologist.

24. These Japanese pejoratives may be translated separately as "juggling concepts" and "desk theory abstractions" or, combined, as "closet philosophy."

Inequality and the Double Bluff

By Paul Davidson

ABSTRACT: This paper demonstrates the role of the distribution of income in promoting or retarding economic growth, in either free market or planned economies. Keynes's view of the importance of the double bluff of income inequality for nineteenth century capitalism is explained in a Harrod growth model. The difference between Harrod's model and the neo-Keynesian emphasis on distribution is explained. Finally, it is shown that, to encourage growth, a rational monetary policy must take into account the fact that the distribution of income can create financial, as well as real, restraints on growth.

Paul Davidson is Professor of Economics and Associate Director of the Bureau of Economic Research at Rutgers, The State University of New Jersey. He is the author of Money and the Real World *and* Theories of Aggregate Income Distribution; *co-author of* Aggregate Supply and Demand Analysis *and* The Demand and Supply of Outdoor Recreation—An Econometric Analysis.

KEYNES attributed the vast accumulation of fixed capital under the capitalist system—which has provided immense benefits to mankind—"on a double bluff or deception":

On the one hand the labouring classes accepted from ignorance or powerlessness, or were compelled, persuaded, or cajoled by custom, authority and the well-established order of society into accepting, a situation in which they could call their own very little of the cake that they and nature and the capitalists were cooperating to produce. And on the other hand the capitalist classes were allowed to call the best part of the cake theirs and were theoretically free to consume it, on the tacit underlying condition that they consumed very little of it in practice. The duty of "saving" became nine-tenths of virtue and the growth of the cake the object of true religion. There grew round the non-consumption of the cake all those instincts of puritanism which in other ages has withdrawn itself from the world and has neglected the arts of production as well as those of enjoyment. And so the cake increased; but to what end was not clearly contemplated. Individuals would be exhorted not so much to abstain as to defer, and to cultivate the pleasures of security and anticipation. Saving was for old age or for your children; but this was only in theory—the virtue of the cake was that it was never to be consumed, neither by you nor by your children after you.

In writing this I do not necessarily disparage the practices of that generation. In the unconscious recesses of its being society knew what it was about. The cake was really very small in proportion to the appetites of consumption, and no one, if it were shared all around, would be much the better off by the cutting of it. Society was working not for the small pleasures of today but for the future security and improvement of the race—in fact for "progress." [1]

1. J. M. Keynes, *Economic Consequences of the Peace* (London: Macmillan, 1971), pp. 11–12.

Thus, according to this double bluff view of economic growth: if significant growth is to be achieved—while resources are scarce and absolute human needs are not easily met out of current production—those consumers whose propensity to save is very low will have to accept a relatively small proportion of gross national product (GNP); those economic units whose savings behavior is strong will be able to call a high proportion of total output theirs, if they do not fritter away on consumption that to which they are legally entitled. If high income groups tend to have high savings propensities, then higher rates of growth may require more unequal distribution of income.

In the 1940s, with the dominance of Keynesian economics and its emphasis on (1) static problems of deficient effective demand and (2) dynamic Harrod growth models, the relevance of the distribution and inequality of income as a prerequisite for rapid growth was lost in the orthodox view of the capitalist economic system. Only dogmatic Marxists and nonscientific radical economists continued to emphasize the double bluff, or deception, which permits a modern capitalist system to accumulate. Recently, however, this view has received a modicum of acceptability as put forth in the analytical views of the English neo-Keynesians: J. Robinson, Kaldor and Pasinetti. In this paper I will attempt to integrate and explain these aspects of income distribution and inequality with the more orthodox Harrod growth analysis and to suggest that the distribution of income can cause financial, as well as real, constraints on the rate of growth.

A MODEL OF GROWTH

In a modern capitalist system, economic growth ultimately depends on the investment decisions of firms and their ability to obtain money with which to implement their investment plans. If firms are in equilibrium, over time, they will be utilizing a stock of capital goods which entrepreneurs believe to be most desirable—least costly—for the current output objectives. In the aggregate, the ratio of desired stock of capital goods to desired output flow per period is Harrod's required capital-output ratio, c_r.[2] If entrepreneurs envision a growth in aggregate demand over time, then the existing stock of capital is unlikely to be deemed appropriate for meeting future market conditions. Thus, given entrepreneurial views about the growth of demand over time and the rate of discount they use to evaluate the ensuing streams of expected profits, and given the inherited stock of capital, its rate of depreciation and the supply price of new capital, entrepreneurs may plan to expand capacity.[3] If they can obtain finance, they will enter into some contractual agreement for delivery of a certain volume of new capital goods— gross investment—during the period, thereby generating a level of aggregate income. If the ensuing level of effective demand merely matches the period's sales expectations, then aggregate income will have been distributed between wages—or contractual income—and profits—residual income—in accordance with the entrepreneurs' expectations.

Given the average, and marginal, propensity to save out of wages, (s_w), and gross profits, (s_c)—and assuming $s_w < s_c$—there is a unique and normally different level of planned aggregate sav-

ings for any given level of gross income and its distribution. This level of planned savings, when expressed as a fraction of current aggregate income, is the planned savings ratio, s_p.[4] In essence, s_p indicates that fraction of aggregate income which the recipients do not use directly to finance their current spending. For endogenous simplicity, Harrod has assumed an unchanging value for this savings ratio for any given level of income.[5] One of the major differences between Harrod's— and Keynes's *General Theory*—analysis and that of the neo-Keynesian's, Robinson, Kaldor and Pasinetti, is that in the former, changes in the distribution of income between wages and profits are implicitly assumed to be connected only with changes in the level of employment; the neo-Keynesian's analysis emphasizes differences in aggregate savings ratios caused by different distributions between wages and profits at any given level of employment.[6]

In any period, the production of the economy can be divided into two parts: (1) available output, which is in a form immediately available for consumption use by households and (2) nonavailable output, identified as the current flow of production from the capital goods producing industry. If the proportion of aggregate gross money income—including gross profits—generated in the nonavailable output sector differs from Harrod's desired or expected savings

2. R. F. Harrod, *Money* (London: Macmillan, 1969), p. 192.

3. In the typical Harrod growth model, the rate of discount and the supply price are assumed constant. Thus, if demand is expected to grow at 3 percent per annum, then capital requirements will grow at 3 percent per annum.

4. Harrod includes planned savings by firms as well as the planned savings out of income by households in s_p. Obviously, s_p is then a weighted average of s_w and s_c.

5. Harrod, *Money*, p. 192. The planned savings ratio can change if either the level of aggregate income changes; and/or if the savings propensities change; and/or if the distribution of income changes.

6. For example, see N. Kaldor, "Some Fallacies on the Interpretation of Kaldor," *Review of Economic Studies* 37 (1970), p. 6.

ratio, s_d,[7] then the realizable level of aggregate demand will differ from the level of demand which entrepreneurs expect, or require, if they are going to hire a particular employment volume. Thus, for a given level of employment, if the proportion of total GNP realized in the nonavailable output sector—the investment sector broadly—exceeds the expected, or desired, savings ratio— that is, if $s_p < s_d$—and if entrepreneurs then undertake the associated hiring and production commitments, they will be exhilarated by purchasers clamoring for their output. Consequently, entrepreneurs will deem the current stock of fixed and working capital goods insufficient to sustain even existing demand and totally insufficient to provide for next period's expected growth in turnover. As a result, according to Harrod, firms will desire to augment their orders for new capital goods in future periods. The additional demand for capital goods in the next period, however, will increase the actual rate of growth even further above the expected, or warranted, rate of growth.[8]

Harrod has defined the warranted rate of growth, G_w, as:

$$G_w = \frac{s_d}{C_r} \qquad (1)$$

C_r equalling the dollar amount of capital goods necessary to generate an extra dollar of output. Given the desired relationship between the stock of capital goods and the output flow per period—as embodied in C_r—the war-

ranted rate of growth in effective demand is that rate which will merely justify the capacity that producers install in each period. Thus, s_d is Harrod's desired ratio of aggregate savings to income, where the desired ratio is implicit in entrepreneurial expectations of short period sales proceeds.

The greater G_w, the higher the expected savings ratio—that is, the greater the proportion of total output devoted to investment-goods activities: entrepreneurs direct a smaller proportion of productive resources to meet current aggregate consumption demand. Hence, a higher G_w involves using a greater proportion of current resources to cater to expected future market demands. Between any two periods, there is some increment in actual demand, which will satisfy entrepreneurs with the net investment commitments they are currently undertaking and entail a coincidence of the actual, and warranted, growth rates—then, s_p equals s_d. If s_p is not equal to s_d, the resulting entrepreneurial action, based on current period surprise, will widen the gap between the actual rate of growth and the, assumedly, unchanged warranted rate.

Finally, Harrod has developed the concept of a natural rate of growth, G_n, which is determined by the growth in the working population and the current potential for technical progress. G_n represents the potential growth in total output in the economy, if it is already at full employment. In Harrod's view, G_n "is not determined by the wishes of persons and companies as regards savings."[9] Therefore, in a free market economy, it would be fortuitous if either the warranted or the actual rate of growth were to equal the natural rate. Given Cr, G_w determines which savings ratio, s_n, is compatible with growth at

---

7. Entrepreneurs' expected, or desired, savings ratio, s_d, is the complement of entrepreneurs' expectation of the proportion of gross income which will be spent on consumer— available output—goods. If s_p is greater than (less than) s_d, then total sales in the consumer goods industries will be less than (greater than) entrepreneurs expect.

8. R. F. Harrod, *Towards a Dynamic Economics* (London: Macmillan, 1948), p. 86.

9. R. F. Harrod, *Money,* p. 195.

full employment—a Golden Age. In the Harrod-Keynes analysis, there is no automatic mechanism which assures that a Golden Age will result from the aggregate of individual planned savings decisions, where actual, warranted and natural growth rates are equal.

As long as there is a unique distribution of income at full employment—s_c and s_w remaining constant—there is a unique planned savings ratio, s_p; s_p may, or may not, equal s_n, the G_n savings ratio. In Harrod's view, if it is socially desirable to keep an economy on a G_n growth path—and if $s_p > s_n$—then government dissavings, via fiscal policy, can operate as the balancing wheel to lower the aggregate planned savings ratio. On the other hand, if $s_p < s_n$ so that demand exceeds supply at full employment, inflationary forces, which raise profit margins relative to money wages and/or increase tax revenues relative to government expenditures, will increase s_p until it equals s_n.

In any modern free market monetary economy which deviates from Keynes's double bluff nineteenth century capitalism, the planned savings ratio can become so great that the intended investment in plants and equipment will be insufficient to employ all the workers willing to offer their services on the market, at the going wage rate. Even if entrepreneurs perceive the situation correctly, the warranted, and actual, rate of growth will be less than the natural rate. The consequent limping Golden Age follows from the fact that —given the distribution of income— income recipients, in the aggregate, desire to save via nonresource utilizing things at an excessive rate, relative to the economy's full employment growth potential.

The ability to transfer purchasing power over time in the form of money and securities can cause a rich capital-istic economy to suffer the fate of Midas. This occurs whenever the aggregate supply price of bringing up the stock of production facilities to the necessary level for providing full employment output is less than the value of:

the aggregate desire on the part of the public to make provision for the future, even with full employment. . . .This disturbing conclusion depends, of course, on the assumption that the propensity to consume and the rate of investment are not deliberately controlled in the social interest but are mainly left to the influences of *laissez-faire*.[10]

Changes in the distribution of income in the private sector can alter the propensity to consume, thereby altering s_p at any level of employment. Alternatively, changes in government expenditures can alter the aggregate planned savings ratio. Thus, if s_p is initially greater than s_n in the wealthy economy, the traditional Harrod-Keynes solution is to increase the aggregate spending via government purchases of new output, financed by deficits which give the public "marketable bits of paper"; these then can be held by the public as a means of transferring command over time.[11]

In a centrally planned economy, on the other hand, if s_p does not equal s_n, changes in the mark-up of market prices over unit labor costs can—by changing the distribution of income between wage and nonwage elements—provide a regulatory mechanism for changing the aggregate planned savings ratio as long as different savings propensities are associ-

10. J. M. Keynes, *The General Theory of Employment, Interest and Money* (London: Macmillan, 1973), pp. 218–19.

11. Harrod, *Money,* p. 199. Harrod, of course, would not deny the possibility of altering the planned savings ratio by redistributing income.

ated with each type of income.[12] In an underdeveloped planned economy, if s_p is initially less than s_n, mark-ups would have to be raised to reduce the proportion of real income going to workers, while in a wealthy planned economy, which has a tendency for $s_p > s_n$, mark-ups would have to be lowered.

Ultimately Keynes's view—of the necessity of the double bluff of income inequality to stimulate capital accumulation—implies a poor economy in which demand tends to outrun supply as a result of greater income equality at full employment. In an affluent economy, however, where s_p tends to exceed s_n, a lesser income inequality may be desirable in a market economy, where consumption spending reflects discretionary, more than biological, expenditures.

FINANCIAL INTERMEDIARIES AND THE DISTRIBUTION OF INCOME BETWEEN FIRMS AND HOUSEHOLDS

In a modern money economy, financial intermediaries and the banking system play an involved role which can facilitate the installation of productive capacity and the expansion of output. Our financial institutions can assist firms in obtaining immediate command over resources, thereby inducing s_d to rise towards s_p. Accordingly, the presence of a banking system and the associated financial institutions carries a potential contribution to economic growth. If a society is fortunate to have both a spirit of enterprise and financial institutions, in times of confidence, it may be doubly blessed—although, in uncertain times, it may be doubly cursed. Through

12. Ibid., p. 197. Kaldor, however, has insisted that there is a mechanism that operates—even in a free market economy—to assure that the warranted rate adjusts itself to the natural rate; see, Kaldor, "Some Fallacies," p. 6.

the operation of financial intermediaries, enterprise often may be encouraged to accumulate real wealth at a rate otherwise incompatible with normal planned savings and bond—equities—money portfolio desires of households. At times of general insecurity, the financial institutions may magnify the rush to liquidity and thereby accentuate slumps. Hence, it is essential to account for, explicitly, the way in which these institutions link the industrial and financial circulation; even though society may desire to save a proportion of income which is compatible with the natural growth rate, a Golden Age may not be attainable without the support of the financial intermediaries and the federal reserve monetary authorities.

In a free market economy, there is no mechanism which automatically assures equality of the actual, warranted and natural rate of growth. In an uncertain world, errors of foresight are inevitable, hence, the probable inequality of the actual and warranted rate. Even if entrepreneurial views of consumer behavior are correct—so that $s_p = s_d$—the distribution of income between households and firms and the behavior of financial institutions may create financial—liquidity—difficulties; these can cause the warranted rate to deviate from the actual and/or natural rate. A rational monetary policy to promote growth must take these distributive elements into account.

Given gross investment expenditures, savings behavior determines total spending and, therefore, realizable aggregate demand. Given entrepreneurial long-run profit expectations, the portion of income recipients' savings which is transferred, via financial institutions, to firms is one of the major sources of production financing. The other major sources of monetary finance are: (1) the creation of new bank debts by commercial banks, (2) the bear hoards of economic units and (3) internal finance by firms. Since corporations make the major capital formation decisions in a modern economy, and since growing corporations normally retain a significant portion of gross profits for internal financing purposes, the corporate profits savings propensity, s_c, may play a crucial role in capital accumulation and growth. Firms:

find it necessary in a dynamic world of increasing returns to plough back a proportion of the profits as a kind of prior charge on earnings. . . . This is because continued expansion cannot be ensured . . . unless *some proportion* of the finance required from expansion comes from internal sources. . . . Hence the high savings propensity attaches to profits as such, not to capitalists as such.[13]

In a stationary economy, each firm's need to replace fixed and working capital per period could be financed from sales receipts over time. Even in a stationary economy, as long as production takes time, firms may be required to make payments to resource owners before sales revenues are received. The financing of these factor payments could be accomplished via short term loans from banks. When—at the end of the production period—sales expectations are met, sales revenues will be sufficient to repay the firms' short term obligations to the banks and to yield a normal profit. Under these conditions, the volume of available short term credit

facilities is a revolving fund of a more or less constant amount, available to finance the working capital expenditures of the next period.[14] In equilibrium, in a stationary economy, there will be neither a flow-supply of securities—new issues—nor a flow-demand for securities by the public out of household savings; net savings and net investment are zero. In a growing economy, on the other hand, there may be a flow-supply of securities, if firms choose to fund a portion of net investment externally,[15] and a flow-demand for securities, if households wish to acquire securities out of net savings.

If at the initial price of securities, excess flow-demand for securities fortuitously happens to be zero, so that

$$iI = ms_hY_h \qquad (2)$$

where: i is the fraction of investment expenditures; I, that which entrepreneurs in the aggregate wish to finance externally; m, the marginal propensity to purchase securities out of aggregate household savings; and s_h, the public's planned savings ratio out of household income, Y_h. Then, the aggregate planned net debtor position of firms will grow *pari passu* with the aggregate planned net creditor position of households.

If the funds used to finance investment spending internally are equal to corporate savings out of profits—s_cP, where P equals aggregate profits, that is, if $s_cP = (I - i) I$—and if entrepreneurial expectations of sales proceeds from current production are being realized—

13. N. Kaldor, "Marginal Productivity and Macroeconomic Theories of Distribution," *Review of Economic Studies* 23 (1966), p. 310. In an uncertain world, firms must guard against illiquidity, while lenders will fear the possibility of firms being unable to meet long term obligations. Thus, both the entrepreneurs and the lenders are anxious to see that some proportion of net investment is funded internally. Internal and external finance are complements, rather than substitutes.

14. Amortization of the outstanding long term debt can also operate as a revolving fund for the replacement of fixed capital; compare, Keynes, "Alternative Theories," *Economic Journal* 47 (1937), p. 247.

15. In a growth context, the ability to obtain finance is related not only to the cost of borrowing, but to the proportion of the total value of the firm which has been internally financed—that is, to the retention ratio.

so that $s_p = s_d$—then aggregate savings out of household income must be equal to the fraction of I spending which is being externally financed—that is, $s_h Y_h = iI$. This implies that m must equal unity, if the warranted, or equilibrium, growth path is to be maintained while excess flow-demand for securities is zero and if security prices are to be unchanged. Of course, even if households do not wish to hold additional idle balances—$m = 1$—as their wealth-holdings increase with growth, demand by firms for increased money balances to finance higher payrolls and other expenses will require the monetary authority to provide more money to support the output expansion. In a monetary economy, however, there is no reason to expect m to equal unity. In fact, it is more reasonable to assume that, as household wealth increases, a portion will go to the accumulation of idle balances. Hence, the money supply would have to be enlarged even more.

If the firms' demand for external funding exceeds households' desire to purchase additional securities out of savings at the current placement price, financial conditions will cause the economy to slow down—even if the banking system is responding to the needs of industry for working capital. In these circumstances, security underwriters will find it increasingly difficult to float new issues and, in an attempt to protect their goodwill with normal customers who bought previous new issues at higher prices, financial intermediaries will (1) discourage other firms who desire to float new issues to finance investment expenditures in the future and (2) increase their indebtedness to the banking system to finance an undesired increase in dealer inventories of securities in order to support the market. The financial conditions created by a negative excess flow-demand will ulti-

mately force entrepreneurs to cut back on investment spending, thereby retarding growth—unless the banking system acts promptly to maintain orderly security markets by buying from the public those securities which it does not wish to hold. Even if $s_d = s_p = s_n$, a Golden Age would be prevented by financial problems when the excess flow-demand for securities is negative. Thus, as Keynes declared:

The banks hold the key in the transition from a lower to a higher scale of activity. . . . The investment market can become congested through a shortage of cash. It can never become congested through a shortage of savings. This is the most fundamental of my conclusions in this field.[16]

On the other hand, if firms' demand for external funding is less than households' desire to purchase additional securities out of savings, this will be symptomatic of a lack of effective demand, since $s_h Y_h + s_c P > (1 - i)I + iI$. Unless easier financial intermediaries stimulate additional investment, sales expectations of entrepreneurs will be disappointed and employment will decline.

There is an asymmetry about financial matters. If excess flow-demand for securities is negative, more rapid expansion of the money supply can maintain growth; if excess flow-demand is positive, monetary policy may be powerless to encourage expansion. This is the analysis which ultimately lies beyond the old monetary theory adage, "You can't push on a string."

In the real world, new issues and household savings are trifling elements in the securities market. Security markets are likely to be swamped by the

16. J. M. Keynes, "Ex Ante Theory of the Rate of Interest," *Economic Journal* 47 (1937), pp. 666-8.

eddies of speculative movements made by the whole body of wealth-holders constantly sifting and shifting their portfolio composition. Consequently, in an uncertain world where financial market expectations are especially volatile, the relationship between increases in the quantity of money and the needs of the financial circulation are too complex and capricious to be handled by any simple rule—even if growth in the real factors underlying the needs of the industrial circulation could be accurately forecast. The solution lies:

in letting Finance and Industry have all the money they want, but at a rate of interest which in its effect on the rate of new [externally financed] investment . . . exactly balances the effect of bullish sentiments. To diagnose the position precisely at every stage and to achieve this exact balance may sometimes be, however, beyond the wits of man.[17]

Any rule for expanding the money supply at the same rate as the growth in output—as recommended by Professor Friedman, for example—will only fortuitously promote a steady rate of capital goods accumulation, since the demand for securities out of households' savings, and/or the public's liquidity preference proper, may be changing at a different rate than the supply of securities.

CONCLUSION

A necessary condition for equilibrium growth is $s_p = s_d$. The higher the rate of equilibrium growth for any given level of resource use, the higher the planned savings ratio must be. The high propensity to save by capitalists and the unequal distribution of income in the nineteenth century were

compatible with rapid economic growth. This is the basis of Keynes's justification of the double bluff.

Often, in the current economic literature, it is argued that an unequal distribution of income favoring profits is still required for rapid growth. This claim is based upon two implicit assumptions: (1) full employment is readily attainable in a decentralized modern economy and (2) households in general—and those of the poor in particular—are instant gratification machines, unwilling voluntarily to forego current consumption. Nonetheless, the existence of gigantic financial institutions, such as life insurance companies, mutual funds, finance companies and Christmas clubs, which arrange for the contractual commitment of savings from most households' income in addition to corporate financial prudence—and tax advantages of rapid amortization of capital suggests that the early Keynes view of inadequate private sector savings is unrealistic. "In contemporary conditions the growth of wealth so far from being dependent on the abstinence of the rich, as is commonly supposed, is more likely to be impeded by it." [18]

Growth is more likely to be stimulated by redistributing income toward those who would consume more, rather than to those who would consume less or to those who would use current resources to order armaments, space shots and other dubious outlay forms, which do little to improve the commonweal. Only if we are convinced that the public wishes to consume too much out of full employment income need we encourage savings via income redistribution towards the rich and thrifty, in compliance with Keynes's double bluff. Only if we are convinced that the public will never consume enough out of full em-

17. J. M. Keynes, *A Treatise on Money* (London: Macmillan, 1930), vol. II, pp. 254–5.

18. Keynes, *The General Theory*, p. 373.

ployment income need we direct income to wasteful forms, tested by any standards of reasonableness. Finance and financial institutions play a vital and unique role in a growing economy. Finally, if the excess flow-demand for securities is negative, then even if s_p equals s_n, financial constraints can retard accumulation and growth. Only if the monetary authority is prepared to increase the money supply more rapidly than the growth in output, can the economy maintain its equilibrium growth course.

A Living Wage

By Daniel R. Fusfeld

ABSTRACT: The only effective way to eliminate poverty in the United States is to pay all workers a living wage, defined as one that would enable a worker to maintain an urban family of four in health and decency. In 1972 that implied a minimum wage of 3.50 dollars per hour. Such a minimum wage would have important repercussions on the low wage industries and the workers they employ. The impact on business firms can be eased by special tax and loan programs. The most important problems will arise from loss of jobs as the low wage industries adapt to the high minimum wage. A three-pronged program is called for: (1) full employment, (2) public service employment and (3) education and training. A sharply accelerated equal opportunity employment program will also be needed, because many low wage workers are Blacks, Latins and women. This program implies a redistribution of income in favor of the low wage worker that could be negated by wage increases for other workers, triggering price increases throughout the economy. Reduced income taxes for workers with annual incomes above 7,000 dollars and up to perhaps 15,000 dollars will be needed to overcome that effect. The net result would be an end to poverty and to many of its social evils.

Daniel R. Fusfeld is Professor of Economics at The University of Michigan. His most recent book is The Basic Economics of the Urban Racial Crisis. *He is the author of* Economics, *an introductory textbook, and* The Age of the Economist, *and he has published a variety of articles in professional journals. Educated at George Washington and Columbia Universities, he was a recent President of the Association for Evolutionary Economics.*

THE only effective way to eliminate poverty in the United States is to pay all workers a living wage. As long as working people labor in jobs in which earnings are inadequate to meet even poverty standards of income, their families will remain poor; furthermore, their poverty will be reproduced from one generation to the next. Our society will continue to suffer from all the ills associated with poverty: disease, degradation, crime, hostility and anger.

These conditions need not exist. The history of industrial society is one of continuous movement upward in real incomes and living standards for one group in the labor force after another. The low wage worker of a hundred years ago is often the labor aristocrat of today; the steel and meat-packing industries, in which the bulk of the workers are now relatively well paid while fifty or more years ago they were almost at the bottom of the wage-level distribution, are good examples.

Changes of that sort are usually accompanied by significant structural changes in the affected industry or in the economy as a whole. Bituminous coal mining is a good example. A sick, low wage industry in the 1930s, the union drive for high wage rates forced the industry to transform itself into a modern, capital-intensive industry of large producers. In the process, employment of bituminous coal miners fell from over 1,500,000 to under 250,000; many workers in the isolated mining areas were left to eke out a miserable existence on various forms of dole. Yet, in the long run, a great amount of poverty was eliminated: 250,000 prosperous families in place of some 1,500,000 poor ones. It would have been more humane to deal with the transition problems of the displaced workers; furthermore, one has no way of knowing whether some of those displaced workers simply moved into another low wage occupation elsewhere. The transformation of coal mining illustrates a basic principle: low wage employment can be eliminated. However, there are several subsidiary propositions which also emerge. Transition problems must be faced realistically. Furthermore, if low wage employment is not to be merely shuffled onto another sector of the economy, all low wage jobs will have to be eliminated.

THE PERPETUATION OF POVERTY

Although the long run economic development of modern industrial society would suggest that further economic growth might ultimately eliminate poverty, there are several important reasons to believe that the normal, or natural, processes of economic change will not continue to erode the hard core of poverty that has shown up over the last quarter century of prosperity and economic expansion.

1771051

1. Technological change, a concomitant of growth, continuously displaces workers and provides additional recruits to the low wage sector of the labor force.
2. Crowding of racial and other minorities into menial occupations, and discrimination in other sectors of the economy, preserves a large body of workers for the low wage industries and occupations.
3. Inability of the economy to achieve full employment levels, with particularly high unemployment rates for minorities, tends to keep wage rates in the low wage sector from rising.
4. Welfare programs and similar income supplements preserve the conditions of poverty out of which come further recruits for the low wage labor force and, by helping

to support the wives and children of low wage workers, provide an indirect subsidy to low wage employers.

Patterns of income distribution also tend to preserve the low wage sector. Wide income disparities, in addition to rising standards of living in the economy at large, create a demand for services that is satisfied, in large part, by the low wage sector. A low wage labor force provides an expanding supply of services for a technical and managerial elite and its concomitant white-collar administrative cadres. We are seeing the emergence of a master-servant society on an impersonal, market-oriented scale—what some Swedish economists call "the English sickness."

The forces creating and preserving a low wage sector in the labor market—and conditions of poverty for 10 to 20 percent of American families—appear to be strong enough to perpetuate present conditions indefinitely. It is interesting to note that the estimates of poverty in America made in the decade before World War I show approximately the same proportion of families in poverty as there are at present—but we must recognize that those estimates were very rough. More sobering is the fact that standards of living for the poor in 1970 were no different from standards of living for the same group in 1945. The families making up the cohort of the poor may have changed, but the poverty remained.

Present methods of alleviating poverty have failed. Amelioration through provision of public services, such as health services, education and welfare payments, may have stabilized the situation and ended the riots of the sixties. But these services represent indirect subsidies, from the rest of the economy, to both the employers of low wage labor and the users of products and services produced in the low wage industries. As for the hope that economic growth will trickle down to the poor, the last quarter century has shown that such a policy has severe limitations with respect to both the magnitude of its effect and the time needed to resolve the problem. The time has come for a new approach: a direct attack on the chief source of the problem—the low wage sector of the economy—supplemented by a broad program of supporting policies that would assure its success.

THE PRESENT MINIMUM WAGE

A living wage should enable a worker to maintain an urban family of four in health and decency. According to the Bureau of Labor Statistics an annual income of a little over 7,000 dollars would have been required in 1972; rising prices have already pushed the figure to higher levels. Reduced to a wage rate for a fully employed person, working forty hours a week for fifty weeks in the year, the 1972 minimum health and decency income for a family of four comes to 3.50 dollars per hour, or 140 dollars per week.

The present federal minimum wage is 1.60 dollars per hour. Various proposals are before the Congress to raise it to 2.50 dollars within two years or to 2.30 dollars over five years. To provide some perspective on these proposals, one should note that a 2.00 dollars per hour wage rate provides a fully employed worker with an annual income of 4,000 dollars—about 95 percent of the 1972 poverty line income for a family of four, as calculated by the Social Security Administration. Admittedly, that is a low estimate for the minimum income needed by a family of four to survive. At these levels, our minimum wage legislation tends to preserve poverty by legitimizing poverty level wage rates. It is incredible that a nation as wealthy as the United States should have an official policy of paying wages that are at, or below, the poverty level.

PROPOSAL FOR A NEW MINIMUM WAGE

The proposal set forth here, then, is to change the federal minimum wage legislation to provide an hourly wage rate that would enable a worker to maintain an urban family of four in health and decency, as estimated by the Bureau of Labor Statistics for the nation as a whole. We might use the wording of the Australian minimum wage legislation, which is designed to maintain wages that provide for "the normal needs of an average employee regarded as a human being living in a civilized community."

A minimum wage of 3.50 dollars per hour would have important repercussions on the low wage industries and the workers they employ. In those industries, such as retail and wholesale trade, food services, medical services, hotels, restaurants and even some manufacturing industries, we could expect a series of adaptations resulting in higher prices and lower output. Rising labor costs in these labor-intensive industries would force higher prices, and higher prices would bring reduced sales. Some firms would go out of business; employment would be reduced. In the longer run, one could expect a general reorganization of the former low wage industries: substitution of capital for labor; more capital-intensive methods of production; reorganization of enterprises to achieve greater efficiency; and, in all probability, an increase in the average size of firms. These are the patterns that have historically been followed as industries have been modernized to use more advanced techniques of production.

The extent of these effects is diffi-

cult to estimate. Previous increases in the minimum wage have not shown any significant impact on either industrial structure or employment; but most studies of these effects have been flawed, and the increases themselves were quite small compared to those envisaged here. In view of these uncertainties, it would seem wise to increase the minimum wage relatively slowly, by stages. My proposal would entail an immediate increase to 2.00 dollars per hour from the present 1.60 dollars, to be followed by further increases of 50 cents per hour each year for the following three years until a level of 3.50 dollars per hour would be reached by July 4, 1976—just in time for the bicentennial of the Declaration of Independence.[1]

Steps can be taken to ease the impact on business firms. Tax credits can be provided for a limited number of years to firms heavily affected by the increase. Special tax allowances can be made for investment designed to modernize production methods. Low cost loans could be provided for the same purpose. By far the most important of the adaptation problems, however, will arise from loss of jobs by workers laid off as the low wage industries adapt to the higher minimum wage. A three-pronged program will be called for: (1) full employment, (2) public employment and (3) education and training.

Full employment

Perhaps as many as 5 million jobs may be threatened by the minimum wage levels envisioned here. Some of those workers will be able to obtain new jobs if the economy is functioning at

1. The figures given are based on 1972 price levels. If the cost of living should rise, the minimum wage should be increased proportionately in order to maintain progress toward a level that would assure a living wage. For 1973, it would move up to 1.65 dollars.

close to the full employment level. To achieve that goal, we need a mix of monetary and fiscal policies designed to bring unemployment rates down to the frictional level of 1.5 to 2 percent for the prime labor force—that is, white men between the ages of twenty-four and forty-five. A level of aggregate demand above the level necessary to achieve those conditions in the labor market is likely to be inflationary and politically unacceptable. This would leave unemployment rates for other cohorts in the labor force above the frictional level. The unemployment rate for the economy as a whole would probably remain at 4.5 to 5 percent; the rate for minorities, at 8 to 10 percent; and for young people, at 15 to 20 percent. A higher minimum wage would probably not increase the difficulties encountered in reducing unemployment to the frictional level for the prime work force, but it would undoubtedly leave other cohorts in the labor force at higher unemployment rates.

Public service employment

Assuring all workers of jobs would require substantial programs of public service employment. Any worker not employed or enrolled in a training program should be eligible for public service employment at the minimum wage of 3.50 dollars per hour—in 1976 and after. Public service agencies at all levels—local, state and federal—would be employers of last resort, with public service employees also earning the minimum wage or more.

This program could be moderately expensive. For example, if 5 million persons were employed at full-time jobs in public service employment at 3.50 dollars per hour, the annual cost would be 35 billion dollars. That total would be reduced by lower costs for welfare and other social services to the poor,

police protection, subsidies for housing and other ameliorative programs; thus, the additional costs might total about 15 to 20 billion dollars annually—and that total would diminish as the economy adapted to the higher minimum wage and was able to absorb more of the displaced workers in the private sector.

Education and training

A comprehensive and extensive program of education and training can speed the adaptation process, particularly for youth and minorities. The program suggested here is modeled after the only successful large scale manpower training program this country has ever had: the G.I. Bill after World War II. Any unemployed worker, or a worker earning less than the proposed 3.50 dollars per hour minimum wage, should be able to enroll in an educational, vocational training or career development program of his own choosing. He or she would be eligible for a training grant equal to a wage of 2.00 dollars per hour or less. If the worker was formerly earning more than 2.00 dollars per hour the training grant would equal his former earned income. Of course, the purpose of the training grant is to encourage as many workers as possible to seek the education and training necessary to upgrade their skills and make them employable in the new and higher wage structure.

Equal opportunity employment

A sharply accelerated equal opportunity employment program, strongly enforced by government at all levels, is needed to supplement the programs described here. A very large proportion of the low wage labor force are Blacks or Latins. If they are to be absorbed into the high wage private sector of the economy with a minimum of public service employment, the present barriers to their entry into many jobs must be eliminated. If they are to enter training programs, opportunities must be provided for entry into open-end, high wage employment. A homogeneous labor force would not require the special equal opportunity programs that would be strongly needed in the present situation in which artificial barriers are created for racial minorities.

A training program of this scope would also be expensive. Assume that some 5 million workers would require training, at an average cost of 5,000 dollars per worker. The total cost would be 25 billion dollars. Spread over a five-year period, the cost would come to about 5 billion dollars annually, for five years. Spread over three years, it would amount to about 8.33 billion dollars annually.

When added to the net costs of a public employment program of some 15 to 20 billion dollars each year, an estimated annual cost of about 20 to 25 billion dollars would be added to government budgets for the first years of the program, diminishing to zero as the economy adapts to a high wage structure over a period of, perhaps, ten years. These amounts are considerably less than the annual costs of the Vietnam War in 1968 to 1971 and would probably require lower military and defense spending in order to avoid additional taxes or inflationary pressures.

PROBLEMS RAISED BY ADJUSTING THE MINIMUM WAGE

A health and decency minimum wage implies a significant redistribution of income toward the poor and near poor, and away from those with higher incomes. Consider the following scenario. An increase in the minimum wage will trigger demands for wage increases by workers whose wages will now no longer be above those of the workers affected by the increase. As wage differentials are reduced, there will be a large demand for increased pay among workers throughout the economy that will tend to reestablish the former wage structure. Employers, also, will try to reestablish the former wage structure in order to retain workers with higher skills and greater productivity. These forces within the labor market could bring cost increases, which will be reflected in price increases. After all of these adjustments have run their course, the poor may be no better off then they were originally. The wage structure will have moved up, and prices will have risen to eliminate the initial effects of a higher minimum wage.

There is much to this argument, even though we must recognize that labor markets and wage differentials are affected by forces other than the purely economic ones implied by the simple adjustment process described above. Along with a variety of other structural factors, unions and their bargaining power, the extent of monopoloid market control in an industry and the nature of production process, all affect wage differentials.

Nevertheless, it would be useless to raise minimum wages if long run economic forces were ultimately to overtake the short run effects. Those long run forces can be neutralized by using the tax system to keep workers' incomes after taxes in approximately the same relative positions as those in which they were before the minimum wage was increased. The federal income tax can be used for that purpose. For example, tax rates can be reduced for all families with annual incomes under 15,000 dollars with the reduction for 7,000 dollar incomes being approximately the same as the increase in income earned by a fully employed worker earning the new minimum wage. The tax rate reductions would be gradually diminished for higher income classes up to a zero reduction in tax rates for 15,000 dollar incomes. Tax rates for incomes over 15,000 dollars would have to be increased in order to avoid loss of revenue. Whether tax revenues as a whole were increased or decreased would depend upon the mix of macroeconomic policies adopted. It might be desirable to reduce tax revenues as a device to obtain voter approval for the whole program.

A shift in the tax structure of the sort envisioned here would minimize changes in the relative incomes of wage earners—after taxes—particularly in those sectors of the labor market that would be most heavily affected by an increase in the minimum wage. An increase in earned income on the part of the lowest paid workers would be supplemented by reductions both in tax rates for higher paid workers and in actual taxes paid for many. The net effect would tend to keep income differentials much as they were before the increase in the minimum wage and would minimize the spreading effect of an increased minimum wage through the wage structure. It might even be wise to overcompensate workers in the low-middle income levels in order to minimize objections and, for political reasons, to assure reduced tax rates for a great majority of taxpayers.

ELIMINATING POVERTY

A health and decency minimum wage, accompanied by the other measures suggested here, would have a significant effect on the economy. Much of our inner city ghettos would disappear relatively quickly. Low wage employment is the chief source of income for the ghettos, and ghettos are a major source of low wage labor for the economy. A decent minimum wage, in addition to full employment and public employment programs, would pull the ghettos out of their cycle of poverty and underdevelopment. There will be less need for large scale welfare programs. Improved incomes would mean better diets, better health, better housing and more city tax revenues to support schools and other public services. Minority business enterprise will be encouraged. With higher incomes, a good deal of the despair and apathy that lead to drug abuse and crime would be dispersed. Our urban problems would not disappear overnight, but many of them would be greatly alleviated.

One side effect of a health and decency minimum wage is its impact on the welfare system. At the present time, welfare payments and other types of transfers are kept to low levels in order not to spoil the incentive to work in the low wage sector of the labor market. For example, welfare payments are kept below prevailing low wage rates and generally average about half of the necessary minimum subsistence income. Who would work for 2.00 dollars an hour if welfare provided 4,000 dollars annually for a family of four, instead of about 2,000 dollars. If a decent minimum wage were paid, we could afford to raise transfer payments for those who cannot work to at least the subsistence level and, probably, to a little more, without interfering with work incentives. Even the welfare system—what would remain of it—could be humanized.

Other effects will be felt throughout the entire economy. Some goods now produced in large part by low wage labor would be imported. Such items as shoes, clothing and furniture would be produced either abroad or in new plants that had substituted capital for labor on a large scale. A better trained labor force would be more heavily concentrated in the capital-intensive industries. With labor more expensive than at the present time, the service industries would themselves be more capital-intensive: services would be provided from within the family to a far greater extent. One would find that automobiles, television sets, refrigerators and similar consumer durable goods would be made with modular parts that could be replaced at home. Many more durable goods will be made to be junked rather than to be repaired at great expense.

Somewhat more extensive public services would also be provided: voters would probably become accustomed to higher levels of service provided by public employment programs during the transition period and would demand their retention. But most importantly, a strong beginning toward a more equal distribution of income would be made. The low wage sector of the economy would have disappeared. The tax system would have been restructured to weigh more heavily on high income families and less heavily on the middle incomes. The bulk of the poor would be earning a satisfactory income; those not able to work would be receiving decent levels of assistance. It would not be utopia, but it would be the most important step toward a humane economy that could be taken by a private enterprise economy.

Sex and Income Inequality among the Employed

By Mary Townsend Hamilton

ABSTRACT: Discrimination in the labor market has received considerable attention in the last two decades. Racial aspects have been a primary concern, but the question of discrimination against females has assumed an increasing importance. Despite statements of alleged discrimination against women, there is a paucity of empirical evidence. For the most part, the evidence cited—including that in governmental studies—is based upon comparisons of gross earnings by sex obtained from census studies or studies of particular industries. The purpose of this study is to isolate pure measures of wage discrimination on the basis of sex, within narrowly defined occupations. The measures are pure in that factors other than sex, to which wage differentials might be attributed, are taken into account. The results of the analysis of wages in four narrowly defined occupations clearly suggest that wage discrimination has a sex dimension. A sex variable is consistently powerful in explaining wage dispersion. Moreover, the estimated sex differentials generally exceed those related to color, often by considerable amounts. This finding poses obvious theoretical questions. If the wage for labor is determined under free market conditions, the continued existence of discrimination seems implausible in the absence of real differences in productivity among sex and color groups. This suggests that there are differences in the supply and demand curves relating to different groups of labor which arise out of subjective, rather than objective, factors.

Mary T. Hamilton is Associate Professor and Chairman of the Department of Finance, School of Business Administration at Loyola University of Chicago. Educated at Wellesley College and the University of Pennsylvania, she is co-author of The Stock Market: Theories and Evidence *and several journal articles. Dr. Hamilton was a member of the Price Commission during Phase II and is currently serving as Vice-Chairman of the Food Advisory Committee, Phase III.*

DISCRIMINATION in the labor market has received considerable attention in the last two decades. Racial aspects have been a primary concern, but the question of discrimination against females has assumed an increasing importance in recent years. One obvious reason for this is the sex amendment to Title VII of the Civil Rights Act of 1964. More fundamental, however, is the expanding role of women in the labor force.

INTRODUCTION

In 1900, 18 percent of women, fourteen or more years of age, were in the work force. By 1972 the participation rate of women, sixteen or more years of age, was 44 percent. Moreover, married women—20 percent of whom had children under six—were a majority of these workers. The increase since 1947 in workers from this source alone accounted for 15 percent of the total labor force in 1972. Women workers as a whole were almost 40 percent of the working population. In view of these dramatic changes, it is hardly surprising that questions of discrimination on the basis of sex have achieved prominence.

At the same time, controversy over the extent of discrimination on the basis of sex is widespread. A wealth of information about the legal aspects of sex discrimination has appeared since 1964; however, there is still a paucity of empirical evidence relative to race-related statistics. In fact, no testimony regarding the sex amendment to Title VII was heard before either the House Committee on the Judiciary or the House Committee on Education and Labor.

This study focuses on one aspect of sex discrimination—namely, wage or income inequality among the employed. Of course, this is only part of the problem, but a part that should be measurable, to some degree. The statistics cited as evidence of wage discrimination are most frequently either median earnings reported in census data or occupational earnings taken from studies made by the Bureau of Labor Statistics in particular industries or areas. By way of example, aggregate comparisons based on census data indicate that in 1971 the median wage or salary income of female, year-round, full-time workers was only 60 percent of that of males. The ratio adjusted for differences in average full-time hours worked is 66 percent. The gap varies considerably by broad occupational groups; yet within many of these groups, the relative earnings position of women deteriorated between 1956 and 1969. The ratios in 1971 were marginally above those in 1969.

These comparisons are gross; while striking, they are not conclusive evidence of the existence, or extent, of wage discrimination.[1] For example, within a broad occupational group, females tend to be concentrated in the relatively lower paying jobs. This suggests that comparison of wages should be made at a finer occupational level. Moreover, observed differentials within narrowly defined occupations could be explained by factors other than sex, such as those related to worker quality or the establishment of employment. Some have alleged that wage discrimination is illusory in that adjustment for such factors would eliminate the observed earnings gap. However, there is a reverse argument. If, in fact, females

1. An analysis of wage differentials based on adjustments of 1950 census data was done by Henry N. Sanborn. See "Pay Differences between Men and Women," *Industrial and Labor Relations Review* 17 (July 1964), pp. 534–550. A more recent analysis, using 1960 census data, was made by Victor Fuchs. See "Differences in Hourly Earnings between Men and Women," *Monthly Labor Review* 94 (May 1971), pp. 9–15.

are of higher quality or located in high wage establishments, the true wage differential may be obscured in gross comparisons.

SOME EMPIRICAL ESTIMATES OF WAGE DISCRIMINATION

The findings to be discussed are taken from an analysis of wage discrimination in the Chicago area.[2] The study includes workers in four narrowly defined occupations, in a random sample of 75 firms in the Chicago-Northwestern Indiana Consolidated Area. The occupations are: accountant, tabulating machine operator, punch press operator and janitor-janitress combined. The data related to individual workers were collected from company personnel records as part of a larger study of the Chicago labor market.[3]

The purpose of the analysis is to isolate, within each occupation, pure measures of wage discrimination on the basis of sex. The measures are pure in that factors other than sex, to which wage differentials might be attributed, are taken into account. These include individual differences in worker quality associated, for example, with age, education, experience, training and seniority and differences related to the establishments where individuals were employed.

The differentials were estimated by multiple regression techniques that allow for the simultaneous influence of other variables. The observations are individual workers. The dependent variable is wage per hour at work in the last week of June, 1963. The wage,

2. Mary T. Hamilton, "A Study of Wage Discrimination by Sex: A Sample Survey in the Chicago Area" (Ph.D. diss. University of Pennsylvania, 1969).

3. Albert Rees and George P. Shultz (with the assistance of Mary T. Hamilton, David P. Taylor and Joseph C. Ullman), *Workers and Wages in an Urban Labor Market* (Chicago: University of Chicago Press, 1970).

as recorded in personnel records, has been adjusted for hours of work and days of paid vacation and holidays. Overtime pay is not included except in the case of a relatively small number of individuals employed in establishments where standard overtime was part of the regularly scheduled work week. No adjustments have been made for fringe benefits. Although the data were collected, it was impossible to attach any meaningful dollar amounts to the various plans.

The sex variable enters as a 0, 1 dummy. For each occupation, two estimates of the sex-wage differential—the coefficient of the dummy—were made. The first relates to wage differences after standardization for characteristics of the individual workers. The second estimate takes into account, as well, differences between establishments where employment was located. These include size, industry, unionization and location. Since the observations in the regressions are individuals, variables relating to these differences are included by assigning the same value of an establishment variable to each individual within an establishment. In some cases, the second regression does not include all of the variables which appear in the first, because not all may still contribute to the explanation of wage dispersion. This is not surprising: some individual qualities may be important in gaining entry into an establishment, but not important within the establishment.

The regressions are ordinary least-squares estimates; for the most part, the independent variables enter additively. This approach assumes that the relationship between wages and explanatory variables—other than sex—is the same for males and females. Results of analysis of wage dispersion within sex groups are generally consistent with this assumption. An exception, discussed

TABLE 1

Estimated Measures of Wage Differentials Attributable to Sex

	Accountants	Tab Machine Operators	Punch Press Operators	Janitors and Janitresses
Mean wage per hour at work	$3.926	$2.728	$2.591	$2.291
Coefficient of variation ($\sigma/\bar{w}$)	20.4%	18.2%	16.8%	16.1%
Sex-wage differential—actual	$0.687	$0.261	$0.130	$0.372
Percentage of male wage	17.3%	9.4%	4.9%	15.6%
Estimated coefficient of sex dummy				
Individual variables only	−0.440	−0.378	−0.199	−0.409
Including establishment variables	−0.432	−0.330	−0.250*	−0.398
Percentage of male wage				
Individual variables only	11.1%	13.6%	7.5%	17.1%
Including establishment variables	10.9%	11.9%	9.5%	16.7%
Number of observations	228	216	303	646
Percentage female	6.1%	21.3%	39.6%	26.8%
Number of establishments	44	32	14	54
R² of regressions				
Individual variables only	0.404	0.586	0.455	0.422
Including establishment variables	0.444	0.607	0.701	0.561

* This estimate comes from the regression with an interaction term for incentive pay.

below, is the differential impact of incentive pay arrangements on wages of male and female punch press operators.

The results of the regression analysis clearly suggest that wage discrimination has a sex differential. The sex variable is consistently powerful in explaining wage dispersion. The estimated wage differential ranges from 7.5 to 17.1 percent of the male wage in the occupation (these findings are summarized in table 1). It was also possible to make some comparisons between wage differentials attributable to color and those attributable to sex. The latter generally exceed—and often by substantial amounts—the nonwhite differentials. The next three sections discuss the findings in more detail.

White-collar occupations

Accounting is the only professional occupation included in this study. An accountant's duties may be generally described as the application of principles of accounting to install and maintain an accounting system. This may include modification and supervision of an existing system or the installation of a new one. His work requires more skill than that of a bookkeeper who makes routine entries in accounting records. By definition, the sample of accountants in this study excludes financial or corporate officers and accountants who supervise other accountants; those who supervise bookkeepers are included.

The sample includes two hundred and twenty-eight accountants, fourteen of them females—or 6.1 percent of the group. The latter are employed in ten of the forty-four establishments with workers in the occupation. In one of these, the female is the only accountant; the other nine employ men, as well.

The average wage per hour at work

for males in the occupation is 3.968 dollars; for women, it is 3.281 dollars. The differential is 17 percent of the male wage. The estimated coefficients of the sex dummy are −0.43 and −0.44, or 11 percent of the male wage.[4] Although the estimated cost—that is, loss of income—of being a female is below the gross differential of sixty-nine cents, it is still substantial. For example, assuming 2,000 hours of work per year, the annual cost is nearly 900 dollars. Moreover, the stability of the coefficient, when establishment variables are added to the regression, suggests that women are not disproportionately represented in establishments which pay lower wages for other reasons. In other words, for the same wage, an employer can hire females of higher quality than males. However, discrimination is not necessarily inter-firm; females in this sample do not seem to lack entry into high wage establishments.

The results of the analysis for tabulating machine operators support those relating to accountants. A tabulating machine operator wires, installs and operates machines that process data. This may include sorting, interpreting and producing punch cards. Supervisors are excluded from this study.

Twenty-one percent, or forty-six of the two hundred and sixteen tabulating machine operators in the sample are female. In all, thirty-two establishments are represented; ten employ females. In three firms, there are no males in the occupation.

The gross differential between male and female mean wages per hour at work is twenty-six cents, or 9 percent of the mean wage of males in the occupation. The estimated coefficient of the sex dummy is −0.378 in the regression with individual variables and −0.330 in

that with establishment variables. In other words, females earn an estimated thirty-three to thirty-eight cents an hour less than their male equivalents. This is 12 to 14 percent of the male wage, as compared with the 11 percent estimated for accountants. In contrast to the results for the latter, the pure sex-wage differential for tab operators is larger than the gross differential. No doubt, this is due in part to the older age and longer seniority of the females in this sample; the gross comparison of wages does not take this into account.

In this study, tabulating machine operator is the only occupation with a distribution permitting a test of a hypothesis advanced by Donald McNulty and John Buckley.[5] Briefly, the hypothesis is: women in establishments with an exclusively female occupation earn less than those in establishments where the same occupation is mixed; no comparable difference is discernible for males. In this sample, the females are divided equally between the two types of establishments.

In order to test this hypothesis, an interaction term was added to the regressions to permit the coefficient of the sex dummy to be different for the two groups of females. The results do suggest that there is a difference in the relative wage disadvantage of females which is related to the sex composition of the occupation within the establishment where women are employed. The additional argument that the earnings of males are not affected by the presence of females was tested by including, in the regressions for males

4. Both t values are 2.5.

5. Donald J. McNulty, "Differences in Pay between Men and Women Workers," *Monthly Labor Review* 90 (December 1967), pp. 40–43; and John E. Buckley, "Pay Differences between Men and Women in the Same Job," *Monthly Labor Review* 94 (November 1971), pp. 36–39.

only, a dummy taking the value of 1 for individuals in establishments with females in the occupation. This variable contributes nothing to the explanatory power of the regression.[6] Both McNulty and Buckley suggest that this unique finding may be attributable to differences in the industry of employment of the two groups of females. However, the stability of the sex coefficient, when establishment variables are added to the regression, would seem to contradict this view.

Blue-collar operations

The analysis of wage dispersion in the blue-collar occupations has two distinguishing features. First, females are represented in sufficient numbers to run separate regressions for each sex group. In addition, the racial composition is such that some comparisons of estimates of sex discrimination vis-à-vis racial discrimination can be made.

The first occupation, punch press operator, is interesting in that many of the workers were on incentive pay. A punch press operator sets up and operates power presses that trim, punch or shape parts from metal or plastic stock. Presses may differ in both size and weight. Apprentice operators are excluded from the sample.

The observed differential in wages of the two sexes is thirteen cents, or 5 percent of the male wage. This is considerably lower than that of the two white-collar operations. The coefficient of the female dummy has a negative value of −0.199 in the regression with individual variables only and −0.500 when establishment variables are added. These are 7.5 and 18.9 percent of the male wage, respectively. The second

is considerably above the 5 percent differential in actual wages.[7]

The twenty cent differential estimated in the first regression is larger than the observed thirteen cent differential, in part because of the higher seniority of the females. The startling increase in the estimated differential, when establishment variables are included, is due to a combination of factors. One is the incentive pay variable that operates in opposite directions for the two groups. The fact that it appears with a positive coefficient in the overall regression suggests that the sex dummy may be serving in part as a proxy for the negative effect of incentive pay for women. In the separate regressions, incentive pay has a negative effect of twelve cents for females and a positive effect of thirty-two cents for males. In the regression for all workers regardless of sex, the coefficient is again positive, but only nine cents. No doubt, this accounts for part of the large increase in the value of the sex dummy when establishment variables are included.

Since it is possible that the large size of the coefficient of the sex dummy can be attributed in part to the above results, one can argue for the inclusion of an interaction term to allow the coefficient of the incentive pay variable to differ for the sexes. Adding a variable that is the product of the dummies for sex and incentive pay results in coefficients of the expected signs for males and females. The coefficients of the other variables are substantially unchanged, with the exception of that for the sex dummy. Its absolute value is reduced from 0.50 to 0.25. This appears to be more reasonable.

The finding of reverse effects may not be so odd as it would appear at first

6. The t values are 0.6 and 0.2; the inclusion of the variable increases the standard errors of the regressions.

7. The t values of the dummy are quite large in both regressions, 5.1 and 12.7.

TABLE 2

ESTIMATED MEASURES OF WAGE DIFFERENTIALS ATTRIBUTABLE TO SEX AND COLOR

	Punch Press Operators			Fork Lift Truckers	Janitresses and Janitors				
	All	Male	Female	All	Male	Female	All	White	Nonwhite
Mean wage per hour of work	$2.591	$2.642	$2.512	$2.681	$2.390	$2.018	$2.291	$2.284	$2.293
Coefficient of variation ($\sigma/\bar{w}$)	16.8%	18.5%	12.7%	14.3%	14.0%	15.7%	16.1%	15.8%	16.9%
Estimated coefficient of sex dummy									
Individual variables only	−0.199						−0.409	−0.365	−0.514
Including establishment variables	−0.250*						−0.398	−0.393	−0.374
Percentage of male wage									
Individual variables only	7.5%						17.1%	15.3%	21.4%
Including establishment variables	9.5%						16.7%	16.5%	15.5%
Estimated coefficient of nonwhite dummy									
Individual variables only	−0.105	−0.134	−0.057	−0.157	−0.077	−0.162	−0.094		
Including establishment variables	−0.150	−0.223	−0.082	−0.156	−0.090	−0.126	−0.099		
Percentage of white wage									
Individual variables only	4.0%	5.1%	2.3%	5.8%	3.2%	7.9%	4.1%		
Including establishment variables	5.8%	8.4%	3.3%	5.8%	3.8%	6.2%	4.3%		
Number of observations	303	183	120	356	473	173	646	434	206
Percentage female	39.6%			35.1%			26.8%	27.6%	25.7%
Percentage nonwhite		10.4%	22.5%		32.3%	30.6%	31.9%		
Number of establishments	14	12	8	30	52	33	54	49	32
R^2 of regressions									
Individual variables only	0.455	0.483	0.405	0.127	0.317	0.362	0.422	0.447	0.455
Including establishment variables	0.701	0.623	0.781	0.545	0.465	0.629	0.561	0.531	0.686

* This estimate comes from the regression with an interaction term for incentive pay.

glance. If, in fact, men are more productive than women, it would be sensible for an employer—who is prevented either legally or by union contract from paying different rates to males and females—to institute incentive rates. Under such an arrangement, workers would receive uniform piece rates; earnings would be a function of output. If, on the other hand, he pays time rates, the more productive men will be relatively underpaid in that they earn lower wages per unit of output. Conversely, women on time rates will be overpaid relative to those on incentive rates.

The occupation categorized as janitress or janitor in this study may more accurately fit the description—according to the *Dictionary of Occupation Titles* [8] definition—of charwoman or porter, since the sample of firms does not include any that operate apartment buildings. Duties—which may include dusting, trash disposal, floor cleaning and polishing—are related to keeping the premises clean and orderly. Employment may be in factories, office buildings and stores. The treatment of janitresses and janitors as one combined occupation is subject to some limitations. In particular, it is possible that janitors may be assigned heavier duties or be employed in warehouses; janitresses may be employed as office cleaners in buildings. If there is a difference in occupational content, the estimated sex differentials may reflect this.

The mean wage per hour at work for males in the occupation is 2.390 dollars; for females it is 2.018 dollars. The thirty-seven cents differential is 16 percent of the mean male wage. The estimates of the coefficients of the female

dummy are −0.409 including individual variables only, and −0.398 including establishment variables.[9] The coefficients are 17.1 and 16.7 percent of the male wage, respectively. That these are quite close to the actual differential of 16 percent reflects the similarity in individual characteristics of the two sexes.

Color and sex

The nonwhite dimension of sex-wage differentials has two aspects. First, in view of the considerable attention given to wage discrimination on the basis of race or color, it is interesting to compare estimates of the latter with estimates of sex differentials derived in this study. Second, there is the question of the relative magnitude of estimated wage differentials for white females vis-à-vis nonwhite females (table 2 summarizes the findings relating to discrimination on the basis of sex and color).

Within the two blue-collar occupations where both females and nonwhites were included in the sample, the estimates of discrimination based on sex exceed those based on color—and often by considerable amounts. If the comparison is broadened to include the white-collar occupations and two additional male occupations with nonwhite representation—fork lift trucker and janitor [10]—the results are equally striking. Only one of the estimated coefficients of the sex dummy—that for punch press operators in the regression using individual variables alone—is smaller in absolute magnitude, or as a percentage of the male wage, than any

9. The t values are −15.9 and −17.4, respectively.

10. The analysis of these occupations was part of the Chicago labor market study. See also David P. Taylor, "The Market for Unskilled Negro Males in Chicago" (Ph.D. diss. University of Chicago, 1966).

8. U.S. Department of Labor, *Dictionary of Occupational Titles*, 3rd ed. (Washington: Government Printing Office, 1965), vol. 1, *Definition of Occupational Titles*.

of the corresponding estimates for the nonwhite variable. The latter range from about 2 to 8 percent of the mean wage of workers in the occupation. These results suggest clearly that it costs more to be a woman than a nonwhite.

The second issue—the wage disadvantage of nonwhite females relative to white females—was investigated by running regressions within color groups in the janitor-janitress sample. In each group, there is a sufficient number of females to include a sex dummy. It is important to bear in mind that costs of being a female, as estimated from these regressions, are the costs relative to males of the same color.

The mean wage of the whites is one cent lower than that of the nonwhites. By sex, this holds true only for males. The nonwhite males earn 2.406 dollars per hour as compared with 2.378 dollars for whites. The nonwhite females earn 1.968 dollars, or about seven cents less per hour than white females. Within color groups, the wage differential between men and women is thirty-four cents for whites and forty-four cents for nonwhites. These differentials are 14 and 18 percent, respectively, of the mean wages of the male groups.

The estimated cost, without adjustment for characteristics of the establishment of employment, is greater for a nonwhite female—fifty-one cents as compared to thirty-six cents for a white female. These are 21 and 15 percent, respectively, of the mean wage for males in the color group. If establishment variables are taken into account, the estimated costs are more similar; in fact, the differential for a white woman—39 cents—is slightly larger than the estimated 37 cents for a nonwhite. However, the change in the estimated coefficient of the sex dummy in the regression for nonwhites when

establishment variables are included does suggest that nonwhite women, relative to nonwhite men, are more likely to be employed in low wage establishments. This does not seem to be true of the white females.

Although the estimated sex-wage differentials after establishment variables have been taken into account are almost the same for whites and nonwhites, it is important to remember that the female wages have been compared with wages of males of the same color. If the comparison is made between the wages of females and those of males, the cost of being a nonwhite woman includes not only the differential attributable to sex, but also that attributable to color. In this sense, the estimated wage differential for nonwhite women exceeds that for white women.

SUMMARY

In summary, the analysis presented here clearly suggests the presence of wage differentials attributable to sex. The estimates for the four occupations range from 8 to 17 percent of the male wage when adjusted for differences in worker quality.[11] The range is 10 to 17 percent after further allowance for differences between establishments where employment is located.

Observed differentials in wages may be larger or smaller than the pure differentials, depending upon the quality and establishment mix of the workers. In general, it has been argued here that if the observed differential is smaller than that estimated using individual variables only, the females are likely to be of higher quality, in terms of the variables included in the regressions, than the males with whom the comparison is made. In addition, if the

11. The estimate for nonwhite janitresses, when compared to nonwhite janitors, is even higher—21.4 percent.

estimated wage differential is increased substantially when establishment variables are taken into account, the presumption is that the females are disproportionately represented in high wage establishments. Other things being equal, the inclusion of establishment variables—that operate in this direction and that are associated with establishments of female employment—will increase the estimate of the wage differential attributable to sex.[12] Similarly, if the reverse is true and the estimate of the wage differential is reduced by the inclusion of establishment variables, one can argue that females tend to be employed in establishments that have low wages, reflecting factors such as industry and location. Finally, an estimate of wage differentials that exhibits stability suggests that discrimination is not necessarily a barrier for entry into high wage firms, but operates within the firm. The analysis of accountants provides a good example.

One caveat is in order. Estimates are pure only insofar as the statistical analysis incorporates all of the many determinants of wages. A consideration which has been neglected is the employer's appraisal—presumably, according to traits such as willingness to assume responsibility and innovativeness—of the employee. There is no way to incorporate subjective determinants of wages in this study.

In conclusion, one may ask if the results of this study prove the existence of wage discrimination on the basis of sex.[13] If discrimination is de-fined in the narrow sense of paying workers different wages for identical work, the findings of this analysis are not relevant. If, however, one accepts the premise that wage discrimination includes the employment of workers of different quality for the same wage—something more plausible and certainly less visible—the implications of this analysis are clear. Discrimination on the basis of sex does exist, or did in the Consolidated Area in 1963, and often exceeds that related to color or race.

This conclusion poses obvious theoretical questions. If the wage for labor is determined under free market conditions, the continued existence of discrimination seems implausible in the absence of real differences in productivity among sex and color groups. This suggests that there are differences in the supply and demand curves relating to different groups of labor which arise out of subjective, rather than objective, factors. On the supply side, one might argue that females and nonwhites are unaware of true market conditions and therefore offer labor of a given quality at prices below those demanded by white males. On the demand side, assuming an employer has no real taste for discrimination,[14] differences in his demand curves for labor could be due to subjective notions in regard to productivity. For example, it has been argued that there is an addi-

---

12. If the estimated influence of other variables is considerably different in the presence of establishment variables, this may not follow.

13. It should be mentioned that the legality of sex discrimination is not a primary concern in this study. Although the Civil Rights Act of 1964 was not in effect at the date of the wage data, the Equal Pay Act did exist. Of greater relevance here is that many states, including Illinois, had then, and still have, protective laws for women. These often include limitation on the amount of weight women may lift or the work conditions. If heavy work is more generously rewarded, and there are differences in this respect within an occupation, women may legally earn less than men.

14. Gary S. Becker, *The Economics of Discrimination* (Chicago: University of Chicago Press, 1957).

tional cost attached to female labor because of higher absenteeism and turnover. Although this does not seem to be supported by the evidence—if age, skill levels and other factors are taken into account [15]—the effective demand curve for the employer is his subjective one rather than the objective market demand curve. On this view, the existence of discrimination would not necessarily conflict with traditional economic theory.

It seems clear that there is a need for more data and more research on this subject. The latter should focus not only on empirical aspects but also on theoretical issues, since these are likely to figure importantly in prescribing appropriate public policy.

15. An interesting review of some of the evidence is contained in U.S. Department of Labor, Women's Bureau, "What About Women's Absenteeism and Labor Turnover?" (Washington, D.C.: Government Printing Office, 1965).

Some Micro-Economic Reflections on Income and Wealth Inequalities

By Harry G. Johnson

ABSTRACT: Concern about inequality involves naive anthropomorphism and the Judaic-Christian tradition. Both lead to anachronistic images of modern society and to concern with sharing its presumably effortlessly-acquired surplus. Observed inequality in contemporary society is largely the by-product of the success of that society in providing opportunities for self-fulfillment. As examples, consumption needs and income-earning capacity are poorly synchronized over time, implying cross-sectional inequalities between people at different ages; people's consumption preferences also differ early and late in life. People differ in their preferences for either risky or safe occupations. The policy problem of inequality reform is to correct inequalities of opportunity without taxing socially useful exercises of choice and subsidizing socially undesirable ones. One of the major sources of difficulty is the role of the family in the transmission of material property, genetic characteristics—good or bad—and attitudes towards work and life. Few, indeed, would be prepared to alter sufficiently the institution of the family to eliminate these family-transmitted sources of inequality.

Harry G. Johnson is Professor of Economics at both the London School of Economics and the University of Chicago, and was recently Irving Fisher Visiting Professor at Yale University. Educated at the Universities of Toronto, Cambridge and Harvard, he has written widely on both social policy relating to inequality and the pure theory of income distribution; his most recent book is The Theory of Income Distribution.

THE subject of inequalities of income and wealth is of perennial interest, erupting into acute concern from time to time. Such eruptions show a high degree of correlation with two frequently—but not necessarily—related phases of economic and political development: (1) serious, and/or prolonged, depression which both frustrates prevalent expectations of prosperity, security and rising standards of living and generates private and public concern over the growth of income and the exploitation of opportunities for increasing income in the future through application and planning; (2) loss of national self-confidence, with respect to both the purposiveness of the political process and the quality of life provided by the economic system, which the political process is presumed to direct to the service of aims nobler than the mere satisfaction of material wants. In the modern world, with its rapid international communications system, concern with inequality in the United States tends to spread to other countries that lack the same objective domestic reasons for discontent. For example, recent discussion of poverty in Canada and the United Kingdom can be fairly reliably traced back to the United States: first in the case of the early 1960s, to the evident and well-publicized failure of Blacks, and of poor people generally, to participate in the national affluence; and later, to the demoralizing effects, especially upon educated and draftable young males, of the expensive fiasco in Vietnam.

THE FOUNDATIONS FOR CONCERN WITH INEQUALITY

The underlying foundations for sporadic, acute concern with inequality seemingly consists of two elements. The first is a naive and basically infantile anthropomorphism: because men are physically identical—at least, men in reasonably homogeneous ethnic and other social groupings—inequalities in the socially determined capacity to satisfy biological and social wants are considered unjust. Such anthropomorphism either disregards or denies the social role of these inequalities in motivation and reward, which contribute to the organization of the society for survival and progress in the face of erosive internal and external pressures. The second element is the historical, Western inheritance of the Judaic-Christian tradition: the equality of man before God. Originally, this belief was primarily an affirmation of the right to survival and self-fulfillment for a minority group against which there was discrimination; now—following the advent of the Industrial Revolution and the associated rise of popular democratic government—it has been shorn of its countervailing affirmation of the religious legitimacy of duly constituted authority and status differentiation by the materialistic secularization of culture.

In essence, these elements are emotional rather than rational; as a result, they lend themselves both to the interpretation of current social organization in terms of archaic myths and to the projection of personal self-doubts and strains engendered by life in modern society. In particular, there are strong tendencies to interpret modern society in terms of feudal or early industrial structures which were based upon the family inheritance of landed or accumulated property in the nonhuman means of production. This interpretation is especially anachronistic for those societies which are based upon the opportunity for immigrants to escape limitations, imposed by a class structure, on economic and social mobility. American society is an explicit—although not singular—prototype; other societies are also increasingly incorporating elements of social reward for economic achievement. Furthermore, there are tendencies to identify equality with the universal opportunity to enjoy the advantages of cultivation of self—formerly reserved to the few who monopolized the economic surplus above subsistence through capture, accumulation, ownership and careful administration of scarce nonhuman factors of production—without worrying about how a surplus of sufficient size can be created and maintained if no one is entitled to the profits of minding the store.

These misinterpretations of the problem lead to an exaggerated and naive conception of the importance of, and urgent need to correct, inequality. This naiveté is reflected in the use of such superficial and irrelevant statistics as: the top x percent of the population receives a percent of the income—where x is a small fraction and a a sufficiently large integer to convey the impression of obscenity. They also lead to analytically weak or unsupported recommendations for policy, such as remedying inequality by giving large sums, taken from those who currently have high incomes, to those who have not.

PROBLEMS OF DETERMINING INEQUALITY

This is not to deny that there are serious ethical problems of inequality about which something should be done. However, I wish to assert that the problem should not be viewed in terms of the absolute ethical principle that all men should be economically and socially equal, but rather ought to be viewed and analyzed in terms of a sophisticated understanding of the mechanisms of modern society's economic organization. The essential point in this assertion is that observed inequality in income distribution is, to a large extent, a by-product of the modern economic system.

The success of a modern economic system lies in its providing opportunities of free choice and self-fulfillment for man—considered, in the short run, as having diverse tastes, preferences and attitudes; in the long run, as being mortal, with a limited life-span of patterned change in physical, mental and social characteristics; and as having hopes of transcendental immortality dependent upon the procreation of his species. The economic opportunities which the system provides should be consistent with the survival and progress of human society and not dependent upon the institutions of legal or de facto slavery that characterized earlier systems. Therefore, in a broad sense, the problem of inequality is that of determining the areas in which, and the extent to which, modern society falls short of this ideal generalization; of devising appropriate remedies for these shortcomings; and of avoiding the danger of superficial solutions to problems at the expense of creating new and more intractable basic difficulties.

In traditional debates on the subject of inequality, the conservative defense of things-as-they-are rests upon the proposition that inequality is necessary to provide incentives for hard work, discipline, inventiveness and accumulation; the only exception customarily allowed is the legitimacy of the claims of the deserving poor—that is, those who are poor through no fault of character or circumstance of their own—on the conscience of the rich. This position is indefensible not simply because it is easy to pick holes in its almost complete endorsement of all inequalities but, more fundamentally, because it entails an antidemocratic instrumental concept of the relation of the citizen to the state.

The point being made here is quite different: the exercise of the alternatives of choice provided to the citizen necessarily give rise to observed inequalities of income, as conventionally measured. Efforts to prevent this outcome, or to cancel it out by post facto income redistribution, run the serious risk of depriving the citizen of the benefits of freedom of choice and self-fulfillment and of eventually requiring a reversion to a more authoritative, or totalitarian, structure of society and the state.[1] This point rests firmly upon: various recent developments in the micro-economic analysis of the functioning of the labor market, most notably the life cycle theory of the consumption function; the concept of human capital; the analysis of the implications for career choices of varying attitudes towards risk and future, versus present, consumption; and the detailed theory of leisure as a consumption good.

To put the point very briefly and generally, one can ignore differences among individuals in opportunities and capacities for economic performance, for the moment, and concentrate on the implications of significant differences in tastes and preferences. One can expect to observe the following phenomena— as well as others not listed—all of which

1. An important signpost is the tendency for Western governments to be increasingly pressed towards the use of incomes policy as a means of controlling the inflation, consequent on state assumption of responsibility for full employment, as a matter of achieving the two presumed social objectives of economic efficiency and economic equality. What is initially intended as a macro-economic policy for eliminating a socially undesirable side-effect in pursuit of these objectives inevitably becomes a range of micro- interventions in the freedom of individual economic decisions.

would lead to observed differences in labor income on a cross-sectional basis and some of which, to observed differences in wealth and property.[2]

Economic characteristics of the human life span

First, the individual life span is economically characterized by nonsynchronous patterned variation with age, in both material consumption needs and potential productive contribution. On the consumption side, the typical pattern involves limited but gradually expanding needs during a first period of upbringing and education; a multiplication of needs in the phase of family formation, child-bearing and child-rearing; a phasing out of these needs as children, in their turn, mature and leave home; and a subsequent diminution of needs with aging and the approach of death, possibly with a final upsurge of needs for medical attention and physical care. On the production side, the individual begins life incapable of productive contribution and dependent upon parental provision; defers the exploitation of immediate productive potential for the sake of investment in education to increase future productive potential; acquires increasing potential through job experience up to some peak point, after which capacity gradually depreciates; and retires from active participation in production, long before death.

These nonsynchronous consumption and production patterns over the life span would imply cross-sectional inequality of income and wealth. These inequalities would exist because incentives to earn money, rather than to enjoy leisure, vary with age and family

2. For further discussion see, Harry G. Johnson, *The Theory of Income Distribution* (London: Gray-Mills Publishing, 1973), especially the final two chapters.

responsibility—in youth, with claims on family resources. Furthermore, it is rational to convert human capital—earning power—into material capital and vice versa—for example, by borrowing or by investing in income-yielding property in order to finance family formation, possibly education of self, and/or children, and retirement. Obviously, such cross-sectional, statistically-created evidence of inequality, where in essence there is none, should not be interpreted as indicating a significant social problem.

Individual preferences

Second, individual choices reflecting differences in preferences will produce observed inequalities of labor income, property income or wealth among individuals at the same phase of the life cycle. People can legitimately differ in their preferences: some may prefer an early, austere, hard-working and productive life for the sake of a comfortable old age as an independent worker or affluent retired person; others may prefer to live it up in their youth while hoping that their future will take care of itself. They can also legitimately differ in their preferences for either family formation and child upbringing or more personal leisure and material consumption, in the potential child-raising and subsequent phases of the life cycle. They may choose between a fixed commitment to regular, but limited, hours of work and the freedom to work in concentrated spurts, punctuated by periods of voluntary idleness; or between either high material consumption and scanty leisure or low material consumption and ample leisure—where leisure should be interpreted broadly to include such phenomena as: the long paid holidays available to school teachers and civil servants; the opportunity to serve one's fellow men through political,

charitable and civic-minded activity; the opportunity to entertain oneself by exercising one's mental and physical talents.[3]

Risk

Finally, given the uncertainties of career choice in an uncertain world, people may legitimately differ in their attitudes towards risk. Those who dislike risk will settle for careers which offer greater security, at the expense of a lower prospective average income for such people as a group. Those who enjoy risk will opt for careers with a prospect of an exceptionally high income, at the expense of possible substantially lower individual income and also of a lower average income for such people as a group than would be obtainable in safer occupations.

A society composed of a majority of risk-averters would be statistically characterized by the presence of a relatively small number of extremely high incomes and of incomes not far below the average. By contrast, a society composed of a majority of risk-takers would be statistically characterized by a relatively high number of very low incomes and of incomes not much above the average. The former society would presumably view its income distribution problem as one of inordinate income inequality; the latter, as one of unwarranted large scale poverty. In both cases, the statistical facts are the outcome of voluntary choice. To make a social problem of them would require introducing the ad-

3. In place of resenting those people whose life-style involves high and conspicuous consumption of material goods, one might well pity them for the poverty of personal and cultural resources that make this life-style their optimal choice. Some radicals, of course, manage to meld resentment and contempt to a high pitch of moral indignation about those who live more richly and ostentatiously than they, themselves.

ditional—although not unreasonable—assumption that the choices of a significant number of society's members are biased by ignorance of opportunities and risks, a lack of resources to exploit opportunities and/or the fact that inequalities in the achievements of parents are unfairly passed on to their children as inequalities of knowledge and resources for exploiting opportunities.

SUGGESTED REMEDIES FOR INEQUALITY

The conclusion to be drawn from this brief analysis is that ethically-motivated social concern about inequality should properly focus on inequalities of opportunities and the knowledge and resources required to exploit them properly. It should not focus on the statistical facts of measured inequality which indiscriminately reflect both inequality of original opportunities and rational, voluntary choices among available opportunities intended to maximize individual self-fulfillment. Analysis and remedies that focus on the resultant income distribution—and attempt to correct it by redistributive, progressive income and inheritance taxes and social security systems—will, if implemented, have unintended or, perhaps even worse, intended side effects. Such taxation will disproportionately burden those who have preferences for non-procreation—that is, for high-quality, low-number families rather than high-quantity, low-quality, high-public-expense families; preferences for future, over present, consumption; preferences for high-skilled, over low-skilled, careers; preferences for material, over leisure, consumption; and preferences for risky, high-payoff, over secure, low-payoff, careers.

In effect, some of the preferences that would be subsidized are definitely antisocial. Apart from the public or tax-payers' expense imposed by private indulgence in fecundity, losses accrue to society if those with creative talents choose leisure rather than work or further development of their talents through rigorous training. The absence of social devices for pooling many career risks implies that private risk-taking tends to be on too low a scale for social optimality, anyway. Moreover, advocacy of redistributionary taxation and expenditure policies almost invariably assumes that habits of hard work and honesty will survive fiscal mauling; however, tax avoidance and evasion respond readily to profit incentives—especially if the taxes are thought to be unjust—and, in the long run, social institutions and customs adapt to produce the kind of people favored by the fiscal system.[4]

The suggestion to focus equalitarian policies on providing information about, and resources for, exploiting available opportunities carries with it a number of obvious implications for the types of policies that might effectively be pursued: better schooling for the children of the poor; better public health care for all children; loan finance to cover maintenance costs and fees for education for the older children of impecunious parents; earlier and more directive career counseling; and public assistance to, or provision of, more information about available, alternative jobs, coupled with grants or loan assistance to facilitate geographical and occupational mobility.

Even policies of that kind raise questions about how they will operate in

4. The author has encountered complaints in Sweden that the younger generation is unwilling to adopt careers requiring responsibility and hard work, and in the United Kingdom that it is impossible to do the private saving required to attain a modicum of independence. In the United States, complaints are mounting that welfare makes it preferable for inordinately large numbers of people to opt out of work entirely.

practice. A variety of evidence suggests that, as an approximation, existing government tax and expenditure policies redistribute income from the very rich and the very poor towards the middle class. There is also massive evidence from the results of the short-lived War on Poverty, launched by President Johnson in 1964, that crash programs and bright ideas directed at the surface of the problem primarily waste resources. Low and uncertain incomes are not merely low and uncertain incomes; they are a way of life, a culture that will take a long-sustained and expensive effort to transform. A large part of this problem is the role of the family in relation to its offspring in the period of social conditioning which precedes full adulthood, signalled by the entry into the labor force, and which, to all appearances, dominates over the social conditioning provided by the formal education system.

In an important sense, modern society has created this problem for itself. It is a by-product of its success in achieving affluence and a consequence of both the narrowing down of the kinship system to the nuclear family and the social ordering of the community to include only casual social relationships with business acquaintances or a few economically-equally-situated neighbors. The result of this, along with the extreme specialization of parental participation in the economic system, is to limit severely the growing child's knowledge of the economic world—particularly in the least affluent families confined to ghetto life—and the family's resources available for investment in the exploitation of economic opportunities. Furthermore, the pace of economic change and increasing affluence frequently makes the knowledge parents have of the world out of date and misleading; thus, youth is less willing to

take parental advice than was the youth of former days—when both boys and girls could expect to live their adult lives more or less as their parents had—who could benefit from their parents' instruction and example.

The family's role in child-rearing raises two major difficulties for policies seeking to increase equality. One, which is relatively minor, is that the motivation for, or the by-product of, material success is the capacity to accumulate material property and to pass it on to one's children, thereby relieving them of the necessity to work for a living. Much contemporary inheritance taxation—and still more, swingeing inheritance tax proposals which have been advanced—aim to eliminate this effect of economic success as far as possible. Judging from the relative stability of statistics on inequality of ownership of property, the results seem to have been nugatory, by and large. To be effective in decreasing inequality, inheritance taxes should be graduated according to the amounts received by individual beneficiaries, as well as by their individual personal means, rather than by the size of the estate. However, their effect is largely negated because such taxes can be avoided in countless ways by foresighted and perfectly legal action. On the other hand, there is much qualitative evidence that large individual accumulations of wealth tend to be dispersed in a generation or two, frequently into worthy charitable purposes. Excessive concern over unearned economic advantages enjoyed by the first generation of descendants may well be too myopic as a basis for equalitarian economic reform. Of course, it is our own generation of descendants of the rich that irk us the most acutely; only as we age, do we see that their children turn out no better than ours—and sometimes far worse—and then realize, too late, that our childhood resentments were unjustified.

The far more serious problem of inequality associated with inheritance is concerned with the bequeathing of less tangible, but probably far more important, productive assets than material property. In the modern economy—as John K. Galbraith's major life work emphasizes—it is not property as such, but the ability to manage property and to combine it productively with other inputs under shrewd management, that counts. Success in this context depends broadly upon three characteristics of the individual that may be classified, in one way or another, as inherited: native ability, inherited genetically; education which, although nominally provided equally for all through the formal education system, depends upon inheritance—in the sense of a family background of parental interest, encouragement and willingness to spend real resources and time to complement and augment the formal educational experience—for its absorption and effective use; and an elusive quality which incorporates determination and ability to accept responsibility and hard work for no immediate return in discharging it—again a matter of family background and parental example which, unfortunately, does not appear to be communicated equally to children of the same parents.

CONCLUSION

The late Frank H. Knight was fond of pointing out, in criticism of the equalitarians of his day, that there is no more ethical justification for inequality of an individual's capacity to exploit opportunities, derived from genetical inheritance, than there is for inequalities of inheritance of property. This point seems incontrovertible—although it suits the book of society's critics whose superior position in society derives from their intellectual brilliance and literary facility to identify inequality as inequality derived from property income. In fact, such inequality is probably less of a fundamental social problem than the other forms of inherited inequality just mentioned; personal concentrations of material property are probably more easily dissipated by foolishness and force of circumstance than personal concentrations of familial, genetical and behavioral characteristics.

Knight was firmly convinced that it would be impossible to eliminate effectively, or to reduce significantly, inequalities associated with nontangible familial inheritance. Utopian philosophers throughout history have struggled with the problem. However, their thoughts concentrated on the organization of relatively small communities, living an austere life based upon a relatively simple and unchanging economic technology; the societies they idealized were highly regimented and joyless constructions, certain eventually to run out of great ideas whose contemplation would liberate the human spirit. In fact, this has been amply demonstrated by the unhappy experience and eventual collapse of the vast majority of utopian communities.

Today, one could conceivably do far better to ensure equality of juvenile training and opportunity; vast scientific resources of modern genetics are available, as well as material resources and administrative knowledge necessary for the raising of children under far more comfortable regimentation—psychological and physical—than that which is currently provided even by the best orphanages. Yet, which bold, but socially respectable, philosopher—not to mention which political party—would have the courage to suggest seriously the complete supersession of the family by the scientific orphanage, now or in the foreseeable future?

A World of Unequal Incomes

By Irving B. Kravis

Abstract: Income inequality is usually greater in poor countries than in rich countries. Among rich countries, incomes tend to be more equally distributed in those countries which have relatively homogeneous populations, for example, in Denmark. Socialist countries have more equality in income distribution than other countries. These facts suggest that, among nonsocialist countries, incomes should become more equal as the level of income rises. Generally, this has indeed been the historical experience of the advanced industrial countries in the last century or so. However, it is possible that income distribution became less equal at an earlier stage of development. This hypothesis of inequality widening and then narrowing as per capita incomes rise is supported by current comparisons of inequality in different countries. This would be consistent with a tendency for income inequality to increase over time in a number of today's less developed countries (LDCs). It is possible, particularly where the rate of growth in per capita gross national product (GNP) is not rapid, that the real as well as the relative income of the lower income groups may decline. The degree of inequality in the world as a whole seems to be greater than that found within most countries. There does not appear to have been very much change in the degree of world income inequality in the last quarter century.

Irving B. Kravis has been Professor of Economics at the Wharton School of Finance and Commerce, University of Pennsylvania, since 1956. He was Associate Dean of the Wharton School (1958–1960) and Visiting Professor at Harvard, Southern California and Hebrew Universities. Dr. Kravis serves as Consultant to the United States Department of State and the Statistical Office of the United Nations; and as member of the Senior Research Staff of the National Bureau of Economic Research. He was awarded the Guggenheim Fellowship (1967–1968) and the Ford Faculty Research Fellowship (1960–1961). His publications include An International Comparison of National Products and the Purchasing Power of Currencies, The Structure of Income: Some Quantitative Essays, Domestic Interests and International Obligations: A Study of Trade Safeguards, Price Competitiveness in World Trade *and many journal articles.*

The author wishes to thank Irma Adelman, Jacob Meerman, Robert Summers, Sidney Weintraub and Elinor Yudin for helpful suggestions on an earlier draft and Alicia Civitello for performing the statistical work.

THE purpose of this paper is to describe the world distribution of income and to survey some of the influences which work to produce it. Before examining the evidence, it may be worthwhile to look into some of the possible factors which work to produce income inequality. First, however, a brief note on the definition of inequality: income inequality may be defined as the average difference between each pair of incomes in the society. Whereas—as is usually the case—there are well-defined social or economic groups, total inequality can be regarded as composed partly of differences in the average incomes of the several groups and partly of income differences within each of the several groups. Therefore, from the standpoint of the world as a whole, one can examine differences in the average incomes of the various nations and then examine inequality in the distribution of income within nations. Within each nation, the same kind of analysis of the composition of inequality is possible. For example, inequality within the United States may be divided into the difference between white and nonwhite incomes and the differences of incomes within each of these racial categories. Of course, race is not the only possible basis of classification; among the other classificatory attributes which may be used are: rural versus urban, region, sex, industry, occupation, age and educational level.

THE CAUSES OF INEQUALITY

Within a nation

In most advanced market economies, total income is divided between labor and property in proportions that generally fall between two to one and three to one. Since the distribution of wealth is always more unequal than the distribution of current income, countries with private ownership of property and with large accumulations of wealth tend to have a greater degree of inequality than countries in which the private ownership of wealth is limited. This is one significant element in producing a much higher degree of equality in the distribution of income in socialist countries. In very poor countries with private ownership of property, the main form of wealth is often in land holdings which are sometimes concentrated in very few hands. Of course, there is an interaction between the distribution of wealth and the distribution of income. The explanation of the current distribution of wealth requires that historical factors, such as those governing the distribution of land at some early point in time, as well as the laws and customs governing the intergenerational transfers of wealth, be taken into account. Primogeniture, for example, leads to more concentration of wealth than equal division of estates among children; small families among the high income groups and a tendency for mating to occur within income classes lead to more concentration, when there is equal division of estates.[1]

Turning to incomes derived from work, income inequality tends to be relatively small but still significant within groups of income receivers who are homogeneous with respect to occupation, age, sex, education and race. Within such a group, some income inequality is simply a result of the impact of chance factors that affect individual incomes as people find their way through life. In addition, within a group homogeneous in other respects, there are likely to be differences in

1. F. L. Pryor, "Simulation of the Impact of Social and Economic Institutions on the Size Distribution of Income and Wealth," *American Economic Review* 63 (March 1973), pp. 50–72.

abilities which can be expected to produce differences in income. However, inherited differences are small relative to the observed differences in income. For example, the dispersion of after-tax incomes of unskilled laborers in the United States is probably around three times as great as the dispersion of intelligence test scores for four or five year olds.[2]

Natural ability also plays some role in influencing the allocation of persons to different occupations, but family background exerts major influence on the level of education, which in turn affects entry into occupations with differing average incomes. Within each occupation, incomes tend to vary with age—usually reaching a peak somewhere in the thirty-five to fifty age range and subsequently declining.

Although human abilities tend to be distributed according to the familiar, normal—bell-shaped—curve, the typical income distribution does not conform to a normal curve. It is more nearly normal in the logarithms of income, but even in log terms it is usually skewed to the right—that is, there are more very high incomes than one would expect from the log normal curve. A log normal distribution would result from the tendency for the many random influences at work to change each income by an amount proportionate to its size— the law of proportionate effect. It could also result from a number of simultaneously operating independent

influences such as race, age, education, health and hours worked, each of which would have proportionate effects on income.

Finally, intersectoral differences in income, particularly the gap between incomes in agriculture and the rest of the economy, play a large role in producing inequality.

Country-to-country differences in average incomes

Differences in income levels among nations reflect some of the same influences, but also involve some new elements. For example, some inequality in the per capita income of different countries would emerge even if the population of each nation somehow began economic activity with completely equal advantages. Inequality among the nations could be expected to develop purely as a result of chance factors; for example, accidents of weather could cause per capita incomes to deviate from equality.

However, there are powerful systematic forces producing large differences in the per capita incomes of the various countries. One major factor is the unequal distribution of natural resources: to some substantial degree, the United States has high incomes as a result of its low population density in a land area with varied agricultural and mineral resources. Industrially, the United States benefited from the fortunate location of rich deposits of coal and iron ore—two key raw materials—near cheap water transport. At the other extreme, one finds sparsely populated countries which are extremely poor in natural resources, such as Chad, and countries, such as India, which are poor in natural resources if their large populations are taken into account. On the other hand, some countries without

2. The measure of dispersion is the coefficient of variation, defined in note 7. See H. Lydall, *The Structure of Earnings* (Oxford: Clarendon Press, 1968), p. 68; and I. B. Kravis, *The Structure of Income* (Philadelphia, Pa.: University of Pennsylvania Press, 1962), p. 195. The dispersion of intelligence test scores is probably biased upward, because some proportion of it is attributable to environmental influences rather than to natural ability.

varied resources, such as Denmark, Switzerland and, more recently, Japan, have achieved high per capita incomes.

Social and economic organization also plays an important role, although one that is more difficult to assess. Mores that stress competitive individual initiative and materialistic aspirations—the Protestant ethic—are more conducive to high production and high real income levels than are customs that place the family at the center of social and economic life and that emphasize spiritual values. Also, private property and enterprise typically promote higher levels of production than socialized ownership and central planning. On the other hand, one can point to failures of private property and successes of socialism. Private ownership fails to lead to high production where the available forms of wealth are highly concentrated and where access to the economic race is denied to those who are not already wealthy. Latin America seems to provide many examples. In these circumstances, individual initiative is stifled.

The success of socialist countries lies in their improving the economic lot of that segment of the population which was most disadvantaged. It appears that centralized economic planning combined with a high degree of political control can successfully organize a society so that everyone is fed and receives the other minimum necessities, which are often unavailable to the bottom of the income distribution in a poor nonsocialist country and even, to some degree, in a rich nonsocialist country. Cuba, China and, earlier, all of Eastern Europe offer examples. Whether such a command economy can move consumption levels as far, or as rapidly, beyond the level of subsistence or adequacy as can market economies is doubtful. In short, the socialist economies have more

equality but lower average consumption levels.[3]

Instability in political and social organization which produces widespread uncertainty hampers economic growth. Investment, an indispensable ingredient of growth, requires a long planning horizon. Investors will not find it worthwhile to consider the use of today's resources to produce output three, five or ten years into the future if they cannot be sure of reaping the rewards. Periods of political instability in the last ten or fifteen years in China, Zaire and Indonesia, for example, have reduced the rate of growth in, and perhaps even the level of, per capita income.

As noted, some factors which help to explain inequality within nations are also significant in explaining international differences in average incomes. Education, according to one estimate, accounted for one-third to one-half of the differences between the per capita incomes of twenty-four developing countries and the United States.[4] The age distribution, in the sense of life span, is also relevant. Relatively short life spans found in many poor countries reduce society's return on investment in

3. Although data on income distribution in the socialist countries do not include the effects of income in kind and perquisites that form an important part of the real income of the upper income groups, it seems highly probable that inequality tends to be much smaller than in nonsocialist countries, even when these effects are taken into account.

4. A. O. Krueger, "Factor Endowment and Per Capita Income Differences Among Countries," *Economic Journal* 73 (September 1968), pp. 641–659. For a comprehensive analysis of the relationships between various social, political and economic indicators and the level of per capita income, see I. Adelman and C. T. Morris, *Society, Politics and Economic Development* (Baltimore, Md.: Johns Hopkins Press, 1967).

education.[5] Industry and occupation also contribute to international differences in incomes. Agricultural pursuits tend to produce larger incomes than others; with some exceptions, predominately agricultural countries tend to have lower per capita incomes than others.

WHAT THE NUMBERS TELL US ABOUT THE WORLD INEQUALITY

Statistics on the distribution of income may be obtained from a variety of sources, including tax records, payroll information, social security data and sample surveys. Each source has its own biases; problems of the under reporting of income and the under enumeration of recipients—especially at the extremes of the distribution—are common. The degree of inequality that is evidenced by a size distribution of income is also quite sensitive to the particular definition of income (for example, the inclusion or exclusion of nonmoney income) and the concept of the income receiving unit (for example, individual income recipients versus families or spending units).[6] Measured inequality is also affected by population coverage—for example, in the statistics available in poor countries, the rural sector is sometmies excluded.

These statistical problems make it possible for two or more income distributions referring to the same country to reveal very different degrees of inequality. Thus, any attempt at international comparison which ignores the statistical differences between the distributions of the several countries is likely to be unreliable; indeed, even in the most careful international comparisons, it is probably wiser to pay attention to only substantial differences.

An additional complication is that no single summary statistic is completely satisfactory as a measure of the degree of inequality. The shares of aggregate income received by various fractiles of the population, such as the bottom quintile and top quintile, are simple measures that are often employed. So, too, are basic statistical measures of dispersion, such as the standard deviation and the coefficient of variation. Perhaps the single most widely used summary measure of inequality is the Gini concentration ratio (CR). The CR is equal to the mean difference between each pair of incomes divided by twice the arithmetic average income.[7]

Some notion of the sensitivity of measures of inequality to differences in the definition of both income and income recipients may be illustrated by a recent study of Brazilian size distribution for 1960, which used the CR as the measure of inequality [8] (as shown in table 1). In this case, CRs differing by almost 20 percent can be obtained by changing concepts.

5. See the discussion of the effect of the dependency ratio—dependents relative to the labor force—on per capita incomes by W. W. Hicks, "A Note on the Burden of Dependency in Low-Income Areas: A Reply," *Economic Development and Cultural Change* 19, no. 3 (April 1971), pp. 471–472.

6. For further discussion of these problems, see Kravis, *Structure of Income,* pp. 181–191.

7. The standard deviation is the square root of the sum of the squared deviations from the mean divided by the number of observations. The coefficient of variation is the standard deviation divided by the mean. The CR may be explained graphically with the aid of the Lorenz curve which traces out the proportions of total income—plotted on the vertical axis—received by cumulative percentages of income recipients—plotted on the horizontal axis. The concentration ratio is the ratio of the area of actual concentration to the area of maximum possible concentration.

8. A Fishlow, "Brazilian Size Distribution of Income," *American Economic Review* 52 (May 1972), pp. 391–402.

TABLE 1

BRAZILIAN INCOME DISTRIBUTION, 1960

	MONEY INCOME Gini Concentration Index	TOTAL INCOME* Gini Concentration Index
Economically active population	.59	.52
Families	.55	.50

* Money income plus imputed income, with distribution of some fraction of the income of the household chief to family workers.

Aside from data on income distribution, in the following sections I will make extensive use of international comparisons of gross national product (GNP).[9] This measure, in a per capita variant, will be used to rank countries for poverty or wealth. Once again, there are serious grounds for doubting the comparability of the figures.

The quality of the measure of GNP in local currencies varies very widely from one country to another. Furthermore, there is no set of estimates covering all countries which converts GNPs in local currencies into a comparable set of values, while taking account of the varying purchasing power of each currency. The most common method of converting local currencies into comparable units is to use prevailing exchange rates. However, the use of exchange rates underestimates the real GNP of other countries relative to that of the United States to a degree that varies inversely with the level of per capita gross domestic product (GDP). The technical reason for this is that the purchasing power of currencies over services and labor-intensive commodities tends to vary inversely with the level of per capita incomes. Exchange rates

9. Sometimes, only the data for gross domestic product (GDP) are available. This includes the total value of the output in the territory of the country, regardless of the nationality of the recipients of the incomes. GDP less net factor incomes paid to foreigners equals GNP.

are not so much influenced by the prices of services, since few consumer services enter into international transactions.[10]

International comparisons of income inequality

Despite all these caveats about the imperfections of the data, it seems fairly clear that incomes tend to be distributed less equally in poor countries than in rich countries. A number of different studies, including those by Kravis (1960), Kuznets (1963), Lydall (1968), Oshima (1970), Adelman and Morris (1971) and Cline (1972),[11] show that,

10. M. Gilbert and I. Kravis, *An International Comparison of National Products and the Purchasing Power of Currencies* (Paris: OEEC, January 1954); B. Balassa, "The Purchasing Power Parity Doctrine: A Reappraisal," *Journal of Political Economy* 72 (December 1964), pp. 584–596.

11. I. Kravis, "International Differences in the Distribution of Income," *Review of Economics and Statistics* 42, no. 4 (November 1960), pp. 408–416; S. Kuznets, "Quantitative Aspects of the Economic Growth of Nations: VIII, Distribution of Income by Size," *Economic Development and Cultural Change* 11, no. 2, sec. 2 (January 1963); H. Lydall, *Structure of Earnings;* H. Oshima, "Income Inequality and Economic Growth: The Postwar Experiences of Asian Countries," *Malayan Economic Review* 15, no. 2 (October 1970), pp. 7–41; I. Adelman and C. T. Morris, "An Anatomy of Patterns of Income Distribution in Developing Nations," Final Report, Grant AID/csd-2236(Evanston, Ill.: Northwestern University, 1971, part 3; W. Cline, *Potential Effects of Income Redistribution on Economic Growth, Latin American Cases* (New York: Praeger, 1972).

TABLE 2

Inequality and Per Capita Consumption and GNP, Fourteen Countries, 1960s

| | Concentration Ratio | | Per Capita | |
	Date	Ratio	Consumption (1962–63)	GNP (1961)
United States	1964	100	100	100
United Kingdom	1965	95	62	52
Latin American countries				
Argentina	1961	125	31	25
Chile	1968	132	26	20
Venezuela	1962	140	22	34
Colombia	1964	150	13	10
Mexico	1963	154	23	12
Brazil	1960	159	10	8
Asian countries				
South Korea	1966	75*	n.a.	3
Japan	1963	95	40	20
Taiwan	1964	97	12	6
Ceylon	1963	122	9	5
Thailand	1962	135	9	4
Philippines	1965	138	10	7

Sources: Concentration ratios: Comparisons for United Kingdom and Latin American countries derived from W. Cline, *Potential Effects of Income Redistribution on Economic Growth, Latin American Cases* (New York: Praeger, 1972); and for the Asian countries, from H. Oshima, "Income Inequality and Economic Growth: The Postwar Experience of Asian Countries," *Malayan Economic Review* 15, no. 2 (October 1970), p. 13.

Consumption: Estimates by W. Beckerman and R. Bacon, "The International Distribution of Incomes," in *Unfashionable Economics: Essays in Honour of Lord Balogh*, ed. P. Streeten (London: Weidenfeld and Nicolson, 1970).

GNP: Data from *International Financial Statistics*, 1972 Supplement.

Notes: United States = 100.

Consumption estimates, for the United States and eight European countries, derived from a regression equation in which real per capita consumption—estimated by Gilbert and Associates, *Comparative National Products and Price Levels* (Paris: OEEC, 1958); and for nineteen Latin American countries, by S. Braithwaite, "Real Income Levels in Latin America," *Review of Income and Wealth* ser. 14, no. 2 (June 1968)—is the dependent variable and the number of telephones and quantity of newsprint are the independent variables.

GNP: Aggregate GNP converted to dollars by means of exchange rates and placed on a per capita basis.

* Relation to United States based on Oshima's index of decile inequality, which was highly correlated with the CR for the six countries for which both were given.

among the nonsocialist countries of the world, inequality tends to be higher in poor countries.

In the upper half of table 2, the six Latin American countries studied by Cline are listed in order of increasing inequality. Both consumption per capita and GNP per capita tend to diminish as the eye travels down the list. This relationship remains, although slightly al-tered, if one adjusts the per capita GDP to take account of the exchange rate bias. However, the rank correlation is not perfect; the degree of inequality is not a simple function of the real income level even among relatively homogeneous countries. This qualification is underscored by Oshima's comparisons of Asian countries, summarized in the lower part of table 2.

Further evidence of the inverse association between inequality and per capita real incomes is provided by Lydall's careful international comparisons of the size distribution of wages and salaries for more than a score of heterogeneous countries. Lydall's measures of inequality, per capita consumption and per capita GNP are set forth in table 3. The rank correlations between the inequality measures and the per capita measures vary from 0.45 to 0.77.[12]

Inequality and economic growth

If incomes tend to be more equally distributed in high income countries, can it be inferred that economic growth will bring more equality to today's less developed countries (LDCs)? Some years ago, Professor Kuznets suggested that income inequality in the advanced countries may have widened in the early phases of economic growth before it had narrowed.[13]

The factors that determine long term trends in the size distribution are various and offsetting. In the early stages of growth, changes accentuating differences in incomes may be dominant; the increasing differentiation of economic activity may lead to a greater dispersion of incomes even within the agricultural sector. For example, it was recently reported that the "Green Revolution" in India, with its "miracle" rice and wheat seeds, greatly increased the value of land, which in turn resulted in the

12. The Spearman coefficients of rank correlation are as follows:

	P_5	P_{10}	P_{75}
With consumption per capita	$-.62$	$-.73$	$+.45$
With GNP per capita	$-.77$	$-.75$	$+.53$

All the coefficients are significant at the 0.025 level.

13. S. Kuznets, "Economic Growth and Income Inequality," *American Economic Review* 45 (March 1955), pp. 1–28.

tendency of land owners to rid themselves of tenants and to use the plentiful supply of hired labor. Within the cities, economic development tends to bring sharp differences in income levels between those who have jobs and those who do not. Recent migrants from rural areas tend to have the lowest wages, and large income differences also develop between those employed in services and traditional industry, on the one hand, and those employed by modern industry, foreign enterprises and government, on the other hand.

Government development policies in many developing countries have also contributed to inequality. Strong support for industrialization has often resulted in: (1) relative diminution of agricultural incomes, (2) substantial profits in commerce and industry and (3) high income levels for the small proportion of the labor force with jobs in favored sectors.

Economic growth may foster greater equality in later stages of economic development. As industry expands and agriculture shrinks, the number of low income workers in agriculture declines and the difference between income levels in agriculture and nonagriculture narrows. Diminution in underemployment, unemployment, the number of self-employed and the unskilled category also reduce inequality. These changes increase the share of labor income and diminish the share of property income, thus reinforcing the trend towards a more equal income distribution.

Also, account must be taken of the impact of government taxing and spending. In the developed countries, government fiscal policy is an income-equalizing force, although to a lesser degree, this is true in LDCs. Meerman recently reported that the impact of government taxing and spending in the United States was to lower the CR

TABLE 3

MEASURES OF DISPERSION OF BEFORE-TAX-MONEY WAGES AND SALARIES OF FULL TIME
MALES IN NONAGRICULTURAL INDUSTRIES,
TWENTY-FIVE COUNTRIES

COUNTRY AND YEAR	PERCENTAGE OF MEDIAN INCOME RECEIVED BY SPECIFIED PERCENTILE			U. S. DOLLARS PER CAPITA	
	P_5 (1)	P_{10} (2)	P_{75} (3)	Consumption 1960 (4)	GNP 1961 (5)
Czechoslovakia, 1964	165	145	85	—	—
New Zealand, 1960–1	178	150	83	1367	1260
Hungary, 1964	180	155	83	—	—
Australia, 1959–60	185	157	84	1274	1524
Denmark, 1956	200	160	82	1208	1434
United Kingdom, 1960–1	200	162	80	1145	1461
Sweden, 1959	200	165	78	1494	1891
Yugoslavia, 1963	200	166	80	316	—
Poland, 1960	200	170	76	375	—
Germany (F. R.), 1957	205	165	77	1085	1449
Canada, 1960–1	205	166	79	1410	2128
Belgium, 1964	206	164	82	989§	1327
United States, 1959	206	167	75	1860	2830
Austria, 1957	210	170	80	834	982
Netherlands, 1959†	215	175	70	895	1056
Argentina, 1961	215	175	75	569	710
Spain, 1964	220	180	75	522	383
Finland, 1960	250	200	73	1023	1225
France, 1963	280	205	73	1080	1451
Japan, 1955	270	211	64	739	565
Brazil, 1953	380	250	—	190	215
India, 1958–9‡	400	300	65	92	77‖
Ceylon, 1963	400	300	—	170	138
Chile, 1964‡	400	300	—	485	559
Mexico, 1960	450	280	65	436	352

SOURCES: Columns (1)–(3): H. Lydall, *The Structure of Earnings* (Oxford: Clarendon Press, 1968). Column (4): W. Beckerman and R. Bacon, "The International Distribution of Incomes." Column (5): Mainly from IMF, *International Financial Statistics*, Supplement to 1972 issues.

* Income recipients are arrayed from highest to lowest. The P_5 income is the income of the recipient who is 5 percent down the list from the top. For Czechoslovakia, this income was 1.65 times the median—or middle—income.

† Married couples treated as single units.

‡ Very rough estimates based on data for manual workers only.

§ Belgium—Luxembourg.

‖ GDP.

by 11 to 22 percent, depending on the method of estimation, as against 1.5 to 9.3 percent in three developing countries.[14]

14. J. Meerman, "Fiscal Incidence in Empirical Studies of Income Distribution in Poor Countries," Agency for International Develop-

Whether these various influences upon equality actually fall into a typical pat-

ment Discussion Paper no. 25 (Washington, D.C.: U.S. Department of State, December 1972). See also C. McLure, Jr., "The Incidence of Taxation in Colombia," in *Fiscal Reform for Colombia,* ed. M. Gillis (Cambridge, Mass.: Harvard Law School, 1971).

TABLE 4

CHANGES IN INEQUALITY AND IN THE INCOME OF LOWER INCOME GROUPS,
SEVEN COUNTRIES, SELECTED PERIODS

	AVERAGE FAMILY INCOME	% SHARE OF LOWEST 20%	% SHARE OF LOWEST 60%	INDEX OF REAL FAMILY INCOME OF LOWEST 20%	INDEX OF REAL FAMILY INCOME OF LOWEST 60%	CONCENTRATION RATIO
	(1)	(2)	(3)	(4) = (1) × (2)	(5) = (1) × (3)	(6)
Argentina						
a. 1953	1298	7.4	31.9			.412
b. 1961	1454	7.0	30.5			.434
c. Index (b/a)	112.0	94.6	95.6	106	107	
Brazil						
a. 1960	513	1.2	18.2			.59
b. 1970	679	2.1	16.8			.63
c. Index (b/a)	132.4	175.0	92.3	232	122	
Ceylon						
a. 1953		5.20	27.80			.46
b. 1963		4.45	27.47			.45
c. Index (b/a)	113	85.6	98.8	97	112	
Colombia						
a. 1947			57.0*			
b. 1961			54.0*			
c. Index (b/a)	138.5		94.7*		131*	
India						
a. 1951–52 to 1954–55	88.375	4.3	23.5			.40
b. 1955–56 to 1959–60	93.14	3.0	17.4			.54
c. Index (b/a)	105.4	69.8	74.0	74	78	
Mexico						
a. 1950	740	6.1	24.6			.525
b. 1963	899	3.5	21.2			.543
c. Index (b/a)	121.5	57.4	86.2	70	105	
Puerto Rico						
a. 1953	1870	5.6	30.3			.415
b. 1963	2992	4.5	27.8			.449
c. Index (b/a)	160.0	80.4	91.7	129	147	

SOURCES: Argentina, India, Mexico and Puerto Rico: R. Weisskoff, "Income Distribution and Economic Growth" (Ph. D. diss., Harvard University, 1969).

Brazil: A. Fishlow, "Brazilian Size Distribution of Income," *American Economic Review* 62 (May 1972).

Ceylon: *Survey of Consumer Finances, 1963,* (Colombo: Central Bank of Ceylon, 1964).

Colombia: R. M. Bird, "Income Distribution and Tax Policy in Colombia," *Economic Development and Cultural Change* 18, no. 4 (July, 1970).

Index of real GDP per capita for India from *National Accounts of Less Developed Countries, 1950–66,* (Paris: O.E.C.D. Development Center, July 1968). Other data in column (1) are from sources given above.

tern of timing in most countries is an open question, as yet. The historical record does not show a phase of growing inequality in the developed countries, perhaps because the statistics do not go back far enough. Professor Kuznets' study of the record does show narrowing inequality in the developed countries, a trend which occurred mainly since World War I.[15] Oshima has suggested that a narrowing of inequality must have occurred recently in Taiwan and Japan.[16] He infers from the declines in both countries in underemployment, tenancy farming and agricultural-nonagricultural income gaps that incomes during the 1960s were more equally distributed than they were before World War II.

It appears—as Professor Kuznets has pointed out—that the degree of inequality observed in today's LDCs is not so very different from that found in the developed countries in the 1920s and 1930s. However, the level of income in today's LDCs is so much lower that the burden of inequality is a more serious one.[17]

Recently, concern has been voiced about the increase in inequality over time in LDCs.[18] Rapid growth, it is

suggested, has sometimes by-passed the masses, and the fear has even been expressed that not only the relative income of the poor, but even their absolute income, has been declining. Obviously, the most direct evidence of the impact of economic growth on the distribution of income would involve the comparison of income distributions for different points in time within developing countries. Some limited evidence on this point, which relies heavily upon the work of R. Weisskoff,[19] consists of data on seven developing countries—including Puerto Rico; the data are summarized in table 4.

The data indicate that inequality has increased over periods ranging from five to fourteen years in all the countries except Ceylon (see columns 4, 5 and 6 of table 4). In Ceylon the overall degree of inequality has probably diminished more and the share of the low income groups declined less than the figures suggest; this discrepancy is caused by a statistical change in the survey data for the two dates.[20]

---

15. Kuznets, "Quantitative Aspects."
16. Oshima, "Income Inequality," p. 29.
17. Kuznets, "Quantitative Aspects."
18. Mahbub ul Haq, "Employment and Income Distribution in the 1970's: A New Perspective," *Development Digest,* Agency for

International Development, 9, no. 4 (October 1971), pp. 3–8.
19. R. Weisskoff, *Income Distribution and Economic Growth* (Ph.D. diss., Harvard University, 1969).
20. The decline in the share of the lower income groups is at least partly a statistical artifact. The reason is that servants were included as members of the employer's spending unit in the 1953 survey, but were regarded as separate spending units in the 1963 survey.

NOTES: Currency units for family income and concepts for shares as follows:

	Family income	Shares refer to:
Argentina	1960 pesos	Personal income of families
Brazil	1960 U. S. $	Money income of economically active persons
Ceylon	Index of real income per income receiver	Income of spending units
Colombia	Index of per capita GDP	Income of persons
India	Index of per capita GDP	Personal income of households
Mexico	1954 pesos (monthly)	Personal income of families
Puerto Rico	1958 U. S. $	Personal income of families

* Bottom 88 percent.

However, an increase in inequality does not necessarily betoken a worsening of the lot of the bottom groups in the income distribution. The real per capita income of a given percentile segment of the income distribution—for example, the lowest 20 percent—will be greater or smaller depending upon whether the product

$$\frac{S_1}{S_0} \times \frac{\bar{Y}_1}{\bar{Y}_0}$$

is greater or smaller than 1—where the first term represents the ratio of the group's share in the current period to its share in the base period, and the second term represents the ratio of the nation's per capita income in the current period to its per capita income in the base period in constant prices.[21] The data for these ratios are found in columns 1 to 3 of table 4, and the product of the ratios, in columns 4 and 5. For example, for Brazil the figures for the bottom 60 percent are:

$$\frac{16.8}{18.2} \times \frac{679}{513} = 1.22$$

where the data in the first fraction are the shares from column 3, and the figures in the second fraction are Fishlow's data on real per capita income in column 1. The product, the index of real income per capita for the low income group, is entered in column 5. In this

21. Let p = percent of population in the income group; S = share of total income received by population in the group; $\bar{Y}$ = per capita income of nation in constant prices; N = population of the nation. The per capita income of the income group is:

$$\frac{N \cdot \bar{Y} \cdot S}{N \cdot p} = \frac{\bar{Y} \cdot S}{p}$$

The ratio of the per capita income of the group for two years, 1 and 0, is:

$$\frac{(\bar{Y}_1 \cdot S_1)/p}{(\bar{Y}_0 \cdot S_0)/p} = \frac{\bar{Y}_1}{\bar{Y}_0} \cdot \frac{S_1}{S_0}$$

case, the real income of the lowest 60 percent increased by 22 percent over the ten year period.

In India, on the other hand, the data in table 4 indicate sharp declines in the shares of the low income groups over a briefer period. The problems of measurement are extraordinarily great in this populous and complicated country; the possibility of error is correspondingly large. Comparisons of other distributions for India indicate little change in equality for approximately the same period.[22] However, the two estimates in table 4 have the advantage of having been produced by the same author, S. Swamy.

If the countries are ranked according to the per capita rates of growth in real income, the percentage changes in the real income of the low income groups appear as listed in table 5. The main evidence of a decline in real income for low income groups rests on the questionable data for India and on the marked decline among the lowest 20 percent in Mexico. It is possible that additional data, especially for the lowest 5 or 10 percent of the income distribution, would reveal other cases of a fall in real income. Perhaps the best judgment on the basis of these data is that, while there have been some situations in which the real as well as the relative income of the lowest income groups has worsened, such cases may not have been pervasive. There is also a hint that such an untoward development is more likely to be associated with slow income growth—say, of 1 or 2 percent per annum—than with rapid growth—say, of 3 or 4 percent per annum.

The small size of the sample, the

22. See, Weisskoff, *Income Distribution*, p. 112. The Swamy distributions are explained in S. Swamy, "Structural Changes and the Distribution of Income by Size: The Case of India," *Review of Income and Wealth* ser. 13, no. 2 (June 1967), pp. 155–174.

TABLE 5

GROWTH RATES IN REAL FAMILY INCOME AND PERCENT CHANGES IN
REAL INCOME OF LOW INCOME GROUPS

	NUMBER OF YEARS	GROWTH PER ANNUM IN REAL FAMILY INCOME	PERCENT CHANGE IN REAL INCOME OF LOWEST	
			20%	60%
India	4½	1.2	−6.5	−5.4
Ceylon	10	1.2	−0.03	+1.1
Argentina	8	1.4	+0.7	+0.8
Mexico	13	1.5	−2.7	+0.4
Colombia	14	2.4	—	+2.0*
Brazil	10	2.8	+8.8	+2.0
Puerto Rico	10	4.8	+2.6	+3.9

* Refers to bottom 88 percent.

varying lengths of the periods covered and, above all, the uncertainties of the data mitigate against drawing any firm conclusion on the connection between growth rates and changes in the real income of the low income groups. The relationship suggested is not implausible; in the usual pattern of development, it may take rapid expansion to absorb into employment underemployed and unemployed persons to a sufficient degree to raise the average real incomes of the lower income groups.

Less direct evidence on the association between changes in inequality and growth in real per capita GNP may be obtained from cross-sectional studies. A compilation of income distribution figures for forty-four developing countries (see appendix table), by Adelman and Morris,[23] provides a larger number of countries, at the price of a much lower degree of comparability of the data for the different countries.[24] The

errors in the data may be reduced by taking averages for groups of countries; this has been done in table 6. The countries are grouped according to their 1961 GNP per capita in United States dollars.

In some important respects, the lowest GNP class—consisting of Tanzania, Chad, Burma, Dahomey and Niger—is characterized by the most equal distribution. The share of the lowest 20 percent is higher than in any of the other groups. With per capita GNPs below 75 dollars—a survival level which, itself, is difficult for a Western writer to comprehend—the larger share must reflect a downward limit that is nearer to the median income than in countries that are not quite as poor.

The greatest inequality exists for the countries that fall in the 200 to 400 dollar range of per capita GNP. These countries have the lowest fraction of income going to the bottom quintile of

23. Adelman and Morris, "An Anatomy of Patterns."

24. The Fishlow study cited earlier will serve to illustrate the uncertainties of the

data. Fishlow's estimates for Brazil are compared below with those of Adelman and Morris:

	Poorest 60%	Top 20%	Top 5%
Adelman and Morris	22.7	61.5	38.4
Fishlow (families)			
"Original"	20.6	56.7	27.9
"Corrected"	24.9	53.9	25.0

TABLE 6

INCOME SHARES AND AVERAGE DOLLAR INCOME FOR ORDINAL INCOME GROUPS FOR FORTY-FOUR
COUNTRIES CLASSIFIED BY GNP LEVEL, AROUND 1960

1961 GNP PER CAPITA*	NUMBER OF COUNTRIES	ORDINAL GROUPS IN INCOME DISTRIBUTION				
		Poorest 20%	Middle 40–60%	Poorest 60%	Highest 20%	Highest 5%
		A. SHARE OF GROUP IN NATIONAL INCOME				
50–74	5	10.4	11.8	33.0	48.9	29.8
75–99	6	6.8	11.8	27.6	53.2	23.8
100–199	9	5.0	12.7	26.9	56.6	27.4
200–299	8	3.6	10.1	19.9	64.7	38.8
300–399	5	3.6	8.6	18.2	67.1	38.9
400–499	5	7.2	15.4	33.6	66.9	35.9
500–699	3	4.6	12.3	25.5	51.8	21.3
Over 700	3	6.1	16.1	33.1	46.2	21.3
		B. PER CAPITA GNP				
50–74		32	39	36	160	392
75–99		30	59	44	172	199
100–199		41	106	73	465	850
200–299		38	110	77	719	1776
300–399		66	190	125	1030	2093
400–499		100	252	172	1252	3042
500–699		134	436	289	1315	1750
Over 700		254	607	428	2013	4170

SOURCE: Basic data on shares from table 1 in I. Adelman and C. T. Morris, "An Anatomy of Patterns of Income Distribution in Developing Nations," Final Report, Grant AID/csd-2236 (Evanston, Ill.: Northwestern University, February 1971), Part III. The forty-four countries given in this source (see appendix table for original data for individual countries) were arrayed from low to high by 1961 GNP per capita, the latter derived from *International Financial Statistics*, 1972 Supplement.

NOTES: Group shares in Part A represent simple averages of shares in Adelman and Morris table 1 for each GNP class. The data in Part B were derived in the following way: each country's aggregate 1961 GNP in dollars was allocated to each ordinal group in accordance with the shares reported in Adelman and Morris. For the countries in each GNP class, the aggregate dollar GNP for each ordinal group was summed for all the countries in the class and divided by the sum of their populations. The results are entered in Part B.
* Given in United States dollars.

the distribution—about 3.6 percent— and the largest shares going to the top quintile—65 to 67 percent—and to the top 5 percent—nearly 39 percent of GNP.

The income distribution becomes more equal at higher GNP levels; in the two highest income classes shown in table 6, it is not very different from that of the developed countries (shown in detail in table 7). The data thus lend support to Kuznets' hypothesis

that inequality widens and then narrows as per capita income rises.

For the LDCs that are not in the two extreme categories—that is, those with per capita GNPs ranging from 75 to 700 dollars—the most consistent difference between their income distribution and that of the developed countries is, as Professor Kuznets has suggested,[25] that the upper income groups in the

25. Kuznets, "Quantitative Aspects."

TABLE 7

INCOME DISTRIBUTION AT HIGHER GNP LEVELS

	LOWEST 20%	HIGHEST 20%	TOP 5%
500–699 class	4.6	51.8	21.3
Over 700 class	6.1	46.2	21.3
5 developed countries*	4.0	46.3	20.5

* Average of France, Netherlands, Norway, United Kingdom and United States. Derived from U. N. Economic Commission for Latin America, *Economic Survey of Latin America, 1969*, (New York: United Nations, September 1970).

LDCs have income shares that are larger than the corresponding groups in the rich countries. For the top 20 percent, the LDC shares in total income shown in table 6 range from 52 to 67 percent, as compared with 46 percent in the five developed countries.

To see the impact of growth in per capita GNP on the absolute level of incomes of the bottom of the income distribution, average incomes have been calculated in the lower part of table 6 for each ordinal group at each GNP level. There are two cases in which the absolute income of the bottom 20 percent drops, but each decline is small and well within the margins of error that must be associated with the figures; also, the small decline is followed by a substantial rise in each case. Of course, it is possible that more accurate data, particularly data for the bottom 5 or 10 percent of the population, would tell a different story. However, these data do not give much support to the view that growth tends to make the poor poorer. The cross sectional data are more consistent with the hypothesis that increases in the level of average income of the nation as a whole usually improve the lot of all quintiles.

It may be argued that the extent of the improvement for the poorest groups is not enough. With low per capita incomes, the abysmal poverty of the lowest income groups compels priority over any other improvement in the nation's capacity to provide the necessities of life. While few would deny this as a desirable outcome, some think that extensive efforts to increase equality would dry up investment and stunt growth.

Others have argued that the upper income groups in LDCs often use their high incomes for either luxury consumption or accumulation of capital abroad rather than for growth-promoting domestic investment. The first of these criticisms is more likely to be true where the upper income classes derive their incomes from land ownership; the second, where fear of extensive social and political change prevails. It has also been claimed that a rise in real wages is likely to lead to higher productivity—through improving the health and the welfare of the workers and through providing management with greater incentives to economize on labor. Some skepticism has been expressed about the impact of such effects in most developing countries where only a small percentage of the economically active population are wage earners.

A recent pioneering effort by Cline[26] to assess this issue in quantitative terms concludes that the redistribution of incomes is unlikely to reduce growth substantially. In four Latin American

26. W. Cline, *Potential Effects of Income Redistribution*.

countries—Argentina, Brazil, Mexico and Venezuela—Cline estimates that a shift in the income distribution to the degree of equality found in Great Britain would not reduce the annual rate of growth in GNP by more than 1 percent per annum in any of the countries; indeed, in Venezuela there would be no reduction. However, work along these lines is only at its beginning; judgment on the impact of different rates of growth on the real incomes of the low income groups is still tentative.

The world distribution of income

It is possible to construct a world distribution of income by assuming that every person in each country receives the average income of that country. Such a distribution does not fully reflect the degree of world inequality, because it does not incorporate the effects of intra-country inequality. Nevertheless, distributions of this character reflect a degree of inequality that is large relative to that found in individual countries. Attention may be called first to the distribution of income among sixty-two countries in 1949, 1957 and 1970 (columns 1, 2 and 5, respectively, of table 8). These distributions have been estimated by converting each country's per capita income into dollars at existing exchange rates. The overall degree of inequality, as measured by the concentration ratio, is substantially the same in all three years. However, there has been a shift in shares into the fourth quintile from the two lowest quintiles of the distribution and, to a lesser degree, from the highest quintile.

Because of the distortions resulting from exchange rate conversions, estimates of the world distribution of consumption that avoid the use of exchange rates altogether are presented in columns 3 and 4 of table 8. The esti-

mates, by Beckerman and Bacon,[27] are based on so-called short-cut methods of international comparisons. A relationship was first estimated between real per capita consumption, as determined in two careful international comparisons,[28] covering more than a score of countries, on the one hand, and the number of telephones and amount of newsprint consumed in each country, on the other hand. This relationship was then used to estimate real per capita consumption in other countries on the basis of telephones and newsprint. The finding of a lower concentration ratio for consumption than for income is plausible; the fact that the CR changes so little between the two periods accords very well with the lack of change in the CR for income over a somewhat earlier period of similar duration.

An alternative approach avoiding the exchange rate bias also involves an estimating equation based on complete international comparisons of a few countries.[29] Here the relationship is between the "real" per capita GNP, estimated as a result of careful and detailed international comparisons of prices and quantities, and the per capita GNP, converted into dollars by the use of ex-

27. W. Beckerman and R. Bacon, "The International Distribution of Incomes," in *Unfashionable Economics: Essays in Honour of Lord Balogh,* ed. P. Streeten (London: Weidenfeld and Nicolson, 1970). For further discussion of these methods, see, A. Heston, "A Comparison of Some Short-cut Methods of Estimating Real Product Per Capita," *Review of Income and Wealth* ser. 19, no. 1 (March 1973), pp. 79–104.

28. M. Gilbert and Associates, *Comparative National Products and Price Levels,* (Paris: OEEC, 1958); S. Braithwaite, "Real Income Levels in Latin America," *Review of Income and Wealth* ser. 14, no. 2 (June 1968), pp. 113–182.

29. For an example of this approach, see P. David, "Just How Misleading Are Official Exchange Rate Conversions?" *Economic Journal* 82 (September 1972), pp. 979–990.

TABLE 8

Distribution of World Income and Consumption

Ordinal Groups	Percentage Shares in Nonsocialist World				Percentage Shares in GNP, 1970			
	Income		Consumption		Exchange rate basis		Real	
	1949	1957	1954–55	1962–63	Nonsocialist world	All countries	Nonsocialist world	All countries
	(1)	(2)	(3)	(4)	(5)	(6)	(7)	(8)
0–20%	3.0	2.0	2.5	3.2	1.7	2.2	3.0	3.6
21–39%	3.5	3.0	3.3	3.8	1.8	3.0	3.2	4.9
40–59%	6.2	8.5	9.6	8.8	5.3	4.1	8.9	6.6
60–79%	17.2	20.5	24.4	25.8	25.4	21.2	29.3	25.9
80–100%	70.1	66.0	60.2	58.4	65.7	69.6	55.6	59.0
Total	100.0	100.0	100.0	100.0	100.0	100.0	100.0	100.0
Addendum: Concentration ratio:	.636	.637	.570	.567	.630	.649	.525	.528

Sources: Columns (1) and (2): S. Andic and A. T. Peacock, "The International Distribution of Income, 1949 and 1957," *Journal of the Royal Statistical Society* ser. A, 124, part 2, (1961).

Columns (3) and (4) W. Beckerman and R. Bacon, "The International Distribution of Incomes."

Notes: Columns (1) and (2): Include sixty-two countries with slightly more than half of world population. China, USSR and Eastern Europe are the main omitted countries. National income in domestic currency was converted in source to dollars at existing exchange rates.

Columns (3) and (4): Include seventy-two countries with nearly 60 percent of world population. Major omissions as in columns (1) and (2), except that Poland and Yugoslavia are included.

Column (5): Includes same countries as in columns (1) and (2). GNP per capita as reported in IBRD, *World Bank Atlas: Population, Per Capita Product and Growth Rates*, 1972.

Column (6): As in column (5), but includes all of the nearly 200 countries and territories in the *Atlas*; China, USSR and other centrally planned economies are included.

Column (7): Country coverage as in column (5), but World Bank GNP estimates, derived mainly from exchange rate conversions from domestic currencies, are corrected for deviations of the exchange rate from the true purchasing power parity. The formula, derived by S. Ahmad for his doctoral dissertation on the basis of preliminary findings of the International Comparison Project, is

$$Y_i = Y_s \Big/ \left[.736 + .432 \frac{Y_s}{Y_i^x} \right]$$

where Y_i = real per capita GNP in U. S. dollars, Y_i^x = per capita GNP in U. S. dollars converted by the exchange rate, and Y_s = U. S. per capita GNP. There were ten observations and R^{-2} = .95.

Column (8): Country coverage as in column (6), GNP as in column (7).

change rates. This relationship is then used to estimate a real per capita GDP for other countries from their GNP converted into dollars via the exchange rate. The results, based upon the work of S. Ahmad, are shown in columns 7 and 8 of table 8. Because the internal purchasing power of the currencies of poor countries tended to be much larger than would be suggested by their exchange rates, the shares of the lower ordinal groups in the distribution are higher than on the exchange rate basis, and the concentration ratios are the lowest found in table 8. If it is indeed true that there has been little change in world concentration since the 1950s and 1960s, these results are not consistent with the concentration ratios for consumption shown in columns 3 and 4. The "real" distribution is based on a regression that includes a wider range of per capita GDPs, but fewer observations than the consumption distribution. However, both are based on inadequate data and methods that are not thor-

TABLE 9

GROWTH IN REAL GNP OF DEVELOPED AND LESS DEVELOPED COUNTRIES,
1950–60 AND 1960–71

	DISTRIBUTION OF 1970 GNP	RATE OF GROWTH*			
		GNP per Capita		Total GNP	
		1950–60	1960–71	1950–60	1960–71
Developed countries					
Total	100.0	2.8	3.6	4.1	4.7
United States	47.9	1.4	2.7	3.2	3.9
All non-United States	52.1	4.0	4.4	5.1	5.5
Canada	4.0	2.1	3.4	4.3	5.2
Europe	38.1	4.1	3.7	4.8	4.6
EEC (the Six)	23.8	5.0	4.1	5.9	5.1
United Kingdom	6.0	2.3	2.1	2.7	2.7
Other	15.0	4.4	6.6	6.1	8.0
Japan	9.7	7.1	9.5	8.2	10.6
Less developed countries					
Total	100.0	2.5	3.1	4.8	5.6
Latin America	33.8	2.1	2.8	5.0	5.6
Argentina	6.3	0.8	2.5	2.8	4.0
Brazil	8.6	3.8	3.7	6.8	6.5
Chile	1.8	1.2	2.9	3.8	4.8
Mexico	8.2	2.6	3.5	5.8	6.8
Venezuela	2.4	4.2	2.4	8.2	5.9
Asia	45.6	n.a	3.1	n.a	5.6
Israel	1.4	6.5	4.9	10.0	8.3
India	16.4	2.3	1.5	4.2	4.0
Taiwan	1.7	4.3	7.0	7.7	9.7
South Korea	2.5	2.1	6.8	4.9	9.3
Philippines	3.2	3.4	2.5	6.5	5.9
Thailand	2.0	n.a	4.4	n.a	7.7
Africa	10.9	n.a	2.0	n.a	4.5
Other	9.7	n.a	5.9	n.a	7.1

SOURCE: Agency for International Development, *Gross National Product Growth Rates and Trend Data* (May 10, 1972).

NOTE: Data refer to forty-four less developed countries and to twenty-two developed non-communist countries.

* Given in percent per annum.

oughly reliable; thus, it is hard to defend the conjecture that the CR for consumption is too high rather than that the CR for real GNP is too low.

The distributions which have been discussed relate to a group of mainly nonsocialist countries which accounted for 50 to 60 percent of the world's population. In column 6 of table 8, the distribution on the exchange rate basis is extended to all countries of the world, and in column 8, the adjusted distribution is so extended. The effects of the additions—of which the most important are China, the USSR and Eastern Europe—is to raise the CR slightly.

Further light may be shed upon the trends in income equality, or inequality, among nations by comparing growth rates for rich and poor countries. Data (listed in table 9) support the often repeated statement that world income inequality has been increasing as a result of more rapid growth rates in per capita GNP. The differences are not as large as those which are often implied, but even so one may ask why this trend toward inequality is not more evident in the CRs of the income distributions in columns 1, 2 and 5 of table 8. One possibility is that the distributions are unreliable evidence of changes in the true world income distribution; an alternative explanation may be that the growth rates involve equalizing changes as well as changes that produce greater inequality. Thus, within the developed countries, the below average growth rates of the United States and Canada—high income countries—and the above average growth rates of Japan and the six Common Market countries operated in an equalizing direction.

Among the LDCs, there were also some differences in growth rates that tended to diminish inequality. Some high income LDCs, such as Argentina and Chile, had low growth rates in per capita GNP, while others with relatively low beginning per capita incomes, such as South Korea, Thailand and Brazil,

had rapid growth. Of course, differential growth rates also operated in the opposite direction; India, a very poor country from the start, lagged in its growth rate behind the average for developing countries.

Even if the relative growth rates within each of the two groups of countries reduced overall inequality, no one can look with equanimity on the growing polarization of income levels in the world. Indeed, it is a sad gauge of world economic progress that the per-capita GNP, measured in terms of the value of 1970 United States dollars, was 110 dollars or less for one-fifth of the world's population, 165 dollars or less for two-fifths and 310 dollars or less for three-fifths. The inescapable conclusion is that the benefits of economic progress have been confined to a minority of the world's population. The application of modern science and technology has not, nearly three-quarters of the way through the twentieth century, provided anything which approximates the Western minimum standard of living for the substantial majority of the human race.

APPENDIX TABLE

INCOME SHARES RECEIVED BY VARIOUS ORDINAL GROUPS, CIRCA 1960, AND PER CAPITA GNP, 1961, FORTY-FOUR COUNTRIES

| | ORDINAL GROUPS | | | | | |
	Poorest 20%	Poorest 60%	Middle 40–60%	Highest 5%	Highest 20%	1961 per capita GNP*
Tanzania	9.75	29.25	9.85	42.90	61.00	53.6
Chad	12.00	35.00	12.00	23.00	43.00	63.0
Burma	10.00	36.00	13.00	28.21	48.50	66.3
Dahomey	8.00	30.00	12.00	32.00	50.00	71.6
Niger	12.00	35.00	12.00	23.00	42.00	74.0
Malagasy	7.00	23.00	9.00	37.00	59.00	75.0
Kenya	7.00	21.00	7.00	22.20	64.00	75.3
Nigeria	7.00	23.00	9.00	38.38	60.90	75.6
India	8.00	36.00	16.00	8.00	42.00	76.6
Pakistan	6.50	33.00	15.50	20.00	45.00	81.0
Sudan	5.60	29.30	14.30	17.10	48.10	97.9

APPENDIX TABLE (*continued*)

	ORDINAL GROUPS					
	Poorest 20%	Poorest 60%	Middle 40–60%	Highest 5%	Highest 20%	1961 per captia GNP*
Sierre Leone	3.80	19.20	9.10	33.80	64.10	100.0
Bolivia	4.00	26.60	8.90	35.70	59.10	117.0
Ceylon	4.45	27.47	13.81	18.38	52.31	137.9
Morocco	7.10	22.20	7.70	20.60	65.40	150.0
Taiwan	4.50	29.00	14.80	24.10	52.00	159.8
Philippines	4.30	24.70	12.00	27.50	55.80	186.7
Ivory Coast	8.00	30.00	12.00	29.00	55.00	192.1
Senegal	3.00	20.00	10.00	36.00	64.00	195.7
Ecuador	6.30	42.60	26.10	21.50	41.80	195.7
Rhodesia	4.00	20.00	8.00	60.00	65.00	203.1
Iraq	2.00	16.00	8.00	34.00	68.00	205.3
Tunisia	4.97	20.57	9.95	22.44	65.00	211.9
Brazil	3.50	22.70	10.20	38.40	61.50	214.9
Peru	4.04	17.10	8.30	48.30	67.60	225.4
El Salvador	5.50	23.60	11.30	33.00	61.40	227.0
Lebanon	3.00	23.00	15.80	34.00	61.00	268.5
Colombia	2.21	15.88	8.97	40.36	68.06	282.1
Zambia	6.27	26.95	11.10	37.50	57.10	305.7
Gabon	2.00	15.00	7.00	47.00	71.00	339.2
Libya	0.11	1.78	1.28	46.40	89.50	340.1
Mexico	3.66	21.75	11.25	28.52	58.04	351.9
Costa Rica	6.00	25.40	12.10	35.00	60.00	362.6
Surinam	10.70	37.00	14.74	15.40	42.40	404.4
Jamaica	2.20	19.00	10.80	31.20	61.50	412.0
Panama	4.90	28.10	13.80	34.50	56.70	415.8
South Africa	1.94	16.27	10.16	39.38	57.36	454.0
Greece	9.00	34.10	12.30	23.00	49.50	475.4
Chile	5.40	27.00	12.00	22.60	52.30	558.9
Japan	4.70	31.10	15.80	14.80	46.00	564.7
Trinidad-Tobago	3.60	18.52	9.16	26.60	57.00	597.2
Argentina	7.00	30.40	13.10	29.40	52.00	710.0
Venezuela	4.40	30.00	16.60	23.20	47.10	968.1
Israel	6.80	38.80	18.60	11.20	39.40	1334.9

SOURCES: Shares: I. Adelman and C. T. Morris, "An Anatomy of Patterns."
1961 GNP: International Monetary Fund, *International Financial Statistics,* 1972 Supplement.

* Given in United States dollars.

Measured Inequality of Income:
What Does It Mean and What Can It Tell Us?

By ROBERT J. LAMPMAN

ABSTRACT: What can be called the American standard method of reporting income inequality needs to be seen as a highly simplified treatment of a complex matter. Broad generalizations, particularly with regard to changes in inequality over time, are to be mistrusted. Special purpose distributions, including one on the distributional effects of a broadly conceived system of transfers, might be more useful than the one overall distribution. The latter does not significantly help in understanding the causes of, and justifications for, existing income inequalities. It has had only limited use as a performance indicator for the national economy and is seldom referred to when decisions about specific legislative measures that have redistributional effects are made. This may be because public concern does not focus upon overall income equality as such, but upon particular differences.

Robert J. Lampman is Vilas Professor of Economics at the University of Wisconsin, where he is also a Fellow of the Institute for Research on Poverty. He is currently serving as Visiting Professor at the New York State School of Industrial and Labor Relations, Cornell University. He is author of The Share of Top Wealth-holders in National Wealth *and* Ends and Means of Reducing Income Poverty, *and has served as Editor of the* Journal of Human Resources. *He has also been a Research Associate at the National Bureau of Economic Research and a staff member of the Council of Economic Advisers.*

IN this country, the size distribution of income is most commonly represented by what may be referred to as the American standard distribution. The Bureau of Census developed this method; since 1947, the bureau has used it in annual sample surveys of households to determine how families and unrelated individuals share the nation's income.[1] These surveys are based upon key concepts which will be discussed, following a brief review of some of the leading findings of the surveys.

THE PATTERN OF INEQUALITY

Between 1947 and 1972 the per capita income, adjusted for price increases, went up about 2 percent per year, on the average, or a total of 50 percent. In 1970 the median family income was about 10,000 dollars. However, some families have incomes below zero—that is, they experience losses—and some receive incomes almost one thousand times the median. If one arrays all incomes from highest to lowest, converts the array into a frequency distribution and then charts the numbers—income-receiving units on the vertical axis against absolute income on the horizontal axis—one finds that the vast majority are clustered within a narrow range of incomes; 80 percent have incomes between 4,000 and 20,000 dollars. This chart will show a distribution that is not normal or bell-shaped, as are many distributions found in nature, but has a distinct skewness to the right.

A frequency distribution highlights the range of incomes, but does not summarize well the manner in which total income is shared. For that purpose, it is best to array the income-receiving units by size of income, select, perhaps, the top 10 percent of such units and compare their share of total income with that of successively lower ranked 10 percent groups. In 1970 the top ten percent, with incomes above 20,000 dollars, received 28 percent of total income; the bottom group, with incomes under 4,000 dollars, had 2 percent of the total. This ratio of 14 to 1 has been relatively constant, as has the ratio of 42 to 5 for the top fifth and lower fifth.

A graphic representation of this sharing of income can be illustrated by what is known as a Lorenz curve. To set up this graph, one starts with cumulative percentages of income on the vertical, and cumulative percentages of income-receiving units on the horizontal, axis. Next, a forty-five degree line is drawn connecting the left hand corner point of zero percent of income and income receivers with the upper right hand corner point of 100 percent of income and income receivers; this serves as a reference line of zero inequality. One then plots the actual percentages of income received by the lowest 10 percent, the lowest 20 percent and so forth, connecting at the upper right hand corner with 100 percent of receivers getting 100 percent of income. This gives a picture of income inequality which can be summarized by comparing the area below the actual Lorenz curve with the area below the zero inequality reference line. This comparison is called the Lorenz or Gini concentration ratio.

In recent years this ratio has been approximately .360 in the United States—that is, 36 percent of the way between perfect equality, wherein each unit would have the same income, and perfect inequality, in which case one unit would receive all the income. Between 1947 and 1964 the Gini ratio for families varied from a low of .351 in 1957

---

1. Results of these surveys are reported in, U.S., Department of Commerce, Bureau of the Census, *Current Population Reports,* Series P-60 (Washington, D.C.: Government Printing Office).

to a high of .379 in 1949.[2] There is no conclusive evidence that income inequality was ever substantially lower than these recent ratios indicate; however, there is a basis for believing that World War II produced a shock effect which reduced the income shares of the top 5 and 10 percent groups from higher prewar levels without changing the share of the lower half.

The Gini ratio is somewhat lower in the United Kingdom and in other Western European nations than it is in the United States. It is generally thought that this ratio is greater in most less developed countries. However, such comparisons have limited value since the data are incomplete and the institutions noncomparable. Some crude data suggest that, for the more than three billion people in the world, the United States— with but 6 percent of the world's population—may have 40 percent of the world's income; China and India—with a third of the world's people—have about 20 percent of the total.

KEY CONCEPTS USED IN THE AMERICAN STANDARD DISTRIBUTION

The Gini ratio for a given year and changes in it from year to year are determined, in part, by key definitions used in constructing an income distribution. This means that if one is to appreciate the specific and limited meaning of the income inequality reported by the American standard method, one must comprehend its concepts of income, income period and income-receiving unit and its method of ranking income receivers. It is also

2. U.S., Department of Commerce, *Trends in the Income of Families and Persons in the United States, 1947–1964*, Technical Paper 17, prepared for the Bureau of the Census by Mary F. Henson (Washington, D.C.: Government Printing Office, 1967), pp. 176–179, table 24; see pp. 34–36 for a good exposition of the computation of the Gini ratio.

helpful to consider some alternatives to the American standard distribution.

The census concept of income is total money income, which includes: money earned by labor and through property ownership; government cash transfer payments, such as social security benefits; private pensions and annuities; and alimony and regular contributions from persons not in the household. It excludes: capital gains and losses; insurance benefits other than annuities; nonmoney items, such as undistributed corporate profits, employer-paid fringe benefits, imputed rent from owner-occupied housing and consumer durables; home production, such as child care services; and government noncash benefits, such as food stamps, public housing, health care and education. No correction is made for taxes paid—except for the corporation income tax— contributions to private pensions and annuities or contributions to other families; nor is deduction made for the expenses of earning income, such as commuting costs and payments for child care. No correction is made for differences in experience of work satisfaction, leisure or disamenities, such as air pollution.

Modifications of the total money idea would, in some instances, lead to a finding of more income inequality. For example, this would follow from inclusion of capital gains, undistributed corporate profits and employee fringe benefits. However, accounting for other items, such as income taxes paid, receipt of government noncash benefits, home production and expenses of earning income, would intimate less inequality.

The income period used in the American standard distribution is one year, which seems reasonable enough at first glance. However, it should be noted that it produces a specific pattern of inequality different from that based on a shorter, or longer, period. Some types of income—for example, farm income—are realistically calculated over a longer investment period than one year. Also, some people enter, or leave, the labor force or form new family units during the year in question. For these reasons one can expect to find more inequality using a one-year income period than a two- or three-year period span. To compensate for these timing problems, some have advocated measurement of a family's permanent, or normalized, income purged of transitory ups and downs. On the other hand, some policy purposes demand an income period of less than a year—for example, public assistance benefits are calculated against one month's income.

Similar plasticity of observed inequality may be noted with respect to the definition of the income-receiving unit. In the American standard distribution, this unit may be one unrelated person or it may be a group of persons living together—related by blood, marriage or adoption—and pooling income or expenses. There may be subfamilies within the unit; of course, there may be more than one person receiving income within the unit. As has been noted, there is no subtraction from income for contributions made to persons outside the unit; nor is there any income adjustment for special needs of members of the group.

A more basic consideration is the lack of adjustment for the number of people in the receiving unit. A single person with 10,000 dollars of income is richer, in a certain sense, than is a family of eight at the same income level. There are two alternative ways to handle this problem: (1) convert income to an equivalent level of living basis—in this case, reducing the income rank of the family of eight persons and recalculating the degree of inequality;

and (2) alter the income-receiving unit from family to individual and assign some income to children, as well as adults, ranking all individuals. The matter of ranking, then, is entangled with the definitions of income and receiving units.

Thus, key definitions and methods influence our impressions of inequality within a nation at a moment in time and cloud our comparisons over time and across nations. Some people may shift their income from included to excluded items, or vice versa; the timing of income may change; the amount of doubling up and sharing of income among relatives may change. Such changes have been considerable in the American economy in recent decades, and they compel caution in the examination of claims of clear findings of change, or constancy, in income inequality. Since the underlying role of the family, the employer, the insurance company and the government are all changing, any single measure of income inequality is likely to be an illusory measure of an elusively moving reality.

THREE ALTERNATIVE DISTRIBUTIONS

Because of the complexity of these matters, students of income distribution tend to shy away from use of one single, all purpose measure of inequality and to offer a variety of special purpose distributions aimed at particular issues.[3] We may classify these as producer, consumer and power distributions. The first seeks clues about how the interaction of supply and demand for productive factors—some 85 million workers and 3 trillion dollars of personally-owned wealth—determines earned incomes. In this instance, income is defined as pretax earnings, with each earner

3. Robert J. Lampman, "Recent Changes in Income Inequality Reconsidered," *American Economic Review* 44 (June 1954), pp. 251–268.

ranked as a separate receiving unit. Nonearners might well be omitted from such a distribution; attention might be confined to men of prime working age who worked a full year, in order to get a picture of prime earnings inequality.

On the other hand, inequality of consumer power would best be indicated by measuring posttax, and posttransfer income, and adjusting income or rank for family size. An interesting application of the latter adjustment is the setting of poverty lines for families of different sizes in connection with President Johnson's War on Poverty.[4]

If the policy interest is not reduction of poverty but restraint of the rich, then a more appropriate distribution might aim at general market power. Here, the income definition should include capital gains and other changes on capital account; the time period should be relatively long; and the income-receiving unit should be broad enough to catch strategic interfamily and interfirm connections. There is no official line separating the rich from the nonrich at present; however, such a line would presumably pay attention to net worth, as well as to current income.

This review of variants of the American standard distribution suggests that there are numerous reasons for concern with inequality of income and that there is some merit in constructing a special distribution to reflect each basis for concern. There is also analytical interest in how a producer, or primary distribution, is transformed into a consumer, or secondary distribution.[5] This transformation is akin to a chemical process, since income changes form as it is redistributed; family units shift in numbers as new devices for sharing of income are invented. One can visualize a system of transfers as mediating the primary and secondary distributions. This system includes a set of taxes and contributions in dollar terms which necessarily equal the aggregate value of public and private benefits in money and nonmoney forms. The American system of transfers, rather broadly defined, redistributes almost 20 percent of the gross national product (GNP); in the process, the pretransfer poor— those with primary incomes below the official poverty lines—who have 3 percent of primary income, end up with 9 percent of the secondary distribution.

THE CAUSES OF INEQUALITY

The particular pattern of inequality captured by the American standard distribution of income is the result of a conglomerate of component distributions, each having a different median and different Gini ratio. For example, the income distribution for the aged has a lower median and more inequality than the distribution for the working age population. The distribution for metropolitan communities is more unequal than that for small towns; for nonwhites, more unequal than for whites; for more educated people, more unequal than for the less educated. Some occupations show more inequality than do others. Of course, property income is far more unequal than is labor income. Only about one-half of all families receive any dividends, interest or rent income, and only 1.5 percent report more than 10,000 dollars of such income.

The existing pattern of inequality is also better understood by a look at the differing compositions of the several income groups. The top 10 percent is

4. Social Security Bulletin, January 1965, "Counting the Poor: Another Look at the Poverty Profile." Also, Current Population Reports, Series P-23, No. 28, "Revision in Poverty Statistics, 1959 to 1968."

5. Robert J. Lampman, "Transfer Approaches to Distribution Policy," American Economic Review 60 (May 1970), pp. 270–279.

disproportionately comprised of families headed by white, prime-age, working males; multiple-earner families; families residing in Northern metropolitan areas; and families headed by those of high educational attainment who are in managerial, professional and technical occupations. The bottom 10 percent of families—which is not quite the same as the 12 percent of the population currently below the official poverty lines—is disproportionately made up of aged, nonwhite, and female-headed families; Southern and nonmetropolitan residents; and those with low educational attainment and relatively unskilled occupations. Contrary to popular impression, income increases with family size up to five persons. The top fifth of families ranked by income has 20 percent of all the children and 27 percent of the earners; the lowest fifth has 16 percent of the children and 11 percent of the earners.

To know if someone is actually rich or poor, some would want more indicators of prosperity than current money income. Before classifying a family with 50,000 dollars of income as really rich—only .5 percent have incomes that high—one might ask how many years has family income been that high; how many earners and how many family members are there; what is their net worth? What extraordinary medical or other needs do they have? Before agreeing that a family with 4,000 dollars of income is really poor, one might ask several of those same questions and also some about age and education—for example, a medical student has human capital as a basis for borrowing. Are there any reasons to expect that the low income is voluntary—for example, chosen in preference to living with affluent relatives, having a wife or mother work, living in a different region or changing occupations?

Needless to say, many of these questions are difficult to answer. But they do point up the idea that some of the inequality which is observed is the result of people having free choice and diverging consumer and producer preferences. It is not simply the mechanistic outcome of unequally distributed talents and property. Also, some of the income differences are what would be agreed upon as equalizing differences—that is, some people with currently high incomes are being compensated for long years of training and low incomes. Others are in high risk occupations with highly variable income. Conversely, some people in low income occupations have pleasant work in attractive surroundings. To the extent that those with high incomes are compensating for their high incomes and others are being compensated for their low incomes, the money income distribution may overstate the real inequality in the society.

Some writers [6] emphasize the role of personal choices in determining inequality, pointing to differences in preferences for present, over future, consumption— as manifested in willingness to forego income for education or to save out of income—in taste for risk and in competitive spirit with regard to income. People differ, it is alleged, in the extent to which they take the economic game seriously. Other writers emphasize differences in genetic ability, acquired skills and inherited and accumulated wealth. The demand for these abilities, skills and wealth arises out of business managers' calculations that employment of them will be productive of goods and services that consumers will buy.

6. For a good collection of writings from differing points of view on this point, see Edward C. Budd, ed., *Inequality and Poverty* (New York: W. W. Norton, 1967).

Critics of the personal preference and productivity schools of thought stress the significance of forces which distort the distributional inequalities that would arise in a perfect market. They point to luck, nepotism, discrimination, monopoly, fraudulent or unethical business practices, governmental favoritism, unfair advantages of the rich and acquiescence of the poor in, what R. H. Tawney called, a "religion of inequality." These critics reject the notion that gross inequalities of income are necessary as part of a functional set of rewards and punishments; they seek ways to modify the prevailing reality.

From the discussion to this point, we can conclude that the American standard distribution of income is a highly simplified statement of a complex reality. It is hardly an ideal measure of inequality for all purposes. It may, however, be useful as either (1) a performance indicator for the national economy or (2) a road map for social intervention. It is to these matters that I will now turn.

INCOME INEQUALITY AS INDICATOR OF PERFORMANCE OF THE ECONOMY

Economists, at least since Jeremy Bentham, have regarded the distribution, as well as the·level, of income to be of importance in judging the functioning of an economy. The Gini ratio is sometimes accorded importance as a performance indicator along with the level of, and changes in, the GNP, the rate of unemployment and the balance of payments. This concern with performance goals is matched by concern for appropriate structures and processes, such as competition and freedom of choice. Perhaps, one should classify equality of opportunity as a process goal and limited inequality of result as a performance goal.

One can justify prominence for a measure of income inequality on the grounds of a historical shift of opinion.[7] Although the ancient Greeks envisioned men—excluding slaves—as equal before the law and early Christians saw them as equal in the sight of God, it was not until recent centuries that clerical hierarchies were broken down and civil rights and voting rights were established for commoners. With the transformation to a modern industrial society, the egalitarian impulse has shifted to economic relationships.

Some see the concept of every man being entitled to socially assured minimums of income and services as merely a new flowering of the concept of citizenship. In the eighteenth century, it was persuasively argued that if people were provided with similar environment and opportunities their conditions would become similar. According to Irving Kristol,

It is a distinguishing characteristic of the modern age that "equality" should be not merely an abstract ideal but also a politically aggressive idea. It is generally accepted—it is, indeed, one of the most deeply rooted conventions of contemporary political thought—that the existence of inequality is a legitimate provocation to social criticism. Every inequality is on the defensive, must prove itself against the imputation of injustice and unnaturalness. And where such proof is established, it never asserts itself beyond the point where inequality is to be tolerated because it is, under particular conditions, inescapable. That inequality may be per se desirable is a thought utterly repugnant to the modern sensibility.[8]

7. Compare, Josef J. Spengler, "Hierarchy versus Equality: Persisting Conflict," *Kyklos: International Review for Social Science* 21 (1968), pp. 217–238.

8. Irving Kristol, "Equality as an Ideal," *International Encyclopedia of the Social Sciences* (New York: Macmillan, 1968), pp. 108–111.

Certainly, John Rawls, the contemporary philosopher, speaks for many in asserting that justice requires that: "All goods are to be distributed equally unless an unequal distribution of any or all of these goods is to the advantage of the least favored." [9]

While those statements may be a fair reflection of the drift of political philosophy, it is interesting that political activists have not focussed on a particular concept, or measure, of overall income inequality. No political party has adopted a slogan of "A .300 Gini ratio, or fight!" John K. Galbraith wrote, in 1958, that ". . . few things are more evident in modern social history than the decline of interest in inequality as an economic issue." [10] Martin Bronfenbrenner describes that interest as "dormant throughout most of this century in the United States." [11] James Tobin concludes that "Americans accept and approve a large measure of inequality; the differential earnings of effort, skill, foresight, and enterprise are seen as deserved, just so long as the earnings were legitimately and fairly won. Even lucky winnings are sanctioned by most Americans." [12] It is not popular to say that since private incomes are socially determined, in small or large part, society has a right to redistribute them in accord with social priorities.

Perhaps one of the reasons for caution in adopting change in the American standard distribution as a goal is that it measures inequality of result, while political interest attaches to the processes that limit inequality of opportunity. It is interesting that we do not have a good index of the latter type of inequality. Even here, however, interests tend to be particularized and to be most sensitive when income inequality is incongruous with lessened inequality on other counts. Thus, differential earnings of Blacks and whites become more significant as an issue when the educational attainment of Blacks comes to approximate that of whites. Similar anomalies arise with regard to income difference by age, sex, occupation or region.

Perhaps another reason for lack of interest in the Gini coefficient is its apparent stability, according to income distribution students; nonetheless, the notion that "the rich get richer" remains a sturdy part of American folklore. While the failure of inequality to decline is viewed by some as an affront to the future, it is considered by others to be a denial of the proposition that ever worsening inequality of income will arise from, and bring about, the downfall of capitalism. [13] Keynesian economic theory denies that high degrees of income inequality cause the imbalances between savings and investment propensities that either lead to recession or impede recovery. The same need for government management of aggregate demand could exist even with less income inequality. Most have resisted the theory that the recent rise in the crime rate and mental illness or other signs of social pathology can be traced to the failure of income inequality to decline. [14] This theory seems to rest upon the assumed importance of

9. John Rawls, *A Theory of Justice* (Cambridge, Mass.: Harvard University Press, 1971); see his discussion of the "difference principle."

10. John K. Galbraith, *The Affluent Society* (Boston, Mass.: Houghton-Mifflin, 1958), p. 72.

11. Martin Bronfenbrenner, *Income Distribution Theory* (Chicago, Ill.: Aldine-Atherton, 1971).

12. James Tobin, "On Limiting the Domain of Inequality," *Journal of Law and Economics* 13 (October 1970), pp. 263–277.

13. Bronfenbrenner, *Income Distribution,* chap. 5.

14. Herbert J. Gans, "The New Egalitarianism," *Saturday Review* 6 (May 1972), pp. 43–46.

changing expectations of economic success on the part of low income people.

Finally, it can be claimed that economic growth is an alternative means to achieve most of the same results as those desired by advocates of redistribution. Growth in all incomes, given stable inequality, will improve the lot of the poor. It will enable them to consume more of the necessities of life, to compete more effectively in the economic process and to participate as full citizens in public affairs. Only when economic growth becomes extraordinarily difficult to sustain, or when it becomes politically unacceptable as a goal, would redistribution become an exclusive remedy for poverty.

It is true, of course, that every society—even those experiencing rapid economic growth—undertakes some redistribution, and social scientists need to have some theories about why this happens and what the results are. Some speculate that redistribution arises from altruistic motives and is in the nature of a public good—similar to national defense—enjoyed by all, including donors.[15] Others argue that redistribution results from bargains between hostile social classes.[16] These classes are not easily identified on the American standard distribution of income.

A ROAD MAP TO SOCIAL INTERVENTION?

Measured inequality of income has had only limited use as a performance indicator. Also, it has had only scattered use as a road map to social intervention on behalf of the economic losers and in restraint of the winners.

The interpretation given to any set of facts is often determined by preconceptions formed even before the investigation of the facts; similarly, one is sensitized to certain facts by the policies one has in mind. Some see income inequality as capitalism's unremovable badge of shame. Marx asserted that "to clamor for equal or even equitable retribution on the basis of the wage system is the same as to clamor for freedom on the basis of the slavery system. What you think is just or equitable is out of question. The question is: what is necessary and unavoidable with a given system of production." [17] For Marxists, the road map is clear: the first step in reducing inequality is socialization of the means of production, hence, the abolition of private property income. Since property income is highly unequal in its distribution, this should eliminate a considerable portion of observable inequality. A second step is the socialization of some—or all—consumption, with state distribution to families on some basis other than market earnings. Moreover, it implies some strong system of nonmonetary rewards and punishments for differential efforts in production.[18]

Short of complete socialism, governments can intervene to minimize inequalities of opportunities or to reduce

15. To sample this literature, the reader may look to Harold M. Hochman and James D. Rogers, "Pareto Optimal Redistribution," *American Economic Review* 59 (September 1969), pp. 542–557; Gordon Tullock, "Public Decisions as Public Goods," *Journal of Political Economy* 79 (1971), pp. 913–918; Lester Thurow, "Toward a Definition of Economic Justice," *Public Interest* 31 (Spring 1973), pp. 56–80.

16. Hirofumi Shibata, "A Bargaining Model of the Pure Theory of Public Expenditures," *Journal of Political Economy* 79 (January 1971), pp. 1–29.

17. Karl Marx, "Wages, Price and Profit," in K. Marx and F. Engels, *Selected Works* (Moscow: Foreign Languages Publishing House, 1962), vol. 1, p. 426.

18. In the Soviet Union, entitlements to social insurance benefits are conditioned upon fulfillment of the obligation to work as specified in Article 12 of the Constitution. See Gaston V. Rimlinger, "Social Security, Incentive and Controls in the U.S. and U.S.S.R.," *Comparative Studies in Society and History* 4 (November 1961), pp. 104–124.

differences in consumption—or both. The implication of the first strategy is that if there were genuine equality of opportunity, then there would be less inequality of result; however, it is not altogether clear that this would follow. Nor is it clear that equality of opportunity for children is achievable without considerably less inequality of results among parents; thus, the two strategies tend to overlap. Policies aimed at equalizing opportunity, however, might conceivably include the following: prohibit monopolies, racial and sex discrimination and other unfair restraints of trade; set a maximum on inheritance of wealth; assure full employment and the availability of education. Policies to limit inequality of result might include: progressive income taxation, social insurance, public assistance and other cash transfers. For those whose earnings and cash transfers are not enough to buy what are judged to be necessities of acceptable quality, the state may undertake to provide those goods at zero, or subsidized, prices. For example, health insurance may be offered on an income-conditioned scale of charges. Low income consumers may be bribed to take their full quota of such merit goods as preschool training and higher education.

James Tobin queries, "Can we somehow remove the necessities of life and health from the prizes that serve as incentives for economic activity, and instead let people strive and compete for nonessential luxuries and amenities?"[19] Of course, limiting the domain of inequality in this fashion will blur the meaning of differential earnings. How far do we want to go in breaking the tie, as Christopher Jencks puts it, "between vocational success and living standards?"[20]

Interestingly, in actually legislating and administering programs with redistributive effect, much overt attention is seldom given to the facts revealed in the American standard distribution of income. Moreover, large changes in such programs may do relatively little to alter the distribution. Consider the income tax and public assistance systems. In either system, families with equal money incomes may pay different taxes or get different benefits—negative taxes. Income taxation is justified on grounds of ability to pay, with consideration of expenses of earning income, casualty losses, socially preferred uses of income and family relationships. Considerable debate goes on over horizontal equity between taxpayers who are similar in all regards but one. For example, suppose a woman works out of the home and has child care expense. If that expense were made deductible from the family income tax base, would it be fair with reference to another woman who produces her own child care—which is not counted as taxable income—and gets no deduction?

The point is that the classification of rich and poor for income tax purposes hardly duplicates the American standard distribution. The same point applies with reference to the determination of public assistance benefits. Here, the theory is that a family is to be helped if its needs exceed its resources. Careful attention is paid to family size and composition and needs for special things, such as medical care. Resources are defined to include assets, as well as cash income, and, in some programs, potential to earn.

Each program for redistribution, be it public education, unemployment insurance or public housing, has its own phi-

19. Tobin, "Domain of Inequality."
20. Christopher Jencks," *Inequality: A Reassessment of the Effect of Family and School-* *ing in America* (New York: Basic Books, 1972); see especially chap. 7 on income inequality.

losophy which may have little in common with the philosophy that informs the design of the American standard distribution of income. The latter is, then, a performance indicator to which no social policy is directly keyed. The hiatus is significant. It means that the income distribution is not used in deciding who should help whom; apparently, it is not considered to be a reliable road map for social intervention. It may also mean something else: namely, that Americans don't really seek any particular degree of income equality, but rather seek a system of sharing that recognizes human needs, restrains certain arbitrary or capricious inequalities and serves social purposes.

The Strategy of Economic Policy and Income Distribution

By HYMAN P. MINSKY

ABSTRACT: In a capitalist economy, income distribution is compounded out of the distribution of capital income, the distribution of labor income and the shares of capital and labor in total income. As capital inequality is much greater than income inequality, a decrease in capital's share would decrease income inequality. Keynes held that euthanasia of the rentier —that is, a decrease in capital's share of total income—would result from the investment that takes place during sustained full employment. Tolerably full employment has been sustained ever since World War II, but capital's share of income has not fallen. Full employment over the postwar period has been the result of policy which conformed to a private investment strategy. This strategy operates by sustaining and increasing the returns on capital and also carries threats of financial instability and inflation. An alternative public employment strategy for full employment policy is available. This strategy would probably lead to a partial euthanasia of the rentier and would tend to diminish the likelihood of financial instability and inflation. Highly stylized examples show that the effects of a partial euthanasia of the rentier, when combined with mildly equalitarian taxes, transfers and government services, can lead to a substantial decrease in income inequality.

Hyman P. Minsky is Professor of Economics at Washington University in St. Louis, Missouri. Educated at the University of Chicago and Harvard University, he is the author of a forthcoming volume that presents an alternative interpretation of Keynes's The General Theory of Employment, Interest, and Money. *Although his primary interest is in monetary theory and banking, he served as a Consultant to the Office of Economic Opportunity in its early days and to the President's National Advisory Commission on Rural Poverty.*

IN the first paragraph of the last chapter of *The General Theory of Employment, Interest and Money,* Keynes announced that there were two lessons to be learned from his theory:

The outstanding faults of the economic society in which we live are its failure to provide for full employment and its arbitrary and inequitable distribution of wealth and incomes. The bearing of the foregoing theory on the first of these is obvious. But there are also two important respects in which it is relevant to the second.[1]

The first lesson has become part of accepted wisdom. As a result of policy measures that owe their legitimacy to *The General Theory,* a closer sustained approximation to full employment has been achieved during the period since World War II than in any previous era. On the other hand, Keynes's belief that his theory would enable us to ameliorate the "arbitrary and inequitable distribution of wealth and incomes" has not been realized. Over the postwar period no significant progress has been made towards improving distributional equity.

INTRODUCTION

The two lessons have enjoyed such disparate theoretical, and practical, success because the standard interpretation of Keynes which has guided economic policy has ignored those aspects of the theory which make income distribution dependent upon the mode of operation of the economy. In an age of active economic policy, income distribution is inevitably affected by the policy strategy that is adopted.

To recapture some lost features of Keynes's theory and its implications for income distribution policy, a financial instability hypothesis which integrates the neglected features of his theory will

be advanced. Of course, the important issue is not whether this alternative view is an accurate reproduction of Keynes's theory; the main issue is whether the alternative is a better theory for the class of economies with which we are dealing—advanced capitalist economies with sophisticated financial systems.

Keynes gives two reasons why his theory applies to income distribution policy: (1) it refutes the defense of inequality that rests on the need to release resources from consumption activities to investment outputs; (2) more importantly, his theory points towards the imminent euthanasia of the rentier. Since capital income is more unequally distributed than labor income, decreasing the weight of capital income in total income would tend to decrease inequality.

The euthanasia of the rentier is one of Keynes's concepts which has been lost. It points to the power of policy to affect income distribution by affecting the share of capital in total income. To point up the power and relevance of this idea, I will consider some highly stylized material on income and wealth distribution in the United States.

Two policy strategies for full employment are distinguished.[2] The first, which dominates the policy thrust in the United States since World War II, emphasizes private investment. This strategy reflects an effort to achieve both full employment and accelerated growth. A side effect of this strategy is an intensified tendency towards financial instability, as well as increased income inequality. The second policy strategy, which largely characterized recovery policy in the years just prior to World

1. J. M. Keynes, *The General Theory of Employment, Interest and Money* (New York: Harcourt, Brace, World, 1936), p. 372.

2. A policy strategy is the broad structure and thrust of the measures adopted. A particular strategy can be affected by various mixes of policy measures.

War II, emphasizes public employment. My argument is that this strategy, appropriately implemented, can decrease inequality by decreasing capital's share of income. A public employment strategy also decreases the likelihood that serious financial stringency will occur.

The operation of the economy generates initial income shares compounded out of the distribution of capital income, the distribution of labor income and the relative weights of capital and labor incomes in total income.[3] Income distribution policy can ignore the way in which the initial distribution of income is obtained and operate to alter the initial distribution by means of tax, transfer and government services in the effort to achieve a desired distribution. The various negative income tax, or guaranteed income, proposals which had a run of academic, but not of public, acceptance in the recent past embodied this approach to income distribution policy.[4] Policy designed to expedite the euthanasia of the rentier modifies the initial distribution by decreasing capital's share. For the United States, a significant decrease in inequality can be achieved by combining a partial euthanasia of the rentier with a rather modest equalitarian bias in taxation, transfer payments and government service programs.

THE FINANCIAL INSTABILITY HYPOTHESIS

The financial instability hypothesis underlies this paper.[5] This interpreta-

tion of Keynes's *The General Theory* ties aggregate demand to the financing and speculative pricing of assets.

A key proposition in this hypothesis is that full employment is itself destabilizing—that is, it is a disequilibrium state, because sustained full employment induces speculation which transforms otherwise stable growth into an euphoric investment boom. In such a boom the cash payment commitments of firms and financial institutions increase more rapidly than cash receipts from participation in income production. A sustained investment boom requires two things: (1) that investing units commit ever greater cash flows to debtors; and (2) that an ever larger, and more closely articulated, set of financial markets function properly. These developments increase the likelihood that financial distress will occur. Such distress or crisis triggers a falling away from full employment.

As a result of these interactions, income in a capitalist economy moves in a cyclical fashion. The economy transits among various system states: full employment, investment boom, financial crisis, debt-deflation, recession, depression, stagnation and recovery. These various states need neither occur nor be of the same intensity in every business cycle. Each system state is a disequilibrium state, which carries the seeds of its own destruction. The transit among system states is an endogenous phenomenon.

The path of income, employment and debts after a financial crisis, as well as the likelihood and severity of the crisis, is sensitive to the behavior of the Federal Reserve System and the fiscal posture of the federal government.

---

3. This initial distribution is conditioned by institutional and fiscal features of the economy.

4. For the taxation and transfer approach, see Christopher Green, *Negative Taxes and the Poverty Problem* (Washington, D.C.: The Brookings Institution, 1967).

5. See H. P. Minsky, "Financial Instability Revisited: The Economics of Disaster," in *Reappraisal of the Federal Revenue Discount*

Mechanism, Board of Governors of the Federal Reserve System (Washington, D.C.: June 1972), vol. 3, pp. 95–136.

Prompt intervention by the Federal Reserve System can abort the more serious financial consequences, such as those which have often followed a crisis. Large government expenditures, combined with consumption supporting transfer schemes, set a high floor to income and introduce safe government debt into portfolios. Thus, the postwar combination of federal reserve sophistication, large government expenditures and substantial transfer payments has succeeded in changing the shape, but not in eliminating, the business cycle.

As decisions to invest and hold assets are based upon uncertain expectations, the market price of equities—common stocks—and prices of real assets are not precisely determined by the technical characteristics of capital assets in production. Investment, capital holding and liability structure decisions are based upon speculative considerations which dominate productivity. These speculative considerations take the form of conjectures about: (1) the cash flows that capital assets generate when used in production, (2) the cash payments required by liabilities, (3) the market price of capital assets and (4) the market conditions for the liabilities of the asset holders. As the subjective estimates are based upon flimsy evidence, events can trigger rapid changes in the decision determinants, thus, in investment and desired asset holdings.

In a world with cyclical expectations and experience, the ratio of employed to available capital and labor services has been, and is expected to be, variable. As a result, the distribution of income between, and within, capital and labor is not determined by production function characteristics. In standard economic theory, the initial, pretax, distribution of income between capital and labor and the size distribution within labor are determined by endowments and production function characteristics. In the financial instability view, production relations do not dominate in determining income distribution. In particular, profit expectations induce investment, and the pace of investment determines the share of profits in income. Thus, policy is not restricted to the use of tax, transfer and government services to modify some technologically determined distribution of income. Policy can affect the within labor distribution of income and the weights of labor and capital incomes in total income, as it affects the structure of demand.

THE EUTHANASIA OF THE RENTIER

In the cited passage, Keynes writes that there are "two important respects" in which his theory is relevant to the goal of a just and logical distribution of income. One is that inequality is unnecessary in generating the savings required for investment and growth. The other is that accumulation during sustained full employment eases the chronic and oppressive shortage of capital, resulting in a decrease of scarcity rent which capital commands.

Logically, these two grounds are quite different. The savings and investment argument points out that a barrier which was believed to exist, in fact, does not exist. Nevertheless, it remains a policy decision whether this opening will be used. On the other hand, the euthanasia of the rentier argument represents a positive view about the economy. It presumes that a sustained approximation of full employment, relieved of the waste of war, will soon lead to full investment—that is, a regime in which the scarcity rent of capital is drastically reduced.

Keynes's distributional optimism was based upon a belief that: "The demand for capital is strictly limited. . . . it would not be difficult to increase the stock of capital up to a point where its marginal efficiency had fallen to a very low figure." [6] Rentier income disappears once capital ". . . ceases to be scarce, so that the functionless investor will no longer receive a bonus." [7] Keynes held that the investment which would take place under full employment and without war and excessive population growth would lead to ". . . the euthanasia of the cumulative oppressive power of the capitalist to exploit the scarcity-value of capital." [8]

Since World War II, a generation has passed without a major war or a serious depression. Nevertheless, the euthanasia of the rentier remains as remote as ever; if anything, the share of capital in total income may have increased over this period. Military expenditures and the increase in population explain part of the continued scarcity of capital, but the enormous rate of accumulation necessitates a deeper explanation.

Keynes approached the question of the ultimate required capital stock with a view that human wants, for those items that use economic resources, are satiable:

Now it is true that the needs of human beings may seem to be insatiable. But they fall into two classes—those needs which are absolute in the sense that we feel them whatever the situation of our fellow human beings may be, and those which are relative in the sense that we feel them only if their satisfaction lifts us above, makes us feel superior to, our fellows. Needs of the second class, those which satisfy the desire for superiority, may indeed be insatiable; for the higher the general level, the higher still are they. But this is not so true of the absolute needs—a point may soon be reached, much sooner perhaps than we are all of us aware of, when these needs are satisfied in the sense that we prefer to devote our further energies to non-economic purposes." [9]

Experience has not validated Keynes's view about the satiation of human needs. The universal satisfaction of the absolute needs lies within the capacity of the affluent countries, such as the United States, Western Europe and Japan; this objective was within the technical capacity of the affluent economies when Keynes wrote.

Nevertheless, capital continues to be scarce and commands a substantial positive return. Relative needs have grown, and these needs are so structured as to induce demand for capital. The apparently insatiable demand is what it is because income distribution enables the rich and near rich to consume capital absorbing goods at an ever expanding tempo. Via demonstration effects and the course of social prestige, demand for such goods trickles down from the few to the many. The result is a demand for capital assets that sustains the shortage of capital. Consequently, growth and affluence—instead of bringing satisfaction—requires the cultivation of dissatisfaction.

SCHEMATIZED VIEW OF INCOME DISTRIBUTION

Conditioned by the impact of monopoly, trade unions and government, the economy generates an initial distribution of income. Taxes, transfer payments and government services transform an initial distribution of income

6. J. M. Keynes, *General Theory,* p. 375.
7. Ibid., p. 376. The elimination of rentier income does not mean that entrepreneurial income will disappear.
8. Ibid., p. 376.

9. J. M. Keynes, "Economic Possibilities for Our Grandchildren," in his *Essays in Persuasion* (New York: W. W. Norton, 1930), p. 326.

into a final one. In a capitalist economy, the initial distribution is compounded out of three factors: the distribution of labor income, the allocation of capital income and the relative weight of capital income to total income. Net worth—and, by inference, capital income—is much more concentrated than total income; whereas the top fifth receives 40 percent of income, the top fifth owns 80 percent of net worth.[10]

As the distribution of net worth is more concentrated than that of income, any increase in capital's share of total income reenforces inequality. If we assume that our distribution of income is the result of capital receiving 30 percent of the total income, by making quite heroic assumptions that the distribution of capital and labor income completely overlaps the distribution of income with capital's share, 20 and 10 percent of total income can be computed. These computations indicate that if the data which show that the top fifth receive 40 percent of income are the result of capital receiving 30 percent of income, then a decrease of capital's share to 20 percent would lower the top fifth to 35 percent of total income. A decrease of capital's share to 10 percent would lower the top fifth to 29 percent of total income. The income of the bottom fifth in the income distribution would increase from 6 percent, to 7 percent and finally to 8 percent as the share of capital income in total income decreases from 30 percent, to 20 percent and finally to 10 percent. The ratio of the top fifth's total income to the bottom fifth's total income would fall from 6.7, to 5.0, to 3.6

10. U.S., Congress, Joint Economic Committee, *The American Distribution of Income: A Structural Problem,* prepared by L. C. Thurow and R. E. B. Lucas (Washington, D.C.: Government Printing Office, 1972).

as the weight of capital income would decrease.

It is evident that an improvement in distribution can be effected if capital's share decreases. It is also evident that a partial euthanasia of the rentier— that is, the reduction of capital's share to 20 percent or 10 percent of total income—would have to be supplemented by tax and transfer measures, if a more substantial increase in the income of the very lowest income groups is the objective. Euthanasia of the rentier is more effective in cutting the income of the very top income groups than it is in raising the income of the very lowest groups.

THE DISTRIBUTIONAL IMPACT OF STRATEGIES FOR FULL EMPLOYMENT

For full employment, the gap between consumption and full employment output must be filled by a combination of private investment and government demand. During the recovery period of the 1930s a public employment strategy was prominent. However, on the whole, policy since World War II has emphasized a private investment strategy.

Private investment strategy

Underlying the emphasis upon private investment as the preferred way to achieve full employment is the view that economic growth is desirable, and that the growth rate is determined by the pace of private investment. Furthermore, permeating standard economics is the preconception that the distributive shares are determined by technical conditions; hence, it is believed that the only effective way to improve the absolute lot of the poor is to increase total income.

The cash flow—gross profit—expected from owning capital assets is the proximate determinant of private investment.

If the aim is to increase investment, measures to increase the size and certainty of capital income are required. Included are tax devices which give capital income favored treatment—that is, accelerated depreciation and investment tax credits and spending programs that take the form of contracts with guaranteed profits, such as defense and space procurement, highway construction, housing subsidies and research. The tax breaks directly increase inequality. Contract spending, especially on sophisticated defense and space systems, tends to generate demand for short-lived and high gross profit outputs. Furthermore, the associated labor demand is for skilled, high wage labor, which increases the intralabor inequality of income.

High capital incomes lead to opulent consumption by the rich which induces imitative consumption by the less affluent, high paid workers. The rising consumption demand, which is a product of inequality, in turn sustains the shortage and income of capital.

Capital yields two kinds of returns: profits and interest, which are the result of participation in income production, and capital gains, which are the result of the revaluation of asset prices. An investment strategy sustains income earned in production by capital assets. An enlargement of capital income increases the value of capital assets, in particular, stock exchange equities. An increase in the surety of profits raises the rate at which income is capitalized. Thus, sooner or later, an investment strategy results in capital gains. Widespread realization and anticipation of capital gains fosters an increase in speculative debt financing of ownership of capital assets and of investment. A private investment strategy contributes to a speculative, debt-financed investment boom. The ratio of contractual cash payments in debts to cash receipts from normal income related services is increased.

The greater the ratio of debt payments to income receipts, the more fragile the financial structure. Inevitably, monetary policy is handcuffed by an awareness that monetary restraint may ignite a debt deflation process, difficult to control. Monetary and fiscal policy must then maneuver ever more delicately to prevent unemployment. Furthermore, each success in avoiding a debt deflation makes subsequent policy more difficult to execute.

A private investment dependence is fraught with inflationary contingencies. The rising desire to consume which is induced by capital gains during booms makes it likely that the growth in aggregate demand will outpace aggregate supply. This generates a demand-pull inflation. In addition, the investment strategy can impel a special type of cost-push inflation, if, as is true for the United States, some trade unions have relatively greater market power than other trade unions.

For example, the combination of an investment strategy and uneven trade union power in construction can force a rise in construction wages relative to other wages and, thus, in the price of the building trade output relative to other output. This, in turn, increases the cash flows that must be realized if investment is to be sustained. For this to happen, it is necessary that the price of output rise to a level that is consistent with construction wages. An investment strategy breeds a likelihood that both inflationary pressures in investment production and a need to generalize this inflation—in order to service the debt used in financing investment—will exist. Furthermore, as construction workers' income is high relative to other workers' income, the private investment strategy, within the context of the greater relative power of trade unions in the building trades, tends to advance high wage incomes relative to low wage workers. The private investment strategy, as it works in the United States, tends to sharpen intralabor inequality.[11]

Thus, the private investment strategy has four flaws:

—it breeds fragile financial relations that threaten full employment and financial stability;
—it evokes inflationary pressures;
—it enlarges capital income in total income;
—it fosters inequality in labor income.

Public employment strategy

The basic ingredients for a public employment strategy are to be found in the Works Projects Administration, National Youth Administration and Civilian Conservation Corps of the 1930s. The philosophy underlying this strategy takes the unemployed as they are and fits public jobs to their capabilities.[12] Such public employment for adult workers would be at the national minimum wage; part time work to supplement social security and child maintenance allowances would be available; youth wages could be at some discount from the legislated minimum wage. This is analogous to farm price supports: the legislated minimum wage is replaced by a wage floor set by an always available alternative. Jobs will be available to

11. H. P. Minsky, "Effects of Shifts of Aggregate Demand Upon Income Distribution," *American Journal of Agricultural Economics* (May 1968).

12. H. P. Minsky, *Labor and the War Against Poverty* (Berkeley, Calif.: Institute of Industrial Relations, Center for Labor Research and Education, 1965).

all; there would be no means test for participation.

The employment available would be in labor intensive services that lead to readily visible public benefits, such as cleaner, safer cities, more and better-maintained parks and recreational facilities. As there will be a continuing minimum amount of public employment, certain services of public concern might well have a permanent cadre of such workers—that is, in hospitals, schools and on police forces. The income received, while presumably more than adequate for the absolute needs of which Keynes spoke, would not generate opulent incomes for any, not even for administrators of the programs.

An employment strategy is consistent with constraints upon private speculative finance. Speculative finance not being required, developing liability structures would not jeopardize the success of this strategy. Tax policy need not be conditioned by the necessity to induce private investment and to sustain the cash flows required to service debts born of speculative finance.

A public employment strategy imparts a strong underpinning to demand. As it does allow technical progress to induce investment and does not foster speculative booms, this strategy can underwrite a steady pace of investment. The tax schedule could be devised to balance the budget whenever public employment is consistent with what would now be a 4.5 percent measured unemployment rate. Whenever the pace of private investment increased to force public employment below this level, the budget would quickly move to a surplus; whenever private employment decreased, the budget would move to a deficit. As a fiscal device, an automatic public employment policy could be an effective stabilizer. As capital shortages and large capital rents are superfluous for this program—and because the emphasis in policy shifts from more to better use of existing capabilities—a rather quick partial euthanasia of the rentier should occur once this strategy is adopted.

With a public employment strategy there is no need to stimulate investment by allowing large intergenerational inheritance transfers. Thus, truly progressive and effective death duties can be instituted. Furthermore, corporate income taxes—especially the definition of nontaxable corporate income—no longer need be determined by a need to sustain corporate cash flows. Capital gains for rentiers would not be a necessary driving force, and the need for the protective treatment of such income would vanish. For example, as construction would be removed from the arena of privileged output, the power of construction unions to force inflation and inequality would be attenuated. Since it is more sustainable and less inflationary, a public employment strategy may be preferable to a private investment strategy. In addition, it holds out the promise that by a partial euthanasia of the rentier it will ease the burden of income inequality.

CONCLUSION

A partial euthanasia of the rentier, which would accompany a shift to public employment strategy, can contribute to equalizing income. A reduction of capital's share of total income from 30 percent to 20 percent will lower the ratio of total income in the top fifth to total income in the bottom fifth from 6.7 to 5. Further reductions in inequality could be accomplished by quite modest tax, transfer and service programs. In the examples that follow, a partial euthanasia that lowers capital's share from 30 percent to 20 percent is assumed.

Let us call a fair shares program one in which there is a proportionate tax on income and an equal per capita distribution of benefits. If the total collected in this manner is 10 percent of total income, then the ratio of the top fifth's total income to that of the bottom fifth's will drop to 3.7.

In a mildly progressive scheme, 10 percent of total income is collected by tax rates that range from 13 percent in the highest fifth to 3 percent for the lowest fifth, and transfers and services are distributed so that the top fifth receives 10 percent of the total—50 percent of their fair share—and the lowest fifth receives 30 percent—150 percent of their fare share. This scheme combined with a partial euthanasia will lead to a top fifth to bottom fifth ratio of 3 to 1.

Substantial progress towards a more just and equitable distribution of income can be achieved by a modest partial euthanasia combined with either fair shares or mildly progressive tax, transfer and service programs. To effect such a transformation it is necessary to design policy with these specific objectives in mind. A public employment strategy is consistent with the goal of distributional equity—a private investment strategy is not.

A public employment strategy directly affects the distribution of income by setting an effective floor to wage income. In addition, the services produced by public employment will be distributed at least on a fair share basis and, more than likely, on a progressive basis. The areas, neighborhoods and population groups with the highest unemployment would naturally receive a larger portion of the useful output produced by such employment.

A public employment strategy implies a significant reordering of priorities. A private investment strategy promises pie in the sky—that is, skimp today for tomorrow's abundance. A public employment strategy aims at a better application of current capabilities and a more equitable distribution of current output. A public employment strategy also removes constraints upon tax policy: it is not necessary to compromise justice and equity because of an overriding need to induce investment.

A final note: the private investment strategy was fully institutionalized during the Kennedy regime with its emphasis upon growth. The liberal economists of that administration apparently did not realize that the measures they pressed to increase growth had the additional effect of increasing inequality. The current financial instability—first evidenced by the crunch of 1966, repeated in the liquidity-squeeze, Penn Central crisis, of 1970 and succeeded by the dollar crises in 1971 and 1973— indicates that the private investment strategy to maintain full employment is running out of steam. The question that we may soon have to face is not whether there will be increased public spending, but what kind of public spending will be selected. The big choice will be between public contractural spending—for defense, highways and so on—and public employment.

The Fall of the House of Efficiency

By Edward J. Nell

ABSTRACT: Under competitive conditions, in capitalist and market-socialist societies, income is said to be paid in approximate proportion to productive contributions. This doctrine is the rock upon which the House of Efficiency is built. The geology implicit in the reswitching controversy suggests that this rock is sedimentary, indeed, loosely packed sandstone. As the rock crumbles in the harsh Cambridge weather, it reveals the outline of the real forces determining the distribution of income.

Edward J. Nell is Professor of Economics and Chairman of the Department of Economics of the Graduate Faculty at the New School for Social Research. He has held teaching positions at Wesleyan University and the University of East Anglia. Educated at Princeton and Oxford Universities, he is author of many articles and reviews for both scholarly and popular journals.

A S shadows lengthen across the Republic, we may deplore protest; however, we still deem our system to be Protestant. No one gets something for nothing—at least, not in the long run and in equilibrium. We work for our livings; we get what we pay for; tit for tat. Income is earned and paid in proportion to productive contribution, even where measurement is inexact. Of course, there are imperfections and blemishes, and not all productive contributions involve work; some kinds of income are earned through the productive services of wealth embodied in capital goods. It is certainly questionable whether people should receive incomes simply because they own equipment which makes productive contributions. What is not questioned is that income is paid in rough proportion to productive contribution, whether of labor or of capital equipment.

INTRODUCTION

This doctrine is the rock upon which the House of Efficiency is built. Resources, whether of labor or of capital, are shifted by their owners in response to incentives which are offered in anticipation of productive contributions. Resource owners will settle upon the most efficient combination of resources because they will thus maximize their net incomes. Output as a whole will be as large as possible and will be produced most efficiently because all individual outputs will be maximized in response to income incentives. This makes sense only if income is proportional to productive contribution.

This curious doctrine is not exclusive to capitalism. In socialist societies, it is sometimes said that income is, or should be, proportional to contribution. Increases in incomes are not awarded to those who work harder or to those most in need of extra consumption or to those whose work is most unpleasant, but to those whose work adds most to increasing output—managers and General Secretaries of the Party.

According to this doctrine, socialism must be efficient and must plan the allocation of its labor force. To some extent, this can be done by assigning workers to jobs; for the most part, however, this will not provide adequate incentives. Hence, to create an efficient labor market, individual incomes or at least increases in such incomes must be made proportional to individual outputs. There is dispute whether the same could, or should, be done for capital; also, it is certainly arguable whether present arrangements result in a very efficient allocation of labor. But whether labor could be paid in proportion to its productive contribution—and if it were, whether efficient allocation would then be possible in principle—is not normally questioned.

The idea that income is a reward for productive contribution is deeply ingrained in our culture. A little reflection should suggest that it is totally implausible. Of course, total output results from the total productive work of society, using the total means of production; and more work, done with proper equipment, results in more output. Yet, certain kinds of work may be quite unproductive, even though respectable. In any case, the doctrine is neither that total output is proportionate to total input—which is true—nor that total income must equal total output in value—also true, indeed, a logical consequence of combining the institutions of property and monetary exchange. Rather, it is that the incomes of individual factors will be proportional to their separate and individual contributions. It is a theory of the distribution, not of the size, of the total product. It is primarily this doctrine which, on the face of it, is so implausible.

Nancy Mitford, in *The American Way of Death*, relates the story of undertakers, who—by becoming first morticians and then funeral directors—raised their incomes relative to those of other professional groups. Does she also describe an increased productive contribution? Garbage collectors have recently become sanitation engineers and increased their incomes, in some cities, above those of most school teachers; their improved productivity is less conspicuous. During the 1960s, the salaries of university teachers made enormous—no doubt wholly deserved—gains while the average teaching loads steadily diminished. Over a six-year period in the late 1960s, the share of profits in the national income suffered a steady erosion and then, after a phase, began a rapid rebound.[1] Did the aggregate capital of the nation steadily decline in productive powers—on average and at the margin—for six years and then suddenly grow fertile again?

IMPLICATIONS OF INCOME DISTRIBUTION

In society

Not only is the claim that incomes are proportional to contributions unconvincing, but a careful scrutiny also reveals unattractive moral and social features. One can assume, as is widely conceded, that a worker's productivity reflects his social, as well as his biological, heritage; indeed, it is not always easy to separate the two. "Man is what he eats," said Feurbach, and he is also what his mother ate during her pregnancy. Perhaps, one can separate out genetics? However, a person's ge-

netic heritage reflects the marriage patterns and habits of the social class from which his ancestors were drawn. Moreover, worker productivity depends not only on physical qualities and native wit, but also on character traits—which are transmitted through family and formal education. Hence, low productivity in this generation will reflect the low consumption, constricted opportunities for development and limited genetic pool of previous generations. Payment of low incomes in proportion to the low productive contributions would then perpetuate this syndrome, visiting the inequity of the fathers upon the children unto the third and fourth generations.

Even assuming that the genetic heritage of low productivity classes is poorer than average in some ways, there still appears to be approximately the same range and distribution of intelligence and physical abilities in this class as in others not impaired by poverty. Such abilities, more often than in richer classes, lie untapped. Their development in children requires a higher standard of living for parents. Paying low incomes to the parents ensures that the Miltons among their children remain unsung, mute and inglorious. In the long run, proportioning income to productivity is wasteful of human resources.[2]

In economics

Yet, the idea that individual income is, and rightly should be, paid to every factor in proportion to its productive contribution is deeply rooted. In economics we commonly estimate changes in productivity by changes in factor in-

---

1. Compare, E. J. Nell, "Introduction: Profit Erosion in the USA," in *Capitalism in Crisis*, ed. A. Glyn and R. B. Sutcliffe (New York: Pantheon, 1972).

2. Household incomes, mostly wages and salaries, are spent in consumption. Health, education and welfare tend to be proportional to consumption. Thus, the distribution of income is the production function for the population.

comes. For example, Solow and his followers have used data on wages and profits to draw conclusions about the relative importance of increases in the skills of labor, on the one hand, and capital accumulation, on the other, in the growth of the American economy.[3] Edward Denison followed a similar procedure in his studies of Organization of Economic Cooperation and Development (OECD) countries.[4] Many studies of education and human capital assume that if education leads to higher incomes, ipso facto, it has also increased outputs. It is hardly worth detailing the point further—any issue of almost any journal for professional economists contains evidence of the widespread acceptance of this assumption.

This assumption is equally pervasive in our culture. Consider the Quaker pacifist who refuses to pay taxes on the grounds that he will not permit his money to be spent in support of the Vietnam war. The money is "his" because he earned it; he contributed his work and received income in return. The same reasoning underlies conservative outrage over welfare cheats who have contributed nothing productive to society, yet are supported by taxes on the income of hard-working security analysts, insurance executives and advertising men. The same outrage spills over into the tax system, itself. Income is paid for productive contributions, but some productive contributions are taxed twice: once as corporate income and then as dividend income. This is unfair. There is only one productive contribution, that of the shareholder's assets which the company manages for

him. Hence, the same money is taxed twice.

In each of these cases we find the same underlying idea. Income is received in an exchange which leaves the recipient quits with society, since value equivalents have been traded. To drop this idea will require us to alter our views about nothing less than the relation of the individual to the social system. Drop it we must; for, the theoretical foundation of this idea, the theory of supply and demand for factors of production, has collapsed.

NEO-CLASSICAL THEORY OF DISTRIBUTION

Neo-Classical economists have held that distribution was determined in the factor market in the same way that prices and quantities were determined in the product market. The theory of marginal productivity, which has always been the foundation of this view, holds that: (1) in competition each unit of a factor will receive the value of the extra product the employment of an extra unit of the factor brings as reward and (2) that as employment of a factor increases, with other factors constant, the amount of extra product from further employment declines. This can be shown easily in a diagram. Plot output per employed plant, Y/K, on one axis, and amounts of labor per plant, L/K, on the other. As we apply more men to the factory, output goes up, but by a smaller amount each time. For a certain ratio of labor to capital, L^*/K, there will be a corresponding Y^*/K. The tangent to the curve at that point will measure the marginal product, and the point where the tangent intersects the vertical axis will divide the output of the factory between wages and profits. The slope of the tangent is

$$\frac{\text{wages}}{K} \bigg/ \frac{L^*}{K} = w,$$

3. Compare, the review of this work by Lester Lave, *Technological Change: Its Conception and Measurement* (Englewood Cliffs, N.J.: Prentice-Hall, 1965).

4. E. Denison, *Why Growth Rates Differ* (Washington, D.C.: Brookings Institution, 1967).

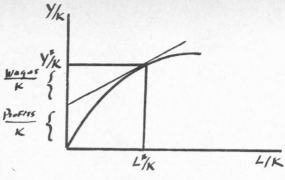

Figure 1

the wage rate, and by definition:

$$\frac{Y^*}{K} = \frac{\text{wages} + \text{profits}}{K}$$

These basic ideas can be developed in a number of ways, for instance: the relationship may be conceived as one between aggregate output—the whole capital and entire labor force of the society; total wages, profits and output can be determined together with investment, savings and growth.[5] Whatever method is used, the ultimate thought remains that factor rewards represent productive contributions at the margin and that these contributions diminish as factor employment increases.

The claim that distribution is really a form of exchange and that factor incomes are proportional to contributions has always encountered opposition. In the past, this centered on the difficulties in separating the contributions made by the various contributing factors. Cassel has commented that "If a pit

has to be dug, the addition of one more man will make little difference . . . unless you give the man a spade."[6] A homely illustration; yet, one can translate the example to the modern factory and consider adding a man to a well designed, properly running assembly line; his marginal product will be zero. Subtracting a man—if the plant is well designed, without redundant workers or featherbedding—will bring the process to a halt; the marginal product will equal the total. Sir Dennis Robertson, commenting on Cassel's observation, provided the neo-Classical answer:

If ten men are to be set to dig a hole instead of nine, they will be furnished with ten cheaper spades instead of nine more expensive ones; or, perhaps, if there is no room for him to dig comfortably, the tenth man will be furnished with a bucket and sent to fetch beer for the other nine. Once we allow ourselves this liberty, we can exhibit in the sharpest form the principle of variation—the principle that you can combine varying amounts of one factor with a fixed amount of all the others; and we can draw, for labor or any other

5. This may be done in a Cambridge manner or it may be combined with Fisherian ideas about time preference and present and future consumption, or it might be done in the manner of J. B. Clark. But the two make uneasy bedfellows; compare, E. J. Nell, "Two Books on the Theory of Income Distribution," *Journal of Economic Literature* 10, no. 2 (June 1972).

6. E. Cassel (*Theory of Social Economy,* vol. I, p. 172), as cited by Sir Dennis Robertson, "Wage-Grumbles," in *Readings in the Theory of Income Distribution,* ed. W. Fellner and B. Haley (Homewood, Ill.: Richard D. Irwin, 1951), p. 225.

factor, a perfectly definite descending curve of marginal productivity.[7]

Robertson admits that where the technique of production is rigidly fixed, marginal productivity theory is inapplicable; he claims that it applies where technique is variable and that under such conditions, a unique inverse relation exists between the wage and the labor to capital ratio.[8]

Examination of Robertson's claims

One can adapt some well known theorems from current literature and analyze these three claims. With a little mathematics—but not much—the results will prove to be of striking simplicity, yet great generality. Start with the income identity in real terms:

$$Y = wN + rK \qquad (1)$$

where Y is output; w, the wage; N, the number of workers; r, the rate of profit; and K, the total capital stock. Then, dividing by K:

$$\phi = wn + r \qquad (2)$$

where ϕ equals Y/K and n equals N/K. Differentiating:

$$d\phi = ndw + wdn + dr \qquad (3)$$

from which it follows that

$$w = \frac{d\phi}{dn} \qquad (4)$$

if and only if $-n$ equals dr/dw. This is to say that the wage will equal the marginal product of labor if, but only if, a certain special condition is met. This condition is that all sectors in the economy must have the same capital to labor ratios—a most unlikely circumstance. In general, therefore, with a given technique—or, for that matter, if techniques vary—the wage will not equal the marginal product of labor.[9]

Consider the second claim and suppose there are two techniques, competitive in the sense that for a given wage both return the same rate of profit:

$$\phi_1 = wn_1 + r$$

and

$$\phi_2 = wn_2 + r \qquad (5)$$

This means that below the given wage technique 1 would yield a slightly higher r, than would technique 2. Combine the two equations and regroup:

$$w = \frac{\phi_1 - \phi_2}{n_1 - n_2} \qquad (6)$$

At the so-called switching point, the wage identically, even trivially, equals the marginal product of labor. Lest anyone think this somehow profound,[10] observe that equation (6) states no more than that when two techniques, operating at a given rate of profit and paying everything out as wages or profits, also pay the same wage, then the technique using more labor per unit of capital must produce proportionately more output per unit of capital.

Modern analysis confirms the first two of Robertson's propositions. What about the third? When methods of pro-

---

7. Robertson, "Wage-Grumbles," p. 226.

8. In fact, Robertson qualifies the claim considerably, admitting "that there seems to be a certain unreality about the assumption [that the forms of capital and organization can change without the amounts changing]" (Ibid., p. 228).

9. With technique constant, the value of output and of the stock of capital will vary because of relative price changes—price Wicksell effects. When techniques can be varied, there are, in addition, real Wicksell effects, due to physical amounts changing. Compare, G. C. Harcourt, *Some Cambridge Controversies in the Theory of Capital* (Cambridge: Cambridge University Press, 1972), chap. 4.

10. As Robert Solow has. Compare, "The Interest Rate and the Transition Between Techniques," in *Capitalism, Socialism and Economic Growth*, ed. C. H. Feinstein (Cambridge: Cambridge University Press, 1970).

duction can be varied—that is, when nine expensive spades can be turned into nine cheaper ones, a bucket and beer—is the result a "perfectly definite descending curve of marginal productivity?"

The answer is devastating, unambiguous and by now well known. The law of scarcity requires that as labor becomes more plentiful with respect to capital, the real wage should decline and the marginal product diminish. However, the distribution variables (w and r), the real wage rate and the profit rate—defined as identical with marginal products at switching points—move in a capricious and haphazard way as the relative scarcity of labor to capital varies. In fact, the marginal product might rise, jump about discontinuously or move in any imaginable manner, without apparent rhyme or reason. There appears to be no way that a monotonic, inverse relation between the real wage or profit rates and relative scarcity can be derived; therefore, most neo-Classical writers introduce it simply as a postulate, a method which has the authoritative support of Bertrand Russell: " 'Postulating' what we want has many advantages; they are the same as the advantages of theft over honest toil." [11]

11. B. Russell, *Introduction to Mathematical Philosophy* (London: G. Allen, 1919), p. 71.

These are strong words, but the demonstration is remarkably simple. One does not need complex multisector models and elaborate matrix algebra. Two sectors—agriculture and industry—and high school algebra will suffice. Let Roman letters, a and b, stand for machine inputs and labor inputs, respectively, in machine production; the corresponding Greek letters, α and β, for machine and labor inputs into grain production. For simplicity, the output of each sector will be taken to be unity and relative prices will be expressed in terms of the price of grain. There will therefore be only one price, p, the price of machines in terms of grain. The equations for the economic system showing revenues equal to cost-plus in each sector are:

$$p = rap + wb$$
$$1 = r\alpha p + w\beta \qquad (7)$$

Solving each for p, equating the results and fiddling a bit:

$$\frac{(1/\beta - w)(1/a - r)}{rw} = \frac{\alpha/\beta}{a/b} \qquad (8)$$

This can be illustrated by a simple, very instructive diagram which shows the relatedness of prices, profits and wages. Plot w against r, marking off $1/\beta$ and $1/a$ on the w and r axes, respectively: $1/\beta$ is the maximum wage rate; $1/a$, the maximum rate of profit consistent

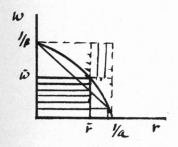
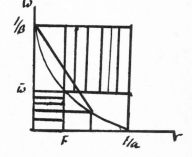

Figure 2

with positive prices; α/β is the machine to man ratio in agriculture; a/b, the machine to man ratio in industry. Consider the shaded portions of the diagrams; they represent the left side of equation (8). When $\alpha/\beta < a/b$, that is, whenever industry uses more machines relative to manpower than agriculture, the curve bulges outwards; when $\alpha/\beta > a/b$, that is, when agriculture uses more machinery per man than industry, the curve bends inwards. This means that, for a given real wage, the rate of profit will be higher for both sectors whenever industry is more heavily mechanized than agriculture.

Prices

Now for prices. Income, by definition, equals wages and profits—ignoring land and rents. In equilibrium, income also equals consumption and investment. Dividing all these magnitudes by the total labor force:

$$y = rk + w$$
$$y = gk + c \qquad (9)$$

where y is output per man; k is capital per man; g is the growth rate $gK/N =$ Investment/Labor Force; and c is consumption per head. In general, it follows that:

$$k = \frac{c - w}{r - g} \qquad (10)$$

In particular, however, ratios of capital value to labor for techniques producing the same good are to be compared. Let this be the consumption good, grain. Then g equals 0; so, $c = 1/\beta$ is the maximum value, the same as the maximum wage. Hence:

$$k = \frac{1/B - w}{r} = \frac{1}{n} \qquad (11)$$

and k, the capital to labor ratio, will be indicated by the dotted lines in the diagrams.

Clearly, when the curve bulges out— when industry is more mechanized— as w increases, the slope measuring k gets flatter. That is, as w increases, the ratio of labor to value of capital also increases. Thus, contrary to accepted opinion, the wage varies directly, rather than inversely, with the ratio of labor to capital. Honest toil is not producing results; if purity of doctrine is to be preserved, there will have to be resort to theft.

Before the dunce cap is placed on the heads of the wise men of modern economics, one had better look again at those switch points. We saw earlier that if $dr/dw = -n$, the wage would equal the marginal product of labor. A close look at equation (8) gives a clue: when $\alpha/\beta = a/b$, equation (8) will be a straight line:

$$w = \frac{1}{\beta} - \frac{ar}{\beta}$$

or rearranging:

$$\frac{-a}{\beta} = \frac{1/\beta - w}{r} \qquad (12)$$

and

$$\frac{dw}{dr} = \frac{1}{n} = \frac{-a}{\beta} \qquad (13)$$

The straight line case is a good candidate for the neo-Classical conditions. Consider two such techniques which cross. As the wage falls, it becomes profitable to switch from technique I to II—that is, from a technique with less labor to capital to one with more plentiful labor in relation to capital. This confirms the neo-Classical picture, although in but a very special case.

Suppose that technique I bends inwards and II outwards; for low levels of the wage, technique I will be most profitable. For middle level wages,

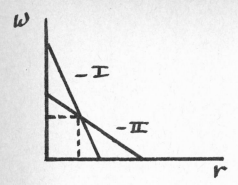

Figure 3

technique II will be best; finally, for high wages technique I will be best again.

At the high wage switching point, the system moves from a more labor-using technique to a less labor-using one as the wage rises. At the low wage switch-

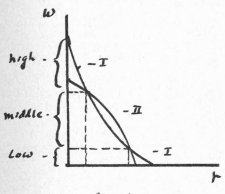

figure 4

ing point, the movement is reversed. As the wage rises, the highest profit is obtained if more labor-intensive techniques are used. As the wage rises, it becomes profitable to adopt a method of production which uses more labor in relation to capital. This result simply cannot be reconciled with neo-Classical doctrine, and there is no way to avoid a plentiful supply of such cases.[12] The

12. Compare Murray Brown, "Substitution-Composition Effects, Capital Intensity Unique-

only thing the faithful can do is bury their heads in the sand, into which the House of Efficiency is sinking.

CONCLUSIONS

The long and short of it is that individual incomes are not, and cannot be made into, "rewards for productive contributions," if they are to be awarded in "proportionality to productivity" at the margin. This is not to deny the obvious. Total income certainly mirrors total output, and changes in output are reflected in changes in income. Specific acts or developments which increase productivity can be encouraged and rewarded with incentives and bonuses, other things being equal. But in Robertson's words, "What we are in search of is the principle governing the level of wages *as a whole*," and when we are looking for this, other things cannot, in principle, be equal. This general principle cannot be based on the idea that wages and profits are proportional to the respective productive contributions of labor and capital.[13] Instead, it must be recognized that a productive economic system turns out a surplus which is the joint product of all the contributing elements.[14] The value of this surplus must be distributed according to the rules of property, the respective manipulative skills of the parties involved and

ness and Growth," *Economic Journal* (June 1969).

13. The argument is easily extended to take into account land and rents, though this introduces some new matters. Indeed, it may change our view of Ricardo quite considerably. Compare, Piero Sraffa, *Production of Commodities by Means of Commodities* (Cambridge: Cambridge University Press, 1960).

14. Observe that not all parties who work, contribute. There is a perfectly clear distinction, in principle, between productive and unproductive labor—even though there may be some difficult borderline cases, in practice.

the effects of the price mechanism through the pressures of effective demand.

Once we admit all this, the true complexity of the distribution question becomes evident. Looking to the w-r diagrams (figures 1, 2 and 3), the monetary sector may determine a rate of interest, giving a point on the r-axis. There then will be a corresponding choice of technique—the technique permitting the highest wage, as employers compete for labor—a point on the w-axis and a value of capital per man. Alternatively, bidding for labor may determine a real wage, w; a most profitable technique, a rate of profits and value of capital will then follow. Finally, investment and savings, given the capacity of the investment sector, may determine the price ratio of capital to consumer goods. It will then follow that only one wage—and corresponding rate of profits—is compatible with matching profit and wage rates in both sectors. In short, distribution can be determined in any one of three ways, each of which represents real forces operating in the economy. There is a monetary system, employers and unions bargain and investment and consumer goods demands press against, or fall short of, the respective capacities in those sectors.

Now wisdom begins. All these institutions exist, but they cannot all function together. The real wage cannot be determined in the labor market if the price mechanism at the same time sets the price ratio of consumer and capital goods according to relative capacity and demand. Since wages are mostly consumed and profits saved and invested, a certain level of the real wage—entailing a profit rate and value of capital to labor—can easily result in a pattern of demand in relation to capacity that will, through the price mechanism, lead to a different ratio of capital to labor. Similarly, the rate of profit cannot be determined by the money rate of interest, for profits are saved; and the rate of profit determined by monetary considerations might result in too much, or too little, savings.

The first thing that gives way is the price level. Modern monetary institutions permit the price level to adjust in relation to money wages and adjust company profits to provide savings to underwrite investment plans. Only the money wage is determined in the labor market, and the theory of distribution has led to a theory of inflation: when wages are too high, there will be a shortage of saving compared to investment; hence, the price level must rise to raise profits and, thus, savings. When wages are too low, there will be a shortage of demand for consumer goods; however— for Keynesian reasons—employment, rather than the price level, will fall. Here one begins to see the connections which can provide modern economics with a unified theory of distribution, employment and inflation, once the faith that our works will be duly and proportionally rewarded is abjured.

Inequalities: Open and Hidden, Measured and Immeasurable

ABSTRACT: The paper discusses which inequalities can, and which cannot, be measured by the economist's data. Among the inequalities of wealth, income and consumption, the second is shown to be the most relevant, although it must be corrected for the redistributive effects of taxation and transfer payments and then summed with both the distribution of public goods and services and the distribution of freely rendered non-market private services. Beyond the distribution of these measured and measurable components of satisfaction, account is also taken of nonmeasurable sources of welfare, such as work and leisure. Their distribution is shown to be positively correlated with the unequal distribution of money income, and guesses are made concerning their relative importance.

Tibor Scitovsky is Eberle Professor of Economics at Stanford University. He has also held teaching positions at Yale University and the University of California, Berkeley. Educated at the University of Budapest and the London School of Economics and Political Science, he is author of Welfare and Competition, Economic Theory and Western European Integration, Papers on Welfare and Growth, Money and the Balance of Payments, *and co-author of* Industry and Trade in Some Developing Countries. *He has also served as Fellow of the Development Centre of the Organization for Economic Cooperation and Development in Paris.*

CONCERN over the inequality of man naturally leads to a desire for a measure or index of inequality; there are only too many of these. In this paper, I will not be concerned with the great array of statistical indicators of varying degrees of sophistication; I will be concerned with the proper choice among a variety of existing statistical data which measure different causes, attributes or consequences of inequality. For example, it is clear that some inequalities are avoidable while others are not; one should focus on those inequalities about which something can be done. Hence, our preoccupation with economic inequalities. But even in the realm of economics, there are many variables. Wealth, income and consumption—to mention merely three—are all unequally distributed; the first much more so than the second; the second, more so than the third. Which of these is the most meaningful?

INEQUALITIES OF INCOME AND CONSUMPTION

Both the man in the street and the economist seem most concerned with inequalities of income, which they usually explain by the unequal distribution of wealth, ability, drive, educational opportunity and luck. If the distributions of these contributing factors overlap only partially, the explanation for the lesser inequalities of income in comparison with the greater inequalities in the distribution of such a causal factor as wealth becomes apparent. The American dream of free and equal educational opportunity for all is an important leveller, as would have been John Stuart Mill's dream of confiscatory inheritance taxes. Therefore, inequalities of wealth and of educational opportunity are worth watching, if only to explain inequalities of income.

The difference between inequalities of income and the somewhat lesser inequalities of consumption is explained by some economists as fluctuations in the same person's income—over both his life cycle and short run changes in luck and employment—for which prudent people are expected to compensate by saving in fat, and dissaving in lean, years, thus maintaining a more stable flow of consumption. If this were indeed the explanation, one would opt for the distribution of consumption as the more meaningful and relevant measure of economic inequalities. Why should one worry about differences in income that merely reflect fluctuations over time in the same person's income if such a person can average these out and maintain a steady level of consumption in the face of fluctuating incomes?

Unfortunately, further study and more detailed information are beginning to discredit this explanation. For example, it is contradicted by the finding that many more of the old are poor, and many more of the poor are old, than would be expected if these two conditions were not causally related.[1] We are beginning to realize that maintaining steady consumption, in the face of variations in income and lack of it during old age, is a luxury of the rich alone —and the reason for their high saving out of high income. The poor and the not so rich seem to be spending most of what they earn throughout their active years, even at the height of their prosperity; thus, they are forced to pull in their belts during retirement and times of unemployment. Such improvidence on the part of people who are rather

1. Almost half the old are poor, although the poor are only one fifth of the total population; one third of the poor belong to families whose head is 65 or older, although such families constitute only one sixth of the total population. Compare, the chapter on poverty in *The Annual Report of the Council of Economic Advisers* (1964).

prosperous by most standards—both by those of other countries and by our own earlier standards—is an interesting and puzzling phenomenon which lies outside the scope of this paper.

A high income provides not only high consumption but the assurance of continuing a comparable level of consumption into retirement as well. Lower incomes do not carry a corresponding assurance of a comfortable old age. If this is so, then income distribution does seem more relevant than consumption distribution as an index of economic inequalities. Also, people's great concern about their position on the income scale seems quite independent of the standard of living their income buys. Whether this is so because they consider income a status symbol or a token of society's appreciation of their services is immaterial. As long as income is valued not only for the consumption it yields but for other reasons as well, it is that much better as an index of satisfaction.

Public services

So far, the discussion has dealt with only money incomes received and market goods and services consumed. Welfare, however, even economic welfare, has many other components as well. One of these is public services, available free or below cost and paid by taxation. As a rule, these services are fairly equally distributed; therefore, the greater their importance in total output, the lesser the inequalities of economic welfare. This is an important argument for the public and free provision of services which formerly were private; it is also the reason for believing that inequalities of welfare are smaller in countries with large public sectors, because inequalities of income are of less consequence. Such thinking also lies behind the heavy subsidies many European countries pay to public transportation, communications, the performing arts and the production of bread. The poor may be deprived of comfort, but should have access to at least the basic nourishments of body and spirit.

In the United States, 45 percent of total—federal, state and local—public expenditures on goods and services is estimated to provide present or future benefits to the general public. The rest is expenditure on "regrettables," such as defense, prestige and diplomacy, which make no direct contribution to the welfare of households. These expenditures add 12 percent to the disposable money income of households—a relatively small addition and a very small mitigating influence on inequalities of income distribution.[2]

While the equal distribution of public amenities may be the rule, there are exceptions, some bad and some good. For example, one of the more depressing aspects of poverty in Harlem is the dirtiness of its streets and the sights and smells of uncollected garbage. The blame lies not so much with the low income or dirty habits of the inhabitants as with the sanitation department of New York City. Although one can hardly accuse the city of discrimination in the distribution of its favors, it does seem that services are provided in proportion to geographical area rather than population density.

Another, and very different, example is the distribution of eligibility for subsidized low rent housing under the federal housing program. A recent study shows that those with higher incomes among the eligible groups are clearly

2. Compare, W. Nordhaus and J. Tobin, "Is Growth Obsolete?" in National Bureau of Economic Research, *Economic Growth, Fiftieth Anniversary Colloquium V* (New York: Columbia University Press, 1972), tables A.1 and A.15.

favored, in the sense that they have a better chance of becoming tenants. Once in the program, however, the poor receive a greater average subsidy.[3]

The opposite type of exception to the rule of equal shares is distribution according to need. From the point of view of social justice, this is clearly preferable to equal distribution. Yet, it is usually impracticable in view of the difficulty of objectively and fairly ascertaining individual differences of need. However, where differences in need are self-evident or ascertainable by objective tests—as in the case of education, medical care and legal representation—distribution of free public services according to need is quite practicable. Indeed, this is one of the strongest arguments in favor of bringing such services into the public sector. Economists tend to be hostile to the provision of free public services as a means of mitigating inequalities on the ground that it is an inefficient means—compared, say, to progressive taxation—because it imposes on the individual a consumption pattern that is generally different from the one which he, himself, would have chosen. The objection is valid, but surely outweighed when the aim is not equality but distribution according to need—which is best accomplished by free distribution on the basis of a separate criterion of need for each of the services so distributed.[4]

Private services

Another, and much more important, component of economic welfare is the unpaid services people perform for each other and themselves. These mitigate inequalities because their distribution typically goes counter to the distribution of bought goods and services. Empirical data show that people in the higher income groups spend less time doing work around the house and favors for friends and relatives than do those at the lower end of the income scale. The value of such services is estimated to add about one half to disposable income after taxes.[5] As to their impact on inequality, a 1964 questionnaire study shows that while the poorest and the richest 25 percent of families earned 6 and 52 percent of society's money income, respectively, their shares in the sum of money income and the value of nonmarket services were 10 and 46 percent, respectively.[6] This indicates a substantial lessening of inequality.

If public services are equally distributed, their value can be added to obtain a further correction of the estimate of inequality. This correction will be very slight, since the value of public services is only about a quarter of the estimated value of nonmarket services. The estimate is that the poorest quartile

3. Compare, E. Smolensky and J. D. Gomery, "Efficiency and Equity Effects in the Benefits from the Federal Housing Program in 1965," in *Benefit-Cost Analyses of Federal Programs*, A Joint Economic Committee Print, 92nd Cong., 2nd sess. (Washington, D.C.: Government Printing Office, January 2, 1973).

4. An alternative means of distributing a specific service according to need is insurance. For a rigorous theoretical argument in favor of the free public provision of such services, see the discussion of national health insurance in K. J. Arrow, "Uncertainty and the Welfare Economics of Medical Care," *American Economic Review* 53 (1963), pp. 941–973.

5. W. Nordhaus and J. Tobin, "Is Growth Obsolete?" Table 1 gives estimates closer to two-thirds of disposable income; for a probably more reliable estimate, which puts the value of nonmarket services at 48 percent of disposable income, see I. A. H. Sirageldin, *Non-Market Components of National Income* (Ann Arbor, Mich.: Institute for Social Research, The University of Michigan, 1969), tables 4 and 5.

6. Compare, Sirageldin, *Non-Market Components,* chap. 4.

of families receives 11 percent and the richest quartile 44 percent of the sum of private, public, market and nonmarket goods and services.

Leisure

Some economists go one step further and add another component, leisure, which is valued at the income given up to enjoy it. Typically, such computations show leisure to be worth one and a half times the disposable money income; its inclusion in the total is believed to reduce inequalities further—although only slightly, because the amount of leisure enjoyed by rich and poor is just about the same, if the involuntary "leisure" of unemployment is not included. It would appear that some higher providence compensated the poor for their low money income with more generous rations of both nonmarket services and the enjoyment of leisure.

Government policies

So far, the effects of government policies directly aimed at mitigating inequalities by progressive taxation and by transfer payments, such as old age and disability insurance and public assistance—have been ignored. Economists disagree on whether the cumulative effect of all taxes in this country—federal and state income, Social Security, real estate, excise and sales taxes —is progressive or regressive. The Council of Economic Advisers, in their 1963 Report to the President, estimated it to be regressive; many other economists believe it to be progressive. Excise and sales taxes and Social Security contributions are so regressive that they more than offset the progressivity of income taxes—especially because income taxes contain major loopholes for the very rich. Differences of opinion center on who ultimately pays real estate and profit taxes. If these really taxed wealth as they were meant to, then the entire tax system will tend to be progressive and to mitigate inequalities. A detailed, careful appraisal of the system and its effects is now in progress at the Brookings Institution. So far, no results are available, and no guesses will be offered here.

Less controversial, and probably more important, are the redistributive effects of transfer payments. It has been estimated that without them the poor would constitute not a fifth, but a fourth, of the total population and not one third, but two thirds, of the aged population.[7]

Unfortunately, it is too early to rejoice over the increasingly favorable picture of our economy that these estimates give. First, there is a flaw in the estimation of the value of leisure. Furthermore, this list of items, comprising disposable income, public services, nonmarket services, leisure and transfer payments, is still incomplete; for, it omits an item which could be as important as all the others combined, but which tends to be overlooked and has defied measurement: the impact of work on satisfaction.

WORK SATISFACTION

Work, the meeting of its challenge and the sense of accomplishment which arises from it are considered the main sources of human satisfaction by at least two philosophical schools: (1) the Puritan ethic, to which we are heirs and (2) Marxism, to which much of the rest of the world is heir. Marx's main objection to modern capitalism and the factory system was not that they led to

7. Compare, B. A. Okner, "Transfer Payments: Their Distribution and Role in Reducing Poverty," *Brookings Institution Reprint 24*. These figures refer to 1966; they show no change from the 1964 data cited in footnote 1, above.

inequalities of income, but that they tended to change the nature, conditions and organization of work in a way which destroyed satisfaction derived from work; thus, it became an unpleasant chore performed only for income and valued only for the product it yielded. This seems to be the original meaning of that fashionable word, alienation.[8] Modern economics seems tacitly to have accepted Marx's view—at least, to judge by its always implying that work is unpleasant and its avoiding the subject.

Work, however, is economic activity; therefore, its direct effect on man's well-being—whose incidence must be considered in a discussion of inequalities—is part of economic welfare, the more so because it is increasingly evident that much can be done to mitigate the unpleasantness of work. There is a wealth of evidence of great differences in different people's attitude to, and satisfaction from, work: less absenteeism among functionaries than among production workers; more unpaid voluntary work performed by the higher, than by the lower, income groups; the failure of near confiscatory tax rates to dampen the work incentive of professionals; the much longer work week of independent businessmen, the free professions and higher civil servants than of lowly wage and salary earners; the great secular shrinkage of the latter's work week in contrast to the complete absence of any such trend among independents and professionals. All such evidence shows (1) that those with more initiative, more responsibility and more control over what they do and how they do

it also find their work more enjoyable and (2) that these are usually the people with the higher incomes. Such economic data are amply corroborated by questionnaire surveys. Not only are quantitative differences great between different people's marginal satisfaction, or dissatisfaction, from work, there seem to be differences even in sign.

Inequalities of work satisfaction

Such inequalities in the satisfaction, positive and negative, generated by work are quite distinct from the inequalities so far considered; since they are, by and large, positively correlated with inequalities of income, they aggravate measured inequalities. To make matters worse, they also call for a correction of the valuation of leisure and its distribution; for, a rational person will so divide his time between work and leisure as to make the satisfaction of the last hour of leisure equal to the sum of satisfactions from the last hour of work and the income earned. This means that people who like their work also get more satisfaction out of their leisure than do those for whom work is a chore. Lucky are those who enjoy their work, because they enjoy leisure even more; leisure, for those who consider work a burden, is quite often merely a lesser burden.[9] Since work satisfaction is positively correlated with income—and the amount of leisure available to rich and poor is about the same—one may conclude that the rich are likely to be favored even in the enjoyment of their free time.

8. Compare, E. Fromm, *Marx's Concept of Man* (New York: Ungar, 1961); and E. J. West, "The Political Economy of Alienation: Karl Marx and Adam Smith," in *Oxford Economic Papers* (Oxford: Oxford University Press, 1969).

9. That this is a correct inference is strongly suggested by a recent questionnaire survey of work satisfaction which shows a high correlation between workers' negative attitude to work and their negative attitude to life. Compare, H. L. Sheppard and N. Q. Herrick, *Where Have All The Robots Gone? Worker Dissatisfaction in the 1970s* (New York: Macmillan, 1972), p. 193, appendix table A.

It is now time to take stock and see where we stand. I listed and measured, in very simple terms, the inequality of distribution of the measured and the unmeasured but measurable sources of satisfaction. The effects of monetary redistribution on inequality ought also to be measurable; however, one could quote estimates only of the effects of transfer payments—and even of these, not in a form comparable to the other measures of inequality. I then discussed the unmeasurable factors and listed the indirect evidence of inequalities in their distribution, noting that they go the same way as inequalities in the measurable differences. The question is how great are these unmeasurable inequalities and how important are they compared to the measured and measurable inequalities? On this subject, one can only hazard a guess; I am offering mine with due warning of its subjective personal nature.

Importance of work satisfaction

There seems to be no doubt that differences in different people's work satisfaction can be very great, ranging from the person who hates his job and finds it completely boring and monotonous to the person who enjoys every minute of it. Of course, many people are somewhere in between, enjoying part of their work and chafing under the dull routine of some of its aspects. What percentage of the labor force constitutes this middle mass and what are the bordering percentages on each side we do not yet know, but the answer may be forthcoming on the basis of the many sample survey studies of work satisfaction and work attitudes now in progress.[10]

More important perhaps, as well as more difficult to answer, is the question of the weight which should be attached to differences in work satisfaction compared to differences in income and distribution of the things that money will buy. The Puritan tradition of American society stressed work satisfaction and disapproved and discouraged just about all other sources of worldly satisfaction. To what extent are our lives in present day America still dominated by the Puritan ethic and its scale of values? There are many signs that the Puritan influence is still strong. We take fewer vacations, spend less time at active sports, seek less entertainment and spend a significantly smaller percentage of our income on recreation than do Europeans; we even pay less heed to the pleasures of food—to judge by the much shorter time we devote to both the eating, and the preparing, of it.[11] Yet, our real income is much higher than theirs, and they often accuse us of being excessively fond of money. A tempting resolution of this seeming contradiction is that we are interested in money income more as a symbol of society's appreciation of our work than for the goods it will buy. The great importance of do-it-yourself activities among our pastimes—the one pastime that most resembles work—and the amount of time we devote to adult education—two-thirds of which is aimed at vocational training and imparting production skills [12]—are further evidence of the great importance we attach to our work, its satisfactions and its appreciation by others.

A second piece of evidence is much

10. The work cited in the last footnote gives 14 percent as the proportion of employees with negative attitudes toward work.

11. Compare, Tibor Scitovsky, "What's Wrong With The Arts is What's Wrong With Society," *American Economic Review* 53 (1972), pp. 62–69, for these and similar data and their sources.

12. Compare, the report of the Commission on Nontraditional Study, as reviewed in *Saturday Review of Education,* April 1973, p. 56.

more direct and to the point. Appendix table A, in Sheppard and Herrick's *Where Have All the Robots Gone?* (cited in footnote 9), shows—for thirty-two different groups, classified by age, sex, marital status, color, education, income group and occupation—the percentage of workers with negative attitudes toward work and the percentage with negative attitudes toward life. The two percentages are so very close for all thirty-two groups that one cannot help feeling that those who dislike their work are the same people as those who dislike their lives. The text discussion bears this out, but the data to clinch the matter are missing. Also, this is only one of many such studies still in progress; one has to wait and see how the others will confirm, modify or contradict the results of this one.

To conclude, let me mention one more piece of evidence. Over the past twenty-five years, ten sample surveys were conducted in the United States at fairly regular intervals in which the respondents were asked, among other things, to state their income and to rate their satisfaction with their own lives on a three-point scale. As could be expected, the highest proportion of the "not very happy" were to be found among the poor and the highest proportion of the "very happy" among the rich. Of the entire population, slightly less than 50 percent were in the middle group; slightly less than 10 percent

were "very happy"; and slightly more than 40 percent were "not very happy." Surprising, however, was the finding that this distribution of the population remained amazingly stable over the entire period between 1946 and 1970, although per capita income in real terms rose by 62 percent.[13]

There are at least three possible explanations of this puzzle. One is that concurrently with the measured rise in our real incomes, the unmeasurable quality of our lives worsened to an extent that offset that rise. The second explanation is that we are so competitive, so much concerned with matching or outdoing the Joneses, that our happiness depends on our relative position in the income scale rather than on our absolute standard of living. The third explanation is that correlated with the distribution of income there also exist inequalities in some other source of satisfaction, such as the enjoyment of work, inequalities in whose distribution have persisted over time and whose contribution to happiness is much more important than that of income. Needless to add, nothing is ever so simple that a single explanation will adequately explain it.

13. Compare, R. A. Easterlin, "Does Economic Growth Improve the Human Lot?" in *Nations and Households in Economic Growth: Essays in Honor of Moses Abramovitz,* ed. P. A. David and M. W. Reder (Palo Alto, Cal.: Stanford University Press, forthcoming).

Poverty, Propinquity and Policy

By Eugene Smolensky

ABSTRACT: There is no necessary connection between poverty and income distribution. When poverty is defined by relative measures, the proportion of impoverished families is the same as it was in 1950. As a result, the urban problems of the United States have been exacerbated. What people spend on house paint, how they travel to work, how long they send their children to school, what public facilities they ask for, how much idle time they will have as adults and how they spend that idle time, all depend at least in part on family income. While tastes vary greatly, differences in consumption patterns, in human capital investments, in political demands and in propensity or willingness to steal depend importantly on income. Furthermore, if people of very different income levels live close to one another—as they do in cities—these different choices exacerbate class conflict. To escape, those with the means to do so seek to segregate themselves and to surround themselves with moats. They also turn to government for relief. The Great Society programs constituted a use of the political process to ameliorate class conflict by lowering the cost of goods to the poor which the nonpoor wanted them to buy. Nevertheless, the poor did not become acceptable neighbors for the rest of the nation. Now, the Nixon administration seeks to terminate a good part of the effort. The problems remain; for the moment, however, we as a nation have decided to live with them.

Eugene Smolensky has been Professor of Economics at the University of Wisconsin since 1968; and has also taught at the University of Chicago, Haverford College and Pennsylvania University. He has served as Economist for the United States Bureau of the Census and Consultant to the Bureau of Labor Statistics, the Social Security Administration, the American-Yugoslav Project, the Council of Economic Advisors and the Economic Development Administration. Professor Smolensky is the author of Adjustments to Depression and War, 1930–1945 *and author of many articles for scholarly and economic journals.*

SINCE inequality refers to the whole income distribution and poverty refers to only a small part of the low end of that distribution, there is no necessary connection between the two. For example, if the poor grew poorer while the rich grew poorer faster, one might conclude that poverty had become a more serious problem than inequality. Also, it is easy to imagine the reverse situation. As a matter of fact, during the postwar period income inequality has not changed significantly. Yet, depending upon whether an absolute or a relative measure is used, the incidence of poverty has either declined or remained unchanged.

POVERTY AND INEQUALITY

Figure 1, which illustrates the distribution of income in 1950 and 1970, was made in the following way. I transferred onto a piece of cardboard a figure from a statistics text which approximated the shape of the United States income distribution in 1950. I then cut the cardboard so that I would have a template and used the template to draw the two distributions of the figure so that one would stand for 1950 and the other for 1970. It should be emphasized that my drafting procedure accords with reality. In the mind's eye, one should see a distribution rigid in shape moving toward ever higher incomes through time: a picture of uniformly rising income for the nation as a whole, although not necessarily for any individual.

That the same distribution with a higher average can satisfactorily represent those two years so widely separated in time is of great importance for understanding the historical relationship between poverty and inequality. If poverty is defined as some fixed real income—for example, 3,000 dollars in 1962 prices—then as the distribution moves along over time, the number of impoverished people declines. Because of its shape, if the distribution moved rightward at a steady rate, the decline in the absolute number of families in poverty would decrease year by year; however, the decline would be continuous. Thus, in figure 1, if the distribution moved rightward at a steady rate—the distance from A to B and B to C being the distance traversed over two equal time intervals—then, as the diagram indicates, there would be a substantial fall in the number of families in poverty over the interval from A to B, a small one over the interval from B to C and so on. By the nature of the distribution, poverty appears to become increasingly intransigent over time. If a recession occurred along the way, the rightward movement of the distribution would be interrupted or reversed for a short period, as would be the decline in the number of families in poverty.

Were we to define poverty not as a

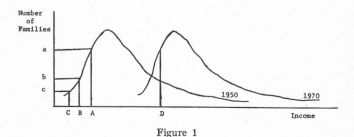

Figure 1

fixed amount of purchasing power, but rather as a fixed proportion of average income, then between 1950 and 1970 the proportion of families in poverty would move not as implied by the interval from A to C on the 1950 distribution, but rather as implied by comparing A on the 1950 distribution with D on the 1970 distribution. That is, the proportion of families in poverty would not have declined.

How, then, should poverty be defined: (1) as a fixed amount of income or (2) as some fixed relationship to the average? Since all poverty definitions are arbitrary, they are determined by the intended use of the data. If the main concern is with the standard of living of the poor, some fixed measure —at least over modestly long intervals —is the one which is appropriate. The Office of Economic Opportunity (OEO) poverty line is of such a kind. While one can argue with the method of determining the poverty line, the purpose is unchallengeable. The intention is to set a target which, if universally achieved, would permit everyone to live at a level that someone has determined to be minimally decent—that is, permitting a particular diet, pattern of clothing expenditures, housing and so on. Alternatively, the main concern may be with income equity. One can believe that justice requires an increase in poor families' share of the pie, and, furthermore, that this share certainly ought to increase when the pie is growing, even if by some reasonable standard the poor are living very well.

Over any long period of time, humanitarianism and egalitarianism must converge, since the concept of minimally decent is as relative to time and space as is the share of income going to the bottom tenth of the population. Thus, more than 60 percent of Americans in the very prosperous year of 1929 would be categorized as impoverished by the official definition of poverty adopted in 1962. If a new exponent of the Great Society were to be elected president in 1976, I would expect a new official definition of poverty in 1977 based on some new concept of minimally decent, which would put us right back to where we were in 1960—with 20 percent of families in poverty. The growth of income in the United States since the Second World War has been prodigious and very widely distributed even among those who do not work and who do not own capital. By the humanitarian standard, there has been considerable progress; by the more stringent egalitarian standard, there has been none.

POVERTY AND PROPINQUITY

The invisible hand piles up the urban poor in the center of cities and strings them out along the mass transit routes, the most prosperous being the farthest out. Fairly well to do people, particularly those who are youngish and oldish, are also piled up near the city center and then strung out along what passes for an amenity of that city, such as a lake shore, a park or a ridge. Middle income people get whatever remains. This distribution puts the poor cheek by jowl with fairly high income people in some places and with middle class people elsewhere. Even with the most judicious placement of freeways, graveyards, public housing, urban renewal, schools, parks and bus routes, many who are not poor must frequently come eyeball to hackles with poverty. But poverty is more than a pain in the eye; it hits many who are not poor in the pocket book, in the class room and on the back of the head, even though they have located their homes and places of business with full knowledge of where the poor are.

If poverty, in the egalitarian sense, had been declining over the last two decades, the nonpoor would undoubtedly be better off today even if their own incomes were lower. This would be so not merely because rapidly rising income puts more paint on the walls and higher aspiration levels in the kids; there are two additional factors at work.

One is that with incomes rising all around, the nonpoor put greater demands on the poor. When a fellow's income rises steadily for a time, he puts part of the additional money into fixing his house. His neighborhood also improves, since his neighbors, whose incomes are also rising, put some money into their homes. The same thing is happening in the local stores and at the local school. However, if all incomes rise at 2 percent per year, the family whose annual income started at 15,000 dollars will put more money into their house each year than will the family whose income was initially 7,500 dollars. Across that extra wide street that separates these two neighborhoods, the gap is widening. If, on the other hand, incomes of the 15,000 dollar family rose by 1.8 percent per year and the 7,500 dollar family rose by 2.2 percent per year, the gap might not widen and both families might have felt better off today. The record is clear enough on one point: higher income families are willing to accept less income than they would otherwise have—that is, to pay higher taxes—to get the poor to buy more of a selected list of things.

The nonpoor would also have benefited from a decrease in poverty because the adjustments made by households, business and government as a response to the failure of the poor to do voluntarily what the nonpoor wanted could have been avoided. For example, more suburbanization, than there would otherwise have been, occurred. In and of itself, this is costly; furthermore, the costs pyramid as suburbanization accelerates the deterioration of the central business district, promotes the proliferation of political jurisdictions and one party rule and contributes to the freeway congestion problem. Of course, while it is unlikely that growing income equality would have prevented all this, there would have been less of it.

POVERTY, PROPINQUITY AND POLICY

Since 1963, the Great Society programs—housing subsidies, medicare and medicaid, food stamps and school lunches, scholarships for higher education, municipal waste-treatment plants, community health centers, grants to encourage urban planning, training of medical-related personnel, economic development assistance and manpower training—have grown from 2 to 14 percent of federal expenditures, or by 34 billion dollars. While cash transfers, such as social security and other federal retirement plans, aid to families with dependent children, public assistance and veterans payments, have risen by even greater dollar amounts, the proportion of aid to the poor in the form of goods and services has obviously risen dramatically.

President Nixon identified this trend with paternalism. It may be that an arrogant majority has, in fact, decided that it knows better what is good for the poor than do the poor, themselves. However, there is an alternative explanation. It may be that the majority does not really care one way or another about the poor: the nonpoor may simply have preferred to bribe, rather than to coerce, the poor into behavior that promised to make their own daily lives more pleasant.

If the anguish of the impoverished pains those who are more fortunate, the solution is more cash. Except in extreme cases of discrimination, giving the poor cash and letting them choose what to buy is obviously the best way to raise their welfare. If one really wants the poor to be happier, the giver should not care if the money is used for booze, betting or bedding. If one finds neighboring slums offensive, giving cash is not an efficient way to be rid of them, precisely because some of that income will be wasted on food. Regulation building codes are conceptually capable of eliminating those slums, but such measures will raise housing costs and constitute a heavy tax on the poor. Subsidized urban renewal, combined with public housing construction, could eliminate the slums, lower the price of standard quality housing to the poor and—as long as the total stock of housing in the rental range of the poor did not decline and no one was forced directly or insidiously to live in the public housing—leave the poor no worse off than they were. Furthermore, the housing could be fortuitously placed to make the poor relatively invisible to the nonpoor. Collecting the poor together would have the further advantage of reducing the costs of administering other bribes, such as compensatory education and family counseling.

The grand scheme failed for a variety of reasons. The central cause was that it could not be adequately funded in this federal system. The political system not only forced the expenditures to be spread over too many programs, but perhaps more importantly, the funds were distributed over too many political jurisdictions. To make a visible impact, whole slums would have to be eliminated; relocating every third family does not help significantly. Public housing expenditures have been sufficient to aid only three out of every hundred eligible families. Moreover, this piddling 3 percent was drawn from more than 2,000 public housing authorities.

What has been true of housing has been true of most other transfer programs, and the president has called a time out. He hopes to be able to dump the problems and some money to meet them onto the states and the cities. State and local expenditures are already rising considerably faster than federal outlays, and the governors and mayors are enormously confident of their ability to do good. They may have a right to their self-confidence, but that rigid income distribution just keeps on rolling along. It is likely to roll right over them.

Education and Equality

By Robert J. Staaf and Gordon Tullock

Abstract: It is fairly clear that higher education, among other things, works a considerable income redistribution. In general, this redistribution is from the poor to those people who would be very well off even without education. The higher educational system increases the degree of income differentiation in the society. People who have considerable natural talent, who would therefore have high incomes in any event, are given higher incomes at the expense of the taxpayer. There is a secondary aspect of income redistribution related to the higher educational system. It has been argued that the children of upper class parents gain more than the children of poor parents and that this difference is greater than the difference between the taxes paid to support education by these two groups. It is not certain that this is so; in any event, the question of the wealth of the parents of the students who receive the taxpayer's gift seems less important than the actual potential lifetime earnings of the recipients. Of course, it is possible to offset the regressive nature of the higher educational system by progressive measures in other parts of government; however, it would seem simpler to convert the higher educational system to one which provides less in the way of benefits for the rich at the expense of the poor.

Robert J. Staaf is Assistant Professor of Economics at Virginia Polytechnic Institute and State University. Currently, he is on leave at the Western Interstate Commission for Higher Education, Boulder, Colorado. Educated at the University of Delaware and Temple University, he is co-author of The Economics of Education *and author of a number of articles in this general area.*

Gordon Tullock is University Professor at Virginia Polytechnic Institute and State University. Educated at the University of Chicago, Cornell University and Yale University, he is editor of Public Choice *and author of numerous books and articles.*

MANY different justifications are given for higher education. The first, and most obvious, is that it teaches an individual skills which will make it possible for him to earn a better living. Second, it may teach him consumption skills: he may be a happier man because he has learned to appreciate Shakespeare. Third, it may produce information for potential employers about his ability—that is, it classifies him so that he can be given more suitable employment. Finally, the fact that he has been educated may benefit other people in some way—for example, it may mean that he votes in a more intelligent way than he would otherwise; hence, government policy is marginally better. Although these are the positive benefits normally expected from higher education, in modern times government policies are judged, in part, by their effect on income distribution.

INTRODUCTION

When the government provides a large subsidized education sector, one would be interested in—among other things—whether education increased or decreased inequality. The theme of this article is that, as far as we now know, higher education increases inequality. College professors are engaged in assisting those who are well-off to exploit the poor.

It should be noted, of course, that none of the objectives given for education necessarily have anything to do directly with equality or inequality. For example, giving people a taste for Shakespeare, presumably, does not particularly affect their income. We could, if we wished, use higher education in a way that would increase income equality. We could lavish our educational resources on those who seem to have the poorest prospects in life in order to bring them up to equality with their more talented fellows; alternatively, we could tax the more talented in order to neutralize their talent. Obviously, we do not do this, but there is nothing impossible about it.

In the Western world, higher education began as an activity for members of the upper class: at first, for younger children of the nobility who were thinking of going into the church and, later, to train nonclerical leaders of society. Granted the aristocratic nature of society until very recently, this is not surprising. The tradition has continued to exist. Higher education is still basically designed to increase the inequalities of income in society, although most college professors are not aware of that fact; on discussion, most college professors strenuously deny the fairly patent and obvious fact that they are doing what they are doing.

It is true that the present higher education system is not basically aimed at the well-being of the very wealthy. However, it is clearly aimed at the well-being of the middle class. It is not obvious that the poor have gained from this change in emphasis. The tax cost of maintaining a college like Cambridge or Harvard for a few wealthy students would have been very modest compared with the amount which is now being spent in our massive state education systems. The wealthy are willing to finance lavishly the education system in which they gained their education. Generally speaking, this financing came in terms of gifts after they had left school rather than payment of tuition; however, in practice, the net effect of institutions such as Cambridge and Harvard was that the upper class received a gentleman's education, while financing it so lavishly that there were a certain number of scholarships for talented people from relatively impoverished backgrounds. Needless to say, the people who were sufficiently talented to obtain such scholarships would normally have done well in life in any event. Yet, it can be said that the net effect of institutions such as the privately endowed schools of the last century was a very mild redistribution of income, mainly by private charitable gifts, from the very wealthy to the moderately well-off classes.

CRITERIA FOR SUBSIDIZING HIGHER EDUCATION

The present situation is almost directly reversed. There may still be some transfer of funds away from the very wealthy who contribute gifts to schools or pay heavy taxes, but it is clear that the middle classes benefit greatly from the institution and that, in general, the poor lose.[1] This latter point is a little confused in discussion, because the poverty or well-being of the student's parents is frequently confused with the poverty or well-being of the student, himself. It is not obvious

1. See, W. Lee Hansen and Burton A. Weisbrod, "The Distribution of Costs and Direct Benefits of Public Higher Education: The Case of California," *Journal of Human Resources* 4 (Spring 1969), pp. 176–191. This article has generated considerable discussion, see, Joseph A. Peckman, "The Distributional Effects of Public Higher Education in California," *Journal of Human Resources* 5 (Summer 1970), pp. 361–370; Elchanan Cohn, Adam Gifford and Ira Sharkansky, "Benefits and Costs of Higher Education and Income Redistribution: Three Comments," *Journal of Human Resources* 5 (Spring 1970), pp. 222–237; Robert Hartman, "A Comment on the Peckman-Hansen-Weisbrod Controversy," *Journal of Human Resources* 5 (Fall 1970), pp. 519–523; Joseph A. Peckman, "The Distribution of Costs and Benefits of Public Higher Education: Further Comments," *Journal of Human Resources* 6 (Summer 1971), pp. 375–377; W. Lee Hansen and Burton A. Weisbrod, "On the Distribution of Benefits of Higher Education: A Reply," *Journal of Human Resources* 6 (Summer 1971), pp. 363–375.

whether in subsidizing the education of the poor one should be interested in the wealth of the parents or in the potential lifetime earnings of the student. In general, the man who is able to get a full time scholarship from Harvard, even though he comes from a poor family, has enough human capital in the form of natural talent to do very well in life, anyway. The Harvard education, at best, merely improves a lifetime income stream which would have been well above average without it. Thus, if we look at the subsidy which he has received—in this case from private rather than government sources— as equalizing total income, we must consider not his income but the income of his parents. In other words, we think about the scholarship which he receives as, in essence, a gift to his parents who are indeed poor people.[2]

It is not obvious which of these two criteria for income redistribution should be used. As it happens, however, it makes little difference. Under either criteria, the net effect of our present educational system is a transfer of funds which injures most of the poor. If we regard the educational subsidy to a talented son of poor parents as a subsidy to the child, then all the poor are in-

2. The point was made very clearly in E. G. West, "Efficiency versus Equity in Higher Education" (Paper delivered at Virginia Polytechnic Institute and State University, Blacksburg, Va., 1973). West remarked that he had met a fifty-year-old Canadian doctor whose income—the result of his education in medicine—when computed back to the time he took his education, would have had a present value of about one million dollars. On being asked why he thought his education should have been subsidized, the doctor pointed out, quite correctly, that his father had been an agricultural laborer. However, it is not clear why the class status of the father is relevant in determining whether or not this doctor should have been given a gift by the state that generated one million dollars of wealth.

TABLE 1

ILLUSTRATION DISTRIBUTION OF BENEFITS AND TAXES
FOR PUBLIC HIGHER EDUCATION

LEVELS	NUMBER OF POTENTIAL STUDENTS	TAX PER FAMILY (Dollars)	BENEFITS PER FAMILY (Dollars)	NET BENEFITS (Dollars)	AVERAGE NET BENEFITS (Dollars)
$2,000	3	100	0	−100	
		100	0	−100	
		100	500	+400	
Total		300	500	+200	+ 67
$10,000	3	400	533	+133	
		400	533	+133	
		400	533	+133	
Total		1,200	1,600	+400	+133
$30,000	3	1,200	1,500	+300	
		1,200	1,500	+300	
		1,300	0	−1,200	
Total		3,600	3,000	−600	−200

Source: Robert Hartman, "A Comment on the Peckman-Hansen-Weisbrod Controversy,"
Journal of Human Resources 5 (Fall 1970), table 1, p. xxx.

jured because his lifetime income would clearly have been high without the subsidy: he, unlike his parents, is wealthy. If we regard it as a subsidy to his parents, then some few poor parents may gain from the present subsidy arrangement. The middle class and most of the wealthy—with their individual gains in monetary terms being larger than those of the middle class—gain from the present subsidies. Some of the wealthy choose, for one reason or another, to send their children to private schools; of course, these particular individuals do not receive any subsidy.

The general situation can be seen in table 1. This is a synthetic table created by Hartman to reconcile the views of Hansen and Weisbrod, on one hand, and Peckman, on the other.[3]

These scholars examined the California public higher education system and came to the conclusion, respectively, that it was regressive and that it was progressive. The figures used are designed to approximate those found in empirical studies. As can be seen, most of the poor are injured by the system; most of the wealthy gain; and all of the middle class gain.

Whether one wants to call these kinds of transfers a progressive or regressive system depends upon, first, the decision that the wealth of the parents, rather than the potential wealth of the child, shall be taken into account in determining whether the subsidy goes to well-off or less well-off people. If the students or potential students are considered, the system in California under which more expensive education is given

3. See, Hansen and Weisbrod, "Costs and Benefits of Public Higher Education" and

Peckman, "Distributional Effects of Public Higher Education."

to people who can pass more difficult entrance requirements clearly transfers funds from the poor to the wealthy.

With respect to the parents, it is more or less a question of what one means by progressive and regressive. The bulk of the poor receive a small loss on the public educational system, but an occasional poor parent finds that his child receives a subsidy.[4] Similarly, the bulk of the wealthy and middle class receive a substantial gift from the taxpayer. Some wealthy people, however, find themselves making a substantial contribution to the system and getting nothing in return. As do the poor, the wealthy who take advantage of public education receive a sizable net transfer.

HIGHER EDUCATION IN DEMOCRATIC COUNTRIES

This situation is more or less typical of modern higher educational systems found in most democracies. It has been carefully studied only in a few places, such as California, but anyone examining the data and comparing it with most other democracies would reach the conclusion that while the numbers would be different, the general structure would be the same.[5] Why do we accept this

4. On the average, approximately six out of ten high school graduates attend college; a large percentage of the students receive subsidies. In the lower income brackets, approximately two out of ten attend, or are eligible to attend, public colleges.

5. George Psacharopoulos, "Rates of Return to Investment in Education Around the World," *Comparative Education Review* 16 (February 1972), pp. 55–67. The case of Turkey is an extreme example of higher education promoting inequality; tuition charges are nominal in public universities and there are a number of indirect subsidies to students, such as low fares for transportation, subsidized lunches and housing. In addition, the scholarships average about 50 percent of foregone income. We suspect there may be a considerable number of professional students in Turkey. See, A. O. Krueger, "Rates of

tendency of the educational system to generate inequality? No doubt, the historical origins of the system are important. Most of the objectives for higher education, which were listed at the beginning of this paper, are either maximized by education that aims directly at greater inequality or are such that their maximization is irrelevant to inequality. However, the basic reason for this inequality-generating activity is simply that the voters want it. The voters perceive the educational system not as a way of generating equality, but as a way of transferring income to themselves. Therefore, the powerful middle class is able to achieve a transfer from both the poor and the wealthy by way of the current educational system.

Quality of Education

Before discussing this in detail, it is necessary to deal with a technical problem. It has been suggested by at least two studies that the quality of education may not make any difference in individuals' well-being as far as their income is concerned. First, the well-known Jencks study,[6] partly based on the Coleman report, shows no evidence that differences in the quality of education as measured by per student expenditures have any particular influence. The significant factor is that which the student brings into the educational process. A somewhat similar study of higher education indicates approximately the same thing. Harvard turns out far better quality graduates than does Clinch Valley Community College because students entering Harvard are of much higher quality or

Return to Turkish Higher Education," mimeographed (Minneapolis, Minn.: University of Minnesota, 1971).

6. Christopher Jencks et al., *Inequality* (New York: Basic Books, 1972).

have other attributes valued in the market.

Indeed, it is possible that the actual education given at Clinch Valley Community College is better than that given at Harvard. A professor at Harvard—living under an extreme variant of the publish-or-perish doctrine and with little monetary gain from teaching—who teaches students bright enough to learn more or less on their own may, in fact, devote very few resources to teaching. The Clinch Valley Community College professor, on the other hand, has little to distract him from devoting all of his time to education. Furthermore, the Clinch Valley Community College teachers are selected, albeit in a very inept way, on the grounds of their ability to teach; the Harvard professors are selected because of their research ability. It is obvious that, under the circumstances, the teaching ability of the Harvard faculty is not necessarily higher than the teaching ability of the Clinch Valley Community College faculty.[7] This is, of course, one explanation of the phenomenon that quality of education as measured by expenditures does not seem to make much difference.[8]

Quantity of Education

On the other hand, there is overwhelming evidence that the quantity of education does change income. It would appear from the existing data that the income of any individual rises with every additional year of education, regardless of which institution the individual attends. One explanation of this phenomenon is simply that, as a matter of fact, the quality of education does not vary much from school to school; Jencks argues that the quality variations are too small to show much effect on the outcome. The second possibility is that since we know so little about education, what we think is high quality education may not, in fact, be so. In 1800, a patient probably was more likely to be killed by the best doctor in London than by a village herbalist. Whatever else happened, the village herbalist would not bleed you with an unsterilized knife which had been used eight times earlier that day to bleed eight different patients with eight different diseases.

In any event, whatever the explanation, the payoff for attending school—which is high—and the lack of payoff for selecting a particular school seems to be reasonably well established in the present data. This suggests that the third objective of higher education—producing information for potential employers about the ability of the student—may be its actual purpose. Regardless of which school is attended, the student is compelled to carry out a number of tasks which test his intelligence, industry and, furthermore, his initiative in doing various types of activity.[9] Thus, the longer he has stayed in school, the more he has demonstrated his talents; the level at which

---

7. We are assuming that teaching and research are not complementary activities. Siegfried and White's study of the economics faculty at Wisconsin suggests that there is no significant relationship between good researchers and good teachers; see, John J. Siegfried and Kenneth J. White, "Teaching and Publishing as Determinants of Academic Salaries," *The Journal of Economic Education* 4 (Spring 1973).

8. Another explanation is that, since teaching effort is not rewarded, any effort devoted to teaching is simply charitable behavior.

9. Nationally, students switch broadly defined curricular groups from their freshman to senior year on the average of 50 percent. Statistical relationships between academic grades and success as measured by income or status are misleading. The real information that may be valued by firms is the ability of students to survive in a particular curriculum.

these talents are tested rises steadily as one goes up in the educational system. Our society may be using its educational system basically as a testing device to classify people according to their native talent. If this is so, there is some social payoff, since our economy will work better if people are properly classified. However, it appears to be a terribly expensive method of classification.[10] Also, it is clear that this classification, although raising the total of national product, tends to increase, rather than decrease, inequality.[11]

GENERATION OF PUBLIC AND PRIVATE BENEFITS

There is one argument which could, perhaps, be used to justify higher education's systematic generation of greater inequality: the generation of public goods. The educated person may somehow benefit other people, as well as himself, as a result of his education. The classic example of this kind of spillover is improving the quality of voting through education. Concentrating education on the best and brightest might conceivably generate more benefits for the whole population than attempting to distribute the educational resources in either an egalitarian or inegalitarian way. If education offsets the natural inequality among individuals, the outcome of the process will be more egalitarian than the input.[12]

Unfortunately, although this seems to be a theoretical possibility, we are unable to find any clear-cut examples. If we consider such things as improving the vote, it is fairly obvious that the vote of the relatively unintelligent counts as much as the vote of the very intelligent. If we were thinking of improving the quality of the vote by education, we would probably concentrate on the untalented, because this is where we would feel they needed improvement the most. In listing areas where we might wish to subsidize education in order to generate public benefits, education should either be concentrated on the less talented or be distributed by a more or less egalitarian method. There does not seem to be any case where public goods could best be generated by concentrating on the most talented.[13]

---

10. Said another way, the information may be attained more efficiently in the private sector in the absence of subsidies to higher education.

11. For a detailed discussion of the social benefits of rationing, see Joseph E. Stiglitz, "The Theory of Screening, Education, and the Distribution of Income," unpublished manuscript (New Haven, Conn.: Yale University, 1973).

12. To our knowledge, no one has ever seriously proposed that education be used to generate equality, although it is quite possible. In a very modest way, our present system does do it. People at the absolute bottom of

the intellectual level are sometimes given educations which are more expensive than those given to the ordinary student. However, this is confined, in general, to the grade school and high school level, and there is nothing equivalent to college. It is clearly possible to use the educational system to equalize the intellectual capital held by people. For example, if we devoted large resources to educating the relatively unintelligent and very few resources to educating the well-off, it seems likely that lifetime incomes would be more equal. Since almost all of the people who are associated with higher education are in the upper IQ levels and also expect their children to be in the upper IQ levels, there is absolutely no support for this policy. See Hansen and Weisbrod, "Costs and Benefits of Higher Education" and Jencks et al., *Inequality,* for a discussion of the distribution of talent as defined by admissions criteria as it relates to the distribution of income.

13. Bowen has offered a list of public goods arguments for higher education. We see no reason that these benefits are unique to the most talented. In fact, some of the public good arguments—for example, reduction in crime and unemployment—suggest that resources be concentrated on the less talented; see, Howard R. Bowen, "Finance and the Aims of Higher Education," in *Financing Higher Education: Alternatives for the Federal Gov-*

Superficially, there are a number of cases where there seems to be an argument for concentrating education on the most talented; however, such arguments confuse public and private benefits. For example, the United States will have better engineers if we concentrate our resources on brilliant people. The problem is that the engineer, himself, is the principal beneficiary of the education. He sells his services at their marginal value, and there is no particular public good of a nonpecuniary nature generated by his education. Society makes a capital investment—in this case, in the form of education— gives it to the individual, but gains little. We could, for example, give the people to whom we now give engineering educations a capital sum equivalent to the value of their education. Clearly, they would spend it more wisely and would become wealthier than duller individuals. There could be no argument for this policy in terms of generating public goods.

CONCLUSION

If education in democracy normally increases the degree of inequality, this in itself raises a problem. Societies in which the university as an institution originated distributed their resources in a way that increased inequality, but democracies talk a great deal about being committed to egalitarian policies. Why, then, do democracies distribute their education in this manner?

First, it should be said that, in general, democracies are not particularly egalitarian, regardless of the language of the politicians. For example, Professor Abel-Smith, a supporter of the Labour government in England, stated in 1959 that: "The main effect of the postwar development of social services, the crea-

tion of the 'welfare state,' has been to provide free social services to the middle class." [14] Webb and Sieve, also supporters of the British Labour Party, agree with Abel-Smith and claim that the situation remains unchanged. [15] The United States is in a somewhat similar situation. [16]

In general, democracies do take money from the wealthy—although there are some who feel they should take more and others who feel they should take less—and make some redistributions to the poor; however, these redistributions are modest. Indeed, redistribution of income in democracies characteristically takes the form of shifts back and forth within the middle income groups who control the bulk of political power and taxable capacity. Education is a rather good example of this phenomenon. Although almost everyone engaged in the education business—the taxpayers who subsidize it, the college professors and the students— are interested to some extent in helping the poor, none of them are willing to make really large sacrifices.

Students, for example, are sometimes in favor of open admissions. Since the capacity of the universities is not large enough to take everyone who applies, this policy usually implies that those who apply for admission should be selected at random rather than by talent. In conversation with students who favor this program, we have suggested that the random selection process be applied not only to next year's enter-

14. B. Abel-Smith, "Whose Welfare State?", in *Conviction,* ed. N. McKenzie (London: MacGibbon and Kee, 1959), p. 57.
15. Adrian L. Webb and Jack E. B. Sieve, *Income Redistribution in the Welfare State* (London: Social Administration Research Trust, 1971).
16. For a broader overview, see, Gordon Tullock, "The Charity of the Uncharitable," *Western Economic Journal* 9 (December 1971), pp. 379–392.

ernment, ed. M. D. Orwig (Iowa City, Iowa: American College Testing Program, 1971).

ing class, but to the class in which they, themselves, are currently enrolled. Needless to say, the result of this suggestion is an almost instantaneous demonstration that they had paid careful attention to their studies, had improved their minds and had become very skilled at producing rationalizations. They want more equality as long as it does not hurt them.

Professors, too, favor more equality in the system only if the terms are general. But they prefer dealing with bright students who put little strain on the teaching capacity of the faculty. As a result, there is normally a good deal of rationalization if the school actually attempts to develop an egalitarian, rather than inegalitarian, education.

The taxpayers, who also vote, are a somewhat more complex problem. First, it should be pointed out that the students and professional staffs of universities are groups who, in net, make large gains from the university—that is, their receipts are greatly in excess of their tax payments. Since they all can vote and are numerous enough to be an important special interest group, their interest in higher education is given careful attention by the politician. In general, what they want is better conditions for the people now in the business. Students want more transfers to themselves and, also, like to have to do less work while they are in school. Professors are interested in increases in salary, lower teaching loads and so on. All of this is rationalized in terms of the public interest. Surely this pressure group—or pressure groups—must be a major determining factor in deciding an education policy in a democracy.

If this special interest group is ignored and a standard median voter model is considered, the first thing that one notes is that the present system does seem to be arranged to benefit slightly more than half of the total population.[17] Furthermore, the people who benefit are the most influential in our society. They are basically prosperous—although not the very wealthy—and bright people who come from all branches of society. Very bright people, who get scholarships or subsidies, are far more likely to win an argument or political debate than dull people who cannot receive such funds. Thus, they have disproportionate political influence. Similarly, the well organized and fairly intelligent middle class is more apt to win in political combat than are the poor. Finally, expanding the amount of education available to the children of the average poor person would not necessarily be of much benefit.

With the present organization of education, requiring the children of the poor to attend college would probably, in net, set them back during the rest of their lives. Also, it is probable that providing college as a free and optional good to the children of the poor would probably not particularly benefit them if, as a result, the tax rate would go up. These arguments assume that the present educational policies will continue. However, if the poor were offered educational opportunities especially tailored to their needs, there is no doubt that their lifetime incomes could be improved;[18] needless to say, a totally new

17. Roughly 60 percent of the high school graduates receive higher education. Of these, only 50 percent graduate. These figures have been relatively stable in the last few decades. Keneth A. Simon and W. Vance Grant, *Digest of Educational Statistics: 1971,* prepared for the United States Office of Educational Statistics (Washington, D.C.: U.S. Government Printing Office, 1972).

18. See, for example, Ismail A. Ghazalah, *The Role of Vocational Education in Improving Skills and Earning Capacity in the State of Ohio: A Cost-Benefit Study* (Athens, Ohio: Division of Business Research, Ohio University, 1972).

educational system would be required. Yet, as has been noted, the reorganization of the educational system to benefit the poor, rather than the talented and well-off, does not seem to be desired by anyone. The poor who would benefit probably do not even realize it is possible.

If we assume that the median voter in society tends to control most policies—which is the simplest model of democracy—the present system of higher education is readily intelligible. It does, indeed, benefit the median voter and most voters who are slightly above the median in income. It injures, in a mild way, most voters who are in the bottom third of the population and, fairly clearly, increases the degree of inequality.

Education and Inequality

By JOSEPH E. STIGLITZ

ABSTRACT: In this essay, I propose first to describe and outline the links between the educational system and the generation of income inequality. The educational system has been criticized as one of the major institutions by which inequality has been perpetuated, especially in less developed countries. In response to this criticism, there have been a number of alternative proposals for modification of our present structure. I shall examine a few of the more important of these proposals and trace through their implications. The desirability of these proposals depends on certain factual assumptions and philosophical presuppositions which may encounter substantial disagreement. Thus, it is not surprising to find disagreement on the nature of desirable reforms for our educational system. This analysis does not lead to any clear-cut policy recommendations; if anything, it suggests that, so far at least, no convincing case has been made for any significant changes in the organization of our educational system.

Joseph E. Stiglitz has been Professor of Economics at Yale University since 1970. He is presently Visiting Fellow at St. Catherine's College, Oxford. He received his B.A. from Amherst College in 1964 and his Ph.D. degree from Massachusetts Institute of Technology (M.I.T.) in 1966. He taught at M.I.T. as an Assistant Professor (1966–1967); was Assistant Professor and then Associate Professor at Yale (1967–1969); and received a Guggenheim Fellowship, which he spent as Tapp Research Fellow at Gonville and Caius College, Cambridge (1969–1970). During the summers of 1969 and 1971 he was Senior Research Fellow at the Institute for Development Studies at the University of Nairobi. His primary fields of research are the economics of uncertainty and information and the theory of public finance. He is presently Co-editor of the Journal of Public Economics, *Associate Editor of the* American Economic Review *and American Editor of the* Review of Economic Studies.

TRADITIONALLY, we have viewed the public educational system as the means by which the children of the poor can improve their status in life. At least in the American mythology, it has been the mechanism to foster a relatively high degree of upward mobility. Equal educational opportunity has seemed at times almost to be equated with equal opportunity.

EDUCATION AND INCOME

More recently, however, the educational system has been criticized as one of the major institutions by which inequality has been perpetuated. There are two important ways that education and income are interrelated. First, the traditional view has stressed education as a process involving the acquisition of skills or the inculcation of better work habits which increase the individual's productivity. Since income is related to productivity, the more education an individual has, the higher will be his income.[1]

Second, education serves as a screening device to sort out different individuals into different jobs; the more highly educated individuals obtain the better jobs. There are three alternative explanations of this: (1) there are marked differences in individuals' abilities. It is often difficult for the employer to identify who will be a good employee; however, firms have observed that the qualities which lead to success in school are related to the qual-

ities which make the individual more productive on the job. Although the correlation may be imperfect, competitive firms can use this information and offer the individuals who do well in school and complete more years of schooling the better jobs. (2) The more educated get the better jobs because they have been made more productive by the schools. Additional years of schooling constitute a signal or an indication of this greater productivity. (3) So long as there is an excess of applicants for a job, the employer has to use some criterion to decide whom to hire. In some economies, it may be the applicant's family connections; in others, the applicant's race or ethnic group; in our economy, it is largely the amount of education. This view is distinguished from the preceding two in that the more educated are not selected because they are more productive, but simply because education is a convenient criterion which most people would regard as fair.

There is a vast amount of evidence that, on the average, individuals who receive more years of schooling earn more income. Unfortunately, most of the empirical studies do not discriminate among the alternative mechanisms by which income and education might be related; thus, at the present time, we simply do not know the relative importance of the direct productivity effect and the screening effects. Indeed, the relationship which presumably exists between income and education could be partially spurious.

Assume, for instance, either that productive capacity is largely inherited or that the employer chooses employees on the basis of family income or status. Also, assume that education is primarily a consumption good not contributing to job skills. The more affluent would give their children more education—just as

1. More precisely, his potential income—that is, the wage he receives per hour worked—is increased. He may choose to work fewer hours, or he may choose an occupation which has more pleasant work conditions—as economists say, occupations with high nonpecuniary returns. Since there are large differences between different individuals' attitudes about work and leisure and about the importance of various work conditions, it is understandable that education and actual income are not very highly correlated.

they spend more on toys, housing and food for their children—and the children of the rich, whether through inherited abilities or inherited status, would go on to higher paying jobs; however, no causal connection between education and productivity would exist.

Statistical studies attempt to avoid these spurious correlations by comparing incomes of individuals of the same ability with different educational levels. But the ability measures that they have used—for example, IQ tests—probably do not accurately reflect those abilities and character traits on which the marketplace puts a high value.

There is another way in which education and income interact: the funds required for the financing of public education must be raised by taxation. To the extent that the beneficiaries of education are not those who pay the taxes, the distribution of income is affected. Some argue that—at least with respect to higher education—since the beneficiaries are mainly children of the middle and upper income groups and state taxes are often regressive, the net effect of state support of higher education is redistribution from the poor to the middle and upper income groups. This is debatable on several grounds. It is difficult to link particular government expenditures with receipts from particular taxes. One could argue that the appropriate question is whether the extra tax revenue paid by an individual to all branches of government as a result of his receiving additional education exceeds the cost to the government. If it does, it is as if the government loaned the individual the cost of his education, to be payed back over a protracted period. To provide the education—if the individual would not, or could not, have obtained it otherwise— is simply a good investment on the part

of the government. Thus, an evaluation of the redistributive effects of public support of higher education requires an analysis of what would have happened in its absence.

PUBLICLY SUPPORTED EDUCATION

Higher education

Any educational system will have effects on the distribution of income through mechanisms of the kind described in the previous section. I will now turn to the particular effects of our publicly supported educational system on the distribution of income. In order to analyze these effects, one must suggest an alternative system to which our present system can be compared. First, consider higher education; assume it receives no public support. Under present institutional arrangements, there would be some individuals who would not be able to go to college. Is it reasonable to assume that institutional arrangements would remain unchanged? For instance, it is likely that use of loan and contingent repayment schemes—loans wherein the amount of repayment would depend on future income [2]—would be more extensive. Since the direct tuition costs are a relatively small proportion of total costs of college education, usually exceeded by the earnings an individual foregoes while in school, is it likely that any individual for whom expected income returns are increased by going to school would not do so under the contingent repayment plan?

It is clear that the contingent repayment scheme will reduce the demand for

2. Yale and other universities have adopted such schemes. In the Yale plan, for each 1,000 dollars borrowed, the individual pays .4 percent of his income annually, until either: (1) he has paid back 150 percent of his loan with accumulated interest or (2) until his class has paid back the total amount borrowed with interest.

education by raising the private costs of education—that is, by imposing the costs previously borne by the government on the individual who is educated. Advocates of the abolition of state support would argue that this is an advantage: if the expected returns fall below the costs of education, including the tuition costs, then it is socially wasteful for the individual to go to college.

The analysis above makes two assumptions. It assumes social benefits do not exceed private benefits. Although there is a widespread belief that strong social benefits are derived from an educated populace, there has been no evidence that social benefits are significantly greater than the private benefits —particularly at the higher education level—except in one respect: increased tax payments result from increased productivity, which results from greater education. On the other hand, if one believes the primary effect of education on income is through screening rather than through the direct productivity effect, there is a strong argument that social benefits may be smaller than private benefits. Assume that schools affect individuals' income by separating out the more able from the less able. Without the sifting, each would receive a wage corresponding to the average productivity of the individuals with whom he is grouped. But if the school is able to identify skills, the more able will receive a wage commensurate with their higher productivity. Thus, by identifying different individuals' abilities, the school system increases inequality.[3]

The fact that the educational system performs this screening function does have an important effect on the demand

for education. Individuals who observe that college graduates earn a higher income do not care whether it is because education has increased productivity or because those who graduate are, on the average, more able than those who do not. To the extent that individuals with a degree receive a higher income because of screening rather than productivity increases, private returns exceed social returns. The effect of the degree is simply to cause a redistribution from the less able to the more able. If this effect is important, there may be too much investment in education.

The analysis also assumes that individuals are relatively well informed about their abilities and are not very averse to risk. Going to college has attributes of a risky investment; most of the returns occur far into the future and, generally, are dependent upon completion of the degree. For a significant fraction of students, the investment does not pay off. No insurance policy can be purchased against this risk, for obvious reasons; the individual must bear the risk himself. There is strong evidence that in such situations individuals will demand a higher average return to compensate them for undertaking the risk. Thus, expected private benefits will exceed private costs at the margin. Even though each individual's risk is important from his own point of view, from the point of view of society the individual risk is small and can be ignored; for example, society would like individuals to invest in education to balance expected social benefits and expected social costs at the margin. To the extent that the risk aversion effect is important, there is too little investment in education and a government subsidy is justifiable.[4]

3. My own suspicion is that this effect is not very important, again, because if the school system did not serve this function, there would be more on-the-job screening; the total amount of screening would not be significantly changed.

4. In this sense, the contingent repayment loan is preferable to a straight loan; for, the amount the individual pays back depends on

My own suspicion is that since individuals from poorer families are likely to be both less informed about their abilities and more concerned about the risk, a contingent repayment scheme is likely to reduce their demand for education and the associated potentialities for upward mobility. However, it is likely to have little effect on the total distribution of income.[5]

Insofar as education serves a screening function, there will be more equality among children of poor families and more inequality between children of higher ability born to poor and to rich parents. Most of us find this kind of horizontal inequity between equals born of different parents far more objectionable than the vertical inequality between individuals of different abilities.

Elementary and secondary education

An analysis of the higher education system differs from that of the elementary and secondary schools because we assume that in the former, the individual is qualified to make decisions while in the latter, parents make the decision. Hence, we cannot compare a system in which the state subsidizes education and one in which each individual bears the cost; rather, an appropriate comparison might be one in which the parent bears the full cost and responsibility for the education of his children.

There are those who have argued recently that our present educational system perpetuates income inequality. For

example, there are large differences in expenditure in different school districts; the high expenditure schools are attended by the children of the rich and the low expenditure schools are attended by the children of the poor. If expenditure is related to school performance, and school performance to productivity —hence, to income—the schools act to perpetuate inequality. This suggests that the public educational system resembles a private school system at the elementary and secondary level. Communities, homogeneous with respect to income and tastes for education, are formed to provide the desired level of education for their children. Thus, the degree of inequality is comparable to that which emerges in a completely private school system—with the obvious exception of the impoverished who would receive no education at all in a private school system. Although the public educational system may not be a great perpetuator of inequality, it certainly is not the great equalizer that its proponents have claimed it to be.[6] Nonetheless, the analysis is open to question. Its validity depends on three factual presuppositions:

—higher levels of educational expenditure purchase higher quality education;
—higher quality education results in higher incomes;
—wealthier communities have higher levels of educational expenditure.

his future income. It reduces the risk the individual must absorb, but does not eliminate it.

5. There are individuals who view education, at least partly, as a consumption good. These individuals would, in a completely private system, invest in education beyond the point where the expected marginal returns are equal to the costs. In the contingent repayment system, these individuals would be subsidized.

6. To the extent to which there are federal or state subsidies to the local community, there is some increase in equality. On the other hand, to the extent that the tax system used to raise revenue for the school system is regressive or to the extent that the beneficiaries of the educational system, particularly of the state higher educational system, are wealthier on average than the community as a whole, the public educational system results in an increase in inequality. The evidence on this score is inconclusive.

To argue that the educational system fosters inequality requires not only that these three propositions be qualitatively correct, but that the children of the rich attend schools with a sufficiently larger level of expenditure per pupil to purchase a sufficiently higher quality of education which results in a sufficiently higher income, to sustain the inequality. Otherwise, the educational system must still be viewed as possessing some equalizing tendencies.

Quality of education and educational expenditures

All three of the propositions have come under strong attack. Obviously, there is a serious problem of measuring the quality of education; performance on the standardized objective tests constitutes an inadequate measure. It would be hard to believe that any properly constructed measure of quality of education would be independent of educational expenditure. To take the matter to its absurd extremes, can one believe that an educational system with one teacher per pupil and an educational system with one teacher per thousand pupils would be equally effective? However, that is not the question we face; the question is: given the kinds of variations in educational expenditure, which perhaps 99 percent of American students experience, the variations in the pupil to teacher ratios and the quality of teaching skill purchased, is the effect on quality significant? The weight of evidence at the present time is that there is not a significant effect.[7]

The communities that spend more on their schools may install better swimming pools or more attractive classrooms; these items may increase the

7. This does not mean, however, that the quality of education is independent of other variables.

pleasantness of school life, but only a fraction of the extra expenditure is directly related to productivity. Diminishing returns can thus set in with sufficient vengeance that even large amounts of increased expenditure result in relatively small changes in productivity.

Higher income and educational quality

The second proposition—that differences in educational achievement have a large effect on lifetime income—has recently come under attack by Jenks and his associates. The weight of evidence, however, is against Jenks; some recent reviews have pointed out that his methodology was faulty in a number of crucial ways. Although the exact mechanism which links education and income is still obscure, plausible evidence creates a presumption of a significant relationship.

Educational expenditure and wealth inequality

The third proposition has also been subjected to extensive criticism. First, the tax base of most educational systems is property; although wealthier individuals own more property—for example, larger houses—they also live in areas of relatively little commercial and industrial property. As a result, the tax base of the community is not highly correlated with average incomes in the community. Secondly, differences in levels of expenditure on education among communities are determined more by labor market factors—for example, general level of wages in different communities—and by socio-demographic characteristics—for example, percentage of parents with high school diploma—than by wealth. Indeed, when proper account is taken of these characteristics there seems to be little systematic relationship between expenditure per pupil and wealth—tax base—or average income in the community.[8]

These remarks suggest that: (1) the inequality of per pupil expenditure which exists at the present time may not be substantially smaller than that which would exist under a completely private school system, but (2) this inequality may have relatively little influence on the perpetuation of inequality. However, the change to a private school system would probably result in less heterogeneity of the student bodies.

GROUPING OF STUDENTS

If education were irrelevant to the income prospects of the children, as some observers have suggested, parents would probably not feel as strongly about education as they appear to. Some schools are better than others, but the differences appear to be more related to the students who attend the school than to the level of expenditure in the school. That is, children of high ability, or potentiality, and motivation tend to improve the performance level of other children in the class. In addition, there is a third factor: a good deal of education occurs outside the school—as informal education. If wealth and education of parents are related to the ability and motivation of their offspring, then the children of the wealthy and educated are likely to bring to the school significant amounts of informal education.[9] It is obviously in the interests of each parent to have his child go to a school attended by children with the highest ability, motivation and informal education. If the parents of the better students could do so, they would form a school consisting only of like students; they would exclude the poorer students.[10] The major mechanisms for exclusion from public school are indirect, such as zoning laws. Although these operate to insulate the communities in which the rich reside, there are many nonrich educated parents, such as teachers, whose children are among the better students and for whom zoning cannot be an effective instrument. They must rely more heavily on grouping within the school district—on tracks. To the extent that the major interactions between students are within the classroom, the good students need not fare badly as a result of the mixing of students within the school district, if tracks are used; to the extent that there are important interactions outside the classroom, such as the general atmosphere of the school, they are worse off.[11] In a private school system, there is some presumption that there will be more homogeneity with respect to quality of students—although, perhaps, less with respect to income of parents—than under the present arrangement.

The effect of better students on improving the performance of less capable students in their class is a classic case of an externality, since the better students contribute benefits for which they are not compensated. Forming homogeneous groups is a mechanism by which the externality gains may be captured, although it may not be the most desirable method of organization from a social point of view.

Economists often divide the effects of

8. These results are based on a study of large school districts. There may be a closer relationship when small districts are included in the analysis.

9. This can be either a result of inheritance or upbringing.

10. They might pay some lip-service to the value of heterogeneity and include a few poorer students.

11. Unless the net returns to heterogeneity are positive. In a heterogeneous society, there are obviously some advantages to heterogeneous grouping. The real question is how large these are compared to the educational disadvantages.

alternative methods of organizing the school system into two categories: efficiency effects, the effect on net national output, and distribution effects, the effect on different groups within the population. From an efficiency standpoint, the acceptability of homogeneous groupings depends on two questions. The first is: to what extent is it more efficient to teach homogeneous groups? If the group is heterogeneous, the teacher must prepare different lesson plans, foregoing the time and thought which could be devoted to either better lesson plans for one group or individual instruction with students. The second question is: what is the relative magnitude of the gains for a poor student and a good student in being in a class of primarily good, rather than bad, students? Both would gain from being in a good class; which gains more is not obvious. If the poor student is far behind the class as a whole, there can be little interaction; he is likely to gain little from the other students' knowledge of Bach and Beethoven. The degree of commonality increases the amount of interaction and, thus, the magnitude of the externality. If at least a certain level of interaction occurs, the poorer student has more to learn from the good student. From this beneficial effect, we must subtract the good students' potential losses resulting from the lower average quality of the class.

There are no reliable estimates of these various effects. My own suspicion is that homogeneous grouping is significantly more efficient than heterogeneous grouping. In any case, it does seem clear that heterogeneous grouping should be within fairly narrow bands. There is little net advantage, and some prospective loss, in mixing the very good and the very bad.

Although there may be some debate about the optimal degree of mixing

from an efficiency aspect, the distributional effects seem clearer. The poor student would be better off in a homogeneous class of otherwise good students, while the other good students would be worse off.

Should the educational system be responsible for the redistribution that is involved in mixing students? If so, how much loss in aggregate overall efficiency should we be willing to pay as the price for increased redistribution? The answer depends on one's view of the responsibilities, and potentialities, of the educational systems.

RESPONSIBILITIES OF THE EDUCATIONAL SYSTEM

The traditional view of the role of the educational system may be characterized, in somewhat stylized form, as follows: everyone has a potentiality—that is, a maximum potential income. To attain this potentiality, two factors are required: the opportunity to acquire the necessary knowledge and skills and the proclivity, or motivation, to do so. An individual who has the motivation but lacks the opportunity will never attain his potentiality, nor will an individual who has the opportunity but lacks the motivation. The traditional view has been that it is the responsibility of the government to provide the educational opportunity; however, it is not the responsibility of the government to concern itself with the extent to which different individuals avail themselves of the opportunity. Indeed, there are as many stories about the children of the rich who turned away from opportunity as there are about the children of the poor who grasped at an opportunity to become rich.

This view is a very individualistic one; each individual has the opportunity to go to college. The system is designed to allow the individual many more chances than do the educational systems of most other countries. He is not confronted with an examination at the age of eleven and shunted into one of several tracks among which movement is essentially impossible. Even if he does badly in high school, he can go to a community college and subsequently transfer to a better college. Ours is a more flexible system, with the focus on individual development.

The objection to this traditional role focuses not on individuals, but on groups. It is observed that children of poor families or children of particular minority groups do not avail themselves of the opportunities as much as do the children of the rich or of other minority groups. Whether this is because the students lack motivation or home education makes no difference; it is argued that the responsibility of the schools is to compensate for these group deficiencies.

Whether schools can compensate for these deficiencies is a moot question. Whether it is the responsibility of the government to bring the lowest group to some minimum level—defined in some way—or to the level of the highest group is usually not clear. Finally, how the groups are to be defined—for example, whether university professors constitute an appropriate group—is not specified.

Leaving these practical questions aside, the desirability of compensatory programs from a purely equity point of view usually depends on whether one takes the family or the individual as the "unit" of society. Consider a set of families living on identical farms. All the farmers have equal capacity to work; some of the farmers, however, prefer more leisure and consequently have a lower income. Should the farmers who work hard be taxed to subsidize the leisure of the other farm-

ers? Most of us would say no. Should the farmer who enjoys leisure be compelled to work hard to eliminate the inequality of income? Or should the farmer who enjoys working be forbidden to work hard and, thus, to purchase the goods he enjoys? Again, most of us would say no. These are matters of individual choice; there is no reason for the government to interfere in the free choice of the individual.

Now, assume that some of the farmers find that they enjoy having large numbers of children; as a result, they have little time to spend with each child. Other farmers decide to have only one child and can thus spend a great deal of time educating him. It takes resources to educate children; the farmer who prefers having fewer children can educate each more adequately. Are there any grounds for saying that one attitude of quality-versus-quantity of children is better than another? Should the government restrict the number of children per family? Should it force some families to have more children? Clearly, a system which forces the parent who has chosen to have fewer children so that he can give each more attention and resources to pay for the education of the children of the parent who preferred the large family is treating the two families inequitably; under identical incomes, there is, in effect, a tax on one kind of parent and a subsidy for the other.

Yet, the child is a member of society in his own right, not only through his membership in the family. To that extent, how can the child who happened to be born into the larger family be fairly treated? Two alternative notions of equity are involved: parental equity and child equity; both represent important moral attitudes.

As a society, we have been ambivalent about which of these attitudes is to be adopted. The parent has a great deal of control over his child, but there are limits: for instance, he must send the child to school. I suspect this ambivalence is a good thing in a pluralistic society, such as ours.

LIMITATIONS OF THE EDUCATIONAL SYSTEM

Even if one agrees that it would be desirable for the educational system to take a more active role in promoting equality, there is the fundamental question of whether, in fact, it can do so within our democratic framework. Consider the consequences of an enforced, uniform level of educational expenditure and heterogeneous mixing of students in every community. Typically, this would require prohibiting communities to increase their expenditures over the prescribed levels. Within the public school system, the objective of uniform levels of educational expenditure would obviously be achieved; whether it would really increase educational opportunity is another matter. The consequence might be a substantial increase in private school enrollment by high demanders of education. This might well curb the education outlay within the public schools, with the overall effect of greater educational inequality.

Several recent court cases have focused on the question of the financing of our educational system. Although there is extensive state and federal subsidization, primary responsibility for financing education has—in most states —remained at the local level. While this has resulted in large variations in the level of public expenditure on education, as has been argued above, there is no strong evidence that this is either a consequence of—or that it results in —significant wealth and income inequalities.

One proposal which attempts to maintain local autonomy and, at the same time, reduce inequality is to permit every school district to pretend that it has a per pupil capita wealth equal to the average in the state. Each state sets a tax rate, then determines its per pupil expenditure and the corresponding tax rate with the difference between revenues received and expenditure either going to or coming from the state treasury. Earlier arguments suggest that it is not likely that this program will significantly alter the inequality in educational expenditures.[12] Although there are doubts about the efficacy of the proposal, it seems to be devoid of serious drawbacks; if its only effect is an increase in the sense of equity within our school system, its adoption may be worthwhile.

Finally, one must ask whether the educational system is the most efficacious way to achieve redistributive goals. For instance, consider compensatory education wherein the government spends more on individuals whose home background is deficient. Although there is some evidence that the compensatory programs introduced so far have had only limited success, with additional resources they undoubtedly could be more successful. Would the cost be worth the additional expenditure? Are there no better programs, such as redistribution through the negative income tax, which would achieve the goals at lower cost?

Again, one must keep in mind the important tradeoff between equity and efficiency. The efficiency question hinges on whether informal education is

12. It should be noted that this is a proposal which is directed more to taxpayer equity than student equity—that is, it ensures that at any given rate of taxation a taxpayer can purchase the same amount of per pupil expenditure. It does not ensure that students themselves receive the same amount of expenditure.

a complement to, or a substitute for, formal education—that is, at the margin, is a dollar spent on the formal education of someone who has a good background and is highly motivated likely to have a greater effect on his earning power than a dollar spent on someone with a poor background who is unmotivated? It is possible that formal and informal education are more likely to be complementary; in other words, that informal education improves formal education. Efficiency would require spending more, not less, on those with a better background. On the other hand, it is clear that such a policy would increase inequality; on those grounds, it might be deemed undesirable.

CONCLUSION

The United States has developed a diversified educational system. It is a mixed public-private school system without the strong class and religious segregation which has characterized the mixed public-private school systems in other places and at other times. It is a school system which has provided a college education to a large proportion of the population without, at the same time, sacrificing the quality of education attained by the best students. It is a system which has the necessary flexibility to focus on the individual and his development.

There are deficiencies in our school systems, and these have not gone unnoticed. Experimentation within our highly diversified system is likely to yield workable answers to these problems. Some of the complaints against the educational system are really addressed to aspects of our economic system, particularly to the degree of inequality which it engenders. Although it has been argued that the educational system is not the cause of inequality, the difficult question remains: is it possible, and/or desirable, to use the educational system to promote greater equality?

The Political Economy of Income Redistribution Policies

By LESTER C. THUROW

ABSTRACT: During the decade of the 1960s, a variety of public policies were adopted to alter the American distribution of income. A history of these policies begins with the manpower programs of the early Kennedy administration and ends with President Nixon's 1974 budget. An examination of the economic and political history of these programs reveals a variety of reasons for their publicly proclaimed failure. Means and ends were never sufficiently distinguished; no consistent decision was ever made about the aspects of the income distribution to be altered; the political process wanted to pretend that income could be redistributed without reducing anyone's economic position; funds could never be concentrated enough to have a visible impact; and the public was simply unwilling to make investments of the size that would have been necessary to solve the problem. The elimination of poverty may be a good investment socially; financially, it is a bad investment. Increases in productivity do not cover the costs of the necessary programs. The Family Assistance Plan was a radical departure from previous attempts to alter the distribution of income, but it was fatally flawed by internal contradictions. Eventually, it proved to be a political liability for politicians of all parties.

Lester C. Thurow is Professor of Economics and Management at the Massachusetts Institute of Technology. He has served as Staff Economist for the Council of Economic Advisers during 1964 and 1965 and during the inauguration of the War on Poverty. Professor Thurow is author of Poverty and Discrimination, *which won the David A. Wells Prize, and* The American Distribution of Income: A Structural Problem.

The author would like to thank Mike Piori for his helpful comments.

WHICH policies should be adopted to alter the American distribution of income? Theoretically, one would specify the income distribution to be achieved and then search for the least costly technique for causing the desired changes. Once costs are known, benefits and costs could be compared. Unfortunately, such a straightforward procedure is not possible. Means and ends are thoroughly interrelated and confused in income redistribution. Value judgements often attach themselves more to the means by which income is to be distributed than to the ultimate distribution of income itself. Since means and ends are interdependent, one cannot specify ends and then search for the cheapest means.

A MUDDLED PROBLEM

Income distributions can also be viewed from many perspectives: personal, family, racial, age, sex, occupation, industry, education and skills. Since movements toward equality from one perspective will often lead to inequality from other perspectives, it is necessary to decide upon the relevant perspectives. For example, equalizing the distributions of male and female income would lead to a more unequal distribution of family income. Since the wives of high income males currently work less than the wives of low income males, equalizing the incomes and working opportunities for men and women would lead to larger income increases for high income families than they would for low income families.[1] In this case, it is necessary to decide whether the primary problem is poverty—low income families—or sexual discrimination—relatively low income women. Judgements about the relevant perspective

must be made, yet, have not been consistently made.

The perspective is relevant to the specification of means and ends, but it also determines whether income redistribution problems fall into a set of problems where solutions are either known or unknown. If the basic income redistribution goal involves reducing mean income differences between groups, such as Blacks versus whites or males versus females, then there are known economic policies which could achieve the desired results. The question becomes one of whether society is willing to bear the economic, social and political costs that these economic policies impose. Hiring quotas are a good example. Is society willing to pay the associated costs?

If the basic income redistribution goal involves reducing the dispersion in income among individuals or families, then there are no known economic policies to bring about the desired results. The lack of solutions springs from the fact that although mean incomes differ across different groups—for example, according to education or skills—the variance, or dispersion, in income within each group is almost as large as the variance in income for the population as a whole.[2] Giving a group of people a college education may increase their average incomes, but it does not reduce the variance among them. As a result, policies to change individual characteristics so that they are shifted from low income groups to high income groups have little impact on the variance of income for the whole society. To the extent that poverty is a dispersion problem rather than an absolute minimum income problem, poverty falls into that category of problems with no known solution.

Because of the sensitive nature of income redistribution goals and policies,

1. This assumes selective mating where men with high incomes are married to women who could potentially earn high incomes if there were no sexual discrimination.

2. This is essentially the argument being made by Jencks. See, Christopher Jencks, *Inequality* (New York: Basic Books, 1972).

political discussions of income redistribution goals and policies tend to be implicit rather than overt. No politician wants to stand up and say that such-and-such a group should have lower incomes, relatively or absolutely. Yet changes that lower someone's income below what it would otherwise have been are a necessary ingredient of any income redistribution policy. A policy of slow income redistribution and rapid economic growth can theoretically prevent anyone's income from falling below what it was in the base period; however, there is no technique for redistribution of income that does not lower someone's income below what it otherwise would have been if the income redistribution policies were not in effect.

In direct income redistribution, income is taken from one person and given to another. In human capital income redistribution, someone's taxes are raised to pay for training someone else. In addition, the taxpayer finds more competition for the jobs that he would like to hold. In legal or administrative income redistribution, someone is hired or promoted into a job that someone else would have had without these regulations. The political process, however, refuses to face up to this necessity. It prefers to pretend that no one will lose. Yet, economic losers are an integral part of income redistribution, no matter how it is done. The inseparability of means and ends, the failure to determine consistent perspectives and the lack of overt discussion of the implications of income redistribution can be seen in the history of the last decade's efforts to alter the distribution of income.

PRESIDENT KENNEDY'S INCOME REDISTRIBUTION POLICIES

The 1950s combination of high growth rates in the USSR and persistently high unemployment and low economic growth in the United States led to Kruschev's promises to "bury" the United States economically and to United States fears that he would realize his threat. One explanation for the poor economic record of the United States focused on the automation crisis. Growth was slow and workers were unemployed because laborers did not have the right skills to match the needs of new technological advances. Round pegs could not be made to fit into square holes.

Slightly later, politicians and the American public discovered regional poverty. Regions existed that were not participating in what little economic growth was occurring in the rest of the country. Interestingly, all of the focus was on regions, such as Appalachia, the Ozarks and upper Michigan, of white poverty. The Black poverty of the deep South and central cities was almost completely ignored.

President Kennedy promised to get the country moving again in his 1960 presidential campaign. When elected, he proposed manpower training programs to match workers with jobs and investment tax incentives to accelerate growth in the mainstream of the economy. Coupled with this were regional development programs—generally in the areas of manpower training and transportation—that were to accelerate growth in underdeveloped regions and tie them into the mainstream of economic development.

Before the programs could reach a scale where they might affect the national economy, the diagnosis of the American growth problem shifted. The economy's failure to respond to investment stimuli and the report of the President's Automation Commission both cast doubt on the proposition that the basic problem was supply bottlenecks. The basic problem was a lack of aggregate demand, not a lack of aggregate supply. Increasing the effective supplies of capital and labor could not solve the growth problem.

Given hindsight, the President's Automation Commission and those focusing on the lack of aggregate demand were clearly right. With the expansion of the economy as a result of the 1964 tax cuts and the expenditures on the Viet Nam War, unemployment fell to approximately 3 percent and growth accelerated. With the high level of aggregate demand, both unskilled people and backward regions began to participate in the nation's economic growth. The acceleration of the United States growth rate coupled with a deceleration in the Russian growth rate led to the realization that the United States was not to be quickly buried; gradually, fear of the Soviet Union ceased to be a motive for manpower training programs.

PRESIDENT JOHNSON'S INCOME REDISTRIBUTION POLICIES

The acceleration of the growth rate left regional poverty as the main problem until the civil rights movement of the early 1960s fostered recognition of a new set of problems: poverty was more prevalent among Black families than white families. The average Black family income was only 50 percent of the average white family income; statistical studies also showed large numbers of poverty-stricken families in the midst of affluent regions. The answer to all of these problems was to be contained in an enlarged War on Poverty under the direction of President Johnson.

While the War on Poverty was overtly color blind and while 80 percent of those in poverty were white, the civil rights movement and urban Black riots rather quickly turned the War on Poverty into a program for Blacks in the eyes of both those who supported and those who opposed the program. This perception, more than the war in Viet Nam, was eventually to lead to its demise.

Although the economic goals had shifted from growth to income redistribution, the programs remained the same. Manpower training, including education, and regional development were the main policy instruments. Regions were simply redefined to include poverty neighborhoods. Community action and model cities were to develop poverty neighborhoods in the same manner as the earlier regional programs were to develop large geographic areas.

President Kennedy could call for overt sacrifices in an effort to beat the Russians, but President Johnson thought that sacrifices could not be called for in an effort to beat poverty or to aid Blacks. Instead of being hailed as heroes, those who were to pay the bills in the War on Poverty were to be told that there were no bills to be paid. Senator McGovern's later lack of success in telling people that their taxes should be increased to solve social problems is some indication that President Johnson was right in his political judgements.

As a result, all direct tax transfer systems were ruled out of the War on Poverty. It was not a welfare system to take money from one individual and give it to another. It would promote economic growth—more for everyone—without lowering anyone's income. To avoid having to raise the taxes of the more affluent in order to pay for the necessary training programs, the War on Poverty was to be financed out of the fiscal dividend—that is, the normal growth in tax revenues—rather than tax increases.

The more affluent groups would either not know that the distribution of income was being altered or would not care, since their own incomes were not falling. For the same reason, a poverty line was set in absolute dollars rather than relative to average incomes. While it was possible to argue that economic growth would eventually raise everyone above 3,200 dollars, it was not possible to argue that economic growth would automatically raise everyone above some relative standard—say, to 50 percent of the median income. The appeal to growth and more for everyone was an attempt to disguise the relative changes in the distribution of income that were to take place.

As a strategy to make changes in the distribution of income more palatable, the there-are-no-losers strategy was a failure from the beginning. The non-poor white population immediately above the poverty line knew what was being done and did not like it. They did not want the government helping others to reach an economic status that they had reached through their own hard work. What is more, they knew that economic status depends upon relative positions rather than absolute incomes. They had something to lose even if their incomes did not fall in absolute dollars and cents.

Essentially, the War on Poverty refused to confront the well-known psychological literature on envy, the sociological literature on relative deprivation and the economic literature on wage contours. Individual judgements about economic success and failure are based on relative incomes compared to some reference group. The reference group tends to be a group that is economically near the person in question. Individuals who do relatively well compared to their reference group, rather than those who do well in comparison with the entire population, tend to be happiest with their economic circumstances. As a result, it is not surprising that upper income whites did not feel threatened by the War on Poverty while lower middle class whites felt acutely threatened.

As some recent research of Harvard sociologist Lee Rainwater vividly illustrated, individuals make judgements about what constitutes poverty on a relative basis and place individuals into poor, middle class and rich categories on a relative basis.[3] Economic growth cannot solve the income distribution problem since we can all become rich by the standards of our forefathers, but not by our own contemporary standards. I am rich only if some large fraction of the population has incomes lower than mine. I feel poor if I have the lowest income in society, regardless of its absolute magnitude.

As a result, poverty is a dispersion, or variance, problem; thus, it falls into the category of economic problems for which there is no known solution. This is especially true if public policies are limited to manpower training policies. Manpower training policies can move people across different groups, but do not attempt, or claim, to effect distributions of income within each group.

While it might theoretically have been possible to forge a political alliance of the poor, Blacks and middle, or upper, income whites to force lower middle income whites to accept a diminution in their relative position, the Johnson administration closed off this possibility by pretending that no one had anything to lose. Perhaps they even came to believe their own rhetoric about no losers.

FAILURES OF THE KENNEDY-JOHNSON WAR ON POVERTY

In theory, the War on Poverty was to start as a highly concentrated war that would eliminate poverty in a few areas. These areas would provide the necessary learning experiences to determine

3. U.S., Congress, Joint Economic Committee, "Poverty, Living Standards, and Family Well-Being," prepared for the Sub-Committee on Fiscal Policy by Lee Rainwater (Joint Center for Urban Studies of MIT and Harvard, June 1972), working paper no. 10.

which programs would work, and their successes would lead to political momentum for large national programs. Political realities stopped such a strategy. No program to help just a few areas could get enough national support to be adopted. Inevitably, the money was split among all areas. This might not have been fatal but for the budgetary constraints imposed by the Viet Nam War. With the budget limitations, there was not enough money to have a visible impact on the entire economy; given the lack of expenditure concentration, there was not enough outlay in any one area to have visible local effects. Since there were few visible effects, critics had no difficulty arguing that the programs had failed— for, given the funding and distribution constraints, they could not have succeeded.

In the War on Poverty there were education and training programs that worked—in the sense that they raised a group's income relative to an identical control group; however, skill augmentation did not prove to be a cheap method for raising incomes. Evaluations indicated that many programs had benefit-costs ratios less than one—that is, more than a dollar had to be invested for each dollar of extra earnings—and few earned high rates of return. This is especially true when one deals with the training of older adults, female household heads or the hard core unemployed. They simply require too many services, such as day care, and too much training, such as literacy, to overcome previous work habits and skill deficiencies. Basically, they require a larger investment than the public is willing to make. The Job Corps is a good example. It was politically unpopular partly because it placed Black teenagers in white neighborhoods. Yet, perhaps a more important objection was that it cost a lot of money; estimates differ,

but costs were approximated at 8,000 to 10,000 dollars per student per year. According to political rhetoric, it was absurd to spend more on a Job Corps camp than it would cost to attend Harvard for a year. Yet, this is faulty logic: if it costs 6,000 dollars per year to educate the brightest and easiest to educate college students, then it surely must cost more to educate the country's hardest to educate young adults.

Unwillingness to raise taxes to pay for either the War on Poverty or the War on the North Vietnamese led to the search for education and training programs that were both inexpensive and earned a high rate of return on investment. While no one can deny that such programs may exist, all of our empirical evidence leads to the opposite conclusion. Undoing low skill levels and poor work habits among adults is simply a slow, expensive job. As our knowledge of education increases, it appears that the critical years occur at ever earlier ages. Head Start was an effort to recognize this fact, but a successful Head Start program would have needed complementary education investments at all succeeding levels of education. Using such a technique, decades of expensive investments would have been needed to raise minority incomes.

Eliminating poverty and equalizing the distribution of income for majority and minority groups may be a good investment morally and socially; financially, it is a bad investment. Increases in productivity do not cover the costs of the necessary programs. If the only justification for the War on Poverty is economic output, then it cannot be justified.

NEGATIVE INCOME TAX

As the expense and difficulties of an education-training strategy became apparent, interests naturally shifted to direct income redistribution techniques. The preferred instrument was always some variant of the negative income tax. The negative income tax appeared attractive for several reasons. First, it was clearly cheaper—even in the long run—to give certain groups of people one dollar than it was to give them enough training and services to increase their earnings by one dollar. Second, there were other groups, such as the elderly and the ill, who could not conceivably be given enough training to raise their income to adequate levels. Third, the existing welfare system was in a mess.

Welfare had been set up to handle the problems of individuals who suffered temporary income loses. It was an emergency system designed to aid the temporarily poor, not the chronically poor. Yet, the welfare system was increasingly being used as a long run income redistribution system in the 1960s. Viewed as an income redistribution system, it was incorrectly structured.

Since welfare was to be a temporary emergency system, it contained a 100 percent tax on earnings. Every dollar earned was a dollar subtracted from a welfare check. This might not be much of a work deterrent to an individual who was temporarily poor with potential earnings far in excess of the welfare level. It is a strong deterrent for the long term poor with potential earnings opportunities less than, or not much above, the welfare level.

When welfare programs were established, society thought that the appropriate place for a mother of small children was in the home. A 100 percent earnings tax on such mothers would encourage them to stay at home and take care of their children. With changing social attitudes about the appropriate role for mothers, demands emerged to eliminate the existing barriers to

work and, in fact, to build work incentives into the program.

Designed as an emergency system, welfare was a categorical system to determine who was in an emergency situation. Emergencies obviously excluded the working poor who were not in an emergency, but simply could not earn high incomes—some 7.2 million Americans earned less than 4,000 dollars for full time, full year work in 1970. As a result, people on welfare often received more income than those who worked hard all year. Viewed as an income redistribution system, this is clearly unfair.

Since welfare standards are set by the states and not by the federal government, the welfare system distributed very different amounts of money to American citizens in different areas of the country. In addition to the resulting inequities, conservatives thought the situation contributed to migration to already overcrowded Northern cities. Empirical studies have always failed to find any significant evidence of the migration effect. But this seems to have little, or no, impact on the political beliefs about the effects of the system.

Under the terms of categorical assistance, women with children but without husbands are regarded as in emergency situations, while women with husbands are not, regardless of the husband's earnings. Consequently, liberals worried about incentives to break up families, and conservatives were searching for husbands under the beds of welfare mothers. Again, empirical studies indicate minimal amounts of voluntary desertion to gain welfare, but such studies have little impact on political beliefs.

Negative income taxes are attractive because they solve all of these problems. Every citizen has the same income guarantee, regardless of where he or she lives. All citizens are treated equally. No incentives exist to migrate. All earnings are taxed at some rate less than 100 percent. Everyone has an incentive to go to work. Those that work always have higher incomes than those who do not work. No purpose is served by family desertion.

PRESIDENT NIXON'S INCOME REDISTRIBUTION POLICIES

A variant of the negative income tax —The Family Assistance Plan—was proposed by President Nixon and twice passed by the House of Representatives. This marked a radical departure from strategies of the 1960s when direct income redistribution was forbidden and all efforts were to focus on changing labor characteristics. Unfortunately, the plan suffered from fatal technical flaws that were a necessary condition of the circumstances under which it was introduced.

To keep federal costs low, the plan was not proposed as a replacement for the welfare system, but as a supplement to it. The guaranteed income was 1600 dollars per year for a family of four. This guarantee would have meant increased welfare levels in eight states, but reduced welfare levels in forty-two other states. The states were expected to supplement the Family Assistance Plan with a welfare program; the federal government would pay 30 percent of the costs of supplementation. To keep federal costs down, the offsetting tax rate was kept high. The basic tax rate was 50 percent in the family assistance part of the plan; in the supplementation part of the plan, the tax rate would be at least high enough to lead to a 67 percent overall tax rate, or even much higher tax rates.[4]

When combined with other in-kind

4. For a discussion of the problems in welfare reform, see, Henry J. Aaron, "Why is Welfare So Hard to Reform," *Studies in Social Economics* (Washington, D.C.: The Brookings Institution, 1973).

assistance programs to aid the poor, the Senate Finance Committee was able to show that many poor individuals would be subject to taxes far in excess of 100 percent of their earnings. When they earned an extra dollar, sixty-seven cents would be taken in the basic grant system. But public housing, medicaid, food stamps and a host of other social programs also had provisions whereby extra earnings reduced benefits. When all of these implicit tax rates were added together, they often exceeded 100 percent for some individuals somewhere in the country. Since many of the programs and implicit tax rates were under the control of state or local governments, there simply was no way to keep total tax rates under 100 percent, except through explicit federalization of the welfare system or implicit federalization through detailed sets of instructions that would essentially dictate how state and local governments were to run their welfare system. Explicit, or implicit, federalization of welfare did not fit in with the Nixon administration's desires for assigning more responsibilities to state and local governments nor with the financial commitments that it was willing to undertake. If the total tax was to be kept well below 100 percent, the implicit taxes in many programs would have had to have been reduced— leading to large expenditure increases in these programs.

Conservatives and liberals were also at an impasse on the size of the guaranteed income. Liberals would not vote for a low guarantee; conservatives would not vote for a high guarantee; neither had the votes to force its desires on the whole Senate.

Not trusting work incentives to keep the population working, a set of compulsory work provisions was also part of the Family Assistance Plan. In theory, everyone in the program who was not working would be required to register with an unemployment office, to be examined for employability and, if in an employable category, to be placed in either work or training. This part of the program was never adequately investigated, since other controversies prevented attention from focusing on it. However, it would have been extremely expensive to implement. In all likelihood, the public would not have been willing to pay the necessary costs, just as it was not willing to pay the costs of the Job Corps.

The stalemate over the Family Assistance Plan was essentially broken by the public response to Senator McGovern's income redistribution proposals. His plan was to federalize welfare, to establish a guaranteed income of 4,000 dollars for a family of four with an offsetting tax rate of 33.3 percent and to raise the necessary revenue with broad tax reform—tax increases on higher incomes. For the first time, the public actually became aware of the proposals of the Family Assistance Plan. The majority of the population, to judge by the election returns, rejected the program. Once again, relative deprivation showed its power: some of the groups that would have financially gained the most—the working poor—seemed most adamantly opposed to the plan. To avoid the odium that surrounded the McGovern proposals, President Nixon backed away from his Family Assistance Plan by refusing to make any compromises that could facilitate its passage; the Republican platform declared that it was unalterably opposed to the guaranteed income in any form, despite the fact that this was exactly what the president's family assistance plan had promised.

While the president was leading the political rush away from negative income taxes as a solution to income distribution problems, politicians of all parties were not far behind. When the president stated that the Family Assistance Plan was not reintroduced because it could not pass, he was correct; if support was not zero, it was close to it. Major national politicians did not want to be tied in with the tax transfer approach to income redistribution.

This retreat, however, did not change perspectives on skill augmentation programs. If they were taken seriously as a technique for aiding low income individuals, they would demand large budgetary expenditures and tax increases. Not thinking that the benefits were worth the costs, the fiscal 1974 budget proposed to eliminate most of the Great Society programs designed to alter work characteristics and the distribution of income. Most of the money is to be given to state and local governments in the form of revenue sharing. They are welcome to use their revenue sharing money for income redistribution programs, but they will have to find a cheap successful program if they are to have enough money to remedy the problem. Since the likelihood of this is small, the political impetus to adopt economic policies that will lead to changes in the distribution of income seems to have completely dissipated.

CONCLUSIONS

Conceivably, the negative income tax systems of income redistribution have been poorly presented—for example, much more than half of the American population would have been better off financially under the McGovern proposals. A better selling job could make them popular. This view, however, assumes that relative deprivation attitudes are mistaken and that people judge their success or failure on their own absolute incomes. A great deal of evidence refutes this hypothesis; very little existing evidence supports it.

Similarly, it is also possible to argue for more experimentation to search for a cheap program that would elevate minority group incomes. Such a program might be funded and might alter the distribution of income before the majority was aware of what was happening. I would argue that we have had enough experiments to know that the probability of such a program is very low. Ruling out either of these possibilities means that the country must face a serious political discussion of whether it is, or should be, willing to make major efforts to equalize the distributions of income across the major groups—such as Blacks, Mexican-Americans and women—in society. Here, the problem is not one of knowledge, but one of willingness to pay the necessary price. Whites will have to sacrifice a lot of their income if Blacks are to earn equal incomes.

The poverty problem is fundamentally one of relative incomes. While there is a verbal attachment to the idea of equal opportunity across different groups, it is not at all obvious what our attachment is to reducing relative income differentials. If we are interested, the basic problem is one of knowledge. Which programs reduce income dispersions? No one knows.

There are grounds for pessimism on the most likely outcome of these political discussions. The majority appears unwilling to make sacrifices in its own economic position to equalize the distributions of income among different groups in society. Verbal attachments to equality and equal opportunity are strong enough only to lead to income redistribution policies that are both cheap and unsuccessful. If a cheap and successful training program were discovered, it would be blocked by the majority. They might not have to make great sacrifices in terms of tax increases, but they would have to be prepared to make great sacrifices in their relative position. Given the fact of relative deprivation, someone always feels that he loses in any income redistribution. Those who feel this way, or who can be persuaded to feel this way, appear to constitute a majority. Wars, revolutions and economic upheavals can change the distribution of income, but historical examples of peaceful changes in the distribution of income are extremely rare.

The "poor are always with us" because the low man on the economic totem pole feels poor regardless of his absolute income. The rest of us insist on having a low man, since we would not otherwise be satisfied with our own economic positions.

Actual, Feasible and Optimal Income Inequality in a Three-Level Education Model

By Jan Tinbergen

ABSTRACT: Incomes should be interpreted as the outcome of demand for, and supply of, various types of labor. Demand is derived from a Cobb-Douglas-like production function with five types of labor characterized by actual education and education required. Supply is derived from a utility function containing income, actual education and education required. One complete model for analytical—explanatory—and one complete model for normative—optimization—purposes are constructed. The former shows the influence on income distribution of given changes in educational level; the latter, the optimal income distribution under two different sets of constraints on education. Figures used are crude figures for the Netherlands around 1962.

Jan Tinbergen is Professor of Development Planning at the University of Rotterdam. He was a founding member of the Econometric Society in Europe, 1931. His main scientific work has been on econometric models, first of business cycles, later of long term growth. Recently, he concentrated on problems of income distribution. In 1969 he shared, with Ragnar Frisch, the first Nobel Memorial Prize for Economics. He is a member of the United Nations Development Planning Committee.

INCOME inequality has again become the topic of the day. It is under continuous discussion in various Western European countries, even though inequality in incomes has been greatly reduced in the last century. The (democratic) Socialist Party of Sweden, in many respects an example for its sister parties of the Socialist International, published a first report on the subject in 1969.[1] In the Netherlands, an intensive discussion takes place on the question of whether employee incomes should be raised by the same percentages or the same amount for all. To a considerable extent, the inflationary policies in Western Europe can be seen as an expression of dissatisfaction with the existing income distribution.

DEMAND FOR, AND SUPPLY OF, VARIOUS PRODUCTION FUNCTIONS

For quite some time, economic science has paid little attention to the explanation of quantitative income distribution. Ever since Marx, distribution between the capital and labor factors has had ample attention. While income from private capital has been practically abolished in the larger part of Eastern Europe, a recent study by Wiles and Markowski concludes that income distribution in Britain approximates that of Poland or the Soviet Union.[2] Figures for several Western countries show that the largest part of income inequality—say, three quarters of it for primary income—is due to inequality in labor income.

Research on the determinants of labor income inequality has long been of a partial character only; one well-known example is that during the period of piece rates incomes of miners were proportional to their physical strength. More general theories, such as those by Van der Wijk,[3] Gibrat[4] or Champernowne,[5] were rather abstract and mainly, if not wholly, probabilistic. A more concrete theory, tested only indirectly, was the one by Tuck,[6] who considered the ability to give guidance to other people—expressed as the number of people one was directly and indirectly able to guide—as the factor influencing both income distribution and the size distribution of enterprises, at the same time.

No doubt, while random elements do play an important role in the short run —as has been demonstrated by Somermeyer[7]—for somewhat longer periods, perhaps of three years and beyond, I wonder whether or not a greater place should be given to systematic forces. In the last few years, I tried to test a theory of income distribution based on a supply and demand mechanism.[8] The recent study by Freeman[9] on college-educated technicians supports this ap-

1. SAP-LO:s arbetsgrupp: Jämlikhet (Working Group of the Socialist Party and the National Trade Union Organization: Equality) (Borås, Sjuhäradsbygdens Tryckeri AB, 1969) (Swedish).

2. Peter J. D. Wiles and Stefan Markowski, "Income Distribution under Communism and Capitalism," Soviet Studies 22 (1970/1), p. 344 ff. and p. 487 ff.

3. J. van der Wijk, Inkomens- en vermogensverdeling (Haarlem: De Erven Bohn, 1939).

4. R. Gibrat, Les inégalités économiques (Paris: Sirey, 1931).

5. D. G. Champernowne, "A Model of Income Distribution," Economic Journal 63 (1953), p. 318 ff.

6. R. H. Tuck, An Essay on the Economic Theory of Rank (Oxford: Basil Blackwell, 1954).

7. W. H. Somermeyer, "An Analysis of Income Variance in the Netherlands," Statistische Informationen 1 (1967).

8. Jan Tinbergen, "The Impact of Education on Income Distribution," Review of Income and Wealth ser. 18 (1972), p. 255 ff.

9. Richard B. Freeman, The Market for College-Trained Manpower (Cambridge, Mass.: Harvard University Press, 1971).

proach for a limited field, considered in substantial detail. Part of my own recent research uses supply and demand factors in an attempt to explain differences in income inequality—between countries and between periods—without going to the scientific bases of demand and supply. Some further studies tried to introduce these bases, basing demand for labor of various qualities on a production function and supply of such types of labor on utility functions.[10]

The present essay constitutes an attempt to add one more step: with the aid of the suggested models, positive and normative approaches to the problem of income distribution may finally be contrasted.[11] The positive approach tries to answer the question of how income distribution will change as a consequence of given changes in data and, more particularly, to instruments of socio-economic policy. The normative approach tries to find the optimal income distribution and the use of instruments needed to attain it.

In order to let the reader judge these new attempts and their results, I am not only going to present the latter, but will also set out the production and utility functions used and the statistical specifications introduced.

THE PRODUCTION FUNCTION

The production function used is of the Cobb-Douglas type, implying that the elasticity of product in respect to the quantities of factors used is constant. The capital factor is introduced in the usual, simplest way and given an exponent 0.2—meaning that capital income constitutes 20 percent of total national

income. Labor is introduced in three different types depending on the schooling completed; levels one, two and three will be distinguished and interpreted as the primary, secondary and tertiary level, respectively. However, for the primary and secondary level, the total quantities of each of these types are split up into two portions of the labor force. People with a primary education presumably work on jobs requiring either primary or secondary education; similarly, people with a secondary education supposedly work on jobs requiring either secondary or tertiary education. These assumptions express the belief that all economies show a scarcity of higher education and, hence, have to operate with insufficiently educated manpower filling part of their jobs. The quantity of the production factor—labor with primary education—is then defined not simply as the sum of the two components, but as one of a sum in which those working in higher jobs have a weight above 1, representing the fact that they are more productive than their colleagues even though they are not fully qualified for the jobs they fill. The same is done with labor of the secondary level of schooling; the weights are called π_{21} and π_{32}, respectively. If the number of people working beyond their education approaches zero, the corresponding weight reaches a lower limit of unity.

There is also an upper limit: people working beyond their education will not be more productive than—but, at most, as productive as—people in possession of the required education. Thus, out of the five groups one can isolate three production factors within labor: those with primary, secondary and tertiary education; their numbers, as just defined, influence total product with constant elasticities ρ_1, ρ_2 and ρ_3. At the same time, these elasticities determine

10. Jan Tinbergen, "Labour with Different Types of Skills and Jobs as Production Factors," *De Economist* 12 (1973), p. 213 ff.

11. Compare, also, Jan Tinbergen, "A Positive and a Normative Theory of Income Distribution," *Review of Income and Wealth* ser. 16 (1970), p. 221.

the portions of national product imputed to each of these three factors; since capital accounts for 20 percent of national product, the ρ's add up to 0.8 and, in the Dutch material used for 1962, amount to 0.648, 0.088 and 0.064. Demand for the various types of education-job combinations by the organizers of production will be based on profit maximization and, as such, primary incomes offered to the five types of labor must be equal to their marginal productivity derived directly from the production function by differentiation with regard to the type of labor concerned. In this process, the π are presumed to be given constants to the single organizer of production. The relationship which is assumed to exist between π and the corresponding proportion ρ of the labor force will be used only when the results in different situations are compared.

The Utility Functions

The utility functions used are based on a recent attempt I made to measure utility functions [12] with the aid of two assumptions not usually adhered to by most economists or, at least, not considered as belonging to the realm of economics as a science. This attempt has been presented as a very first step only on a road of further research which looks promising, but whose results cannot be foreseen. For the time being, only the result obtained from a first illustration based on material for the Netherlands, 1962, is available. Again, it is being used in order to present a first illustration, now directed at the solution of the problems of this essay— that is, the size and nature of actual, feasible and optimal income inequalities. Measurement of utility for individual

households enables us to give concrete content to: (1) the supply of labor for different jobs and (2) a social welfare function conceived, in this essay, simply as the sum of all individual utilities.

In this very first attempt, utility for everybody is presumed to be the same function of the variables: (1) spendable income, (2) education required for the job chosen and (3) actual education completed. In this setup, the latter element—called parameter—is supposedly the only relevant indicator of quality differences among individual households. While this looks like a drastic oversimplification of the real mechanism at work, a number of studies by other authors show that approximately two-thirds of the variance in labor income can be accounted for by variations in schooling.[13] In addition, the overwhelming part of the variance in spendable income can be attributed to variations in earned, or labor, income.

The role played by utility functions in the supply of labor is restricted to the assumption that wherever income recipients of a given educational level have a choice between two types of jobs, the spendable incomes drawn from these jobs must compensate for differences in labor disutility or satisfaction—meaning that utility in the two positions must be equal. As a counterpart to this equality, we have the alternative situation in which income of the less attractive job is too low to compensate for the difference in disutility; then, only the more attractive job will be chosen. This means that the individual with first level schooling will fill a first level job and not a second level job; or, alternatively, somebody with second level education a

12. Jan Tinbergen, *An Interdisciplinary Approach to the Measurement of Utility or Welfare,* Fifth Geary Lecture (Dublin: The Economic and Social Research Institute, 1972).

13. P. de Wolff and A. R. D. van Slijpe, *The Relation between Income, Intelligence, Education and Social Background* (Amsterdam: Institute of Actuarial Science and Econometrics, 1972).

TABLE 1

CHANGES IN INCOMES AND PORTIONS OF MANPOWER IN THE FIVE POSITIONS
CONSIDERED, AS A CONSEQUENCE OF CHANGES IN THE TOTAL
MANPOWER WITH EDUCATION OF LEVELS 1, 2 AND 3

			CASE A	CASE B	CASE C	CASE D
Portion (%) of Active	$E = 1$	F_1	91	88	85	81
Population with	$E = 2$	F_2	6	8	9	11
Education (E) and	$E = 3$	F_3	3	4	6	8
Jobs (J) Indicated	$J, E = 1, 1$	ϕ_{11}	79	76	85	81
	$J, E = 2, 1$	ϕ_{21}	12	12	0	0
	$J, E = 2, 2$	ϕ_{22}	3	3.5	9	11
	$J, E = 3, 2$	ϕ_{32}	3	4.5	0	0
	$J, E = 3, 3$	ϕ_{33}	3	4	6	8
Primary Incomes of	$J, E = 1, 1$	l_{11}	6.2	6.6	6.9	7.35
Combinations J, E	$J, E = 2, 1$	l_{21}	7.9	8.4	.	.
Indicated*	$J, E = 2, 2$	l_{22}	12.5	9.1	8.9	7.35
	$J, E = 3, 2$	l_{32}	14.4	11.15	.	.
	$J, E = 3, 3$	l_{33}	21.4	14.9	9.7	7.35
Total National Product*		Y	9.05	9.35	9.10	9.15

* In thousands of guilders of 1962 per income earner.

second level job; finally, both phenomena may occur. Generally, this situation tends to prevail whenever the supply of lower level educated is not so much above demand, creating relatively small income differences between jobs of the three levels of required schooling. In the case where supply of the less educated is relatively high, their primary income will be depressed and, hence, also their spendable income. Thus, it will be more attractive for part of the group to offer themselves for a job requiring more schooling, even if this by itself increases their labor disutility. In our applications, both cases will be presented in numerical form, which may facilitate the understanding for the two types of conceivable situations.

ACTUAL AND FEASIBLE INCOME INEQUALITY

As announced, the first use made of the model of income distribution sketched before will be called positive and bear on actual and feasible income inequalities. Also, in these cases, the problem posed will be which income inequalities can be explained by given values of the instruments of socio-economic policy. The instruments considered are the tax system and the education system. The former is assumed to be such that differences in spendable incomes between jobs two and one for income earners of first level education will be 85 percent of the differences of their primary incomes and between jobs three and two for income earners of second level education 75 percent of the corresponding differences in primary income.

The education system is presumed to be reflected by the total portions of the active population having finished first, second and third level schooling; these portions will be written as F_1, F_2 and F_3. The results of the use of the model are summarized in table 1, which is largely self-explanatory. Of the four cases shown, Case A coincides with the

TABLE 2

OPTIMAL VALUES OF VARIABLES RELEVANT TO INCOME DISTRIBUTION

Group	b_1 Manpower of Each Level Given and Equal to Initial Values					b_2 Unlimited Shifts Between the Three Levels of Education to Be Possible					Initial		
	l	ϕ	x	t	y	l	ϕ	x	t	y	l	ϕ	y
11	6.1	0.80	8.6	−2.5		7.1	0.835	8.9	−1.8		6.2	0.79	
21	7.7	0.11	10.1	−2.4		—	0.00	.	.		7.9	0.12	
22	12.6	0.035	9.5	3.1	8.9	8.0	0.10	9.8	−1.8	9.15	12.5	0.029	9.05
32	14.1	0.024	10.8	3.3		.	0.00	.	.		14.4	0.03	
33	19.0	0.03	10.4	8.6		9.0	0.065	10.7	−1.7		21.4	0.03	

Symbols: l : primary income; ϕ : portion of labor force in education/job group; x : spendable income; $t = l - x$: tax; y : total product; l, x, t and y in thousands of guilders, 1962.

actual situation in the Netherlands in or around 1962.[14] Case D may be seen as an imaginary case chosen so as to equalize all incomes because, for each level of schooling, supply coincides with demand. Its interesting feature is that it requires less than three times the portion of higher educated individuals than were actually present around 1962. It is also interesting to note that in Case B and even more in Case C income inequalities are considerably lower than in the actual situation A in 1962. Alternative exercises with moderate changes in marginal tax rates have shown a relatively weak influence of existing tax systems on income differences. One possible reason for this result will be discussed.

OPTIMAL INCOME INEQUALITY

Turning now to the normative approach, the problem will be to find the instruments of socio-economic policy conducive to maximum social welfare—defined as the sum total of individual utilities—under the following constraints:

—the production function links factor use with product obtained;

—the balance between supply of, and demand for, manpower either (b_1) separately for three given values of F_1, F_2, F_3 or (b_2) for the sum of all F;

—the balance between production and expenditure from spendable income.

In my technical article "Actual vs. Optimal Income Distribution . . . ,[15] the traditional Lagrangian method has been set out and used to solve the two versions of the optimal problem. Version b_1 considers as given the portions of the labor force with first, second and third level schooling; version b_2 assumes that shifts between these portions are possible without any limitation. Table 2 summarizes the results obtained with the aid of these two policy models.

Due to rounding errors in the computations, done by slide rule, tax figures show differences of one or two decimal places where, in principle, they must be equal—$t_{21} = t_{11}$; $t_{32} = t_{22}$ for b_1; $t_{11} = t_{22} = t_{33}$ for b_2.

We see that optimum b_1 shows small differences in l and ϕ with the initial situation, but large differences in the tax system. For the optimum outcome, taxes must be lump-sum taxes—meaning

14. Income figures are for 1962, education figures for 1960, tax figures for 1966; compare, also, with note 12.

15. Jan Tinbergen, "Actual vs. Optimal Income Distribution in a Three-level Education Model," to be published by the Institute of Economic Statistics, University of Rome, 1974.

that marginal decisions are unaffected by them.[16] In our model, this implies that taxes depend only on the level of education, but not on either the job chosen or the income level. The important practical question arises: in more elaborate models with a larger number of parameters representing quality, can the tax base be determined with sufficient accuracy? Today's accuracy of psycho-technical tests is certainly not sufficient.

Optimum b_2 shows large deviations from the initial situation in primary incomes, namely, a strong reduction of inequalities together with the disappearance of the mixed groups, where job level and education level are different. This is obtained by a size of third level educated manpower 2.2 times the initial size, a size of second level educated manpower 1.7 times the original size and a remaining primary educated group 8.3 percent lower than it was originally. It is interesting that such relatively moderate changes appear sufficient to obtain such a drastic change in primary income distribution. It should be noted that this is not due to our choice of the Cobb-Douglas production function with its high elasticities of substitution between production factors, since a production function without substitution permits any politically desired change in income distribution.

Since in Case b_2 all taxes are negative, one may wonder what the source of such subsidies could be. It so hap-

16. Compare, Jan Tinbergen, "The Theory of the Optimum Régime," in *Selected Papers* (Amsterdam: North Holland, 1959), p. 264 ff.

pens that the total amount of subsidies equals capital income, suggesting that capital income may be used for the financing of subsidies.

Finally, we should observe that the existence of possible limits to the number of people able to absorb a third, or secondary, level education may lead to optimum situations between b_1 and b_2; however, it is striking that the numbers of third level educated in Case b_2 are not unrealistically large; it is smaller than the figure suggested by Case D of table 1.

The impression left by the results is that if demand and supply factors in the markets for productive services were the main factors determining income distribution, a reduction in income inequality should not be too difficult to attain. Even so, a doubling of the portion of manpower with third level education takes time. While in the Netherlands about ten years after the initial situation of our model—that is, in 1972—the number of students has, in fact, risen to twice the initial figure, it will still require about a generation, or a few decades, before the same applies to the labor force as a whole. Over that period, the demand side may also change, however, and the demand for third level educated will probably rise. This would reduce the equalizing tendency emanating from the supply side. Therefore, the next point on our agenda should be to collect evidence about possible changes over time of the exponents in our particular Cobb-Douglas production function, ρ_1, ρ_2 and ρ_3.

The Dialectics of Equality

By Walter A. Weisskopf

ABSTRACT: Equality and inequality are discussed from the philosophical and socio-psychological, rather than from the economic, point of view. Social inequalities are bearable only if they are felt to be legitimate and justifiable in terms of the predominant hierarchy of values. Movements for equality are caused by doubts about the legitimacy of existing inequalities. Modern individualism, libertarianism and equalitarianism were a rebellion against the existing order. In premodern times, inequalities were justified by ascription and were derived from inherent characteristics, such as birth and caste. Industrial society justified inequalities by achievement of economic success. This orientation is reflected in the labor theory of value, as well as in marginalist value theory. In the American creed, equalitarianism was combined with the acceptance of inequalities through the principle of equality of opportunity which justifies inequalities by the assumption of an equal start for everyone. Under the impact of the great depression and of the organizational revolution, economic achievement was replaced by intellectual merit, knowledge and academic credentials as justification for inequalities. Under the impact of growing doubts about this kind of achievement, a new equalitarian trend is under way, supported by the antigrowth and the environmental protection movements, as well as by the tradition of protection for the underprivileged which was always an intrinsic part of the market economy.

Walter A. Weisskopf has been Professor of Economics at Roosevelt University since 1945; he was Chairman of the Department of Economics (1945–1965) and is currently a member of the Board of Trustees of Roosevelt University. Professor Weisskopf has also taught at the University of Omaha, the Central YMCA College in Chicago (1943–1945) and the Salzburg Seminar for American Studies (1952). Born in Vienna, he received a Dr. Juris degree in 1927 from the University of Vienna, but also studied at the Universities of Cambridge and Geneva. He served as a panel member of the War Labor Board of Chicago (1943–1945); currently, he is a member of the American Economic Association, the Association for Humanistic Psychology and the Board of Editors of Journal of Humanistic Psychology. *Professor Weisskopf's publications deal with the interrelations among economics, philosophy and psychology and include* The Psychology of Economics *and* Alienation and Economics.

ECONOMICS developed during a period in which segmentalization became the rule in the social sciences. The fragmented approach makes it difficult for economists to deal with the philosophical, psychological, social, political and economic dimensions of equality and inequality. Yet, the non-economic aspects should be discussed if the purely economic aspects of income inequality are to be understood. The very question of the economic effects of equality or inequality of incomes entails value judgments and transcends, therefore, the realm of economics as it is usually considered. An integrative approach must start with the recognition that equality and inequality are related in dialectical interdependence: they are like two sides of the same coin; they give meaning to each other; one would be senseless without the other.

THE DIALECTICS OF PARTICIPATION-INDIVIDUALIZATION

The equality-inequality dichotomy is one of the many antinomies which beset the human condition. It is related to the antinomy of individualization and participation; this is an existential antinomy, a category of human existence. Man participates in his world, in his environment. He is a part of a whole, a member of a larger entity. This participation is one of the existential roots of the experience of equality. It is the root of the experience of the "I am one with the world," of the "I am thou" and of the unity of all creation. It underlies ideas such as "we are all children of God" and "we are all members of the brotherhood of man."

At the same time, man has the experience of individualization, separateness and distinctness—being one self, and not the other. This is the root of the experience of the I versus the Other, of existing as a person different from other beings and persons. This is the existential source of incomparability and inequality and the idea of the uniqueness of personality—I am I; nothing and no one is, nor can be, like me.

THE SOCIAL DIALECTICS OF EQUALITY

The antinomy of participation and individualization is reflected in man's social existence. Again, one finds centripetal and centrifugal tendencies. On the one hand, men have an innate propensity for solidarity, community and integration and, on the other hand, for separation, distinction and differentiation. Solidarity and community are the basis for the experience of equality. As a member of a family, group, tribe, clan or nation, I am equal to other members; such membership forms a common link which generates the feeling of equality with other members. Each member of a group has common traits with other members. The very concept of society implies an element of equality, consisting in group membership, if nothing else—for example, the concept that "we are all Americans." This element of equality through group membership is enhanced by the inclusion-exclusion principle. A group includes insiders and excludes outsiders; the equality of the insiders is underscored by the inequality, inferiority, of the outsiders.

The centrifugal force in society is related to individualization. In his own life history, and in the history of societies, the individual tends to emancipate himself from the primordial ties with the mother, the parents, the family, the peer group, the home town and even the nation. Self-consciousness leads to a split between individual and group which tends to counteract the experiences of belonging and equality. Insofar as the individual becomes psychologically separated from the community, the common denominator on which equality rests is destroyed. Equality requires comparability; when the individual becomes aware of his separateness and uniqueness, there is no basis for either comparison or equality.

THE HISTORICAL DIALECTICS OF EQUALITY AND INEQUALITY

The conflict between equality and inequality is ineluctable in human existence. However, historical conditions determine when and how this conflict becomes conscious. Under certain historical conditions, there is little awareness of inequalities and, therefore, little desire for equality; under other conditions, existing inequalities are experienced as an intolerable burden and strong equalitarian movements develop. In Western history, such a situation arose in the eighteenth century; during this era, it was assumed that society generates unfreedom and inequalities of power, status and wealth and, thus, destroys the individual's natural state of freedom and equality. This intellectual scheme was developed in the eighteenth century, but had its roots in the thought of the Sophists, the Stoa and Roman law. According to this pattern—clearest in the thought of Locke and Rousseau—the individual surrendered his natural freedom and equality to the state for the sake of economic cooperation and physical safety. This constitutes the famous social contract, which assumes that the accomplishment of common purposes necessitates the voluntary surrender of primary, natural equality and freedom to social inequalities. This ideological scheme underlies most modern thinking about equality and inequality.

The scheme, however, is not borne out by history. Individualism, with its claim to freedom and equality, is a late historical phenomenon. In all cultures, man is originally part of a group, integrated into a community, linked with others and hardly aware of his individual existence. His ties with the group are supported by religious belief, value systems and institutions which are part of an uncritically and unconsciously accepted natural order. The individual becomes aware of himself as a separate entity only when the stable structure of beliefs, values and institutions begins to disintegrate. Then, consciousness awakens and existing institutions are examined by reason. This process may confirm prevailing beliefs, values and institutions. But, sooner or later, it leads to a critique of the existing order and to alienation from it.[1]

This is the point where individualism, libertarianism and equalitarianism emerge. Individualistic and equalitarian thought owes its origin to an intellectual rebellion against the existing order; thus, they began as phenomena of social disintegration and change. Individualism implies a fundamental doubt in the legitimacy and justice of the prevailing social hierarchy. All societies, with the exception of a few small esoteric groups, require some hierarchy of organizational structure with superiority, subordination and a structure of authority, command and obedience. Society, but not community, is synonymous with some unfreedom, inequality, suppression and restriction of individuals. Originally, these restrictions were not experienced as oppressive, because they were presumed to be rooted in divine, or natural, order. When reason is applied to this order, the hierarchy requires rational legitimation and justification; it must appear to conform to principles of justice. In premodern times, such justifi-

1. Walter A. Weisskopf, *Alienation and Economics* (New York: E. P. Dutton, 1971), p. 33 ff.

cation was based on ascription: differentials of power, status and wealth were derived from inherent characteristics such as ancestry, birth or caste; people were privileged or underprivileged because of what they were and not for what they accomplished. During the last four hundred years, modern Western industrial society replaced ascription by achievement: differences were justified by the degree to which different individuals attained social goals and values. Ascriptive aristocracy was replaced by a meritocracy wherein merit consisted of achieving that which society valued most.

It is misleading both to identify inequalities based on achievement with meritocracy and to maintain that inequalities based on ascription have nothing to do with merit. The courtiers in ancient Egypt, the citizens of the Greek Polis, the Senate and the people of Rome, the feudal lords—all groups whose status rested on ascription—considered themselves as the better, more worthy and superior ones and, thus, deserving their privileges because of their inherent merits. In a way, social hierarchies based on ascription are also meritocracies; they rest on the conviction that the existing inequalities are legitimate and just. After all, the Greek word aristocracy means the rule of the best. The difference between ascriptive and achievement-oriented meritocracy lies in the yardstick for merit: in the case of ascription, it is being and belonging to a group; in the case of achievement, it is doing and performing. Hierarchies based on ascription are also more rigid, whereas those based on achievement allow upwards, and downwards, mobility; one can never change what one is, but one can change one's social position by achievement and performance.

Achievement replacing ascription as the legitimizing principle went hand in hand with a class struggle. The bourgeoisie, in its struggle with the aristocracy in England and with the Ancient regime in France, attacked the traditional ascriptive inequalities through their demand for liberty and equality. The ideal of equality had the socio-historical function of attacking the existing inequalities, but it led, in turn, to new inequalities based on achievement.

EQUALITY AND INEQUALITY IN ECONOMICS

The new inequalities are reflected in the history of capitalism and economic thought. The ideas presented by Max Weber, in the *Protestant Ethic and the Spirit of Capitalism*, show the transition from the principle of ascription to the one of achievement. The belief in predestination through the inscrutable counsel of the Lord is ascriptive; one is chosen regardless of one's merit. However, every Calvinist and Puritan tried to prove his salvation by his economic success, achieved by practicing economic virtues: systematic, methodic, unrelenting pursuit of gain combined with intensive impulse control through hard work, thrift, frugality and avoidance of spontaneous enjoyment. Achievement of economic success gradually replaced ascriptive salvation; economic performance became the source of individual worth.

It is important to understand that this transition from an ascriptive to an achievement-oriented society took place hand in hand with the emergence of capitalism; thus, the way for a meritocratic mobile society was opened two hundred years ago. Meritocracy is not an invention of postindustrial society.[2] The achievement orientation of capital-

2. This seems to be the position of Daniel Bell, "Meritocracy and Equality," *Public Interest* 29 (Fall 1972), p. 29 ff.

ism was, and is, supposed to be meritocratic. Merit consists of living up to the work ethic and therefore reaping the reward of one's performance. A change in the basis of merit distinguishes the postindustrial meritocracy of the mid-twentieth century from the bourgeois meritocracy of the nineteenth; the economic virtues have been replaced by the intelligence quotient (IQ) and by educational credentials.

The work and success ethos performed two historical functions: (1) it destroyed the basis for ascriptive inequalities of the old order; (2) it also provided a justification for the new inequalities of wealth and income in the new order of the market economy. The labor theory of value in economic thought reflects this justification.

The pure labor theory of value, as formulated by Adam Smith and Ricardo, justified the inequalities of income. This theory is essentially meritocratic: in an economy of independent producers—without wage labor and without private property of land—prices would reflect differences in effort, measured by labor-time used in production; thus, those who work longer and harder would sell a higher priced product and receive a higher reward. The classics used this theory to justify the existing price system—therefore, Ricardo's desperate, although unsuccessful, attempts to eliminate profits as a determinant of price and his theory of rent which interpreted land income as an effect, rather than a cause, of price.[3] Profit and rent are not earned through labor; therefore, they do not fit into the moral philosophy of the labor value theory. Ricardo thus tried to prove that they were not causal for price differentials. If that were true, such differentials would be caused only by differences in labor-time used in the production of goods; such differentials would be morally justified according to the labor theory of value: more work leads to higher prices and incomes.

Marx used the same theory to castigate the price system. In contrast to Ricardo, he acknowledged the influence of profits on prices. But to Marx, the surplus value—profit—is an unearned increment which the capitalist did not earn by his own labor. Therefore, a profit economy leads to inequalities which are unfair by the standards of the labor theory of value. The union movement and the modern women's liberation movement use the same theory—as in the slogan "equal pay for equal work"—to attain equality. Equality is based on merit and is quite compatible with inequalities of unequal pay for unequal work.

The labor theory of value was later replaced by marginalist value theories. Originally, they also contained the seeds of moral justification of differentials in prices and incomes. When economists state that in a competitive market system everyone's wage, or income, will be equal to one's marginal value product, they actually state: "to each according to his productive contribution." This is a meritocratic justification of economic inequalities.

In the twentieth century, economic thought has become evermore value-neutral and value-empty. Few economists today would openly try to justify wage and income differentials by their proportionality to productive contribution. Their apologetics for the existing income distribution would rest on functional grounds: inequalities are necessary as incentives for increasing the supply of scarce resources. However, the idea that higher income and wealth are deserved and caused by personal

3. Walter A. Weisskopf, *The Psychology of Economics* (Chicago, Ill.: University of Chicago Press, 1955), p. 51 ff.

virtues and higher contributions has been absorbed by popular feeling and vulgar economic philosophizing. Social Darwinism is still very much alive; those who have succeeded in the competitive struggle regard themselves as the fittest and as better than others. This attitude underlies the Nixon administration's attack on the welfare state. The economy is viewed as a meritocracy of the rich; they supposedly deserve their exalted status.

EQUALITY OF OPPORTUNITY

The existing inequalities, however, had to be made compatible with the equalitarian, individualistic and libertarian tradition of the American creed. The combination between egalitarianism and justification of inequalities was achieved by the idea of equality of opportunity. It contains an element of equalitarianism; everybody is supposed to begin at the same starting line; but the inequalities that emerge in the competitive struggle are accepted. The idea of equality of opportunity makes possible the representation of the resulting unequal income distribution as just: because of initial equality, the resulting inequalities are supposedly based on merit.[4]

The idea of equality of opportunity can serve its purpose to justify existing inequalities only if one believes everyone has an equal start and accepts the resulting inequalities as meritorious. Both beliefs are open to grave doubts. There are obvious flaws in the assumption of an equal start; differences in environment, background, education and genes distribute the chances very unevenly, indeed. But the main source of

discontent is the conviction, ever growing in the twentieth century, that the privileges of higher income and wealth are not deserved—that the present form of the free enterprise system is not a meritocracy. Corporate concentration and market power made the inequalities in economic opportunities more visible. The events of the great depression of the 1930s made it obvious that hardly anybody is master of his economic fate and that economic success and failure have little to do with individual merit. Under these circumstances, the Horatio Alger myth and the idea that the higher income receivers are the fittest appeared to be ludicrous. These ideas were supposed to justify economic inequalities, but the underprivileged and the intelligentsia began to reject them. People feel that high incomes are not based on just desert. As long as there was an unspoken, implicit, often unconscious consensus about the justice of income differentials, equalitarianism remained marginal, remedial and ameliorative. When this consensus evaporated, the inequalities lost their psychological base. They can then be maintained only by the power structure of the existing institutions.

MERITOCRACY

A more recent source of discontent with the principle of equal opportunity is found in the changing character of the meritocracy. This term is not usually applied to the merits of the rich and successful, but to what Galbraith calls the "technostructure" and the "education-scientific estate."[5] Previously, merit was based on the virtues of the work ethic and of the adventurous, successful entrepreneur. Since World War II—in what is fashionably called

4. For a critique of the principle of equality of opportunity, see J. H. Schaar, "Equality of Opportunity and Beyond," in *Equality,* ed. J. R. Pennock and J. W. Chapman (New York: Atherton Press, 1967), p. 228 ff.

5. John K. Galbraith, *The New Industrial State* (Boston, Mass.: Houghton, Mifflin, 1967), chps. 8 and 25.

the postindustrial society—merit and differentials in status and power are attributed to the knowledge of the highly educated and trained experts with academic credentials who are supposed to have become the real decision makers and power structure in business, government and even politics. Under present conditions, this further restricts the equal start necessary for real equality of opportunity; higher education and expertise are to many even less accessible than economic success. Equalitarianism, once directed against the rich, is now directed against the status of those with credentials of higher education and expert knowledge.

Trying to justify the existing hierarchy of status and power as an intellectual meritocracy—as does the literary crowd writing in the *Public Interest* [6]— is even less effective than the justification of income differentials on the basis of the work ethic and entrepreneurial success.

First, the trend towards a meritocracy of the intellectual elite has aggravated inequalities in the economy. It has reenforced the dual economy: minority groups have been shut off from the mainstream of the economy; they do not even benefit from expansion and prosperity, because of their lack of background and education. More and more, the better jobs require educational credentials of achievement which these minorities are unable to acquire. Without the certificates they are not needed by the economy. Therefore, they cannot improve their situation by organizing and withholding their services—by strikes. They are not exploited— needed, but underpaid—but discriminated against—discarded, not in demand. This aggravates their unequal status because the system does not pro-

vide any legitimate remedies: they are in the minority, therefore, they have little political power; they do not have an equal start, therefore, they have little upwards mobility. A meritocracy based on IQ and academic credentials condemns these groups to social inferiority.

However, the resentment against the intellectual elite is not confined to the disadvantaged minorities. The resentment is also caused by doubts about the value and meaning of intellectual, white collar work. Recent interviews of blue collar workers in the Boston area have thrown some light on this attitude.[7] After twenty years as a meat-cutter, a blue collar worker—who had been forced to quit high school—became a white collar bank clerk; however, he harbors an innate disrespect for educated white collar work: "these jobs are not real work where you make something—it's just pushing papers." He feels a "revulsion against the work of educated people in the bank, and a feeling that manual labor has more dignity." Children of blue collar workers, with more education than their parents: "feel that they have more opportunity open to them than their manual-laboring parents. At the same time they see their parents' work as intrinsically more interesting and worthwhile . . .". These men see "knowledge through formal education as giving a man the tools for achieving freedom. . . . As things actually stand, however, certified knowledge does not mean dignity . . . it is the reverse, it is sham."

In part, this attitude is a heritage of the industrial society in which production of goods was the main economic activity. It is an attitude reminiscent

6. *Public Interest* 29 (Fall 1972), issue on equality.

7. R. Sennett and J. Cobb, *The Hidden Injuries of Class* (New York: Alfred A. Knopf, 1972), p. 21 ff., from which the following quotations are taken.

of the Marxist glorification of the manual worker as the only real productive factor. However, this traditional belief in the superior dignity of manual work has become amalgamated with a more recent distrust in expertise, intelligent quotients, academic credentials and the achievements of the intelligentsia, in general. The growing resentment of Middle America against the "best and the brightest" seems to bear this out. The issue of postindustrial society is not merely intellectual meritocracy versus equality, as sociologist Daniel Bell maintains, but the growing doubts about the merits of the meritocracy.

Considering the kind of world the experts in science, technology and business have helped to create, these doubts are not without justification. Yet, the source of these doubts lies deeper. They are—consciously or unconsciously— connected with the basic problem of postindustrial society: the longing both for a ground for legitimizing equality and inequality and for the fusion of order and freedom.[8] The postindustrial, meritocratic, intellectual elite owes its high status to its mastery of a restrictive intellectuality of a cognitive, analytical, measuring and technical nature. They use instrumental rationality which can choose means, but can say nothing about ends. This rationality has destroyed a deeper philosophical kind of reason which could deal with ends, goals, purposes and ultimate meanings.[9] The merits of the meritocracy are based on a rationality which makes it impossible to establish standards for any merits, whatsoever. Their high IQs and their academic credentials enable them to serve the existing order,

8. J. Kristol, "Capitalism, Socialism and Nihilism," *Public Interest* 31 (Spring 1973), p. 15.
9. Weisskopf, *Alienation and Economics*, p. 37 ff.

but not to justify it, nor to replace it, by one that can be accepted as legitimate by its citizenry. The hunger for such legitimacy, called by Irving Kristol the dominant political fact in the world of today, cannot be satisfied by the instrumental, technical intellect of the experts. Therefore, their merits are not accepted by the community.

Thus, today's egalitarian resentment of the underprivileged against the privileged is based less on need than on a loss of the belief in the justice, legitimation and justification of existing inequalities. The traditional approach that the starving masses resent the abundance of the rich has become, with some notable exceptions, obsolete in our relatively affluent society. The main cause of egalitarian trends is the disintegration of the belief that the privileges of higher income, wealth and education are based on just desert and merit.

THE TRADITION OF SOCIAL PROTECTION

There is, however, another source of egalitarianism which is related to poverty. It does not originate with the poor, the disadvantaged and the underprivileged, but with society as a whole —or better, with the privileged groups. This is the tradition of charity and compassion and the idea that society has to take care of those who cannot take care of themselves.

In the Middle Ages, the poor were almost exclusively the impotent poor who were not able to support themselves. They were the object of charity which was, and is, a method of practicing a Christian virtue and of assuaging guilt feelings of the privileged. In the free market system, the impotent poor were joined by the able-bodied poor and the unemployed. Various measures were used to force them into employment but they were also made the beneficiaries of charity and compassion through some measure of relief—for example, the allowance system of Speenhamland, 1795. Aside from trying to solve socio-economic problems of poverty, this constituted an enlargement of the group to which charity and compassion was extended from the physically, to the economically, helpless. The reason for this extension was, and is, the guilt feelings of the haves towards the have-nots. This is probably one of the strongest roots of egalitarian welfare measures and of the orientation of social responsibility. Not only does the resentment of the underprivileged, but also the guilt feelings of the haves grow when income differentials are felt to be illegitimate; the less they feel that their privileges are deserved, the more they feel obligated to ameliorate the situation of the poor and underprivileged—for example, as in the 1930s in the United States. It was much less the case early in the nineteenth century when wealth was equated with morality and poverty, with immorality. Thus, demands for a more equal distribution of income originate not merely with those who want more, but also with those who feel badly about having more.

However, there is more to this trend than the guilt feelings of the privileged. The free market system required, almost from its beginnings, a protection of society from the system's detrimental effects. As Karl Polanyi has pointed out, the free market tended to destroy man and his environment by treating labor and land as commodities.[10] When they are used or not used according to the vagaries of the market, human beings and their natural habitat may be injured or destroyed. A countervailing force—which Karl Polanyi calls social

10. K. Polanyi, *The Great Transformation* (New York: Farrar & Rinehart, 1944), part II.

protectionism—was required, including all types of social legislation and welfare measures. Social protectionism forms a necessary counterweight against the free market. Without it, the free market would lose its infra-structure, the supporting framework of a viable society.

Social protectionism, nourished by the Christian tradition of charity and compassion towards the underprivileged, rests squarely on the principle of ascription: we help the disadvantaged not for what they do or achieve, but for what they are—namely, human beings in need. The ascriptive principle has never been completely abandoned as the meritocrats maintain. It has been applied as a countervailing force, as a balance against the ravages wrought by the inequalities of the market economy. Significantly, social protectionism was often supported by non-bourgeois, conservative groups, such as the Tories in England and Bismarck and the Junkers in Germany, and by a growing civil service bureaucracy.

CONCLUSIONS

Where does this kaleidoscopic and dialectical picture leave us, today? The antinomic forces pulling towards greater economic equality, on the one hand, and the counter-tendencies pushing back the equalitarian trend to protect the existing order, on the other hand, are still at work. If the equality-inequality dichotomy is an existential antinomy, the struggle will not cease, whatever the structure of our society and economy. However, the two forces are never in a static equilibrium; there are always trends in one or the other direction. Surface appearances to the contrary, the pendulum will probably swing in a direction of greater equality based on ascription and away from income differentials based on either financial or educational achievement. One of the reasons is that economic growth, at least in the developed countries, may become less and less desirable and possible. Growing affluence makes an increase in the standards of living, in terms of more and more income and wealth, less attractive. This, in turn, may weaken the resistance against measures towards a more equal income distribution, such as a guaranteed minimum income. The economies of the developed countries may turn towards an improvement of the quality of life, which would imply a weakening of the acquisitive ethos. Time and energy—the really scarce resources—may be increasingly devoted to the production of psychic income in the form of playful, artistic and contemplative pursuits to satisfy the higher needs and to games, circuses, fishing and loafing to satisfy lower needs.

The likelihood of such a development is greatly enhanced by the dangers predicted by the ecologists. If population growth, exhaustion of basic resources, pollution and the problems of waste absorption should actually set absolute limits to economic growth, the basic economic orientation of the present economic systems will have to change. Mankind, especially in the West, will have to turn to a life style which consumes less resources and leads to less waste than the present system. Thus, production and income, in the traditional sense, will lose their importance and a more equal distribution of income will be more acceptable merely because there will be fewer uses for money income. The basic values of life may change; market values will have to be replaced by noneconomic values. People will have to pursue goals which will cost more time and energy, but less resources, and will not generate detrimental by-products. Friendship, love, enjoyment of nature, contemplation, mere loafing and so forth will have to become more important than income and purchasing power.

This does not mean an end to inequality, but it will be based on different grounds than income and wealth. Inequalities may be based on noneconomic—such as aesthetic, spiritual and communal—standards. These differences may be based on achievements outside the economic dimension. In the economic field, we may return to the principle of ascription. Income will have to be separated from production of traditional goods and services; meaningful activity will have to be defined as more than the earning of income; and a guaranteed minimum to everyone, with strict regulation of what can be produced and bought without ecological dangers, will have to be instituted. The realm of "goods" will have to be restricted and the realm of "bads" greatly increased. If all this sounds utopian, it is; however, without utopia, there can be no vision and no survival.

The problem of equality is ultimately a philosophical, and not an economic, question. Differences of status, wealth, power, natural endowment and social functions are unavoidable in any society. When people talk about equality and human dignity, they really want acceptance—I shy away from the word love, but that is what it is—in spite of all differences. They want to be accepted and loved as they are, even in spite of what they are. This love and acceptance—Christian theology calls it agape—is not primarily a creation of any social system; it is needed to soften the nonegalitarian harshness of society. This is the real meaning of the longing for a classless society and for a plurality of values. It is expressed beautifully in the brilliant social science fiction of Michael Young:

The classless society would be one which both possessed and acted upon plural values. Were we to evaluate people, not only according to their intelligence and their education, their occupation, and their power, but according to their kindliness and their courage, their imagination and sensitivity, their sympathy and generosity, there could be no classes. Who would be able to say that the scientist was superior to the porter with admirable qualities as a father, the civil servant with unusual skill at gaining prizes superior to the lorry-driver with unusual skill at growing roses? The classless society would also be the tolerant society, in which individual differ-ences were actively encouraged as well as passively tolerated, in which full meaning was at last given to the dignity of man. Every human being would then have equal opportunity, not to rise up in the world in the light of any mathematical measure, but to develop his own special capacities for leading a rich life.[11]

This is, of course, a fable. But where, today, would a description of the ideal be found if not in a fable?

11. M. Young, *The Rise of Meritocracy 1870–2033* (New York: Penguin Books, 1958), p. 169.

Urban Affairs Abstracts

URBAN AFFAIRS ABSTRACTS is *informative*—abstracts inform reader of the suitability of the article to the user's needs.

URBAN AFFAIRS ABSTRACTS is *unique*—UAA is the only weekly abstracting service to cover the urban affairs field.

URBAN AFFAIRS ABSTRACTS is *complete*—UAA provides the user with a complete bibliography of articles relating to the urban affairs field.

URBAN AFFAIRS ABSTRACTS is valuable for its *timeliness*—most abstracts appear within a week of the articles publication.

URBAN AFFAIRS ABSTRACTS provides the user with *easy retrieval*—abstracts include periodical reference including address of periodical.

The **URBAN AFFAIRS ABSTRACTS** is compiled by the NATIONAL LEAGUE OF CITIES and the UNITED STATES CONFERENCE OF MAYORS. This weekly service, which is cumulated quarterly and annually, selects and abstracts articles of general and specific relevance to urban information analysts, from nearly 800 periodicals, newsletters and journals. The periodicals regularly scanned comprise a basic, comprehensive set of current publications on *urban affairs*.

URBAN AFFAIRS ABSTRACTS is arranged according to 50 subject areas including: Community Development, Communications, Criminal Justice, Economic Development, Employment, Environment, Government, Housing, Land Use, Municipal Administration, Public Policy, Social Services and Transportation.

The annual subscription fee of $200.00 includes weekly abstracts, three quarterly cumulations and one annual cumulation.

WHY OTHERS USE URBAN AFFAIRS ABSTRACTS

"URBAN AFFAIRS ABSTRACTS is the only weekly periodical index on the broad subject of urban affairs, so the COG staff relies on UAA to keep them informed on a wide range of interests".
Mary L. Knobbe
Librarian
Metro Washington Council of Governments

"URBAN AFFAIRS ABSTRACTS is an extremely useful tool for keeping up with current trends in the urban affairs field. The currency of the abstracts published cannot be matched by any other abstracting service".
Elizabeth K. Miller
Assistant Librarian
New York University—Washington Square

"URBAN AFFAIRS ABSTRACTS' efficient organization promotes rapid retrieval of information, thus repaying the subscription cost in reduced searching time".
Richard A. Baker
Director of Research
The Government Research Corporation

I am interested in **URBAN AFFAIRS ABSTRACTS**:

☐ 1973 Annual Subscription for $200.00 (includes 52 weekly abstracts, 3 quarterly and 1 annual cumulation)
☐ 1973 Annual Subscription *plus* the 1972 annual cumulation for $225.00*
☐ 1972 Annual Cumulation only for $49.50
☐ Check is enclosed (payable to NLC-USCM)
☐ Bill me
☐ Please send me sample copy

(Special Offer)

URBAN AFFAIRS ABSTRACTS
National League of Cities
U.S. Conference of Mayors
1620 Eye St., N.W.
Washington, D.C. 20006

NAME _____

ORGANIZATION _____

TITLE _____

ADDRESS _____

CITY/STATE/ZIP CODE _____

173b

SOCIAL SCIENCE AND THE NEW SOCIETIES:

Problems in Cross-Cultural Research and Theory Building

Edited by Nancy Hammond

Contributors: Erik Allardt, David E. Apter, Karl W. Deutsch, Max Gluckman, Alex Inkeles, Wilbert E. Moore, Manning Nash, Robert C. North, Peter M. Worsley

SS | SOCIAL SCIENCE RESEARCH BUREAU, MICHIGAN STATE UNIVERSITY
RB | 206 BERKEY HALL ● EAST LANSING ● 1973 $6.00

Urban Studies from Yale

Rio *and* Rome

Two Brazilian Capitals   *Architecture and Urbanism in Rio de Janeiro and Brasilia*
by Norma Evenson
Combining a sympathetic understanding of man's habits and needs as a city user, a year of research in Brazil, and her skills as an architectural historian, Norma Evenson here examines Brazilian urban design and architecture in terms of the modern development of the old capital, Rio de Janeiro, and the new capital, Brasilia. In her analysis of Rio and Brasilia as both functioning cities and symbolic capitals, she illuminates the problems and processes — political, economic, and social — of urbanization in a developing country. Over 200 plans and photographs, many never before published, enhance the text. $19.50

Planning the Eternal City   *Roman Politics and Planning Since World War II*
by Robert C. Fried
There is much to be learned about urban planning and politics from this study of Rome, a very old city now overwhelmed by a very new city that has problems familiar to urbanists all over the world. Mr. Fried's purpose here is to assess the effectiveness of postwar planning in Rome and to identify the factors shaping its performance level. Planning is presented as a complex configuration of bureaucratic organization, inter-governmental relations, private interests, and party politics. Much more than a narrow study of planning, the book provides a comprehensive description of Roman civic culture in all its aspects and sharpens our understanding of what managing cities in the twentieth century is all about. $13.50

Yale University Press   New Haven and London

Kindly mention THE ANNALS *when writing to advertisers*

Book Department

INTERNATIONAL RELATIONS, LATIN AMERICA AND AFRICA

RUSSELL D. BUHITE. *Patrick J. Hurley and American Foreign Policy.* Pp. xiv, 342. Ithaca, N.Y.: Cornell University Press, 1973. $14.50.

Patrick Hurley's seemed a typical American success story—tall, handsome, son of immigrants, self-made millionaire from poor origins on the western frontier. Today his reputation stands and, mainly, falls on his China mission in 1944–45, where he attempted to weld Nationalists and Communists into a unified government with a common war effort. But this book recalls the many other foreign policy problems with which he was involved. As Hoover's secretary of war, as private citizen and then as presidential envoy, Hurley dealt with the American responses to colonial dependence for independence in Asia; with foreign expropriations of American oil holdings and with the problems of the Middle East—getting embroiled with American Zionists on the question of Palestine. The failure in China brought his widely publicized blasts at "pro-communist" elements at the State Department, igniting the right-wing frenzy over who lost China that led to McCarthyism. He helped mangle the careers of the department's China specialists, crippling our China policy for a generation.

Professor Buhite offers a careful, balanced account of Hurley's career, well researched and nicely written. He distributes praise and blame fairly, noting Hurley's better qualities and achievements without slighting the warts prominent in other portraits. He shows that Hurley's unsuccessful China policies often originated with his superiors, while his misconceptions were sometimes widely shared.

Hurley brought his general mistrust of State to one of the few places where it was inappropriate—the "China hands" were dedicated, knowledgeable and articulate—but he displayed no real aptitude for the job at hand. They responded by pressing views contrary to Hurley's, to the point of open disloyalty to him, and he could and did respond vindictively. Buhite spots their occasionally unprofessional conduct and sometimes questionable analyses of Chinese communism, but stresses Hurley's ignorance, misjudgments and extreme sensitivity to criticism. He sensibly avoids sensationalizing the Mao request in 1945 to visit Washington—unlike Allen Whiting and Barbara Tuchman—and corrects the belief that Hurley never pressured Chiang to reform.

Hurley's denigration of the China specialists has been reversed and their view of Hurley as a Colonel Blimp is now widely accepted. Buhite finds him "superficially spectacular but actually rather

174

average." Prior to arriving in Chungking, he managed a successful career on the fringes of important events. Career and reputation tarnished badly in the harsh China mission and its aftermath, making him one of the foremost victims of the China tangle.

PATRICK M. MORGAN
Department of Political Science
Washington State University
Pullman

ELBAKI HERMASSI. *Leadership and National Development in North Africa. A Comparative Study.* Pp. 256. Berkeley: University of California Press, 1972. $8.50.

This study is intended as a contribution to social theory on change and transformation, or as the blurb puts it, "a paradigm for the study of the formation and transformation of national societies"—in Morocco, Tunisia, and Algeria, in this case. As such, the study has considerable merit. A secondary objective, a critique of modernization theory as an approach to an understanding of events in the new states, is less well articulated. In all respects, heavy reliance is placed on Clifford Geertz, and on Huntington, Shils and Apter, to a lesser extent. Here a major criticism is in order.

The author treats purely theoretical excursions as substitutes for empirical proof, expending much effort forcing reality into extremely fragile theoretical vessels, prepared by others, with reference to substantially different contents. Moreover, one is left to wonder whether a sociologist should attempt to study a subject by reference to socio-political theory, when his data actually demand to be tested against socio-economic theory.

Another major and serious weakness lies in the absence of the kind of social statistics one would expect in an elite study. The tables are too superficial to convey much to the expert: it is doubtful that they convey much to the layman. However, to the reader who is capable of separating the gems from the surrounding theoretical waste, the study has much to offer.

Hermassi acquaints us—and he does this exceedingly well—with the historical processes which link, or may link, traditional feuds and internecine wars with the contemporary anti-colonial—and eventually anti-capitalist—movement as in Algeria. In the course of this analysis, the author uncovers a hitherto less well observed specimen—the French "conqueror-ethnologist," a mercenary who, under cover of military preoccupation, works to rearrange ethnic reality to suit colonial designs and purposes. The shock-effect and the consequences of the culture contact between France and North Africa are well covered. However, one question, clearly posed by the evidence offered in this study, remains unanswered: why the same France which is said to have generated forces to destroy traditional culture in the *maghreb* in its favor, would at the same time—through its own political Left in the metropole—train the North African cadres which would eventually reduce French influence in the area. Indeed, was the principal training ground for the final assault on French hegemony in North Africa not metropolitan France herself?

One of the mottoes used in the study is an Algerian proverb: "He who wishes to understand too much will die of anger." The author's attempt to understand his subject by use of paradigms, and scientific inquiry and models, will surely cause him much upset. One can only hope that he is satisfied—without attempting to understand what it all means—to have created, alas with a rather broad brush, a first-rate panorama of the struggles surrounding elite formation, first and second-phase governance and independence in the three *maghribi* states.

HENRY L. BRETTON
Department of Political Science
State University College
Brockport
New York

RAOUF KAHIL. *Inflation and Economic Development in Brazil, 1946–1963.* Pp. v, 357. New York: Oxford University Press, 1973. $35.25.

This book is an important contribution toward the analysis and interpretation of the sources of inflation in low-income nations. Raouf Kahil, who is associated with Oxford University's Institute of Economics and Statistics, sets out to test the "structuralist thesis" in the light of the Brazilian experience from 1945 to 1963. During the early 1960s, a period marked by an accelerated rise in prices in Brazil, two major factions within Brazil's *tecnico* group contended for intellectual and political recognition: the "structuralists"—under the leadership of Celso Furtado—and the "monetarists"—of whom Roberto Campos was the principal spokesman. As Kahil points out, the "structuralists" maintain that inflation in poor countries arises from deepseated "structural factors and the resistance they oppose to development."

In testing the view that inflation in low-income nations like Brazil requires a special theory to explain it, the author has organized the book into four parts: (1) "Geographical and Historical Background," (2) "The Role of Structural Factors," (3) "The Four Phases of Inflation, 1945–63" and (4) "Conclusions." His findings tend to support the "monetarist" position: "No compelling force stemming from structural weaknesses in the economy ever played a significant role in the persistence of aggravation of inflationary pressure" (p. 330). He demonstrates that the general concepts of demand inflation and cost inflation apply to Brazil. Behind the immediate causes of persistent and often violent inflation—such as, public deficits, too rapid expansion of bank credit and exaggerated increases in legal minimum wages—he finds political motivations and pressures.

Brazil's more recent experience, under the tutelary guidance of the "monetarist" *tecnicos*, demonstrates that rapid and accelerated real growth is compatible with a diminishing rate of inflation. This experience also suggests that "structural bottlenecks" are the consequence of faulty economic policies, such as over-valued exchange rates and distortion of the price system generally.

ERIC N. BAKLANOFF
Dean for International
  Studies and Programs
University of Alabama

PETER Y. MEDDING. *Mapai in Israel: Political Organization and Government in a New Society.* Pp. 326. Cambridge, England: At the University Press, 1972. $16.50.

The subject of this book is Mapai, the political party which has kept the reins of Israeli government in its hands, from the beginning of the state's creation and until this very day. The fact that the party has achieved all this in a democratic setting, thus not following the totalitarian path of most new nations, is the central problem that the author attempts to solve throughout the book. To do this, Dr. Medding gives us an analytical account of Mapai's history, from its inception in the pre-state period to its recent merger with two splinter groups and its continuation under the new name of the Israeli Labor Party. The chief emphasis in this account is on Mapai's ability to change and adapt in accordance with an ever changing reality.

In order to account for Mapai's adaptive capacity, Medding turns to its organizational structure, to which he devotes the bulk of the book. He first analyzes the internal structure of the party; the various techniques utilized by Mapai to retain control over its varied constituency; the way in which the parts are woven together to form an organizational unit and, most importantly, how the decision-making process works. Medding then discusses the way in which Mapai deals with, and retains control of, the Histadrut—the labor union complex—and the governmental machinery.

In evaluating this study, let it be said at the outset that it is a first rate work. However, despite its general high quality, Medding's *Mapai* has a few serious shortcomings, two of which ought to be mentioned. The first is a discrepancy between facts cited and conclusions drawn; the second is the absence of a broader theoretical frame.

Throughout the book one finds a marked tendency to paint Mapai in considerably brighter democratic and public-minded colors than seems warranted by the reported details. For example, chapter 10, "The Party Machine," contains a vivid and detailed account of the Mapai machine's long and successful struggle against democratization of the party's structure and process. We find here all the familiar trimmings of machine techniques, such as the carrot and stick of patronage, open booth elections, attended by party activists who are also the voters' employers and who openly oversee the way their employees vote, and so forth. Yet, in the conclusion of the chapter, Medding attempts to soften the impact by pointing out that "the machine strove valiantly to achieve widespread representation of the diverse social forces" and that while the machine helps the established leadership retain its power, it does not attempt to dictate policy. As if sensing something wrong with the latter point, Medding adds: "Of course in the long run the two are interwoven . . . But this is clearly different from influence and control arising from actual participation in the decision making process" (p. 160). (Attention all critics of Chicago's Boss!) Somehow, the sweetener is less than convincing.

A similar situation exists in chapter 2, "Depoliticisation and State Integration," which deals with the painful process of handing over party-controlled areas to the state. The discussion ranges from areas such as defence—which the party has totally released, through spheres like employment—in which the depolitization is only partial, to health services—over which the party still holds a firm grip via the unions. While the author concedes the general desirability of depolitization, in evaluating Mapai's performance he, curiously, applies a double standard. Whereas the relinquishment of the army is praised as "a vital contribution to state building," the retention of party control over other areas is viewed as contributing to "effectiveness of policy making . . . that would have been much more difficult if not impossible outside the Mapai framework." Again, the reader remains somewhat puzzled.

Other examples of the same sort abound in the other chapters, culminating in the conclusion, where Medding assures us that even Mapai's charismatic leaders have led the party "in the direction of firmly established competitive democratic procedures" (p. 300). This conclusion is hardly warranted, in view of such phenomena as Mapai's exclusion of other parties from competition wherever possible (chap. 2), or their utilization of political power to send an appropriate portion of new immigrants to Mapai-controlled settlements where they are involuntarily harnessed into the party network, without consulting the immigrants or giving them a chance to choose. Then there is the decade long succession struggle, so vividly described in chapter 12, the chief earmark of which is the Old Guard's reluctance to allow an internal democratic process to determine the path of succession. None of these seem to be steps toward "competitive democratic procedures."

One more point before leaving this subject: one may wholeheartedly agree with the author that "if the main aim of political parties . . . is to win power in elections and retain it, then Mapai was clearly a highly successful party." What is rather difficult to accept is the disclaimer that, while "there may be other criteria of success"—normative in nature—which if applied may indicate a lack of success, "throughout our analysis we have not been concerned with this type of question" (p. 299). The continuous concern with democratic process, representation and public mindedness; the apologetics that follow every instance of undemocratic and party centered, rather than public centered, behavior; all these squarely contradict Medding's claim of not being concerned with the normative dimension.

Medding's second sin is one of omission. Except for a few opening pages of trite jargon on the function of political parties, the book does not contain any serious theoretical discussion worth mentioning. This is, first of all, an unfulfilled promise. The subtitle *Political Organization and Government in a New Society* as well as the first paragraph of chapter 1—which states the problems of Israel's success in remaining a democratic society—at least imply the promise of a return to the problems. Unfortunately, the subjects are never mentioned again.

Then, promise or not, the failure to offer some broader theoretical insights on the basis of one's findings, constitutes an opportunity missed. This is especially regretful in view of the fact that the case at hand is fascinating and makes one ponder a whole range of problems. What do the flaws of Israeli democracy suggest? Is the only alternative to dictatorship in new societies a partial democracy that allows one party to keep its grip on the governmental machinery through economic and political control, if without resort to the familiar oppressive techniques employed by totalitarian regimes?

Yet, the shortcomings notwithstanding, *Mapai* is an outstanding book, one that no serious student, either of Israel or of political process in new nations in general, will want to omit from his reading list. The reader, however, will be well advised not to seek shortcuts by reading chapter conclusions, and—should he happen to be a theory lover—he will just have to engage in some speculations of his own.

ISRAEL RUBIN

Department of Sociology
Cleveland State University
Ohio

CHRISTIAN P. POTHOLM. *Swaziland: The Dynamics of Political Modernization.* Pp. ix, 183. Berkeley: University of California Press, 1972. $8.00.

Case studies of African political systems have provided the reader with some of the most useful analyses of African politics. They permit the scholar to immerse himself in a manageable area and study the people—or a limited number of peoples—and the influences which mold their political order. The factors unique to the area surface naturally and this is appropriate. Africa—particularly underdeveloped in its communications technology—did not permit a long-term habitual communication among African peoples, with a consequent interpenetration of political cultures which would make comparison particularly insightful.

A case study of Swaziland, unencumbered by the need to impose comparison, is especially suitable. Swaziland is one of the smallest African countries in size and population: it is virtually a uni-ethnic state. The Swazi people make up over 90 percent of the population. Sobhuza II has led his people since 1921—probably the longest reigning leader of our day. The territory is substantially isolated from black Africa and faces the need to develop a tolerable *modus vivendi* with the larger, more powerful white supremacist states which surround it. What emerges from Potholm's analysis is the accounting of a rather successful adaptation of Swaziland, under the leadership of the Ngwenyama, Sobhuza II, to its surroundings and to the demands for modernization. Since independence, in 1968, Swaziland has been stable and relatively prosperous. Stability is not solely a product of ethnic identity and reverence for traditional forms. It arises more importantly—the author convincingly argues—from Sobhuza's leadership, his ability to adapt Swazi tribal forms to the needs of political modernization and the pursuit of development. In contrast to tribal leadership elsewhere, Sobhuza's is dynamic and modernist. Thus the Swazi tribal structure is placed at the disposal of the Imbokodvo National Movement to serve the needs of the political process and to assure the effective functioning of Swaziland's political institutions. Sobhuza's talent for political maneuver leads him into alliance with the European community, to overcome African opposition parties, but later, to refuse Europeans a privileged political status when this would affront the sense of African interest and propriety.

Similarly, in seeking a place for Swaziland in a South African dominated subsystem, Sobhuza utilized South Africa's assistance where this was essential, adapted Swaziland's policy to the realities of South African power but maximized the distance between South Africa—with its hated social order—and Swaziland.

Potholm's study is concise, rather than exhaustive. It presents data sparingly, and as they are related to its main theme—the chieftancy as an effective agent of political modernization. Therefore, the question which naturally arises is: what happens after this aging monarch departs the scene? Here perhaps there is too great an emphasis on the formal complexities of succession and the personalities who could replace Sobhuza. It is not illogical that the system itself will facilitate succession successfully.

This volume has a dual utility. It enhances our understanding of Swaziland and provides us with important case study in the transformation of a traditional leadership into an agent of political modernization.

J. LEO CEFKIN
Colorado State University
Fort Collins

MARSHALL R. SINGER. *Weak States in a World of Powers: The Dynamics of International Relationships.* Pp xii, 431. New York: The Free Press, 1972. $10.95.

Violating, as they do, the egalitarian and democratic concepts prevalent in this country, the realities of international power are very difficult for many people to accept. These realities also "violate the nationalist pride of the leaders and intellectuals of most countries of the world." During the Suez crisis of 1956, prime ministers Eden and Mollet of England and France "refused to see that reality and believed that they could make policy for their countries independently of the wishes of the United States. Both men were wrong, and their errors not only brought disaster to their policy, but ended their political careers as well."

Dr. Singer's personal background—as a professor at the University of Pittsburgh, and years of residence in Ceylon and Malaysia—could not help but underscore in his studies of the dynamics of international relationships, the facts, the sentiments, the traditions, and the imagery of the strong-weak confrontation. In a treatment replete with charts and statistics that add to the impact of the author's theories, the use of jargon and of visual aids in the chapter headed "Perceptions And Communications" is somewhat overdone. Some charts have whorls, convoluted lines and arrows pointing to upsidedown clichés that are far from helpful. A stronger chapter, "Economic Ties,"

explores the realities and explodes some of the mythology of colonialism, mercantilism, imperialism, and the fetish of economic development. In considering foreign aid, Professor Singer shows that there are results tending to support the political regime of the recipient nation— even if it might be militaristic, corrupt, inept or dictatorial—and sometimes binds the recipient to the donor, with unhappy consequences. Contrary to a favorite concept of many Americans, "many weaker countries prefer bilateral foreign aid to multilateral aid, because they often believe they can get more by direct negotiation . . . than they could from a multilateral organization."

Military ties of varied nature yield a network of ties between the weak and the strong. Membership in multilateral collective security agreements—NATO and SEATO—partnership in bilateral defense arrangements—Philippine-U.S.—the protective umbrella of nuclear weaponry—U.S.-Japan—the sale of arms—U.S.-Israel—military grants—to Iran, Indonesia, and others—and training of indigenous military personnel—Latin America—are assessed in depth.

Dr. Singer makes the point that attractive, rather than coercive, instruments of power can be effective in advancing the interests of the larger power in its dealings with a small one. President Truman's assistance "to Yugoslavia to prevent that country from being reabsorbed by the Soviet Bloc" is cited as proof. But in further discussion of attractive or coercive measures in Vietnam, Dr. Singer raises more questions than answers, with confusing results.

After pointing out that institutions for political and economic gain by cooperating weaker states are already in existence, the author concludes that "in many cases there is considerable evidence that the elites are at best ambivalent in wanting to see their countries develop rapidly." Thus, Singer's final conclusion is hardly more than wishful thinking: "Under the guidance of responsible leaders that demand [for change] could be the engine that propels weaker countries out of a condition of poverty and dependence into one of affluence and interdependence."

WILLARD BARBER
University of Maryland

DAVID WELSH. *The Roots of Segregation: Native Policy in Colonial Natal, 1845–1910.* Pp. x, 381. New York: Oxford University Press, 1972. $14.00.

This is a valuable contribution. It would be easy enough to criticize the volume for what it does not include, especially, perhaps, the virtual absence of significant comparisons, save the brief references to the neighboring Cape Colony. This lack is hinted at in the foreword, where the point is made that the reader can be left to draw comparisons. Another criticism which has been made is that the book says little, if anything, that is fundamentally new. It is, however, the great merit of Dr. Welsh's study that he has deliberately set limits to his enquiry, in order to explore at depth evidence which has not been examined, or thoroughly examined, by other scholars.

The central purpose of the book is to depict and to analyze the policies of the governments of colonial Natal towards the African subject peoples, mostly Zulu-speaking, for whom they assumed responsibility. Whenever possible the responses of the Africans are examined and explained. The scope of the study is confined to the successive phases of colonial administration between 1845 and 1910, the years 1856 and 1893 being notable for the constitutional advances of representative and responsible government. Zululand, not annexed to Natal until 1897, is largely excluded.

It will come as no surprise to those with even a slight knowledge of African government in colonial Natal that the center-piece of the whole book is Shepstone—Sir Theophilus to the British, after being knighted by Queen Victoria; Somtsewu to the Zulu. As Dr. Welsh writes of the year 1875, "Shepstone was unquestionably the most famous African administrator of nineteenth century South Africa, and his influence lived on after him in Natal and

elsewhere in South Africa. For thirty years Shepstone and 'native policy' had been virtually synonymous in Natal." Save for Sir Benjamin Pine (1850–1855), who opposed Shepstone and advocated "an entire change" in the system—notably the breaking up of what he called the "enormous and unwieldy" reservations of land and the institution of a form of individual tenure—all the many heads of government who came and went were generally content to accept the specialist guidance of an officer fluent in the Zulu language and possessed of a genuine if conservative understanding of African custom and tradition.

It is disappointing, if understandable, that so little evidence could be discovered of contemporary African views on policy and practice towards themselves during the earlier decades, notably while Shepstone was still in office. It is at this point that the question arises whether, given the shortage of material from Africans, the author might not have done more to bring out the composition and attitudes of the different elements within the dominant white minority. These were so influential over crucial aspects of "native policy," as well as over matters such as the immigration of Indians, workers and merchants—in and after 1860—and too little is said about them, as well as about India and indirect rule.

Another major query which arose in this reviewer's mind was whether Dr. Welsh—possibly in a praiseworthy effort to be self-critical of the British role in South Africa—does not err a little towards falling over backwards to assert that the antecedents of present day apartheid in South Africa "are to be found in Natal rather than in any of the other provinces." Many of us have gone out of our way to direct severe and critical attention—and for much the same reasons—to precisely the same institutions and practices of colonial Natal which he examines, and many of us have also highlighted serious defects in British imperial policy elsewhere and in local administrative policy in colonies other than Africa. But apartheid and its antecedents do demand more specific analysis and the careful establishment of more precise links or causations than he offers, or can offer, in the study of a period which terminates in 1910. Natal's native policy was never monolithic, unilinear or coherent. Rather did it approximate to the United States' Indian policy of which Commissioner Francis A. Walker wrote in 1872: "that the Indian policy, so called, of the Government, is a policy, and it is not a policy, or rather it consists of two policies, entirely distinct, seeming, indeed, to be mutually inconsistent."

Yet the very questions raised by this book testify to its overall worth and to the sustained stimulus of its many important chapters. The wealth of evidence contained in the text is most valuable, and the skillful and modest interpretations are impressive.

KENNETH KIRKWOOD
Oxford University
England

ASIA

S. M. BURKE. *Pakistan's Foreign Policy: An Historical Analysis.* Pp. ix, 432. London: Oxford University Press, 1973. $20.25.

Samuel M. Burke is eminently qualified to explore the subject of the foreign policy of Pakistan. He was a member of the Indian Civil Service and—according to biographical material available—joined the Pakistan Foreign Service in 1948, after a brief interlude in India following partition. He served in a number of senior positions in Washington, London, Ottawa and elsewhere, prior to his retirement in the mid-sixties. Since that time he has been at the University of Minnesota in that institution's South Asia program. He thus combines practical experience with the opportunity for scholarly reflection. It might also be noted that he was one of the very few non-Muslims in the Pakistan service and is perhaps able to see his subject with a view less fully reactive to India than some of his colleagues. He is, so far as this reviewer is aware, the first career

officer of the Pakistan Foreign Service to attempt an analysis.

Burke has organized his study into three chronological segments: (1) the "non-aligned years," 1947–1953; (2) the "aligned years," 1954–1962; and (3) the "reappraisal," 1963–1970. He adds a postscript to cover the events of 1971, ending in the division of Pakistan. Each of the segments is further divided into chapters covering a specific aspect of Pakistan's foreign relations. The chapters, again, are divided into topical units and here the publisher would have performed a useful service had he indicated the chapter divisions in the table of contents. The organizational system is excellent. A user of the book can find a full discussion of each subject with a minimum of effort. Burke's effort to make each division stand by itself does lead to considerable repetition when the work is read as a whole, but this turns to advantage when the work is used for reference.

Burke has documented carefully and has used a vast amount of material, although at times he cites secondary sources, especially *Dawn,* when it would appear that the primary material would have been rather readily available. One notices this most often with speech or press conference remarks by American officials, whose statements are likely to be available verbatime in such sources as the *Department of State Bulletin.* The reliance on primary and secondary documentary sources tends to limit the personal recollections of Burke the diplomat. This has both an advantage and a disadvantage It does permit the researcher to go further into a subject, but the dimension of a practitioner turned scholar is missing.

No writer on Pakistan's foreign policy, not even one who has been detached from day to day operation for several years, can avoid the role of India in the formulation and practice of that policy. Burke spends much space on actions taken in New Delhi and relates, seemingly, every step taken by Karachi and Islamabad to some event in the Indian capital. Alignment is a response to possible Indian attempts to end the existence of Pakistan. Ayub's bilateralism is a response to Western military assistance to India and to the Sino-Indian conflict which preceded the Western action. The disputes on the questions of the division of the waters of the Indus and the Ganges and the primary concern of Pakistan—Kashmir—dominate the book, as they have dominated Pakistan's international position. Burke weaves Indo-Pakistan relations well into the broader picture of his country's relations with the three great powers and the Muslim world. It would seem, however, that some greater attention might have been paid to domestic forces impinging on foreign affairs. *Dawn* is frequently cited and usually went along with whatever the government of the day was proposing. But also influential was the *Pakistan Times* and under the leftists Iftikharuddin, Faiz and Mazhar Ali its views were very different and exerted some influence. Different points of view in the two wings are mentioned, but could have been explored further.

As a chronology, the work is excellent and will be an indispensable volume for those who study the interplay of the countries of South Asia. As an analysis, it relies almost exclusively on Hindu-Muslim differences—as perhaps it must, for those differences are the very *raison d'etre* of Pakistan.

CRAIG BAXTER
United States Military Academy
West Point
New York

MALCOLM CALDWELL and LEK TAN. *Cambodia in the Southeast Asian War*. Preface by Noam Chomsky. Pp. xiii, 447. New York: Monthly Review Press, 1973. $15.00.

Messers. Caldwell and Lek Tan have put together their view of Cambodian history, recent events in Southeast Asia and United States foreign policy with the apparent intent of revealing extraordinary and, one might conclude, quite predictable parallels. This book was undertaken, if the statements on the dust jacket are accurate, ". . . in the spring of 1970, immediately on the heels of the latest American violation of all accepted principles of international law." That is, after the intervention by the United States and allied forces in Cambodia of April 30, 1970.

It is clear, from the start, that this book was written with little or no pretense of scholarly neutrality, disinterest or objectivity. The authors, including the author of the preface, would appear to be writing to an ideological, rather than a scholarly purpose. Indeed, the book is replete with the appropriate catch phrases and cue words, so beloved by neo-Marxists. If glorification of the Khmer Rouge and vilification of all others on the tragic stage of Southeast Asia—save the Viet Minh and Viet Cong—are of interest, then this book should do the trick.

In short, Caldwell and Lek Tan have produced an ideological polemic based upon the conspiracy theory of history and the economics of exploitation and imperialism. The authors seize any pretext to connect useful historical events to the objective development of American imperialism, no matter how tenuous such connections might be. This book is not recommended to the serious student of Southeast Asia, unless he or she wishes to become familiar with the ideological perspectives involved. The book, however, may be suggested to idle students of political psychology.

DAVID R. WEAVER
Department of Political Science
Saginaw Valley College
University Center
Michigan

CHALMERS JOHNSON. *Ideology and Politics in Contemporary China*. Pp. xii, 390. Seattle: University of Washington Press, 1973. $15.00.

This is a must book, prepared under the joint auspices of the American Council of Learned Societies and the Social Science Research Council. It contains ten excellent articles contributed by eminent scholars and is introduced and edited by Professor Chalmers Johnson. Rather than commenting on each essay in a short review, we merely describe the contents of the book as a whole. It is cohesively organized, has a good index, some tables and adequate footnotes.

The first of the three parts into which the book is divided, entitled "Origins and Functions," discusses whether political ideology precedes or follows political activity and whether the two interact on each other and evolve as a movement grows and attains state control. The functions that ideology performed for the Chinese Communists are described, particularly those relating to legitimacy; identity; solidarity; agitation; communication and goal-specification. Mao's reliance on the masses, his belief in protracted struggle and his own attacks on ideological dogmatism are also examined.

Part 2, "Ideology and the Intellectuals," offers a case study of the intellectual process involved in the formation of an ideology which served as a new source of identity for intellectuals alienated from their society's traditions. Also considered are the formulation and development of political concepts which have shaped the perception and policies of the Chinese Communist elite to the present day. The suggestion is that the Chinese intelligentsia, after debating the merits of socialism, democracy and communism—despite their doubts—embraced the last. However, their support was not unequivocal and was not to the ultimate communist objective of one party rule. There is an analysis of why certain ideological principles were reinforced by the failure of the Great Leap Forward and why it was determined that the cultural revolution was necessary to accomplish further political change and halt the slide toward revisionism.

Part 3, "Maoism in Action," relates how previous politics or changes in political environment led to changes in ideology and to a new ideological critique of the past. There is interestingly detailed the effect of Mao's policies on the role of scientists and technicians, and the resultant ideology of mass participation in technological innovation as a method of incorporating native elements into the creation of a modern state. As to foreign policy, the failure to promote revolution abroad—largely through the exporting of Mao's

thought—is ascribed in great part to the non-recognition of the factor of modern nationalism. Finally, the basic question is posed whether the Chinese will continue to conceive of a life in terms of permanent self-criticism and unremitting struggle.

Of necessity, there is some overlapping of ideas and repetition of material. This book, nevertheless, deserves the close attention of all serious students of the Chinese scene and of all those generally interested in the subject of ideology and politics

ALBERT E. KANE

Washington, D.C.

NALINI RANJAN CHAKRAVATI. *The Indian Minority in Burma: The Rise and Decline of an Immigrant Community.* Pp. xxiv, 214. New York: Oxford University Press, 1971. $10.50.

This study is a fine piece of scholarly work. The writer was for many years a resident of Burma and he served as a high-level government servant of the country. The study utilizes most of the relevant sources of data, reports, and books, but, strangely, reference is made to not a single journal article.

The study is a chronicle of the rise of the Indian community in Burma which grew to over one million in 1931 when it constituted 7 percent of the total population of the country. Between 1931 and 1941 the Indian population declined by about 10 percent and an exodus of nearly half a million Indians through overland routes to India took place early in 1942, and many thousands died enroute.

The Indians were never much loved by the Burmese, and the Indians did little to change and did much to strengthen these feelings of the Burmese. Even after the Indian community in Burma had existed for over one hundred years, most of the Indians had not made up their minds to settle permanently in Burma and had not brought their families with them.

During the 1930s there were numerous claims made that the Indians were "flooding into Burma . . . swamping the Burmese . . . squeezing them out of their own country." Chakravarti emphasizes that alarm at Indian immigration was stimulated by virtue of the great concentration of Indians in Rangoon, the country's capital, which had become virtually an Indian city. It might be mentioned in addition that the Indians along with the Europeans and Chinese, controlled much of the country's finance, trade, and industry. The reviewer found, for example, that in 1921, of the 738 industry establishments with ten or more workers on the payroll, in Burma, 42 percent had European or Anglo-Indian, and 33 percent had Indian or Chinese supervisory and technical staff. This is merely one indication of the fact that the Burmese were not masters of their own house.

The long period of subjugation under the British and their retinue and the inferior economic position of the Burmese, the misery of the great depression, and rising resentment toward the foreigners, resulted finally in 1938 in the eruption of violence. However, the violence was directed neither against the imperial rulers of the country, nor against the Chinese, but was directed against the Indians who, in the eyes of the Burmese, represented one of the main causes of the misery, and primary impediment to improvement of their meager lot. The Indians were resented, not only because there were so many of them, but also because they were money-lenders who charged exorbitant rates of interest and dispossessed the Burmese of their land and other wealth, and paradoxically, they also resented them because so many of the Indians were poor and formed a large labor pool available at cheap wages which undercut the Burmese who were less willing to work at arduous tasks for little pay.

Furthermore, the Indians were resented because they never assimilated—unlike the Chinese many of whom intermarried with the Burmese. And they were resented because when Burmese nationalism was on the rise they continued to insist that "as Indians, they had a special position, requiring special safeguards. . . . The Indians insisted upon separate representation in the new legislative assembly. They organized themselves in separate political parties." They even argued for the continued adherence of Burma to India.

Burmese politicians exploited the rising resentment towards the Indians. There were riots and pogroms, discriminatory legislation was passed, the immigration of Indians was severely curtailed, all this while the British still ruled. With the withdrawal of the British and the occupation by the Japanese, hundreds of thousands of Indians fled Burma to return to India. After independence, they continued to emigrate to India or Pakistan under "increasingly intensive efforts to liquidate their presence in Burma." How many remain in Burma is not known, but the reviewer found that the 1953 census round of Burma showed that only 9.8 percent of the country's urban population was Indian or Pakistani, and the corresponding figures for Rangoon was 19 percent, whereas in 1931 these figures were 30.5 and 53.2 percent, respectively.

The tragedy of the Indian community in Burma is not only that hundreds of thousands of Indians and Pakistanis suffered and lost so much, but that they contributed to bring this upon themselves. The tragedy for Burma is not only that it lost so many who contributed so much, and could have continued to contribute more, to the country, but that the Burmese themselves, to a considerable measure, brought about that tragedy.

The tragic play enacted in Burma—and elsewhere—is most recently being reenacted in Uganda with the only difference being that in the Burmese play no actor comparable to the Uganda President, Idi Amin Dada, had performed.

SURINDER K. MEHTA
Department of Sociology
University of Massachusetts
Amherst

JOHN NORTON MOORE. *Law and the Indochina War.* Pp. xxxiii, 794. Princeton, N.J.: Princeton University Press, 1972. $22.50. Paperbound, $9.50.

No more Vietnams? This book speaks for those international scholars who advocate regulating intervention in internal wars, but who also see such intervention as essential to maintaining world order. "In a revolutionary international system constrained by the fear of mutual nuclear annihilation, proxy wars, indirect aggressions . . . covert and limited coercion have become the principal modes of violent conflict" (p. 79). Can such conflict be regulated?

The prospects are not bright. In a series of detailed analyses, Professor Moore concludes that international law has been far too preoccupied with the search for "one rule applicable to all forms of civil strife" (p. 113), its machinery too *ad hoc* for fact-finding and its institutions plagued by weak sanctioning processes. The central thesis of the book—that the Vietnam war "has served as a catalyst for rapid development in the international law of non-intervention"—is disproved by the very force of the analyses of why intervention is both intractable to effective regulation and a crucial ingredient of strategies designed to maintain world order. While President Nixon would find these conclusions reassuring, Richard Falk and much of the United States Congress would not.

Indeed, nearly all of the material has been published elsewhere—though typographical and syntactical errors are legion—sparking lively debate among international legal scholars and between critics and defenders of the Vietnam war. By codifying the arguments used to justify American involvement in Indochina, the book contributes a legal prolegomenon to the Nixon doctrine. By defending the legality of intervention in Indochina based on an all too glib acceptance of the State Department's version of the facts and an all too selective reading of the Pentagon Papers, Professor Moore's analysis compellingly demonstrates how international legal norms are perverted, when used to justify intervention rather than to regulate it. At nearly every turn, for example, assistance to governments, deemed crucial to maintaining world order, is sanctioned, while similar assistance furnished to those challenging the legitimacy of such governments is considered contrary to the principles of international law and order. Thus, to the dictum: "non-intervention is about the same thing as intervention," this book adds that this is particularly so when world order is at stake. As such, it is required reading for those who would defend the Nixon doctrine, and more important, a must for those who would oppose it in its incipiency, unmask its rhetoric, and continue to warn that Vietnam could happen again.

ALLAN E. GOODMAN
Department of Government
  and International Relations
Clark University
Worcester
Massachusetts

MOHUN RAM. *Maoism in India*. Pp. 196. New York: Barnes & Noble, 1972. $7.50.

TAUFIQ AHMAD NIZAMI. *The Communist Party and India's Foreign Policy*. Pp. 282. New York: Barnes and Noble, 1972. $11.50.

No serious student of current affairs can ignore the Communist movement in India. Notwithstanding the factionalized and somewhat failure ridden history of the Communist Part of India (CPI), neither its influence on Indian policies nor its potential for the future are negligible. And despite the dominance of the Congress Party before and since independence, it has yet to demonstrate convincingly that parliamentary democracy and a mixed economy can surmount the social and economic problems of a developing country. We welcome, therefore, several recent publications on communism in India, to supplement old reliables by Kautsky, and Windmiller and Overstreet. Of the two books under review, one is a stimulating account of how the Maoist strategy of people's wars has fared in India, and the other, a less than successful attempt at tracing the attitude of the CPI towards Indian foreign policy.

Mohan Ram is personally involved with his subject and so writes with a certain passion. Perhaps he overestimates his readers' familiarity with the people, events and places he mentions, thus sacrificing clarity. But this might be expected in a slim volume, attempting more than narrative history. What Mohun Ram tries to do is assess the evolution and potential in India of the revolutionary strategy, known now as Maoism. He explains the line of the Communist Party of China (CPC) on India. This was based on Lin Piao's thesis of 1965 on violent revolution throughout the Third World, and led to Chinese recognition of the CPI (Marxist-Leninist) as India's only genuine communist party. Some of the ideological differences between the CPC and the Communist Party of the Soviet Union (CPSU) are spelled out, since the CPC advocated a radical alternative to Soviet supported national democracy and peaceful transition in India. However, this is not the best book available on the triangular relationship between China, India and the Soviet Union.

In continuation of his earlier work, *Indian Communism—Split Within a Split,* 1969, Mohun Ram concentrates on divisions within the leftist movement of the CPI. Doctrinal disputes riddled the CPI, as they did the international communist movement—Soviet revisionism being cast as villain in both. The 1964 creation of the CPI (Marxist) was followed by a further leftward split when the 1967 uprisings of Naxalbari and Srikakulam had been finally crushed. Yet even the CPI (Marxist-Leninist), created in April 1969, lacked the support of all Indian Maoists; to the bafflement of the CPC, among others, it was fragmented from birth. Mohun Ram's apparent preoccupation with the absence of a unified tactical line, leads him to describe events as they appeared to different communist leaders. That approach obviates a more penetrating socioeconomic analysis for the failure of a peoples war so far. Interestingly, Kerala is scarcely mentioned. Chapters on the Naxalbari and Srikakulam movements point out lessons, such as lack of strong organization or mass base, too much formalism, and too little implementation of programs. No solutions are offered for these weaknesses—found alike in the present ruler and rebels of India. Nor is the question posed: how is Maoism to succeed without an authentic Mao-type Indian leader?

The conclusion points out stresses created by state intervention in the economy, India's relative dependence on the super powers, as well as by the Green Revolution. Like many others, Mohun Ram sees a revolutionary potential in the contemporary Indian scene. This could be harnessed by a party functioning outside the parliamentary system and uniting the urban and rural proletariats. However, he wonders, as we do, whether the Indian Maoists will prove equal to the challenge.

Taufiq Nizami's revised dissertation suffers primarily from lack of guidance in its preparation. Its quality could have been improved by deeper research, interviews, and by focusing more closely on the CPI itself. Descriptions-cum-justifications of India's official foreign policy hardly need repeating, especially when given without clarification on how, why, or if at all, the government position was modified by CPI criticism or influence. The CPI's pronouncements on international issues are duly recorded, but we miss analysis of their precise origins or effects. Intriguing questions are, surprisingly, left untackled: by what mechanism do the Soviet Union or China ensure CPI adherence to their world stances? What are the differences on foreign policy between the three different CPI's? How would Indian foreign relations actually be altered if the communists were in control?

Editorially, we suggest cutting most of the etceteras, unscrambling the chronology and consolidating discussion of topics such as the German question. But there is much promising material in this book, and a good revision could transform it from being disappointing to being satisfying.

SURJIT MANSINGH

Delhi University
India

EUROPE

ROBERT H. BECK. *Change and Harmonization in European Education.* Pp. 206. Minneapolis: University of Minnesota Press, 1971. $8.50.

That there is a significant international interest in Europe-wide cooperation in sociopolitical, economic, legal, educational, and other affairs is evident—among other indications—from the publication by the European Community Institute for University Studies of a 335 page volume, *Etudes Universitaires sur l'Integration Européen* (1972). An examination of the quadrilingual references in the section on education, culture and research in this compilation, reveals the uniqueness of the study by Beck, Professor of Education at the University of Minnesota. What he has done, is to present in compact form an analysis of the tendencies, since 1945, toward educational cooperation, coordination, integration, unity and, indeed, "harmonization"—a less familiar synonym—with reference to the impact of such efforts on school reform in west Europe, particularly in West Germany and Sweden.

To Beck, educational harmonization signifies the agreement by European educators "on how to cope with certain common, critical issues," including the policy that "training in other countries should be equivalent to one's own" (p. vii). He highlights various developments along these lines, such as, intergovernmental and interministerial organizations—which meet periodically to deal with educational issues and problems—international schools; the borrowing of innovations by countries, so as to make their school systems more similar than different; the movement toward the revision of textbooks in literature and the social studies; the growth of language instruction, and others. Not that all elements in the process of harmonization are handicap-free; language, for example, frequently involves intranational and international tensions and conflicts. A "frank recognition" of the inherent difficulties in the linguistic situation is a necessity "if we are to be realistic about the chances of harmonization in European education" (p. 43).

The author deals with various problems on a European, or at least a west European, scale and at times considers the other side of the continent. Among the issues are the rising demands for, and en-rollments in, secondary and higher education, with the pressures toward social and educational equality; better vocational-technical instruction and guidance and system-wide educational reform. He makes an effort to present and analyze the data in comparative perspective—briefly, as in the case of teacher education (pp. 123–125), but more substantially in the contrast of school reform (pp. 142–163).

Beck's book is a compact, convenient, competent introduction to some recent developments in several west European school systems, as well as to a variety of educational interrelationships. Because of its limited size, it cannot be expected to be comprehensive. It would be desirable for Professor Beck to build upon this volume and produce one which is more thoroughgoing, with additional historical context—on textbook revision, for instance—and free from periodic elementary content (such as, p. 62) and occasional misprints (such as, pp. viii, 114, 115).

WILLIAM W. BRICKMAN
Graduate School of Education
University of Pennsylvania

CHARLES E. BOHLEN. *Witness to History, 1929–1969*. Pp. xiv, 562. New York: W. W. Norton, 1973. $12.50.

Charles E. Bohlen entered the Foreign Service in 1929, and chose to specialize on Russia. In 1934, he arrived in Moscow with the first American ambassador to the Soviet regime. "The Soviet Union," he writes, "became the central focus of my life in the Foreign Service," and it, too, is the central focus of these engrossing "reminiscences and observations," covering almost forty years. Only one chapter out of twenty-nine is devoted to his five years as ambassador to France in the 1960s and one to his "exile in Manila" as ambassador.

Thus Soviet-American relationships dominate this memoir. Bohlen was witness to every important development in these. In Moscow in the 1930s, he observed the purge trials and the evolution of the Nazi-Soviet collaboration. Through the Second World War and afterwards, Bohlen served the presidents and secretaries of state at the foreign ministry and major summit meetings, including the famous trio of

Teheran, Yalta and Potsdam. Surviving an assault by the Senate's primitives, as Dean Acheson labeled them, Bohlen was ambassador to Russia from 1953 to 1956, in the critical years of change after Stalin and at the time of the Hungarian revolution.

Bohlen's account provides historians, both professional and lay, with a rich source of information. Some of it is new, but he does not stray significantly from the official versions of relationships. Most valuable are his judgments and insights.

A few should be noted. President Roosevelt's "greatest single mistake . . . was his insistence on the doctrine of unconditional surrender. . . ." Avoiding war and doing anything to preserve the Soviet system are the "two cardinal rules of Soviet diplomacy." He believes that the basics of the system have not changed. "The fact of the matter is," he writes, "that ideology is just as important today as it was in 1934, when I first stepped on Russian soil." "Just as Bolshevik ideology has remained intact, so the political structure of the Soviet Union remains virtually unchanged." And "it is my gloomy conclusion that the United States faces decades of uneasy relations with the Soviet Union."

Bohlen has an immense affection for the Russian people. We learn a lot about them. But never was he ever invited to a private home: among Russians, he had no friends, only acquaintances.

Two other features of the book should absorb the .reader. One is the author's appraisal of every significant American and foreign personality he encountered—Bullitt, Davies, Hopkins, Presidents Roosevelt through Johnson, Churchill, the secretaries of state, Stalin, Khrushchev and DeGaulle, among dozens.

The other is the continuing thread of how a public servant goes about the business of learning about a closed system. He has to be a detective, picking up bits of information here and there, reading for nuances between the lines of pronouncements in the Soviet controlled press, and sharing generously with other diplomats. Particularly intriguing is Bohlen's account

of his friendship with a free spirit in the Nazi embassy who kept him informed of the Nazi-Soviet negotiations. The book is a fine tribute to the quality and integrity of the Foreign Service.

HOLBERT N. CARROLL
Department of Political Science
University of Pittsburgh

FREDERICK B. CHARY. *The Bulgarian Jews and the Final Solution, 1940–1944.* Pp. xiv, 246. Pittsburgh: University of Pittsburgh Press, 1972. $9.95.

WILLIAM O. McCAGG, JR. *Jewish Nobles and Geniuses in Modern Hungary.* Pp. 254. New York: Columbia University Press, 1972. $9.00.

It is now more than twenty-five years since the Nazis committed what Adolf Eichmann himself called "one of the greatest crimes in human history," with the systematic murder of Europe's Jewish population. It is only in recent years, however, that objective scholarship has become strongly involved in researching aspects of the life and death of European Jewry, particularly East German Jewry. It has taken this long just to overcome the psychic hesitations, implanted in the collective academic community by the traumatic ramifications of the Holocaust. The erstwhile pioneers in Holocaust research—men like Gerald Reitlinger, Isaiah Trunk, Raul Hilberg, Leon Poliakov, Yehuda Bauer, Nathan Eck, and their colleagues—are finally being augmented by a new generation of scholars, not necessarily young, whose readiness to enter into this "valley of the shadow of death" has now belatedly reached the active stage. Due to the enormous academic research potential contained in the "final solution" process, we can now realistically expect a steady growth in the amount of energy that will be invested in this area of study in the near future.

In *The Bulgarian Jews and the Final Solution, 1940–44*, Professor Frederick Chary presents a comprehensive portrait of the experiences of the Jewish population of Bulgaria during those terrible years. Since the Bulgarian experience was largely a "benevolent" one—seventeen thousand were killed, while forty-five thousand remained alive—Chary adopts as his overarching framework the rhetorical question: "Who saved the Bulgarian Jews?" He presents for analysis the two major schools of response to this question and then advances a third probable cause—one which his own researches have led him to adopt decisively. One school of thought—that of Natan Grinberg—emphasized the enlightened and militant role of the Bulgarian masses in preventing the active collaboration of King Boris' government with the Nazi murder plans. The second major approach—Benjamin Arditi—dwelt on the basically ethical intentions of King Boris, and his shrewd handling of the German demands and pressures for the "resettlement" of the Bulgarian Jews.

Chary refutes these generalizations with the convincing observations that there were very enlightened masses elsewhere in occupied Europe that did not succeed in saving their Jewish populations—such as in Holland and Greece—and that there were some particularly malevolent tyrants in whose realms Jews were not successfully eliminated—as in Laval's France, Quisling's Norway and Mussolini's Italy. He then offers his own explanation for the central question: "The Bulgarian Jews, like a great many Rumanian and Italian Jews, and all of the Finnish Jews, were saved because these countries were *allied* to the Reich rather than defeated by it" [italics added] (p. 194). Because of the added levels of negotiation that were necessary between Germany and her allied autonomous satellites, these nations were able to bargain, postpone and watch the shifting tides of war. In Bulgaria's case, Stalingrad, North Africa, and the other turning points were closely watched by King Boris and his associates, and the survival of the Jews became an item that could carry bargaining points in negotiations with the allies, concerning Bulgaria's options in the post-war world. Chary's conclusions thus coincide with the similar judgments made by the main-stream Holocaust scholars—Bauer, Feingold, Goldhagen and Hilberg.

Professor McCagg's book does not purport to deal with the Nazi Holocaust at all, yet in the final analysis, one of its major conclusions does come to rest on the circumstances of the Hungarian participation in the Nazi's destruction of its Jewish population. The book devotes most of its bulk to a captivating analysis of the historical and economic factors that produced Hungary's Jewish business elite in the nineteenth and twentieth centuries. It draws heavily on archival materials and develops a plausible hypothesis for the Jewish participation in the economic modernization, that took place in Hungary from 1848 to 1918.

The ennoblement of many of the leading Jews during this period, for a variety of reasons, and usually after they abandoned their formal Jewish identity, was clearly a logical development in this well-documented progression. Professor McCagg, however, has sought to go considerably beyond this theme. As the title of the book indicates, he has sought to draw a parallel between the rise of the ennobled Jewish businessmen and the growth of a generation of Hungarian Jewish scientific geniuses, such as Edward Teller, Theodore von Karman, John von Neumann, Georg von Hevesy, Leo Szilard, and so forth: "It is improbable . . . that the same factors which drew Jewish capitalists into ennoblement, and indeed, their ennoblement itself, contributed also to the formation of the Hungarian scientific geniuses" (p. 109).

In his effort to draw this parallel, Professor McCagg seems to have developed an artificial and inadequate connection. Using his own lines of development, the factors that produced the "geniuses" appear quite different from those that fostered the ennobled capitalists. The motifs of modernization, westernization and economic nationalism that developed the acculturated, integrated and eventually ennobled Jewish business elite did, indeed, produce the families of the geniuses. Thereupon, however, a new set of factors, by Professor McCagg's own analysis, gave rise to those free souls, with their broad horizons and unlimited *lebensraum* for their talents.

McCagg describes most suggestively some of the circumstances that produced these Hungarian men of talent: the Budapest *Minta*—model gymnasium—and its great teachers, orginated by von Karman's father; the *Eotvos* annual prize competition; the regular opportunities to study abroad at Vienna, Gottingen, Leipzig and so forth. In addition to these, he adds the decisive point that "in our opinion best accounts for the emergence of the whole galaxy . . . his immigration under special circumstances" (p. 217). The brilliant young men among them habitually left Hungary for advanced training throughout the nineteenth and twentieth centuries, and they were able to do so comfortably, even in the Hitler era, longer and with greater safety than any other Jewish refugee group, since Hitler's "final solution" came to Hungarian Jewry only in 1944, whereas it had overtaken all other Jews in Nazi Europe in 1942–43: ". . . the Hungarian scientists are numberous on the international scene above all because, by quirk of fate, emigration was clearly advisable for them earlier, and comfortably possible for them later than for other East European intellectuals" (p. 229). These factors are true enough, but the link-up of the nobles on the one hand, and the geniuses on the other remains an apparently unnecessary connection in what is otherwise an engrossing and well-researched work.

HERBERT ROSENBLUM
Associate Dean
Hebrew College
Brookline
Massachusetts

LOUIS M. CULLEN. *An Economic History of Ireland Since 1660.* New York: Barnes & Noble, 1973. $8.50.

Since George O'Brien published his three volumes on the economic history of Ireland in the seventeenth, eighteenth and early nineteenth centuries, fifty years ago, a number of articles and monographs have re-interpreted various aspects of Irish economic life since 1660. However, until Dr. Cullen, no one has tried to pull the threads together and present a continuous coherent picture of Irish economic development in modern times. Since his outline history arises out of his earlier work, which concentrated on eighteenth-century Ireland, it is perhaps inevitable that the weight of his discussion is concerned with this century and the remainder of the period between 1660 and 1971 gets briefer treatment. In particular, two chapters and fifty pages are devoted to the sixty-three years between 1730 and 1793, whereas the forty-nine years since 1922 are dismissed in seventeen pages. His story is of the evolution of Ireland from an underdeveloped economy in the sixteenth century— by means of the establishment of manufacturing industries, such as woolen and linen textiles, shipbuilding, whiskey and brewing and the expansion of agricultural production, both for overseas markets—to a position in 1913 where the remarkably high proportion of 50 percent of its agricultural and industrial output was exported. Checked by the contraction of world trade between the wars, Irish prosperity since 1945 has continued to depend, not only on maintaining, but on expanding exports.

Brief though his account is, Dr. Cullen is a cool and almost detached revisionist, with an attitude to the Irish past far removed from the current violence of Belfast and Londonderry. He argues, for example, that the Cattle Acts did not spring from English policy towards Ireland but were the product of the pressure of vested interests; that the Navigation Acts did not adversely affect Irish consumption of colonial produce nor prevent the growth of a significant volume of trade between Ireland and the colonies. Nor did the woolen industry, he suggests, decline in the later seventeenth century as disastrously as is sometimes held. On smuggling, he reiterates his familiar view that it was of modest significance. He argues, too, that the attempts to restrict land ownership by Catholics in the eighteenth century were unenforceable; that, the years of falling prices apart, the condition of rural Ireland in the pre-Famine decades has been painted too darkly; that the rapid rise in population in Ireland 1740–1840 should be seen as part of a Europe-wide phenomenon and that even if the Famine had not intervened, a decline in Irish population in the later nineteenth century was inevitable. But refreshing as all this iconoclasm is, in setting out his views in prose which is sometimes less than lively, Dr. Cullen does not indicate how far his revisionism is accepted. He does, however, provide a useful, if selective, bibliography and a brief but welcome note on primary sources, to aid any who may wish to take the subject further. If this interpretation of the Irish past will not entirely gain universal acceptance, nevertheless we now have a modern single-volume account of Irish economic history which pays regard to economic, rather than to political factors.

W. E. MINCHINTON
University of Exeter
England

PHILIP DARBY. *British Defence Policy East of Suez, 1947–1968.* Pp. xiv, 366. New York: Oxford University Press, 1973. $21.00.

In December 1962, Mr. Dean Acheson created a considerable stir in Britain by saying that the country "has lost an empire and has not yet found a role." Perhaps, however, she could have better been described as someone who, not yet having grasped that she needed a new role in the world, was not looking for one. For, as Mr. Darby makes plain in his well-researched and clearly-written book, the ideas of an earlier age continued to hold sway long after the foundation for them had been surrendered. The old Indian Empire passed out of Britain's control in 1947, and with it went the basis of her position as the dominant state from the Persian Gulf to Australia. But throughout the next two decades, she continued to think in imperial terms, and it was not until January 1968—Black Tuesday as the day was known in the Ministry of Defence—that the prime minister announced that British forces east of Suez would be withdrawn by the end of 1971. Britain had finally renounced her claim to be a world power. But even then, the decision was brought about primarily by reduced economic circumstances rather than by a revised intellectual appreciation of her situation.

There were, of course, other factors which contributed to this postponed response to changed reality. Britain's involvement in various Asian crises helped her to jog along in her pragmatic way. Long-term thinking was discouraged, not only by the natural forces of inertia, but also by frequent changes at the Ministry of Defence and perhaps, the author suggests, by the cabinet system itself. The armed services, not surprisingly, spoke up for the maintenance of their former place in the scheme of things and much keen inter-service rivalry stood in the way of coherent overall analysis of their role. On the other hand, change was facilitated by the successful domestic pressures of the late 1950s for the ending of the draft; the lesson of Vietnam in the mid-sixties and, at the same time, the increasing lure of Europe. Britain's self image was, after all, beginning to alter Up to this point she had tried to maintain her old posture within a changing environment, by varying her defence policy in ways which, in theory, were less than fundamental. Mr. Darby skillfully guides his readers through them all and shows how, in the end, Britain abandoned the emotional heritage of Empire and cut her coat according to her cloth. His book is required reading for all students of British defence and foreign policy in the post-war years.

ALAN JAMES
London School of Economics

EUGENE DAVIDSON. *The Nuremberg Fallacy: Wars and War Crimes Since World War II.* Pp. xii, 331. New York: Macmillan, 1973. $9.95.

Eugene Davidson's monograph is an attempt to analyze the relevance of the principles of the 1946 Nuremberg War Crimes Tribunal to post-World War II international affairs. Davidson seeks to examine the causes and methods of warfare in five major post-World War II conflicts and to use his findings in these five case studies to draw general conclusions about the meaning of Nuremberg principles, for the modern world. It will come as no surprise to readers of this book that Davidson finds that the Nuremberg principles have neither helped to limit warfare, nor to reduce atrocities. Torture of prisoners, slaughter of civilian populations and terrorist bombing have, if anything, greatly increased in number, since 1945.

Davidson's book is, on the whole, a rather disappointing monograph. Although his intentions were good and his theme was highly worthwhile, the book lacks organization and synthesis. His subject matter is too diverse, and he does not provide enough comparative conclusions to prove his thesis. The monograph does, however, provide a wealth of detail about five highly significant cases of aggression in the contemporary era, and it does raise questions about the nature and causes of modern aggression, which scholars of modern international affairs will find illuminating.

Davidson's general conclusions about the five case studies in the monograph, alone, make this a very valuable book. These case studies of contemporary aggression consist of: the Arab-Israeli wars; French warfare in Algeria; the Suez crisis and the ensuing warfare; warfare in Indochina since 1945 and Russian aggression in Czechoslovakia in 1968. Although he fails to synthesize his material, Davidson does provide the interested reader with many controversial judgments about five very violent episodes in twentieth century international affairs. Readers of this work will find it to be rich in relevant detail, filled with controversial viewpoints, well documented and assiduously researched.

JOHN STANLEY WOZNIAK
Dunkirk
New York

JOSEPH R. FISZMAN. *Revolution and Tradition in People's Poland: Education and Socialization.* Pp. xxii, 382. Princeton, N.J.: Princeton University Press, 1973. $15.00.

It must be made quite clear at the outset that, despite the apparent specialist nature of this book, it is more far-reaching in its aims and more ambitious in its task than the title implies.

In essence, Professor Fiszman seeks to juxtapose the "traditional personality type" against some "socialist personality type" and examine the transition, or otherwise, from the former to the latter. This requires a study of the socialization process, as well as the socializers, and to this end we are presented with a very detailed, thoroughly researched and stimulating portrait of the Polish teaching profession and educational system.

It becomes clear that the teaching profession, although prestigious as a whole, is itself internally differentiated along several dimensions: (1) urban versus rural, (2) higher and lower education, (3) specialists versus educators, and (4) those engaged in general education preparing students for university entrance and those employed in vocational training. With reference to the last discussion, this book is particularly timely since the recent Committee of Experts on Education set up by the Central Committee of the Polish United Workers Party in the wake of the workers' riots in 1970, recommended the merging of these disparate groups, which had, until the present, succeeded in maintaining social divisions.

The attitude surveys delivered by Polish sociologists, and supplemented by Professor Fiszman's own in-depth interviews, probe the extent of persistence or change in values relating to sex, religion and the Church, and technical-industrial culture. It is a pity that the last of these is given the least space, since the tenacity of humanist tradition, in the face of the socialist emphasis upon industrialization, is clearly one of the most compelling features of Polish society.

The most satisfying section of the book is the extensive coverage of what it is to be a teacher at the interface of traditional society going through the modernization process. The small town atmosphere, steeped in intrigue—social as well as political—and fraught with danger—even to the extent of assassination—all contribute to make the life of a teacher lonely, problematic and, despite social recognition, highly unrewarding. Contrary to popular opinion in the West, the Church in Poland does present grave obstacles to the Communist socializers. To read of complaints concerning discrimination against party members by Catholic cliques is indeed enlightening. Throughout the book, we are presented with records of interviews, where we learn, for example, that the questions set in school examinations in pre-socialist Poland (1938) do not differ from those asked in 1966, and here we come to the nub of the problem. Whatever else this book does succeed in, the fundamental question as to how the traditional Polish intelligentsia was able to maintain its hold over the educational system, despite the latter's intense "statization," under twenty-five years of party rule is left unanswered.

G. KOLANKIEWICZ
Department of Sociology
University of Essex
England

SHMUEL GALAI. *The Liberation Movement in Russia 1900–1905.* Pp. x, 325. New York: Cambridge University Press, 1973. $22.50.

The domestic "national liberation struggle" of imperial Russia, in the first years of the twentieth century, derived its strength from three social sources. The first stemmed from aristocratic elements dedicated to improving the operation of the zemstvos, established in 1864 to provide a framework for local government in thirty-four provinces, following the serf emancipation of 1861. Independent Slavophile elements, led by Dmitrii Shipov, pioneered private congresses of zemstvo leaders in 1896. In 1898 they founded an informal leadership group, Symposium (*Besada*), to protect the zemstvos from a hostile bureaucracy, in hopes of forestalling a revolution. Shipov, however, was relegated to the background in 1905, as the technical specialists employed by the zemstvos—and the educated professions, the "democratic intelligentsia," generally—assumed ascendency in the movement, demanding that the autocracy be limited by a central, elected, representative body. A third source of leadership was provided by former independent Marxists—such as

E. Kuskova, S. Prokopovich and Peter Struve—the latter of whom edited the emigré newspaper *Liberation* (1902) in Germany, on funds contributed clandestinely from zemstvo circles.

Continuing the counter-reform policies of Alexander III, the government of Nicholas II further restricted the powers of the zemstvos, decreed the forcible conscription of dissident students and brutally dispersed a public protest called by the Writers' Union in St. Petersburg in 1901. A majority of opposition groups, except Social Democrats, met in Switzerland at Schaffhausen in July, 1903, to form an umbrella leadership as the Union of Liberation. As the Japanese war moved from defeat to catastrophe, other white-collar pressure groups were initiated and a conference in Paris in September, 1904—again without Social Democratic participation—agreed to cooperate in the campaign against absolutism. A successful banquet campaign in November-December 1904 shook the self-confidence of the government, to the point at which Bloody Sunday was possible. Subsequently, the ranks of the liberation movement were split by the Bulygin Rescript, which envisaged an elected consultative body. After the Treaty of Portsmouth was signed in August, 1905, renewed student pressure in the universities and a railroad strike escalated rapidly into a general strike. Yielding to Witte, Nicholas issued the October Manifesto, which appeared to represent a commitment to constitutional government.

The present study by Shmuel Galai—currently at Tel-Aviv University—is a revised version of his London dissertation, supervised by Leonard Schapiro. The book is based on a thorough and detailed study of non-archival sources. The role of the Symposium is clarified more than heretofore. Although this study tends to confirm the existing picture of the liberation movement, it supersedes preceding research and will undoubtedly become the standard work on the subject.

DALE T. LABELLE
Russian Institute
Columbia University
New York

CORNELIA GERSTENMAIER. *The Voices of the Silent.* Pp. 592. New York: Hart, 1972. $10.00.

This book is divided into two approximately equal parts: a discursive, roughly chronological, account of the development of the current "intellectual opposition" within the Soviet Union, and a set of documents illustrating this opposition. The historical section seems to have been rather hastily pulled together and does not show any marked degree of political or literary insight. It has been translated and proofread with equal haste and lack of care; there is at least one unbelievable misprint—"doctors" where the context obviously calls for "factors." As to facts, the historical section did not reveal anything new to this reviewer, who does not by any means consider himself a specialist in Soviet internal dissent. The author consciously limits her field by leaving out of consideration both specifically religious dissent and nationalistic agitation by non-Russians—including, in the Soviet context, the Jews. Even so, the people she deals with are a very mixed bag, politically, morally and psychologically. They run all the way from individuals of unquestionable courage and integrity—Solzhenitsyn, Aleksandr Ginzburg, Larisa Daniel—to borderline madmen—or jokers—like Anatoly Kuznetsov and Andrei Amalrik, to, quite possibly, a few out and out opportunists. To treat all of these people successfully, in one frame of reference, would take a great deal more intellectual muscle than the author apparently possesses.

The document section is more worthwhile and contains, in fact, much useful material—although the extensive selections from the Ginzburg "White Book" on the Siniavskii-Daniel trial, which was widely circulated in this country, could well have been omitted. Many of the documents are quoted from the Russian emigré journals *Grani* and *Possey*; from West German newspapers like *Der Spiegel,* and from various anthologies published in Germany and the Netherlands during the late sixties. A minor difficulty arises from the fact that there is no indication, in many cases, as to whether this material has been translated directly out of Russian, or through German. The book, as a whole, is marred by various editorial errors, such as the fact that the system for translating Russian words is not consistent: apparently the publishers merely took over the European system used in the original, but omitted the diacriticals, without which this system makes no sense whatever.

Gerstenmaier has probably performed a service by gathering together a large body of *samizdat* and protest documents in compact form, but this large and fascinating body of literature still awaits even the beginning of a definitive interpretation. In conclusion, the reviewer would like to suggest a distinction—which Garstenmaier unfortunately obscures—between the Soviet "loyal opposition," which takes its stand on the—often mangled—letter of the Soviet Constitution, and the conscious revolutionaries, who want the Soviet Union to have a form of government different from what the Constitution calls for. It seems clear that any intervention from the West, on behalf of the latter, represents a political act, rather than a purely humanitarian one and will appear morally ambiguous in view of the increasing scope and intensity of political surveillance, for example, in this country.

STEPHEN P. DUNN
Highgate Road Social Science
Research Station
Berkeley
California

JEROME M. GILISON. *British and Soviet Politics: A Study of Legitimacy and Convergence.* Pp. 186. Baltimore, Md.: The Johns Hopkins University Press, 1972. $8.50.

ROBERT RHODES JAMES. *Ambitions and Realities.* Pp. 311. New York: Harper and Row, 1972. $8.95.

To a practicing politician, the very name political scientist is a self-contradiction. The attempts to give to the study of political institutions and activities a predictable form by empirical study shows signs of falling flat on its face; at the same time, the older established sociology of politics, through the study of governmental and party structure, is mostly carried out by those with no inside experience and therefore misses the vital element of human motivation. As Mr. Rhodes James remarks in his attractive essay "politics is a very human business."

It is the failure to deal with the effect of people on politics, and politics on people, that makes Professor Gilison's book so arid. His hypothesis is that the Soviet and British political systems, already similar in many respects, are converging. He admits that there are limits to that convergence and, in fact, it would be possible to argue from much of his own text that the systems are so different, both in structure and action, that the limits are very narrow.

On this, opinions will vary according to the criteria by which the comparison is judged. Of course in any modern mass industrial society there are similar problems of economic management and technological choice; and, whatever the new revolutionists may say, equally, any complex society must have a hierarchical structure of government with professional elites in the upper ranks. Professor Gilison rightly draws attention to the part taken by political parties in creating the consensus by which a system of government is legitimized; but governments were accepted by their peoples—either out of tradition, fear, or a mixture of both—before political parties were ever thought of. It is a gross exaggeration to suggest that, because governments in both Great Britain and the Soviet Union sponsor most legislation which their legislative bodies then approve and because the British political parties are constrained by external factors and the need to win the central voter from developing radically opposing policies, there is therefore little practical difference between the two systems. The difference between a single state party supposedly representing the peoples' will and two or more parties competing for popular support is the difference between totalitarian and liberal democracy, with all that flows from the former of oppression and suppression and from the latter of protection of individual rights.

Professor Gilison, while admitting that the Soviet system has led to a bureaucratic conservatism, underestimates the amount of change that a two-party system can achieve. The changes that have taken place in Britain since the war, though not revolutionary in the normal sense, have been substantial in economic management, social welfare, urban planning and education. And surely there is a significant difference between a Parliament which sits and debates policy and criticizes ministers for eight months of the year, and the Supreme Soviet which is in session for one week. The comparison of the work carried out by deputies and Members of Parliament illustrates one of the inevitable weaknesses of a book of this nature. On the work of British politicians and parties, there is a wealth of empirical study; of those of the Soviet Union practically none, although two Soviet surveys of the work of local deputies are quoted. The rest of the sources on Soviet politics are Soviet newspapers and journals. It would be interesting, for instance, to know if there are any studies of backbench revolt in the Soviet Union, comparable to those made in Britain. Moreover, the current criticism of the British parliamentary scene has already led to procedural changes, in an attempt to restore the balance between the executive and the legislature and this is likely to lead to more over the next few years. Can this happen to a body which meets as infrequently as the Supreme Soviet?

Perhaps if Professor Gilison had had the opportunity to read Mr. Rhodes James's book, he would have achieved a better feel for the system of representative democracy in action. Mr. Rhodes James has seen how it works from the inside; both as a clerk in the House of Commons and as a constituency worker supporting a Conservative candidate in a general election. His book covers the period of the last Labour Government and the general election, which returned the Conservatives in 1970 and, although it is apparent that he is much better informed about the inside working of the Conservative party, it is on the whole a fair survey of events and—even more interesting—of leaders. His studies of Harold Wilson and the considerably longer one of Edward Heath are just and tolerant. The only other politician who gets similar treatment is Enoch Powell and his still inconclusive influence on his party is critically considered.

The judgment on Heath—that most unlikely of Tory leaders, with his working class background and, as it seemed at the time, rather doctrinaire attitudes—may need revision in the light of the extraordinary reversal of policies which he has been forced to accept since he came into power. There is a danger, to which the author draws attention, that the two party system may lead to exaggerated emphasis on differences which are not in the national interest, a failing from which the Soviet system is unlikely to suffer. An example was Heath's bitter attack on the Labour government's Prices and Incomes Policy, which has since made his own attempts all the more difficult. This is not to say—as would be said in the Soviet Union—that there is only one public view of what the national interest is.

Both these books must be faulted on editorial grounds. Professor Gilison's academic study has an index of one and a half pages and no index to the copious references. Mr. Rhodes James' book betrays evidence of the speed with which it was written, in a large number of misprints and grammatical errors.

AUSTEN ALBU, M.P.

Sussex
England

BRONIS J. KASLAS. *The USSR-German Aggression Against Lithuania.* Pp. 543. New York: Robert Speller, 1973. $15.00.

W. W. KULSKI. *The Soviet Union in World Affairs: A Documentary Analysis 1964–1972.* Pp. xiv, 592. Syracuse, N.Y.: Syracuse University Press, 1973. $17.50.

The volume of documents on Soviet-German attacks and occupation of Lithuania is in the form of an unofficial white book in support of an independent Lithuania, which became an innocent victim of great power imperialism. The documents have been collected primarily from materials already published, from the captured German archives, by the United States Department of State and by the Lithuanian Government and legations. Essentially, nothing new is revealed by the collection. The introduction provides a short summary of Russian-Lithuanian relations. It is neither exhaustive, nor documented and is written exclusively from the viewpoint of the exiled Lithuanian government.

Certainly few knowledgeable persons in the West doubt, or need to be told, that Lithuania—along with other states in Eastern Europe—were the innocent victims of World War II and the events that followed. Why, therefore, did the author feel the need to collect and republish these documents? In the introduction he argues:

Perhaps the most compelling reason for compiling this collection of documents on the destruction of a small country through the machinations of great powers is to try to harness the widespread tendency to forget the problem of Lithuania and to turn it into nothing more than an artifact for archeologists to ponder on in future centuries. It is worth noting that an active attempt by politicians to "forget" may be quite a reliable indicator that this particular episode ought to be fully remembered and closely examined . . . (p. 5)

Professor Kaslas's reasons may well be true, but it is doubtful that a white book will renew Western concern for the wrongs of World War II, when there still seems to be no viable solution, and new problems are forever pressing for solution.

During the last decade, there has been a marked reduction in Soviet hostility toward West Germany and the United States, and a desire on her part to come to a long term *modus vivendi* with the West. While the ideological filter still colors Soviet attitudes, increasingly, Soviet observers are expressing their views on international relations in non-ideological terms, or in the light of practical politics. Thus, Soviet statements no longer seem to serve only propaganda purposes, but try to be informative and educate the Soviet population in the actual state of world affairs. This volume, by Professor Kulski of Duke University, shows the scope of this change by reviewing a very large part of the Soviet official and scholarly press in the period since Khrushchev's dismissal, 1964–1972. By thorough and exhaustive documentation, Professor Kulski has produced what amounts to an encyclopedia of current Soviet attitudes toward world affairs. Taking each major topic and area of the globe one by one, he summarizes and documents from Soviet sources what is the current Soviet view, also documenting changes wherever there have been any recent major shifts. For the most part, the author is very careful to distinguish between the official views expressed by the leadership and the more official press, such as *Pravda, Izvestia, Tass,* and *Kommunist,* and by those of other commentators and scholars.

This study makes no startling relevations and has no particular thesis, except perhaps an examination of the diversity, scope and depth of Soviet analysis. The volume is primarily a comprehensive description of Soviet views, presented in a manner which is both objective and straightforward. The author's own analysis and comments are sparse; they are not detailed or gone into in any depth. The main use of this volume will be as a reference work: for this purpose it is well organized and documented, and can be highly recommended.

DAVID T. CATTELL
Department of Political Science
University of California
Los Angeles

BRADFORD A. LEE. *Britain and the Sino-Japanese War 1937–1939.* Pp. 319. Stanford, Cal.: Stanford University Press, 1973. $10.00.

If author Lee established as his goal the demonstration of the manner in which the British government muddled through a crisis period with little evidence of great power status, he achieved that end However, this was not his objective. He states that the principal aim of his book is to examine Britain's response to the undeclared Sino-Japanese War, from its outbreak in 1937 until the coming of the European war in September 1939. In a succinct and carefully documented volume, Lee successfully achieves his stated aim. Set in the larger context of the threats from the European dictators, sensitive Anglo-American relations and severe economic and military preparedness constraints, Lee examines the multitude of cross pressures which caused Britain difficulty in developing a coherent policy toward China and Japan.

He persuasively argues that the British response to the East Asian crisis was far different from the response to the German and Italian behavior at the time. Still, while it is evident that the appeasement which was clear in the European policy was not present in Asia, there was considerable vaccilation and uncertainty in British policy toward Japan. This could have affected Japanese extremists in the same way appeasement affected the European dictators. The United States-British relations, in regard to China and Japan, are described as friendly distrust and misunderstanding. Lee treats the implications of the British uncertainty about the United States-Asian policy, especially regarding American proposals for initiatives in Asia. Also, an interesting secondary theme involving attitudes of the British Government toward the Soviet Union emerges. The Soviet military power was clearly underestimated. However, all British relations with the USSR were colored by a considerable fear that communism was a threat to British interests in Asia.

This book is sub-titled: *A Study in the Dilemmas of British Decline.* The volume clearly deals with the final stages of the disintegration of a myth, that for some time had not reflected the realities of Britain's position in the world. Britain did not have the military might necessary to act from strength. Also, the nation's leaders did not have the inclination to take forceful stands, even based on bluffs. Curiously, several of these leaders felt their government's policy was aimed at maintaining Britain's position as a world power and a greater power than Japan in Asia. The book capably describes the awkwardness of this situation.

A lengthy and critical bibliographical note is provided. Scholars will also appreciate the fact that Lee relied heavily on newly opened British Foreign Office and Cabinet papers for the 1930s.

STEPHEN P. KOFF
Department of Political Science
Syracuse University
New York

STANLEY PIERSON. *Marxism and the Origins of British Socialism: The Struggle for a New Consciousness.* Pp. 290. Ithaca, N.Y.: Cornell University Press, 1973. $10.75.

The last two decades of the nineteenth century saw the creation of the popular movement, which became the British Labour party. The story of its progress has often been written in terms of the growth of socialist ideas, but what kind of socialist consciousness was it that inspired the Labour pioneers? Professor Pierson's book provides an informative survey which will be particularly useful to students approaching this question.

In the first part of the book, he gives an agreeable sketch of some of the Victorian prophets who nourished aspirations for social reconstruction, which would dethrone the dominance of the market economy in favor of a sense of community. Coleridge; the Christian Socialists; Carlyle; Ruskin, the Secularists—all were undeniably influential in working within this tradition, and their ideas are duly recorded.

The second part of the book deals with the reception and transformation of Marxist ideas in England, in the 1880s and 1890s. The treatment here is more challenging, for Professor Pierson claims that the characteristic beliefs of the emergent Labour party in the 1890s arose from a crucial modification of the Marxism of the 1880s, into a version of socialism acceptable to native traditions. Marxism, on this reading, developed in three main ways. Hyndman's Social Democratic Federation tried to hold to a strict interpretation; there are some perceptive comments here about his emphasis on doctrinal rectitude— reflecting, however, a mechanistic view which smacked of utilitarianism. The same was, to some extent, true of fabianism, which arose as a version of Marxism with the class struggle left out. The field

was therefore open for a third modification of Marxism, which drew upon the romantic tradition of revolt to produce a more amorphous brand of ethical socialism, with a strong utopian content.

The third part of the book is concerned with the fading of this socialist vision in the late 1890s, as the Labour leaders— with Keir Hardie and Ramsay MacDonald to the fore—came to terms with the exigencies of practical politics. There is a real problem here, which all historians would recognize, in explaining both the visionary impulse behind the socialist revival and its dissolution. For by the time that an independent Labour party was formed in 1900, the political aspirations embodied in it were of a limited and pragmatic kind.

The title of this book could be taken in two senses. First as an examination of how Marxist theory influenced British Socialist thought. This is what Professor Pierson is mainly concerned with, but his assumption that Marxist ideas were in one way or another fundamental, is not really borne out by the evidence he offers. The second interpretation of the title would be to concentrate on the problems of why the British working class movement failed to live up to Marxist expectations. On this he has some interesting reflections to offer, notably in his last chapter, and perhaps the work should have gone further in this direction. One is left with the provoking question, whether we would do better to explain the growth of the Labour party in terms of the rise of socialism, or of its decline.

P. F. CLARKE
Department of History
University College London
England

UNITED STATES

RICHARD DRINNON. *White Savage: The Case of John Dunn Hunter.* Pp. 320. New York: Schocken Books, 1972. $12.50.

In April 1823, John Dunn Hunter's *Memoirs of a Captivity Among the Indians* of North America, From Childhood to the Age of Nineteen was published in London and the twenty-six year old author—then in England—found himself something of a sensation. In the seven years since leaving the life of savagery, he had made remarkable strides in education and self-improvement, and he was now formulating plans for going back to help the Indians improve their lot, through civilization. English society lionized him like a second Robinson Crusoe. He was taken up by such notables as the philanthropist Robert Owen, the celebrated agriculturist Thomas William Coke and his royal highness the Duke of Sussex, brother of George IV.

Hunter's book had appeared in America earlier in the year under the title *Manners and Customs of Several Indian Tribes Located West of the Mississippi*. In it, the author claimed to have been captured by Kickapoos when he was so young he could no longer remember the incident. A roving band of Pawnees took him from the Kickapoos, and he later passed into the hands of Kansas Indians, with whom he remained until he was ten or twelve years old. When hostile Osages cut off this band from the rest of the Kansas tribe, Hunter "was received into the family of Shen-thweeth, [an Osage] warrior distinguished among his people for his wisdom and bravery." While living with this family, the boy received the name Hunter because of his success in the chase. He later joined "a hunting expedition of sixteen moons duration . . . in the course of which he and his party crossed the Rocky Mountains, and reached the Pacific Ocean." He left the Osages in 1816, when he went to warn a white trader on the Arkansas—a certain Colonel Watkins—of an impending attack.

Hunter was so impressed with white civilization, while visiting New Orleans, that he decided to secure a white education. He received instruction from various people and in various schools, for a little over two and a half years. After his first difficulties with English, he made rapid progress, became a prodigious reader and supplemented his formal training with rigorous self instruction. The result was that, on going to Philadelphia in 1821, he

was able to put together his memoir with the help of Colonel Edward Clark, a civil engineer. Meanwhile, he had added to his name that of John Dunn, "a gentleman of high respectability, of Cape Girardeau County, . . . Missouri."

Eventually, on returning to America, Hunter went among the Cherokees of Texas on his self-assumed mission of saving the Indians west of the Mississippi from genocide. Then, as emissary of Richard Fields, a Cherokee chief, he traveled to Mexico City on an unsuccessful mandate, to secure a patent for the lands occupied by Cherokees and other Indians in east Texas. On returning there, he was murdered early in 1827 by a Cherokee confederate, while trying to rally the forces of the "Red and White Republic of Fredonia," which he had helped to organize in rebellion against Mexico.

Meanwhile, unknown to Hunter, he had been branded an arrant impostor and his book a fraud by General Lewis Cass, General William Clark, the linguist Peter Stephen Duponceau, and others. Historians have generally accepted the charges of Hunter's discreditors. On beginning his researches Richard Drinnon assumed the charges were true, but in sifting the evidence he reversed his opinion, and in this book has built a solid and persuasive case in Hunter's favor.

THURMAN WILKINS
Queens College
Flushing
New York

PHILIP S. FONER. *The Spanish-Cuban-American War and the Birth of American Imperialism.* Vol. 1 1895–1898, vol. 2 1898–1902. Pp. vii, 338: 339, 716. New York: Monthly Review Press, 1973. $23.00.

If there exists a recurring style in the writing of American history, then the cyclical appearance of the conspiracy thesis must be the most common. Recently, the debate on the factors underlying this nation's entry into the Spanish-Cuban War of 1895–1898 has been revived. The myth of the yellow press having been deflated by previous revisionists—coupled with a questioning of those altruistic motives ascribed to the intervention, at the time—has left only the conspiratorial theme unstated. That theory now appears in Philip Foner's study: the United States intervened in Cuba in order to crush the insurrection, and annex the island in the aftermath. Political and economic forces motivated this desire which, though thwarted by adverse reaction to the Philippine occupation and Cuban truculence, was closely approximated through the quasi-protectorate status imposed under the Platt amendment.

The alleged conspiracy begins in 1868 when Ulysses S. Grant and Hamilton Fish collaborated with Spain to deny the Cubans a victory in the Ten Years War. Grover Cleveland and Richard Olney are indicted for maintaining the collusion, as is the administration of William McKinley. Confronted by this menace, the Cuban patriots, so the author says, decided upon war in 1895 because of "the growing fear that emerging imperialist forces in the United States would succeed in annexing the island before the revolution could liberate it from Spain."

There is a heavy injection of Cuban revolutionary proclamations, songs, poetry and propaganda throughout the work. The bulk of the evidence is drawn from Cuban sources, many hitherto inaccessible to American scholars. Unfortunately, the author's case suffers from an evident bias which, carried to extremes, results in a periodic assault on historians who hold opposite views, or who missed the "obvious" evidence of Machiavellian design behind America's intervention. William McKinley's support for Cuban autonomy is judged a plot to prepare Cubans for annexation, to cite but one example of preconceived notions. The authors who are attacked, in both the text and the footnotes, are too numerous to list, although it is interesting to note that Winston S. Churchill is criticized for reporting the pre-American phase of the war from the Spanish side, a fault Dr. Foner duplicates in reverse.

In equally poor taste is the author's shrill tone of presentation, making one wonder if he was more concerned with ingratiating himself to the Castro regime than in submitting a balanced view of his subject. His premise, though faulty, could only have benefited, had the incendiary verbage been discarded. "North American colossus" is suitable to *Destiny of a Continent* but not to current writing. In addition, the author should have avoided the frequent digressions on causes alien to his topic. Referring to the Boxer rebellion, Foner says, "War was the imperialists answer to the attempt of the Chinese people to keep their country for themselves." Fortunately the subject of atrocities is not exploited, although the author's remarks on the existing historiography serve to accuse the Spanish and exonerate the Cubans, with the exception of those "irregular units over which there was not sufficient control." General Frederick Funston's *Memoirs of Two Wars* presents a somewhat different view, however.

More common than misstatement is overstatement, such as the description of an "intense" battle resulting in "heavy" Cuban casualties.. On further reading it is seen that the engagement was of skirmish proportions and only thirteen *insurrectos* died. Moreover, chapter 14 could have been deleted altogether, since it contains little more than contemporary socialist views on American intervention. There is no substantial discussion of strategic considerations influencing McKinley's decision for war, and evidence does exist in this area. The author seems to have intentionally avoided this aspect in favor of economic determinism, but, curiously enough, even those cited in support of this theory are admonished for having missed the aroma of villainy, which supposedly tainted the McKinley Administration.

The Spanish-Cuban-American War will undoubtedly ignite controversy. In the tradition of Irving Stone's *Hidden History of the Korean War,* also a Monthly Review Press publication, it provides a convenient contrast to other works on the same subject. Regrettably, a dispassionate study did not emerge from the author's research.

CALVIN W. HINES
Stephen F. Austin State University
Nacogdoches
Texas

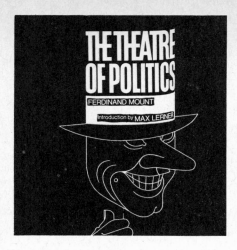

The Theatre of Politics

FERDINAND MOUNT

Introduction by Max Lerner

Hardbound $7.95

From a presidential press conference to a student rally or a civil rights march, there is a strong theatrical element in all political activity. In positing the notion of politics as theater, the author forces us to consider how the theatrical framework limits and influences political theory and practice.

Dealing With Deviants

The Treatment of Antisocial Behavior

STUART WHITELEY, DENNIE BRIGGS, and MERFYN TURNER

Hardbound $8.50

Dr. Stuart Whiteley describes and analyzes the evolution of a therapeutic-community method of treatment at a hospital in England. Dennie Briggs describes how the California prison system has responded to deviants, and the methods employed. Merfyn Turner, founder of a London halfway house for ex-prisoners, tackles the problem in relation to the community-at-large.

Death in American Experience

ARIEN MACK, editor

Paper $2.95/Hardbound $7.50

Contents:

The "Gift of Life" and Its Reciprocation
Talcott Parsons, Renée C. Fox and Victor M. Lidz

The Premature Gerontocracy: Themes of Aging and Death in the Youth Culture
David Gutmann

Death and the Native Strain in American Poetry
Harold Bloom

The Sacral Power of Death in Contemporary Experience
William F. May

Death in the Judaic and Christian Traditions
A. Roy Eckardt

Psychiatric Aspects of Death in America
Vivian M. Rakoff

Being and Becoming Dead
Eric J. Cassell, M.D.

How Others Die—Reflections on the Anthropology of Death
Johannes Fabian

The World of the Office Worker

MICHEL CROZIER

Paper $3.75

This empirical study of white-collar working class, by a leading French sociologist, shows that there is a lack of class consciousness in this sector, that many workers believe that they have a fair degree of freedom, and that the group's loyalties vis-à-vis management are fragmented. Crozier discusses Parisian social status and stratification, and reviews the American and European literature on the subject. "A most useful book for students of work, stratification, and social change."—Choice

Examination copies of paperbacks are available when requested on academic letterhead. Hardcover books are sent on 60-day bill. Write to Dept. 339

Schocken Books

200 Madison Avenue. New York. N.Y. 10016

Kindly mention THE ANNALS *when writing to advertisers*

THE IDEA OF FRATERNITY IN AMERICA

Wilson Carey McWilliams

"This is an astonishing book — in terms of scholarship, of insight, of breadth of vision.

—PETER BERGER

"A vast work . . . it illuminates the whole range of American political thought and its background."

—LOUIS HARTZ

696 pages
$14.95
at your bookseller

UNIVERSITY OF CALIFORNIA PRESS
Berkeley 94720

HENRY J. FRIENDLY. *Federal Jurisdiction: A General View.* Pp. 199. New York: Columbia University Press, 1973. $10.00.

The author—a former pupil of Professor Felix Frankfurter at Harvard and law clerk to Mr. Justice Brandeis, and presently chief judge of the United States Court of Appeals for the Second Circuit—has been interested in the question of federal jurisdiction for a long time, having first written a piece on diversity jurisdiction in 1928 for the *Harvard Law Review*. After forty-four years of judicial experience, Judge Friendly returned to this subject in the James S. Carpentier Lectures at Columbia Law School. Based upon these lectures, this book provides insights into several problems and solutions regarding one of the gravest matters facing American governmental institutions: the burgeoning workload of the inferior federal courts. Judge Friendly views the current situation with alarm; the prospect of a breakdown in the inferior federal courts—and even the Supreme Court—is very real in his opinion. Stating the thesis of the book, he writes that "the general federal courts can best serve the country if their jurisdiction is limited to tasks which are appropriate to courts, which are best handled by courts of general rather than specialized jurisdiction, and where the knowledge, tenure and other qualities of federal judges can make a distinctive contribution."

The mushrooming of federal litigation has been the result of several factors, including the liberalization of the requirement of standing, the growth of class action, and a wealth of new federal statutes emerging from Congress—the important Civil Rights Acts of the 1960s, for example, have spurred a marked increase in civil rights cases. To reduce this intake, Judge Friendly has a number of recommendations, among them the substitution of workmen's compensation for judicial remedies in the cases of railroad workers and seamen on American ships, and the removal of automobile accident litigation from the federal courts, either as a consequence of state no-fault plans, direct legislation, or—as the Judge would prefer—almost complete elimination of diversity jurisdiction. He further urges the creation of a single specialized court to handle all patent questions, and a separate system of trial and appellate courts to decide all federal tax claims. Among other aspects of federal jurisdiction reviewed are problems of civil rights litigation, proposals for upgrading judicial efficiency, standing, federal injunctions against state court proceedings, class actions, and exhaustion of state remedies.

In sum, as seems to be his custom, Judge Friendly has again provided us with a highly informative and lucid discussion of problems facing the American court system. Surely the book will be widely read and, hopefully, its proposals will be carried out.

LOCH K. JOHNSON
Department of Government
Ohio University
Athens

GENE S. GRAHAM. *One Man, One Vote: Baker vs. Carr and the American Levellers.* Pp. 338, vii. Boston, Mass.: Little, Brown, 1972. $8.95.

The special merit of this book is that the author has combined excellent journalistic reporting with superb legal research. Marching through his pages are the unsung heroes and heroines of the legal profession, whose dedication and tireless struggle culminated in the landmark decision of the United States Supreme Court on March 26, 1962, now known as the case of *Baker v. Carr.*

With his experience as a reporter on the Nashville *Tennessean* for seventeen years, Gene Graham was especially qualified to chronicle the inspiring story of the struggle to strip "cow country" political bosses of the inordinate power they had acquired at the expense of the urban centers of population.

Former Chief Justice Earl Warren was eminently correct when he characterized *Baker v. Carr* as "the most vital decision" of his distinguished tenure on the Supreme Court.

The injustice that was finally corrected by the United States Supreme Court stemmed from the fact that, for a number of generations, the population has been shifting from rural areas to large urban centers, and that most of the state legislatures neglected to reapportion the people's representation in both the state legislatures and Congress. In Florida, for instance, a majority of both houses of the legislature represented districts which contained only 15 percent of the state's population. In Georgia, the largest congressional district contained a population of 823,680, while the smallest congressional district—with a population of only 272,154—was also represented by a Congressman. In California, Los Angeles County, with a population of 4,151,687, had a senator in the state legislature, while three other counties with an aggregate population of 14,014 also had a state senator.

Quite apart from the discrimination in representation on both the state and federal level, there was the maldistribution of state funds. In Colorado, for instance, in one year the city of Denver received from the state $2.3 million for its ninety thousand school pupils, while Jefferson County received $2.4 million for its eighteen thousand pupils.

Mr. Graham has told the story vividly, of the tireless struggles in state courts and in federal district courts, which finally culminated in the United States Supreme Court decision of 1962. The story proves that the people can still win victories in struggles for human rights. This book should be read by every person who is interested in the welfare of our country, and we strongly recommend it for both private and public library acquisition.

MORRIS KOMINSKY

Elsinore
California

ALEC BARBROOK. *God Save the Commonwealth: An Electoral History of Massachusetts.* Pp. vii, 220. Lawrence, Mass.: University of Massachusetts Press, 1973. $12.50.

VAN BECK HALL. *Politics Without Parties: Massachusetts, 1780–1791.* Pp. ix, 375. Pittsburgh: University of Pittsburgh Press, 1972. $14.95.

The politics of Massachusetts—the only state in the Union that did not agree that "Nixon's the One" in 1972—is the subject of a once-over lightly study of Bay State electoral history, during the past two generations. Relying heavily on the work of others scholars and on newspapers, Barbrook charts the transformation of Massachusetts, from a Republican bastion before 1930, to a Democratic stronghold since the 1940s. Here is the familiar story of the expansion of Irish political power from Boston across the state in the 1930s, when economic distress enabled Democratic politicians to reach beyond their normal ethnic power base and attract votes from WASPS, and others, that had voted Republican in good times. The Great Depression, for a while, made class or economic status a more important influence on voting behavior than it had customarily been and ethnicity less so. Yet, paradoxically, ethnic politicians, entrenched in the Democratic party, were to be prime beneficiaries of this shift away from the politics of ethno-cultural conflict, so prominent in the 1920s, to a politics of economic interest. Democratic hegemony, however, did not become firmly established until after 1945, and even since then, the party's tight grip on the legislature has not been paralleled with comparable success in electing constitutional officers.

Mr. Barbrook plods through each administration during the last thirty years, suggesting that ethno-cultural conflict, which fed a "politics of revenge" has been giving way to the "politics of discernment." The Irish, and other groups, are becoming more middle class and secularized; prejudice is receding. Moreover, as the Bay State's economy shifts from its nineteenth century factory foundations to technologically advanced firms employing a well-educated professional and managerial class, these elements demand honest, efficient government, that tries to cope with state problems. The Kennedys have presided over this transition, able to appeal to old ethnic loyalties, as well as to the desires of the new groups. The result, Barbrook concludes, is that Massachusetts politics in the 1960s "seems a great deal healthier than it seemed ten years earlier" when tribal warfare dominated the political scene.

Barbrook has put together a useful introduction to recent Bay State political history but this is not the intensive, fresh analysis of politics in an American state that we need. First, it is highly derivative, relying very heavily on other scholars without adding much that is fresh or new to one who has followed the Massachusetts scene in the press. Nor has Barbrook subjected the voting data to systematic analysis—despite the twenty-one tables briefly commented on in the text—that could take one beyond the usual cliches. Nor has the author systematically analyzed the ways in which social structure and constitutional mechanisms have shaped Bay State politics, though he alludes to these variables often. Organized business and labor, for example, receive only a glancing mention. A study of the long battle over the sales tax versus the income tax might have shed light on the role of economic interests in state politics. Why, for instance, was the majority Democratic party—most of whose leaders strongly opposed the sales tax—unable to head it off with a more equitable source of additional funds? Similarly, Barbrook notes the weakness, if not the absence, of well-disciplined political organization, especially among the Democrats, even decades ago when machines were still powerful in other states. Yet he does not convincingly account for this phenomenon. As elsewhere in the Northeast, the Democratic Party lives off the votes of ethnics and working people, but in the absence of responsible party government, they get sales taxes; cronyism; corruption and business-oriented government. The result is voter alienation, something Barbrook ineffectively disputes, and susceptibility to the likes of George Wallace.

Mr. Barbrook, however, thinks that Massachusetts government is improving. Principles rather than personalities; programs rather than ethnic loyalties, are increasingly shaping the state's politics. The time is passing when one can say of Massa-

chusetts—as did Elliot Richardson in 1961, then a rising Republican politician—that "the most striking feature of the Massachusetts political scene, as I view it, is the subordination of programs and principles to personal relationships." Whether Massachusetts was unique, as Mr. Richardson then thought, or is changing, as Mr. Barbrook now believes, are propositions deserving of healthy skepticism.

This book is an important contribution to the reconstruction of American political history, a task rendered imperative by the demolition of the interpretive frameworks with which Beard and Turner and their followers organized the evidence. Professor Hall has written an exhaustive and persuasive study of Massachusetts politics in the 1780s, combining traditional historical methodology with an apt use of quantification. The findings are neither novel nor surprising. They, in fact, substantiate the contentions of other recent students of the Bay State in the Revolutionary era, but they do so with a precision and in a systematic way that quantification makes possible.

Recognizing the importance of factions, personalities and regionalism in Bay State politics, Hall focuses, however, on socio-economic cleavages that proved to be decisive. First, he identifies the towns of Massachusetts along a commercial-cosmopolitan spectrum, from the most commercial—such as Boston—to the least commercial—such as Mount Washington, Berkshire county. This procedure rescues us from the too simple and unworkable radical-conservative, agrarian-mercantile categories on which Beard's work foundered. Moreover, it makes clear the decisive role played by towns in the center, when the extremes polarized during Shays' rebellion. Hall also shows that urban artisans, sailors and petty tradesmen usually identified their interests with those of the urban mercantile elites who dominated their communities, thus foreclosing the possibility of a union among the lower strata, rural and urban. Within the rural populace there were significant distinctions, depending on whether farmers were more, or less, enmeshed in commercial relationships.

Hall has systematically analyzed roll call votes in the Massachusetts legislature, to determine how socio-economic differentiation among the towns influenced voting. He finds that, on many issues, representatives from the most and the least commercial towns agreed: granting commercial powers to the Confederation and adopting anti-British trade regulations, for example. Many of the least commercial towns often went unrepresented, or were content to send placeholders—local worthies who tended to identify with the elites in the commercial centers. The indifference of voters—who ordinarily did not think that politics mattered—and acquiescence in elite rule, generally permitted commercial-cosmopolitan interests to run the Bay State. But when they saddled farmers with new taxes to pay for the public debt and denied them relief from paying private debts during the hard times of postwar economic readjustment, conflict erupted. In the absence of political parties to provide farmers with an organization and a common platform, the least commercial towns were at a disadvantage in the struggle with the urban elites and their placeholding followers. The result was a political system that frustrated the discontented who seemed incapable of working effectively within the system. Though the Shaysites were put down, the crisis politicized the least-commercial towns, which then successfully used the ballot to redirect state policy and pacify debtors. Defeated at home, Mr. Hall tells us, the most commercial cosmopolitan interests—which had only slowly and indecisively come to favor a strong central government—now pinned their hopes on an invigorated Union to solve the Bay State's most pressing problem, the public debt. The lines of division over the federal constitution largely paralleled the polarization in state politics, yet the cleavages did not endure. As the new federal regime moved swiftly to fund the state debt without relying on direct taxes, it removed the

major source of conflict in Massachusetts. The Shaysites had resorted to violence, but they had limited objectives and like other agrarian protest movements in America, they "had no intention of destroying the social or political structure of the commonwealth. They merely desired certain reforms." Instead, the new national government—which they feared and fought as an instrument of their rivals—accommodated warring interests and facilitated the restoration of tranquility.

All of this story rests on massive research, documented in mammoth footnotes, reported in eighty-one tables, and expounded in a dense text that tells us more about Massachusetts than most would care to know. As scientific history, this monograph deserves high marks. As a tale, interestingly told, it falls short. Though clearly written, it is too detailed and, stylistically, plods along. There must be a better way of saying: "The least commercial farmers, the largest single element in the least commercial category of interests, had their greatest strength in the western group C towns." If not, the new history will surely forfeit history's claim to being both a science and an art.

PAUL GOODMAN
Department of History
University of California
Davis

ROBERT W. JOHANNSEN. *Stephen A. Douglas.* Pp. xii, 993. New York: Oxford University Press, 1973. $19.95.

LEWIS PERRY. *Radical Abolitionism: Anarchy and the Government of God in Antislavery Thought.* Pp. xvi, 328. Ithaca: Cornell University Press, 1973. $14.50.

No matter the role assigned to Stephen A. Douglas by earlier writers, Professor Johannsen believes that the Little Giant "was probably the most widely-known political figure" in America in the 1850s. He clearly shows that Douglas was always in the spotlight, due to his political activism; his ardent support of western interests; his ultranationalism in foreign affairs; his presidential ambitions and particularly his key position on the Senate Committee on Territories, where the slavery issue was centered.

To Douglas, politics was all consuming. He spent his fortune and health on it. From earliest manhood he was in the thick of politics, as an organizer, wheeler-dealer, and office-holder. He was elected to three different offices before he was thirty, and in 1852—at the age of thirty-nine—he might have been nominated for president, but for the ineptitude of his campaign managers. In 1856 he narrowly missed the prize, due in part to untimely Anglophobic outbursts of his own.

As Douglas loudly, vigorously and consistently supported popular sovereignty, he increasingly became the center of controversy. The year 1858 was crucial to his career. His debates with Lincoln—they were longtime opponents—and his open break with Buchanan over LeCompton, cast him in a different light before the public. Johannsen says: "Douglas found this altered image appealing . . . He became more openly and unabashedly a defender of principle, struggling for popular sovereignty and the Union against increasingly vicious attacks from all sides" (p. 618). He and the abolitionists hated each other.

Douglas was energetic—despite frequent bouts of ill health—resourceful, an easy mixer—even with political opponents—coarse in manners and dress, an excessive drinker, sometimes unscrupulous and demagogic, but most always the skilful pragmatist. Nevertheless, at times he underestimated the intensity of sectional feelings generated by the slavery issue. He kept thinking the issue could be laid to rest.

Although the debacles at Charleston and Baltimore dimmed his chances for the White House, he was still "grimly determined to win, if not the presidency then that other prize, control of the Democratic party. Either way, the nation could yet be saved" (p. 775). But upon realizing his cause was lost, Douglas spent the last days of the campaign fearlessly touring Dixie in a vain effort to bolster unionism. Shortly, he was even willing to sacrifice popular sovereignty, if necessary, to save the Union. He was dead a few months later.

This is a superb political biography, although perhaps too detailed in places. Johannsen's account of Douglas' activities, drawn mainly from a wealth of primary sources, is objective and well balanced. Nevertheless, the author admits that "it is doubtful that the key to [Douglas'] personality will ever be found to the satisfaction of all. Certainly I make no claim of discovery" (p. ix).

Perry's monograph impressed this reader with its wealth of detail about abolitionists' views, their confusion and contradictions, the idealism of the nonresistants, and the fact that abolition was only part of their program. They wished to achieve the millenium—the government of God on this earth. Those who held anarchistic views did not believe in violence, but they opposed authority—of church, government, or any sort. In general, they longed for a simple, sinless society.

Nonresistance was replaced on the abolitionists' agenda by disunion in the 1840s and by a surrender to violence in the 1850s. Perry writes that "little of the anarchistic tendency to champion the government of God and denounce all human coercion can be followed beyond Harper's Ferry" (p. 302). He believes these radical reformers were too few in number to be classed as an anarchistic wing of the abolitionist movement. However, he argues "that certain of the most basic ideas honored throughout abolitionism turned out in experience to have anarchistic implications" (p. x). He believes it is difficult to understand antislavery properly without considering its anarchistic offshoots.

Perry discusses the philosophy of many of the greater and lesser reformers, from Garrison, Phillips, Weld, and Ballou downwards. Most were eccentrics. He also includes brief accounts of the little-known reformer communities of Hopedale and Modern Times. This monograph is heavy reading, and the author probably tells the generalist more than he wishes to know about anarchistic tendencies in the abolitionist movement. Be that as it may, this study will be valuable for specialists, and its admirable summary in the last chapter will be helpful to others.

ERNEST M. LANDER, JR.
Clemson University
South Carolina

CLYDE E. JACOBS. *The Eleventh Amendment and Sovereign Immunity.* Pp. 216. Westport, Conn.: Greenwood, 1972. $9.50.

This volume is a splendid addition to the relatively scanty literature of the Eleventh Amendment. There were no great discoveries made in the course of his research, but digging deeply and perceptively into the cases, Professor Jacobs has given us an enlarged understanding of the amendment, its origins, and its subsequent history.

It is a reminder to college professors of American government and constitutional law that (1) the clauses in Article III extending the jurisdiction of the federal courts to "controversies between a state and citizens of another state . . . and between a state . . . and foreign states, citizens or subjects," were full of ambiguities admitting of different interpretations; and that (2) the amendment was not a cease and desist order, settling forever the problem of sovereign immunity.

Were these Article III clauses to apply to all cases in which the state was involved whether as plaintiff or defendant? Or were they to apply only to cases in which the state was the plaintiff? Were they subject to an implied state immunity? Or did they constitute "a waiver of the state's immunity from suit?"

Professor Jacobs writes: "Textual analysis . . . by itself . . . yields no answer. Moreover, the records of the convention simply do not cast any direct light on the question. . . ." Nor are the debates in the ratifying conventions of much help.

Despite the apparent absence of precise knowledge of what the framers had in mind, the United States Supreme Court had no doubts. Beginning with *Vanstophorst* v. *Maryland* (1791) the court, exercising its original jurisdiction, entertained "suits instituted against various states by citizens of other states and by foreign-

ers. . . ." Of the seven suits in which a state was the defendant, *Chisholm* v. *Georgia* looms large in our minds, because of the furore it created; but in most of the seven cases the defendant state protested the court's jurisdiction.

Supported by Federalists and Anti-Federalists alike, the Eleventh Amendment was proposed and ratified, becoming operative in 1798. The Constitution being a document of many ambiguities—a source of its strength—one ambiguity was replaced by another. Did the Eleventh Amendment mean what it said?

Again, was the amendment merely a reaffirmation of "a general understanding existing at the time the Constitution was ratified," namely, "that the states were to be immune from suit by individuals, in spite of the clauses in Article III . . .?" Or was the amendment adopted "because the states were fearful that they would be compelled by the Supreme Court to pay certain debts . . . to noncitizen creditors?" Professor Jacobs holds neither explanation to be satisfactory; but he provides us with no definite exegesis. Lacking documentary evidence, the author must necessarily conjecture: the nationalists

may have understood quite well that federal judicial protection against impairments of contracts, tender laws, and other state infringements of property rights was possible, whether or not the states could be impleaded as defendants in the Supreme Court in suits instituted by individuals. To the nationalists, the amendment's implicit concession to state sovereignty may have seemed more formal than substantial. . . .

During the Marshall period, the Supreme Court "formulated the basic law of the amendment in three opinions sharply circumscribing its potential impact upon the scope of the federal judicial power." In *United States* v. *Peters* (1809) it was held that

the amendment did not bar a proceeding in whose outcome a state was consequentially but significantly interested. In *Cohens* [1821] the Court had, in effect, denied the applicability of the amendment as a limitation upon its appellate jurisdiction over federal-question cases. Finally, the general doctrine of *Osborn* [1824] that a state officer may be sued in law or equity for wrongs done or threatened, even though his acts are defended upon the basis of official but constitutionally defective authorization, afforded a potential remedy that partly mooted the issues of a state's suability under the federal-question clause.

This problem of the suit against a state officer is amply discussed by Professor Jacobs in chapter 5. In 1868, there came the Fourteenth Amendment, followed by several cases relating to the Eleventh Amendment, including *Ex parte Young* (1908). "The doctrinal development wrought by *Young*," writes Professor Jacobs, "reflected the sympathetic pre-occupation of the federal judiciary with the substantive rights secured by the Fourteenth Amendment." As Mr. Justice Black declared in *Griffin* v. *School Board* (1964), "It has been settled law since *Ex parte Young* . . . that suits against state and county officials to enjoin them from invading constitutional rights are not forbidden by the Eleventh Amendment."

Professor Jacobs' last chapter explores, all too briefly, the theories "supporting the doctrine of sovereign immunity."

Professor Jacobs brings a fine analytical mind to bear upon his subject. This is an important book for the scholar of American constitutional law. Those who read it will gather new insights into the significance, past and present, of the Eleventh Amendment.

GORDON C. POST
Department of Political Science
Wells College
Aurora
New York

HENRY S. KARIEL. *Saving Appearances: The Reestablishment of Political Science.* Pp. 154. North Scituate, Mass.: Duxbury Press, 1972. $3.95. Paperbound.

Henry Kariel has opened himself up again and is happily on display. His analysis of appearances is a brilliant challenge to political scientists to open up stale paradigms for fresh air, to encourage the development of repressed human capacities, to politicize what is masked as "nonpolitical" and to find new forms to express themselves politically.. Kariel encourages all to do as he does: to perform in new directions and to risk new logics, new languages and new experiences—both in and out of the field of political science. Anyone who cannot tolerate the tangential brilliance of Kariel's thought is probably in the process of closing his mind. But if Kariel, in turn, cannot get beyond his tangents to write the great contribution many have expected of him, narrower minds are likely to dominate the most important institutions and paradigms of the field of political science.

Structurally, Kariel's book is broken into eight parts, which symbolize points of pause in the exciting intellectual journey which he offers the reader: "The Finality of Beginnings," "The Quest for Meaning," "The Cultivation of Reality," "The Recovery of Experience," "Inconclusiveness as Ideal," "The Transformation of Reality," "Political Science as a Form of Action" and "Political Education." No political scientist who wants to know where the boundaries and paradigms of his field are going can afford not to read this book. It calls for an open-ended discipline, tolerant of interdisciplinary excursions, thirsty for insight and depth, and relevant to basic human needs and everyday experience.

Logically, Kariel's work is based on undermining the prescriptive grammar implicit in the following, widely-accepted distinctions: objective fact/subjective value; description/prescription; theory/practice; value-neutral means/value-permeated ends; impersonal detachment/personal involvement; behavior/action; public knowledge/private opinion; the knowing scholar/the known subject matter and scientist/citizen. According to Kariel, the grammar of these descriptions dictates the style and content of political science publications and articulates the political roles to be played. In so far as such distinctions maintain the scientific goal of neutrality, they divorce the order of science from the subjective opinions, interests, and choices of academic and non-academic human beings. In refuting the logic of such repressive dichotomies, Kariel cites interdisciplinary authorities ranging from Jorge Luis Borges to Jürgen Habermas, from Joseph Brakman to Clifford Geertz, from Friedrich Nietzsche to John Dewey.

This is a little book of incisive quotes, each a gem. Indeed, at times Kariel's own phrases outshine the perceptive sources he feels obliged to cite. His own logic, therefore, becomes a buckshot anti-logic—extremely open-ended, mind-stretching and humanizing. But such scattered incisions necessarily lack the Apollonian clarity and coherence that the academic reader has been conditioned to respect. No department of political science in the country should be without the Dionysian perspective provided by a free-wheeling character such as Kariel. But no such Kariel character will be able to make a Nietzschean contribution to the history of intellectual thought, without submitting to the logical constraints of Apollo, for at least one major work in his life.

Finally, Kariel argues that there is no such thing as finally. All endings become new beginnings. Likewise, the end of this review should consist of the twelve beginnings to which Kariel invites political scientists:

(1) Let convention be no more than a point of departure for defining the basic units of political inquiry
(2) Assume that the subject matter of political science is unavoidably variable and equivocal
(3) Assume that political life is constituted by symbols that mediate between the knower and the known
(4) Assess propositions by involving others and yourself in the process of testing, inquiry, and speculation
(5) Treat those parts of experience which defy comprehension as a functional system, using terms that keep you from acquiescing in its incomprehensibility
(6) Define men as actors whose conduct—whose movement through time and space—is self-reflective and self-determined
(7) Seek to understand political phenomena by empathetic acts

(8) Regard your formulations as always incomplete acts
(9) Express yourself in terms no more clear than you must to win and hold others
(10) Accept procedures—constraining practices—which facilitate continuous expression and lead to increasingly ambiguous formulations
(11) Work on problems set by your need to give shared meanings to transactions with seemingly intransigent nonpolitical environments
(12) Welcome whatever clues for reality-expanding action are offered by other reality-constructing communities

This is one of the most creative and constructive books on the field of political science that I have read. It is now up to the rest of the political science community to test its coherence, in terms of their own everyday needs and political experience.

ROBERT A. ISAAK
Fordham University
New York

PETER KOLCHIN. *First Freedom: The Responses of Alabama's Blacks to Emancipation and Reconstruction.* Pp. xxi, 215. Westport, Conn.: Greenwood Press, 1972. $10.00.

In Reconstruction studies, as this provocative monograph notes, the revisionist triumph has not moved historians much beyond the older concern with white political action. Black responses to emancipation have not received much study, and if Professor Kolchin is correct, this has thoroughly obscured the extent, speed, and processes of social change during the immediate post-emancipation period.

In the work under review, a meticulous study of the years from 1865 to 1870, the author focuses particularly on changes in the mobility, labor system, social institutions, class structure and political behavior of Alabama's Blacks. In each sphere, he finds, the period was characterized by the rapid emergence and solidification of new and quite different social arrangements; in forging these, he also finds, the blacks themselves played major roles. Far from being mere objects of manipulation, they quickly grasped the essentials of freedom and moved rapidly to achieve greater mobility and independence, create stronger family structures, set up independent churches and seize educational, economic, and political opportunities. The real revolution—that involved in destroying the pre-war structure and shaping this new set of relationships—was virtually complete before the radical Republicans came to power. And while white actions helped to shape the new order and insure that it would be accompanied by oppression and discrimination, its main features cannot be understood apart from the actions and attitudes of Blacks.

These findings, the author also argues, undercut both the "Sambo" thesis of Stanley Elkins and the view that black family weakness can be explained as a legacy of slavery. In Alabama at least, slavery had not transformed the blacks into good-natured, docile, lazy "Sambos." This was a pose that they quickly dropped when emancipation came. And among those studied, the family arrangements of slavery quickly gave way to relatively strong family structures, modeled along white lines. It was the urban ghetto, not the slave heritage, that produced the later disintegration.

It is possible, of course, that these provocative generalizations rest upon too narrow a base. Kolchin has studied only Alabama, and given the dearth of historical materials left by Blacks, he has been forced to infer much from documents generated by white participants and observers. But still, his reconstruction of Black behavior is a careful and persuasive one, likely at least to stimulate similar studies of other areas. And if these find similar patterns, it seems likely that another broad re-examination of the conventional wisdom concerning the Reconstruction era will be in order.

ELLIS W. HAWLEY
Department of History
University of Iowa

RICHARD KUNNES. *The American Heroin Empire: Power, Politics and Profit.* Pp. 215. New York: Dodd, Mead, 1973. $5.95.

"The American heroin empire" says author Dr. Kunnes, "is literally just that, an empire based on heroin . . . ." And this book, I admit, is a powerful, provocative and remarkable identification and description of the reality of an empire based on dealing death for huge profits.

Possibly the most fascinating aspect of the whole problem of drug abuse is related to the strange manner with which it has emerged in the collective conscience of the American people. And as I have observed, through personal involvement in a variety of research activities, the vast majority of our personnel and the largest share of our monies are incoherently and spastically applied, with little net result in either understanding or treating the problem and the persons that are involved in it.

At last, Dr. Kunnes has put forth a simply written, easily read account of the heroin problem. I am sure that professionals and non-professionals will appreciate some two hundred pages of "proof" that ". . . The empire involves American governmental officials, important foreign political figures in numerous countries, as well as Mafia and organized crime. The empire also includes numerous American industries and institutions. The empire is a worldwide operation, complete with colonies and client states, with expeditionary forces and foreign markets."

Within the jackets of the book, the reader will encounter such provocative chapters as "Junk and Genocide: Ghetto Counterinsurgency" and "Law and Medicine: Professional Failures" as well as "The Addiction-Education-Industrial Complex." Within each chapter, courageously, the author points the finger of accusation to a problem that is not simply a manifestation of personal maladjustment, but, on the contrary, an exhibition of society's structural dysfunctions.

One could find fault with the fact that the author bases both his descriptions and analysis mostly on periodical literature and newspaper articles—running, therefore, the risk that his work will not be thought scholarly and not taking into account scientific knowledge and published research results.

I feel that this is not a shortcoming, but rather another significant innovation in perceiving the problem of heroin abuse in its fullest context. And—though I do not place it in the same category—I cannot overlook the fact that neither the Bible nor The Communist Manifesto are authenticated with adequate bibliographical sources and research findings.

The fact is that Dr. Kunnes has written a remarkable book. A book that provides enlightening reading and destroys the myopic security of carefully controlled scientific experimentation. He tells us boldly and eloquently:

Heroin addiction is not a criminal problem, though criminals and crime are involved. Nor is heroin addiction a medical problem, though medical symptoms are produced. Heroin addiction is ultimately a political and economic problem created by, and controlled for, wealthy criminals with political connections, political officials with corporate and criminal connections, and corporate officials controlling the priorities of our society. . . .

To use the expression of a resident of one of the therapeutic communities for drug addicts, where I acted as research and evaluation consultant: "[Dr. Kunnes] . . . tells it like it is . . . Man, he is telling us where its at and where we are . . . ." I feel we should listen to the message of this book.

GEORGIOS PAN PIPEROPOULOS
Director, The Branch of North Greece
The National Center of Social Research
Salonica

J. STANLEY LEMONS. The Woman Citizen: Social Feminism in the 1920s. Pp. vii, 266. Urbana, Illinois: University of Illinois Press, 1972. $9.50.

"What Happened after the Nineteenth Amendment?" asks J. Stanley Lemons in The Woman Citizen. "When the suffrage crusade ended, social feminism tended to resume its previous interests and multiple purposes. . . Success would have to be measured by hundreds . . . of little items from 1920 onward." Success could be so measured, argues the author, thus challenging the prevailing notion that feminism faltered and died in the twenties. It is a

significant thesis, and well argued. The Woman Citizen is an important, albeit modest, contribution to feminist history, as well as to the history of the progressive movement, the 1920s, and the New Deal.

In support of his argument, Lemons assembles an impressive body of material painstakingly culled from primary sources. He argues that socal feminists continued to promote reform in the 1920s, thereby contributing to a basic continuity between progressivism and New Deal liberalism. Women entered the political arena, not only as voters, but as candidates, office holders, members of the newly formed League of Women Voters, and—most significant—as lobbyists for such reform legislation as equal citizenship for women, protective labor laws for women and children, and infant and maternity protection.

In addition to its persuasive thesis, the felicitious qualities of this book include a good preface, Lemons' clear, straightforward prose style, and his Herculean investigation of primary sources.

Four unfelicitous qualities render the author's contribution more modest than it could have been. First, the book is dull. Nowhere is there a hint of the sprightly style with which some other historians have written of this era. Second, the book lacks analysis. Regarding progressivism, Lemons states, "It was believed that facts and statistics, when properly collected and published, would mobilize the public to reform." An analysis of the shortcomings of such an approach would be welcome. Yet it is not forthcoming, in this, as in other instances in the book, for Lemons shares the fatal belief that facts and statistics alone will do the job. Third, the book would be enhanced by smoother transitions, a more comprehensive prefatory overview, and—for the general reader—a brief introductory survey of events within the progressive and feminist movements which antedated World War I.

Finally, the book could be much more sensitive to the personal psychodynamics of feminism. It is one thing to carefully delimit one's subject. It is another thing to write a book on social feminism in the twenties without even a hint of the personal odysseys and philosophies of these remarkable women citizens.

Joy Miller Huntley
Ohio University
Athens

Jackson Turner Main. *Political Parties Before the Constitution.* Pp. xx, 481. Chapel Hill, N.C.: University of North Carolina Press, 1973. $15.95.

This impressive work is the most comprehensive study ever published of political parties in the United States, prior to the development of the first national party system in the 1790s. Advising that the phenomena under investigation are not modern political parties but legislative parties, or blocs, Professor Main has painstakingly set out to determine if legislative blocs did, in fact, exist in the state legislatures of the 1780s and, if so, who composed them and what factors influenced legislative voting patterns. A great merit of the work is that it does not follow the frequent design of concentrating on a single state, but embraces all of the thirteen states, though detailed analysis is limited to seven states: Massachusetts, New York, New Jersey, Pennsylvania, Maryland, Virginia and South Carolina.

This ambitious plan involved the collection of individual data on 1503 legislators in the seven states and computer analysis of their responses to the issues recorded in legislative roll calls. In examining the composition of the state legislatures, Main has assembled data on each member to indicate residence, economic status, religion, political experience, occupation, age, military service, social origin, intellectual interest, education, world view and other information. The result of this extensive compilation of data and its systematic analysis is a study, so solidly based on the obtainable evidence, that its judiciously drawn conclusions command scholarly respect and widespread attention.

Main's key finding is that two legislative blocs existed in every state, and everywhere these blocs divided on the same issues and contained the same sorts of people. In every assembly there were legislators not aligned with either bloc, but two major legislative parties regularly confronted each other on most of the major issues of the Confederation period, with similar alignments in every state. Main labels the two blocs Localists and Cosmopolitans. In the seven states exhaustively examined, he identifies 539 Localists, 522 Cosmopolitans, and 412 neutrals.

In analyzing the sources of these political alignments, Main finds that the most influential factor determining a delegate's voting record was that of residence. This factor included a member's own environment and the kind of constituency he represented, and could generally be described in terms of urban versus rural, commercial versus agrarian, and cosmopolitan versus localist. Other major factors which strongly influenced legislative alignments were world view, occupation and economic status. The proportions of these factors varied from state to state, but Main's analysis for the nation as a whole ranks their influence in the order listed above. Compressing the major influence under the most encompassing labels, Main suggests that the two blocs might most accurately be called agrarian-localist and commercial-cosmopolitan. He projects the continuing influence of these alignments in the Antifederalist and the Federalist positions of 1787–88.

Noble E. Cunningham, Jr.
Department of History
University of Missouri
Columbia

Huey P. Newton. *Revolutionary Suicide.* Pp. 333. New York: Harcourt, Brace Jovanovich, 1973. $8.95.

The title, *Revolutionary Suicide,* is not a very accurate reflection of the content of this book. Although the author devotes a considerable amount of effort, in the first part of this work, to differentiating "revolutionary suicide" from "reactionary suicide," a title more in keeping with its content might have been: Poverty, Policemen, Courts, Schools and Prisons.

The author makes a determined effort to convince the reader that death, to a black man in pursuit of a revolution aimed at eradicating social and economic injustices, is a great and noble thing. He is persuasive in his efforts to create an image of himself as a courageous and dedicated man, willing to die in the struggle to improve the lot of black people. His willingness to challenge the laws which he deems unjust; to spend hours of his time consulting and assisting those involved in legal difficulties and his willingness to fight and to go to prison, reflect a more than usual concern about improving the quality of life for the Black.

His efforts to justify the use of force by the Black Panther Party, to attain its goals, are not very convincing. In developing programs and political strategy to deal with the political and economic needs of the poor, Newton would have done well to have consulted with some of the black political pragmatists, such as Carl Stokes, former mayor of Cleveland; Mayor Hatcher of Gary, Indiana and the newly-elected Mayor Bradley of Los Angeles. All of these men have demonstrated their astuteness in interpreting the mood, the needs and aspirations of black people.

Newton's comments on the thoughts, emotions and frustrations of those constantly confronted with the problems of poverty are colorful and provocative. To escape from poverty, he rationalizes to the point of justifying crimes against the poverty of white people. Robbing parking meters and helping himself to the merchandise in the neighborhood stores was not "looked upon as stealing or anything wrong." In prison he expressed no need for rehabilitation because, to him, his only crime was "to speak in defense of the people."

His commentary on the schools, reflects a deep and bitter resentment against an educational system oriented, primarily, to the values of white society. If his contentions are accurate, that his junior high school "teachers attempted to embarrass and humiliate" him, and that, even though he was a high school graduate, he was not able to read, his resentment is easily understood.

When Newton confines his remarks and explanations to domestic problems and institutions with which he is familiar, his style and the substance of his arguments is at times informative and persuasive. Unfortunately, he succumbs to the temptation of pontificating on a variety of complex national and international political and economic problems. His arguments in relation to these problems are shallow, and his sweeping unsubstantiated generalizations are unimpressive. His political and philosophical intoxication with the economic concepts of Castro and Mao Tsetung tend to blur his objectivity, in his attempts to analyze the strengths and weaknesses of the American economic system.

ERNEST M. COLLINS
Department of Government
Ohio University
Athens

DAVID E. PRICE. *Who Makes the Laws? Creativity and Power in Senate Committees.* Pp. ix, 380. Cambridge, Mass.: Schenkman, 1972. No price.

This book is an ambitious, and, for the most part, successful treatment of Congress's role in policy making. Based on case study materials, Price's study examines several conceptions bearing on Congressional policy making, tentatively confirming some and revising others.

The book examines thirteen domestic policy bills in three Senate Committees— Commerce, Finance, and Labor and Public Welfare—during the Eighty-ninth Congress (1965-66). The author was, at that time, legislative aide to the late Senator E. L. Bartlett of Alaska. In terms of an abundance of factual information, the book demonstrates the advantages of writing about Congress with an insider's perspective. At the same time, the author has maintained a very nice balance in presentation—indeed, just about the best I have seen—between an abundance of factual material, and the requirement for systematic treatment of facts imposed by an academic discipline. The conceptual threads that weave the facts together remain prominent and the whole study is written in a prose style of uncommon clarity and precision.

Price examines the opportunities for, and constraints on, congressional policy making by examining Senate action on the thirteen bills across six phases in the policy process: formulation, instigation/publicizing, information gathering, interest aggregation, mobilization and modification. Despite variations in involvement, depending on the particular committee, issue, or individual personality, Price finds that, overall, United States senators make valuable contributions to the shaping of important domestic policies at critical junctures in the policy process. This finding is particularly important, inasmuch as the period of the Eighty-ninth Congress was seen by some analysts as the apogee of presidential domination over the legislative branch. In the current Washington context of a president deeply wounded by scandal, the nation could ill-afford a docile, ineffectual, legislature. The strength of the nation's political system, in the immediate future, could well depend on the strength of Congress. Price's study, and subsequent events, would suggest a congressional capacity to act that critics were certain was lost.

Price's study clearly displays both the advantages and limitations of the case study approach. As with all good case studies, this one is rich in detail and consistently interesting. On the other hand, although Price pays far more attention to conceptual matters than most case study authors, he quite correctly shies away from making formal theoretical generalizations. Price suggests that this is necessary because of the phenomenon under study; that policy making is "singularly resistent to generalization and theory." But it may be less a problem of the phenomenon studied, than of this particular way of studying the phenomenon. The case study approach, by definition of its singularity, tends to treat as unique, phenomena that may not be unique, even when more than a single piece of legislation is under consideration, as it is here. It is this orientation toward uniqueness that has always hindered the case study and restricted its use for purposes of building formal theories. Case study conclusions are usually hedged with qualifications and caveats that the findings

from the case under examination may not apply uniformly across all cases, and formal theories, of course, must be based on uniformities. To my way of thinking, this does not necessarily diminish the quality or importance of a case study if it adds useful increments of information on important political institutions or events. Price's study does this, and does it well. As nothing more nor less than a quality case study, it is a welcome contribution to the literature on Congress, particularly in highlighting some evidence that Congress has not gone the way of the Edsel. The only unconvincing part of the study is Price's assertion that policy making resists theorizing because of the "peculiarly creative and purposive character of 'policy entrepreneurship.' " What is peculiar is not the process, but Price's slice of it—thirteen bills out of thousands, three committees out of dozens, and one Congress out of eighty-nine. For that slice, however, this study is a thoroughly sound and professional piece of work.

EVERETT F. CATALDO
Director, Institute of Behavioral
  Research
Florida Atlantic University
Boca Raton

CHARLES W. ROLL, JR. and ALBERT H. CANTRIL. *Polls: Their Use and Misuse in Politics.* Pp. xii, 197. New York: Basic Books, 1972. $6.95.

DAVID LEBEDOFF. *Ward Number Six.* Pp. 179. New York: Charles Scribner, 1972. $5.95.

Both of these books are directed towards students of contemporary politics and each provides significant insights into the challenges and frustrations facing those running for political office.

Charles Roll and Albert Cantril are professional poll-takers who have been actively involved in numerous political campaigns and academic surveys. To their study *Polls: Their Use and Misuse in Politics,* the authors bring a wealth of information relating to the formulation, execution and interpretation of public opinion polls and they present their findings in an easy to comprehend, and often humorous, fashion. Some of the most imaginative and useful material can be found in the chapters describing the abuses and benefits of polling in political campaigns. The authors describe techniques used to create a false bandwagon effect for a particular candidate, methods of biasing the outcome through sampling only certain pre-selected populations and misreading responses because of the poor wording of questions. However, they also cite the benefits that polls can bring to candidates and the general public, such as indicating the concerns of the people and finding weaknesses in an opponent's image or campaign strategy. The final segment deals with an area often neglected in the literature surrounding opinion polling: the consequences of polls for society and safeguards that might be introduced to insure that the public receives accurate and unbiased results from the many polls taken.

While Roll and Cantril stress the importance of observation and measurement of political activity and public thought, David Lebedoff emphasizes politics from the viewpoint of the active participant. *Ward Number Six* is a fascinating personal account of the author's observations of the political process at the local, state and national level. Lebedoff is well qualified to lead us through the labyrinths of a presidential campaign. He is presently a close advisor to Governor Wendell Anderson of Minnesota and was intimately involved with the McCarthy and Humphrey efforts during the 1968 election. The story he tells is one of a blending of the new and old style American politics, the personalities of two major democratic presidential aspirants and the behind the scene maneuvering that ultimately culminated in the nomination of Hubert Humphrey. It is particularly refreshing to find an author who retains a healthy skepticism of the political process, and yet does not see the necessity of denouncing the many behind the scene agreements reached because of the realities of electoral politics. Lebedoff strongly attacks the press coverage afforded the 1968 convention, and cites several examples of what he clearly views as distortion of events by the news media. Many may disagree with this assertion, or others made throughout the book, but probably few will deny the value to be gained by reading the author's narrative account.

There are naturally several areas in which both volumes are open to criticism. One might wish, for example, that Roll and Cantril had examined in more depth many of the technical aspects of sampling and survey interpretation that they condense into a relatively limited space. Similarly, Lebedoff's personal analysis would have been enhanced by presentation and analysis of pre and post election voting and opinion data, as well as some reference to the campaign tactics and objectives of other presidential candidates. Both studies, however, provide excellent examinations of the art and science of politics. They can be highly recommended to those seeking further knowledge of the workings of the American political system now and in the future.

RICHARD D. FELD
East Texas State University

DAVID LEE ROSENBLOOM. *The Election Men: Professional Campaign Managers and American Democracy.* Pp. ix, 182. New York: Quadrangle Books, 1973. $6.95.

RALPH M. GOLDMAN. *Behavioral Perspectives on American Politics.* Pp. xvi, 379. Homewood, Illinois: The Dorsey Press, 1973. $5.95.

Professor Rosenbloom has directed attention to an important phenomenon in American politics: the emergence of a relatively new type of political animal—the professional campaign manager. He says: "The professional campaign managers are a small group of businessmen-politicians who are taking control of the electoral process in the United States."

Professional campaign management was born in California, with the founding of the renowned firm of Whitaker and Baxter in 1934. Since that time, a professional campaign management industry has grown from that one firm, operating in one state, to several hundred firms, operating in most states at all electoral levels. It was not

until the 1950s, however, that professional campaign management really burgeoned on a national scale. Mass-merchandising techniques to sell political candidates began to develop.

The practitioners of this industry have emerged from a variety of backgrounds: journalism, public relations, advertising, radio and television, and traditional political party or staff positions. And as a group they have come increasingly to perceive of themselves as skilled professionals. Rosenbloom says: "The most unanimous finding in this entire study revolves around the managers' self-image of professionalism. . . . They argue strongly that they bring scientific, or at least objective, views into an arena long dominated by myth and incompetence."

Rosenbloom sees a serious threat to democracy in this phenomenon. He writes: "A new political elite is developing at the very core of democracy that does not meet a crucial test, a relationship of responsibility to the people. . . . The campaign managers are increasingly accountable only to themselves and to their own vision of politics." The lack of true accountability on the part of those who increasingly dominate our electoral processes is indeed a cause for concern in a democratic society.

An analysis of American national government and politics from the perspective of a series of behavioral concepts, is the task undertaken by Professor Goldman in the present volume. Thus, he is focusing on the institutions of our national political system, the major behavioral concepts which he dealt with in his earlier work, *Contemporary Perspective on Politics*. It is an imaginative and illuminating approach to the study of American politics.

The principal concepts used by Goldman for his analysis are the following: Group and Organization; Communication and Information; Definition and Proposition; Transaction and Marketplace; Decision, Role, and Reference Group; Collective Decision and Decision Rules; Leadership and Followership; Socialization and Politicization; and Conflict and Game Theory. He has applied each of these concepts to an examination of two types of political phenomena: (1) the constitutional organizations of the national government—presidency, congress, the federal judiciary; and (2) the quasi-constitutional organizations of the nation's political life—organized interest groups, political parties, the electorate and the mass media of communication.

The author states in the preface that his purpose is "to stimulate the student of politics and society to see familiar phenomena in the new ways and new relationships suggested by contemporary behavioral theory." I believe that he succeeds in that effort.

Among the particularly strong segments of the book are his treatment of the decision making process and the modes of handling conflict in American politics. The chapter glossaries add to its utility as a teaching resource. Each chapter also contains a series of analytical exercises which may be performed by the student on an individual basis.

Goldman's book will not, of course, be every instructor's cup of academic tea. But for those seeking to approach the study of American politics, in a manner that blends institutional and behavioral considerations, it is a useful and skillfully done book.

RAYMOND H. GUSTESON
Department of Government
Ohio University
Athens

JOSEPH R. STAROBIN. *American Communism in Crisis, 1943–1957*. Pp. 331. Cambridge, Mass: Harvard University Press, 1972. $12.95.

This study, prepared under the auspices of Professor Zbigniew Brzezinski's Research Institute on Communist Affairs at Columbia University, is an important addition to that organization's anti-Communist literature. The author—who lives in Massachusetts but who teaches in York University, Toronto—is an ex Communist party minor functionary, who looks back with a mixture of sorrow and anger on the "god that failed." The book is no recanting *apologia pro fide sua;* nor, on the other hand, is it a history of the party between 1943 and 1957. Starobin centers his view on the labyrinthine contortions of party policy between the 1943 Teheran Conference and the virtual disintegration of the American Communist party after its sixteenth national convention in 1957.

Professor Starobin obviously feels a greater affection for the "right-wing revisionist" heresy, than for the vacillating "left sectarian" views of some of the party's leaders. Thus, he finds Earl Browder being somewhat shabbily treated by the party in 1945 and Browder's successor William Z. Foster lacking both in imagination and decisiveness. In brief, the Communist Party of United States of America was destroyed—according to the author—as much by its own inner contradictions as by external opposition.

Internally, the party was torn during the later 1940s by, (1) the desire of party purists for a go it alone policy, confronted by the desire of revisionists to join forces with the Murray-Hillman faction of the Congress of Industrial Organizations, (2) the objection of some intellectuals in the party to the decree that art be judged solely according to the dictates of Marxism-Leninism and (3) opposition by racial integrationists to the proposal to redraw state boundaries in the Black Belt so as to create a Black Republic within the South. The ignominious showing of Henry Wallace at the polls in 1948 signaled, concludes the author, the rout of the American Communist party. "From this point on, the American C. P. became at least a case in civil liberties, at best an object of sympathy, but no longer a power."

This is a carefully and gracefully written book, by an author in whom many of the old wounds created by his identification with the Communist party are not yet closed. As a publisher's venture in bookmaking it regrettably falls short on several counts. Besides several awkwardly contrived chapter headings, the typography—including a number of typographical errors—leaves much to be desired, esthetically. And one wishes Mr. Starobin's interesting explanatory footnotes, seventy-three pages

in all, had not been condemned to the Siberia of backnotes.

WILLIAM M. ARMSTRONG
Department of History
Clarkson College of Technology
Potsdam
New York

HAROLD C. SYRETT, ed. *The Papers of Alexander Hamilton.* Vols. xvi and xvii. Pp. 664. Columbia University Press 1972. $30.00.

These two volumes cover the hyperactive career of Alexander Hamilton, from February to December 1794. As in previous volumes, they include letters to, as well as by, him and the more important of his official and other writings. Throughout that year he remained secretary of the treasury, though he had indicated to President Washington his wish to retire; his enemy Jefferson had already left the government in December 1793 and he himself was to follow suit in January 1795, finding his official salary of $3,500 alarmingly inadequate.

It was a strained and gloomy period. Abroad, there was the problem of how the United States—still formally allied to France—should maintain genuine neutrality in the Franco-British struggle. This problem heightened the mutual suspicions of Jeffersonians and Hamiltonians. Excellent editorial notes reveal the tensions surrounding the president's decision to send John Jay to England to try and negotiate a treaty. Jefferson, regarding Hamilton as an "Anglomaniac," was quick to interpret the whole affair as a disgraceful plot in which Hamilton was maneuvering to secure the appointment for himself.

At home, the biggest controversy was over the Whiskey Rebellion in western Pennsylvania. Here the volumes contain no startling revelations, but they provide as much information as we are ever likely to get on the inner workings of the Washington administration. What actually happened is still something of a puzzle. Possibly the president, increasingly wearied by the strains of office, overreacted to the crisis. The excise tax that provoked the rising was ill-considered, but Washington thought he detected a conspiracy and that the only way to restore order was through a show of force. It is understandable that, given this reaction, he should have decided to call out the militia in considerable numbers and prepare to lead them himself. One can also appreciate why he let Secretary of War Knox go off to Maine to deal with personal financial problems. The curiosity is that he allowed Hamilton, not only to replace Knox as organizer of logistic aspects, but also to assume actual command of the troops, when he well knew that the treasury secretary was a controversial and unpopular figure.

The reason seems to be that Hamilton was so inescapably there—so eager, so competent, so authoritative. A tired president, aware that Hamilton was potentially dangerous, nevertheless found him indispensable for the moment. Once again, this admirable edition brings out the extraordinary centrality of Alexander Hamilton in the formative years of the new nation. If he did not always get his own way with Washington and others, he did impose his sense of the vital issues upon the direction of policy. Few men in American history have made such an impact: few are so endlessly fascinating.

MARCUS CUNLIFFE

University of Sussex
England

HOWARD TOLLEY, JR. *Children and War: Political Socialization to International Conflict.* Pp. vii, 196. New York: Teachers College Press, 1973. $9.50. Paperbound, $4.95.

No doubt, the future of humanity's interrelationships—particularly at the level of the artificial territorial creation of the nation state—depends partly upon how the young child and future citizen learns to view war. This book, which is devoted to the subject of how children develop their views of international conflict, is informative and interesting, though limited. The data—a questionnaire survey of 2,677 children aged seven to fifteen from public, private and parochial schools located in urban, suburban rural portions of New York, New Jersey and Maryland and collected from January through March, 1971—are interesting, in that they represent one of the largest and most comprehensive analyses of how children learn to view war. While one could argue, and the author stresses, that the data base is limited in terms of sampling procedures, this is less disturbing than the absence of theory. Data, even those collected methodically and analyzed using the most sophisticated bivariate and multivariate methods, speak for themselves in only the most limited sense. Hence, while it is interesting to note that all children do not hate war, and that "three factors contribute most to children's acceptance of war: school, parents, and age of the child," the reader is left to wonder just how important—not interesting—are such findings?

Based upon the assumption which underpins most work on childhood political socialization, that is "that childhood socialization influences adult political beliefs," this book is not well grounded in the theory necessary to validate that rationalization. While the author has surveyed previous studies of children's views of international conflict, he has not plugged this work into a schema that could account for the processes at work. Thus, this book joins most other socialization studies, in their primary emphasis on what children know or feel about certain pre-selected political objects. The data reported do, on the other hand, assume some importance in thir own right. It is, for example, interesting to find that "children almost unanimously condemn war on principle," but qualify their objections in specific cases. It is also important to note how the results of the present study fit into the historical climate of opinion on war. The author notes that "Our survey reveals, in the face of recent anti-war protest, about the same proportion of avowed pacifists as do studies conducted before World War II." The present study also raises serious questions about some of the findings of earlier studies conducted in "more stable" times, which noted that children agreed with and idealized political authority figures. The respondents in the present survey are not nearly so acquiescent as those interviewed by Hess, Easton and Greenstein.

Using age, sex, and race as the basic control variables, other interesting findings emerge. Black children, for example, appear as less supportive of war than most white children, even though these findings are complicated by parental views and attendance in Quaker, Catholic, public, or military schools. Enter here, however, one of the major problems in conception and interpretation. The author states that his analysis of attendance in military as opposed to other schools "confirms" the hypothesis that *"Experience with military routines at school fosters an acceptance of both war and patriotic values"* (Tolley's italics). The author does not account for the possibility of prior selection, except in the limited sense of examining children's perceptions of parent's views on war. Moreover, finding no stastically significant differences between teachers in the four different types of schools, leads one to speculate further that prior selection, or perhaps personality differences, are involved in the results and that the family and possibly children's peers—which are not examined in the present study—are more important socialization agents than given credit for by the present author.

In short, this book, while limited theoretically, is an informative, interesting and valuable addition to the existing body of data on political socialization.

HERBERT HIRSCH
Department of Government
The University of Texas
Austin

BETTY ZISK. *Local Interest Politics: A One-Way Street.* Pp. v, 184. Indianapolis: Bobbs-Merrill, 1973. No price. Paperbound.

Local Interest Politics is a study of the impact of interest groups on policy-making of city councils. It is based on data collected by the City Council Research Project, Institute of Political Studies, Stanford University. Most of the data came from extensive interviews of city councilmen in eighty-two of the eighty-nine cities in the San Francisco Bay area, with some data drawn from city budgets and the United States Census.

The author's thesis is that three sets of data are required to explain group influence on city councils: (1) socio-economic statistics *à la* Thomas Dye; (2) descriptions of group activities and (3) descriptions of the councilmen's attitudes toward interest groups. These data sets are closely related in a number of ways. First, groups tend to be more numerous and active in large cities than in small ones, although groups are by no means always active in large cities. Second, councilmen in large cities tend to be more favorably disposed toward interest groups than councilmen in small cities, although this, too, is only a statement of tendency and councilmanic attitudes are not completely dependent on socio-economic factors. Thus the author demonstrates that socio-economic factors are important, but she directly challenges Dye's thesis with her findings that group activities—and councilmen's attitudes toward those activities—have an independent impact on policy outcomes.

While this study is an important contribution to the interest group literature, it is not without weaknesses—most of which are openly discussed by the author at several points in the book. The most severe problem is that, except for socio-economic input and policy outcome statistics, data is derived exclusively from interviews with city councilmen. Considering that eighty-two out of the eighty-nine cities in the Bay area were covered, it would appear that the researchers' energies would have been more economically utilized by studying fewer cities and interviewing a wider range of political influentials. This is especially critical, since one of the study's major findings is that approximately three-quarters of councilmen are unaware of, or hostile to, group activity. There appears to be no substantial reason to believe this finding. The reviewer has had considerable experience in interviewing and observing legislators in four states, and their statesmen-like poses of interest group independence are often belied by their actions as group representatives and members. It is possible that some of the interview results were biased by councilmanic lies and self-deception; without other data sources we cannot know. The same criticism applies to the author's data concerning interest group activity, which was obtained from councilmen only. In the reviewer's experience, politicians consistently underrate the importance of interest groups, stressing instead the critical nature of public opinion and the public interest.

Despite these problems, this is an important work. The author asks perceptive questions, if not always of the right people.

CARL GRAFTON
Department of Political Science
University of Houston

ECONOMICS

JA NGOC CHAU. *Population Growth and Costs of Education in Developing Countries.* Pp. 313. Paris, France: International Institute for Educational Planning, 1973. $7.00.

JOHN VAIZEY. *The Political Economy of Education.* Pp. 297. New York: Halsted Press, 1973. $14.95.

The Chau book will be both welcomed and criticized for its handling of the important question of how population growth affects education. Perhaps this is unfair, since it is aimed at an audience of educational planners who presumably are content to anticipate additional costs, numbers of students and teachers—in short the bare statistical increments of their trade. The cases discussed—Ceylon [sic], Tanzania, Columbia and Tunisia—intend rather modestly ". . . only to show the sensitiveness of educational expenditures to various population projections . . ." (p. 281). In order to do this some basic assumptions must be made, which are not easily accepted. First, the role of technology in future development is ignored since, for the next two decades—the usual projection dates used in the book—things are expected to remain very much as they are. Secondly, only primary level education is considered and although the reasons for this are clearly stated on page 14, they

must be considerably qualified, namely, second-level enrollment is more dependent on government policy than population trends, government costs are largely concentrated at the first level and, finally, changes in fertility would not be felt for twenty years beyond first level.

Besides this ambivalence between the aim of the book and its reasons for focusing on a particular level, there is an additional difficulty between the model showing the effect of demographic growth at the back of the book and as it was applied in the countries studied. Although we are cautioned to apply the model separately for rural and urban populations (p. 282)—which often differ in terms of natural growth, migration, opportunity and other factors—this is only partially done for Columbia and not for the other countries. One wonders how meaningful the projections are for, say, Tunisia where 70 percent of the population live in rural areas. Although these are certainly serious shortcomings, it would be unfair not to commend the International Institute for Educational Planning for taking up this important topic.

Also a word should be said concerning the excellent case study chapters, which are of a uniformly high standard. They combine useful and detailed cost and enrollment data on each country, that are not otherwise readily available.

The Vaizey book is at once a more sophisticated work and, at the same time, a less coherent one. It suffers from sounding like a textbook when surveying a wide range of relevant materials of direct interest to educational economists—such as the "social demand" models of Correa-Tinbergen, Tinbergen and Bos and Stone (p. 80 ff.). Elsewhere, there is the most exhausting detail which would be better left in a special monograph; for example the discussion of income differentials due to status and those which might be mistakenly attributed to education. At no place in the book could this reviewer find the least relevance of the title to the text material and can only conclude it was a mistake. It is unfortunate, because one looks in vain for a discussion of the interrelations between educational needs and political realities by an obviously gifted and dedicated author. A more proper title would be the already familiar titles of Vaizey books, such as *The Economics of Education*.

Though much of what is written in this volume has been said before, there is value in repeating the need to combine theoretical sophistication with intimate knowledge of how schools operate. At times Vaizey is both clear and precise, as in the discussion of teacher salaries in six European countries, where average salaries are skewed by different national teacher age distributions, and by the nature and degree of overtime payments. Elsewhere, when dealing with educational "effectiveness" there is a tendency to rely on costs and degrees for answers, rather than the student "subjective" enjoyment which Vaizey claims to be important. Perhaps he would not consider this an economist's proper focus. He does say, "The real problem of educational innovation is probably an administrative rather than an economic one" (p. 220).

Of considerably less importance, though no less bothersome, are the numerous errors which indicate careless editing. There is no list of tables, so table 6, referred to on page 195, may be missing. On page 236 there are two footnotes numbered 2 but only one cited; more curious, subscript 1 comes at the end of a sentence which talks about growing teacher numbers between 1965 and 1980 and then is documented by a table showing the number of pupils from 1920–1969. One wonders if these faults also characterized the extensive Gulbenkian research project on which the book is based.

JOSEPH DI BONA
Department of Education
Duke University
Durham
North Carolina

DONALD J. CURRAN. *Metropolitan Financing*. Pp. 166. Madison: University of Wisconsin Press, 1973. $11.50.

Much has been written about the complex economic and social problems which beset the metropolitan areas of the United States. Seldom, however, has the historical evolution of such problems been in the primary vehicle of their analysis. Yet, this is the methodological approach followed by Donald J. Curran in his study of metropolitan fiscal issues in the Milwaukee area, as they have developed over the fifty year period between 1920 and 1970. In all, the author successfully utilizes the historical perspective and, by so doing, adds further insight into the nature of metropolitan fiscal problems and their possible solutions.

Since the study deals exclusively with the development of metropolitan fiscal problems in the Milwaukee area, the actual data presented in the study are of little interest to other metropolitan areas. However, this in no way detracts from the overall usefulness of the study. For example, since the application of historical analysis adds further insight into metropolitan economic problems in Milwaukee, there is justification to use the same methodology for similar studies of other metropolitan areas. Moreover, many of the characteristics of metropolitan fiscal issues in Milwaukee undoubtedly are not unique to that area. Thus, a broad understanding can be gained of the nature of these problems and of techniques for their solutions, even though the detailed data are specifically Milwaukee in their orientation.

The author operates under the acceptable assumption that metropolitan fiscal problems can be "improved from within," if the fiscal characteristics of the various units of government constituting the metropolitan area—including those between the central city and suburban government—become significantly more uniform over time. That is, the blending of fiscal characteristics will encourage voluntary solutions to these problems by the local governments themselves, rather than by a reliance upon solutions "imposed from above" by a higher level of government. Unfortunately, he concludes that such has not occurred in Milwaukee. Instead, the "economic unit" which constitutes the Milwaukee metropolitan area is fragmentized in balkan fashion into numerous "political units" with diverse fiscal characteristics and interests. Even worse—as is well demonstrated by the author—state government fiscal policies directed toward local governments in Wisconsin have accentuated this diversity.

Accordingly, the responsibility to coordinate policies for improvement is placed appropriately "at the doorstep" of the Wisconsin State government. This seems to be a logical point of placement, since the local governments are, in fact, political entities created by the sovern state government. Consequently, the state government cannot escape its responsibility for maintaining intergovernmental fiscal efficiency among the local governments.

BERNARD P. HERBER
Department of Economics
University of Arizona
Tucson

J. D. GOULD. *Economic Growth in History: Survey and Analysis.* Pp. xix, 460. London: Methuen, 1972. $7.50.

Economic theory abounds in abstract analytical models of economic growth, constructed with little appeal to historical experience, and in planning theories based on such theoretical models. On the other hand, historical economists did not go far enough in using the theoretical models of growth and planning developed by the theorists. This contribution by Gould is addressed to historical economists, who want to know to what extent pure theory is relevant in the area of economic growth and development, as well as to economic theorists who want to draw benefits from the lessons of history.

The scope of this book is limited to the treatment of a restricted range of economic variables, though the author is fully aware that the search for the sources of economic growth can be carried out on a number of different levels. He realizes that the ultimate causes of economic backwardness might lie in "social and psychological features of traditional societies rather than in characteristics, which fall within the province of the economists." Yet, within this deliberately restricted do-

main, the author skillfully integrates the theoretical and historical aspects of growth.

In his introductory chapter, Gould describes historical aspects of structural changes which took place in the presently more highly developed countries. The main body of the work deals with such topics as the role played by the agricultural sector in economic growth and development; the relationship between rates of investment and rates of growth of the economy; the role of the foreign sector, and the impact of inventions and rate of technological advance on the rate of output. In the concluding chapter, one finds a critical review of several theories of economic growth and development.

Instead of deriving his own theory from available data, the author attempts to test existing theories in the light of historical evidence. Two major obstacles stand in the way of constructing a useful theory of growth and development. First, historical reality is too complex to be adequately accounted for, by even a sophisticated analytical model. Secondly, the nature of the study makes it impossible to subject the contesting theories to adequate empirical testing. Gould's greatest contribution lies in the use of relevant historical evidence to clarify several important relationships among the factors affecting economic growth.

The licidity of style and avoidance of professional jargon make this study readily accessible to both specialists and laymen interested in the fascinating phenomenon of economic growth.

OLEG ZINAM
Department of Economics
University of Cincinnati

DAVID GRANICK. *Managerial Comparisons of Four Developed Countries: France, Britain, United States, and Russia.* Pp. ix, 394. Cambridge, Mass.: The MIT Press, 1972. $15.00.

Comparison is an excellent analytical tool when used by a theorist, or technician, familiar with the elements involved in the problems under investigation. Professor Granick qualifies in all these respects; but, recognizing that many of his readers may not be equally qualified, the author tries to find a basis for common understanding by building a theoretical foundation in his first three chapters. Although not suggested by the author, this reviewer found it necessary also to study the glossary and the well-organized index—found in the final twelve pages of the book—to comprehend and evaluate the broad scope of the statistical tables, management patterns and behavior comparisons, presented in connection with the case studies which follow the theoretical dissertations.

Recognizing that he will have an audience of varying interests, training and experience, the author attempts to assist the reader by choosing the parts of the book which will appeal most specifically to him. This is done in the introduction by grouping assumed readers into three categories: (1) economists, (2) industrial sociologists, and (3) business administration specialists. He also suggests specific chapters for each group.

The source of the material used in the case studies, and the time periods in which studies were made, are also set forth in the introduction. Unfortunately, the years indicated predate the date of publication by five or more years. To up-date his investigations, at least theoretically, the author includes a section at the close of the book entitled "Conclusions and Recent Developments." The following excerpts from that section set the tone for the book as a whole:

The managerial function in a modern industrial society may be viewed as primarily that of adapting the enterprise to changing conditions. The quality of management can be judged primarily by its responses to changes in the technological, social, and market environment. Variations in the standard of management between countries have their most significant effect on the rate of productivity growth rather than upon the level of static efficiency reached at any moment.
Throughout this study, the effectiveness of managerial adaptation to change has been analyzed in terms of two systems of variables: managerial values on the one hand, and the characteristics of managerial organization on the other. Both determine the enterprise's

state of readines to implement successfully alternative projects.

The varying degrees to which the criteria of managerial function are being met in the four countries selected for comparison are discussed and evaluated, which is not an easy task considering the institutional variables among these countries.

GLEN U. CLEETON
Dean Emeritus, Humanities and
   Social Sciences
Carnegie-Mellon University
Pittsburgh,
Pennsylvania

STUART W. ROBINSON. *Multinational Banking: A Study of Certain Legal and Financial Aspects of the Postwar Operations of the U.S. Branch Banks in Western Europe.* Pp. vii, 316. Leiden, The Netherlands: A. W. Sijthoff, 1972. Dfl. 5,500.

This book studies, with an interdisciplinary approach, the legal, financial and economic intricacies and problems of operations of some United States private banks, in four Western European countries, —France, Great Britain and Switzerland.

The problems of multi-national banking for American private banks is an important topic, because their overseas operations —especially in European countries—have undergone a dynamic evolution and growth since 1945. Despite a short period of dollar shortage and exchange regulations in Europe, there has been an inflow of dollars to Europe since completion of the Marshall Plan, so that from 1956 on, all American banks in France, Great Britain and Switzerland had an ample supply of dollar deposits. The outflow of dollars continued until it was restricted in July, 1963 by President Kennedy's retro-active legislation to dampen and slow the United States capital outflow, in the form of interest equalization tax. This was later followed by President Johnson's Voluntary Guidelines, in 1967.

As the author indicates, the American branch banks working in host countries have been extremely active, inventive and flexible, and have been adapting their pace and structure to the various changing situations and circumstances of these countries. They have also used their innovative marketing tools to attract clients, offering more service and better management and control in handling multi-national banking operations.

The book is a well-documented and interesting study and contains numerous guidelines and trends for further study of multinational banking. The author gives much attention to Euro-currency—especially the Euro-dollar—and to various techniques, regulations and rules for borrowing and depositing these currencies in different branch banks of American banks in Europe. He explains in detail how the competition of American branch banks in host countries has been a good and healthy factor in increasing competition among the host countries' banks, in creating efficiency among them and particularly, in expanding the idea of universal banking to the narrow banking concepts of those countries. It would have been more meaningful if the author had given precise statistics as to the increase of shares of the American banks' operations in getting deposits, as well as in lending. One could then have evaluated the trend and compare it with total activity of indigenous banks in host countries. It would have been still more meaningful to study the impact of American competition on the merger movement, especially in view of increasing concentration and merger tendency in these host countries.

There is another topic which the author has not given the full consideration which it deserves: the effects and impact of inflationary tendency and political and economic conditions in the United States on the movement of dollars to and from the United States to the dollar holdings of the American branch banks in host countries. As indicated through the book, the increase of operations of American branch banks has a direct effect on the American economic and monetary situation at home. Besides, the economic political and monetary situations in the host countries are highly relevant to the United States of America. This international interdependence of multi-national banking could have been the subject of a special chapter, emphasizing the need for more economic analysis than has been give by the author. It would have also been interesting to develop, in more detail, the study of the tendency of host countries—like Switzerland, France, and Great Britain—to try to open branch banks in the United States, so as to compete the way American branch banks are competing abroad.

To cover such an extensive subject, the book is well planned and contains much data. It should be studied by all students of international money and banking.

ALLEN O. BAYLOR
College of Business Administration
University of Texas
El Paso

LYNNE B. SAGALYN and GEORGE STERNLIEB. *Zoning and Housing Costs: The Impact of Land-Use Controls on Housing Price.* Pp. iii, 132. New Brunswick, N.J.: Center for Urban Policy Research, Rutgers University, 1973. $5.00.

This is a scholarly investigation of the relationship between exclusionary zoning practices of suburban communities and the high cost of new housing. Numerous housing studies have suggested that affluent communities prevent the intrusion of low-income and minority households, by requiring house lots to be at least one acre in size, and there has been litigation concerning the right of a community to discriminate in this fashion. *Zoning and Housing Costs* does nearly for this issue—perhaps the final distillate of the open housing controversy —what Luigi Laurenti's well-known study, *Property Values and Race,* did for the myth that non-white neighbors cause house values to fall (Berkeley: University of California Press, 1960).

The book reports on a survey covering 153 subdivisions in New Jersey, in 1970. Data were developed on the selling prices of homes; the size and frontage of lots; setback requirements; streets and sidewalks; sewage systems; building code requirements; physical characteristics of the dwellings; the scale of the subdivision and of the builder's operations, and local factors—such as the tax rate, average density and house values and delays in processing development permits. The data were processed by stepwise multiple regression experiments, in which the object was to determine whether circumstances under the control of the local government were validly asociated with the selling prices of new homes.

The conclusion is relatively weak. "Large-lot zoning *alone* does not produce expensive housing . . . it is more probable that the desirable socioeconomic character of the area was a more significant determinant of sales price" (p. 66). The principal determinant of house prices turned out to be—not surprisingly—the floor area of the dwelling, followed by the average price of homes already built in the area. Large-lot zoning has some separate effect on selling prices of new homes, but not enough—in the opinion of the authors— to promise much benefit to even middle-income families through reform of zoning practices. The predicted selling price of a 1,600 square foot house on a one-acre lot is $57,618; for a house half the size on a 12,000 square foot lot the predicted price is $33,843. This is still too high for the median New Jersey household, and most of the reduction is accounted for by the smaller house size in any case.

There is an abundance of other statistical information—which the knowledgable reader may examine to advantage—and it is presented in a fair, forthright and clear manner. The introductory section of the book has an admirable summary of the fiscal and legal arguments about large-lot zoning. There are many useful footnotes, but no index. The study was financed in part by a Department of Housing and Urban Development planning grant, with additional assistance from the state of New Jersey.

This book will be of lasting value to formulators of housing policy in the United States. It is a technical study, however, and cannot be said to lay the issue of exclusionary zoning to rest. If the larger community should determine that socio-economic integration—a mix of housing types all across the urban landscape—is desirable, then stronger means will be needed than attacking the right of suburban communities to zone their land. This book implies that a tactical legal effort will not be productive.

WILIAM F. SMITH
Department of Commerce and
  Business Administration
University of British Columbia
Vancouver

STERLING D. SPERO and JOHN M. CAPOZZOLA. *The Urban Community and Its Unionized Bureaucracies.* Pp. xiv, 361. New York: The Dunellen Company 1973. $12.50. Paperbound, $5.95.

Sterling Spero and John Capozzola have written a treasure trove of a book on collective bargaining in local government; factual, authoritative, hard-hitting and insightful. The senior author is the pioneer scholar in the field and brings to the book a time perspective of half a century. The authors face up squarely to the critical questions. They focus not only on the strike—which is the way collective bargaining mainly surfaces into public view—but beneath the surface, where issues may be equally, if not more, important.

There is the politicization of bargaining. The public employee unions function on two planes: collective bargaining with their employers in the local agencies and a kind of concurrent political bargaining with legislatures and city councils. When the "employee organization exhausts the possibility of greater gains from the management team [it] persists in trying to get more from the City Council" (p. 130).

Collective bargaining in local government, in the view of the authors, is well on the way toward "codetermination." Where collective bargaining implies negotiation over the terms of employment, codetermining implies employee negotiation of the whole range of management decision-making. "The current trend of enshrining into collective bargaining contracts many facets of personnel policy or practice hitherto regarded as the prerogative of public officials has led to forecasts that soon public employee unions will control personnel systems, with the eventual abandonment of the merit principle in public employment" (p. 199).

Codetermination has also penetrated the area of substantive public policy. The "new public worker" is "no longer content merely to implement policies handed down to him, he insists on becoming involved in the what, how, and why of the policy-making process as an active agent of change" (p. 10).

All of these developments raise critical questions about the conduct of public government. Is "Democracy within administration" compatible with "political democracy" (p. 194)? What does what Harold Laski once called "administrative syndicalism" (p. 192), do to standards of management efficiency? Has union power in effect "preempted the budgetary authority of public officials legally vested with power to decide how, when, and for what purposes city funds shall be spent" (p. 215)?

Unionization has made positive contributions. "Good faith bargaining has proved to be an effective means of communications between public employers and employees" (p. 325). It is possible that unionism can imbue increasingly autonomous bureaucracies with a sense of accountability.

The authors are highly critical "of the widespread attitude that special horrors inhere in the public service strike" (p. 317). The important question is whether there is a vital impairment of a necessary service, regardless of its public or private character.

This is a challenging book, written from the viewpoint of scholars who value collective bargaining, but also value effective public administration. Professors Spero and Capozzola have raised the kinds of right questions that must precede the formulation of right answers.

JACK BARBASH
University of Wisconsin
Madison

RICHARD SYMONDS and MICHAEL CARDER. *The United Nations and the Population Question: 1945–1970.* Pp. 236. New York: McGraw–Hill, 1973. $8.95.

PHYLLIS TILSON PIOTROW. *World Population Crisis: The United States Response.* Pp. vii, 278. New York: Praeger, 1973. No price.

With the publication of their respective studies, Symonds and Carder and Phyllis Piotrow have contributed two timely historical analyses of the responses of both the United Nations and the United States to the population problem over a twenty-five year period, beginning in 1945. The almost simultaneous publication of the two works is most fortunate since, on the one hand, Symonds and Carder claim that an important reason for the increased "involvement of the United Nations in population action programmes . . . was the evolution in the position of the United States Government" (p. 140). On the other hand, Piotrow states: "Although the UN process remained throughout the 1960's about two years behind U.S. moves, significant parallels exist in the events and some of the institutional changes that characterized the growth of both programs" (p. 199).

Piotrow makes a deliberate attempt to show how increased United States action over the past twenty-five years has been "a direct response to sequentially-made determinations of relevance, feasibility, priority, and urgency" (p. 55); determinations which, according to her, also conditioned United Nations population policy-making (p. 199). Both studies trace the events, attitudes and influences which led both the United States and the United Nations from the notion, in the 1940s and fifties, that—according to President Eisenhower—birth control was "emphatically a subject that is not a proper political or governmental activity or function or responsibility" (Piotrow, p. 45), to one, in the 1960s and seventies, that accorded the population explosion problem the highest priority in governmental and world political councils.

The Symonds and Carder book attributes the lack of significant action by the UN during the first fifteen years of its existence mainly to sustained opposition of a moral and religious nature. A General Assembly resolution in 1969 makes it quite clear that, even with a change of attitudes regarding the appropriateness of UN action, the world is a long way from the point of permitting the UN to do anything more than aid in the "formulation and establishment . . . of programs in the field of population, *within the framework of national demographic policies . . .*" (Resolution 2542 [XXIV], 1969, p. 173; emphasis mine.) The authors suggest that "it would be somewhat ingenuous to ask 'could the United Nations have done more' to bring such changes about more rapidly, or even to promote a world population policy" (p. 198). They conclude with an admonition not to underestimate the UN's role in national population planning, stating that "as the tide turned in favor of these measures, resolutions of the United Nations gave them international legitimacy which made it easier for national leaders to change course" (p. 205).

Ms. Piotrow's study, the more analytical of the two, sees American population policy resulting from bureaucratic in-fighting among governmental decision-makers faced with two contradictory positions. Formulated as questions, they are: "How can you justify using taxpayers' money for a cause that many taxpayers consider immoral?' and 'How can you justify withholding such important and useful information as birth control from the poor and disadvantaged who want to have it?'" (p. 107). She traces American policy-making to the point where the latter question clearly becomes the more accepted of the two, and both the executive and legislative branches begin responding positively and with determination.

Unfortunately, neither of the two works relates, in any meaningful way, the issue of population control to that of environmental quality. Neither really attempts to correlate attitudes regarding birth control with socioeconomic forces at work in the society. Neither gives a detailed account of what the United States and the UN are actually doing, and whether their respective programs are succeeding in reducing fertility—Piotrow specifically excludes this latter concern from her study (p. xvii). Neither deals with the socio-

economic variables affecting population, nor with the effect of population on social welfare and economic prosperity. Finally, neither looks toward the future to ask questions about the possibilities of regional population planning, of the coordination of national and international endeavors, or of the ultimate creation of a universal master plan for population control.

Ms. Piotrow suggests, in her preface, that "by the end of the decade [of the sixties] ecologists and biologists began to challenge the economic and social science theories of growth with an ecological theory of stabilization" (p. xiv). It is indeed unfortunate that neither her account, nor that of Symonds and Carder, leaves us with any real understanding of where humanity is in its quest for a universally livable world.

RICHARD CONO GIARDINA
Bowling Green State University
Ohio

HOWARD M. WACHTEL. *Workers' Management and Workers' Wages in Yugoslavia: The Theory and Practice of Participatory Socialism.* Pp. xii, 220. Ithica, N.Y.: Cornell University Press, 1973. $14.50.

Professor Wachtel has written a short, but ambitious, book in which he traces the development of the idea of participatory socialism, through a variety of nineteenth century radical movements and their more recent counterparts (chap. 2). He then turns to the development of the theory of a worker-managed enterprise in the writings of Lange, Ward, Domar, Vanek, and Horvat (chap. 3). Except for some consideration of the operation of neoclassical marginal productivity theory in chapter 7, the rest of the book deals largely with the actual operation of the Yugoslav economy, with regard to worker management and wage determination in particular. Professor Wachtel concludes that the director is the most influential member of the managerial system, which also includes a management council and a workers' council. He seems to conclude that managerial interests overshadow worker interests in firm management and that, within the firm, power lies disproportionately with white collar and highly educated or trained workers, rather than with unskilled blue collar workers. He concludes that the influence of external forces—the trade unions, the League of Communists, the economic chambers, the commune—is "problematical" (p. 97).

Turning to wage determination, Professor Wachtel utilized data on nineteen industries in mining and manufacturing since 1956 and concludes that, while there have been changes over time—despite the disproportionate distribution of power noted above—wage differentials are somewhat smaller than in either western capitalist, or centralized socialist, economies. Wachtel notes that the Yugoslav wage is composed of a fixed wage—determined in advance and received periodically—and a variable wage—paid intermittently, as a profit-like reward for risk taking by the worker-manager. Combining the two, Wachtel concludes that the wage differentials—including both of the wage parts but not non-wage payments—widened from 1956 to 1961, if measured as interskill or interrepublic differentials and narrowed after 1961. Interindustry differentials widened from 1956 to 1961 and stabilized thereafter. He finds that average productivity contributed the most to the observed differentials, with industrial concentration and profits contributing somewhat less, after controlling for differences in labor quality and regional concentration among industries.

While there is much that is admirable in this effort at examining existing hypotheses concerning wage determination in an actual "laboratory of participatory socialism," my major criticism is that little effort is made to relate the empirical findings to the theoretical parts. Wachtel largely leaves it to the reader to determine which of the models of worker management, discussed in chapter 3, the Yugoslav case gives most credence to, although the fact that Horvat's model is the only model which is dynamic, makes it a likelier candidate for securing high marks for realism. The failure to relate these models directly to the Yugoslav experience is particularly glaring in the concluding chapter, where the discussion shifts from a summary of the five theories of a labor-managed economy to the Yugoslav experience, without a single reference to the models just summarized.

The least successful part, in my opinion, is the historical chapter on participatory socialism (chap. 2), written in collaboration with William Kruvant. Again, not much effort is ever made to relate this material to the Yugoslav experience and, moreover, it is far too elliptical to offer much to those who do not already have the history of these various radical-socialist movements at their fingertips, and unnecessary for those who do.

Therefore, while Professor Wachtel's book promises more than it delivers and is, additionally, a far from easy book to read, it contains much valuable information and points the way for future efforts at studying evolving systems following new paths, such as is the case in Yugoslavia.

PHILIP A. KLEIN
Department of Economics
The Pennsylvania State University

SOCIOLOGY

ALEXANDER ALLAND, JR. *The Human Imperative*. Pp: viii, 185. New York: Columbia University Press, 1972. $8.50.

An interesting and significant pattern in intellectual history is the long-continued conflict between biological and non-biological—social, environmental and spiritual—explanations for human nature. This applies especially to that part of it which expresses itself in what is deemed asocial or antisocial behavior—evil, in fact. Despite continuing attempts to explain such behavior by invoking non-natural, and thus socially ameliorable, agencies, each new development in biology tempts social philosophers to root man's behavior in a biological system, fixed in the virtually unchanging structure of genetic inheritance and in the vast expanse of evolutionary time. The choice of explanation has important implications for one's view of social behavior: the relative resistance to change of a biological system makes one do with the present, while the implicit change assumed by the social ameliorists provides some hope for the future. While both views have parallel and interlocking histories, each has its own time of popularity, if not of fad. And it is an interesting problem in social and intellectual history to attempt to plot out those cultural forces which lead to such changes in philosophical style.

Most recently, the growing number of decent field studies in primate social behavior has combined with a vastly expanded body of data concerning the earliest of the hominids to produce the popular pastime—often indulged with dramatic fervor—of recasting human behavior in the image of his primate kin. Both the intent and the effect have been to maintain, not only the antiquity, but also the biological inevitability and implied virtue of some of the most cherished of human traits—not excluding violence, agression and warfare, which have come to be of the greatest concern for those who would inhabit a human world.

Robert Ardrey is the most popular of these new philosophers of the jungled man; but with their more respectable scientific credentials, Desmond Morris and Konrad Lorenz have impressed their own territorial imperative upon this reworked land. Against their critics, they build their defences as they build their arguments: an appeal to anti-intellectualism; a call for the recognition of the truth of our animal being for the sake of science; the honesty of recognizing as natural the worst of our nature and the warnings against the seductive and old-fashioned arguments of the soft-headed humanists and "bleeding hearts" among us. The dramatic level of the discussion and the breathless revelation of secrets so jealously guarded by a scientific elitist establishment, have made it difficult for disagreeing scientists to contest the field before the same audience, or with the same appeal.

In *The Human Imperative*, Alland, a bio-cultural anthropologist at Columbia, makes a valiant attempt. It is a small book, but in its five persuasive central chapters it marshals the evidence, especially from anthropology's storehouse of comparative data and from its systemic approach, to combat the biological faith which Ardrey, Morris and Lorenz are preaching. Without denying man's animality, Alland emphasizes the flexibility of his culture, as a system which has adapted, and continually adapts, him to the changing environments he meets. This is a plasticity over which he himself has some control, in contrast to the much slower and more permanent change effected by biological mechanisms. It is not a revolutionary argument, this emphasis upon the human imperative in human evolution, nor is it presented with the zeal of a prophet; it is central to the anthropologist's view of man, which itself has emerged from a century's concern with the scientific explanation of the human condition. As an argument against the popularizing animalists, however, it does not succeed. It is too reasoned, too objective, too full of the humility of the scholar who knows how much we do not know. In short, it is too human to appeal to those whose needs require the drama of Ardrey's world. For the rest, for those who wish to begin to understand something of the nature of the human animal, it is the best of introductions.

JACOB W. GRUBER
Director, Temple University College
　of Liberal Arts
Rome
Italy

JOE R. FEAGIN and HARLAN HAHN. *Ghetto Revolts: The Politics of Violence in American Cities.* Pp. ix, 338. New York: Macmillan, 1973. $8.95.

While engaged in reading this excellent account of the rage that erupted in American ghetto communities during the sixties, I had a distinct feeling that I was looking into a page from the American past. Confrontation techniques have slipped out of fashion, and it seems hardly likely that there would be a reenactment in the foreseeable future—even on a small scale—of the drama of Watts. Then, as I was about to sit down and compose a few words about this book, history proved me wrong. A ten year old child was shot and killed by a policeman, in an incident which I should prefer at this time not to describe further, inasmuch as criminal action against the police officer is pending. However, I shall add—although it is tragically unnecessary, for anyone would be aware of this without knowing a single fact of the case—that the child was black and the police officer white. To exacerbate an already volatile situation, white policemen demonstrated in solidarity with the arrested officer, and the Patrolmen's Benevolent Association came to his support. No wonder, then, that New York City witnessed a couple of evenings of looting—a minor Watts.

Feagin and Hahn, sociologist and political scientist respectively, have written a remarkably dispassionate account of the ghetto revolts. They have absorbed the literature; looked at the evidence; sifted polemic and ideology from research and science and have produced a study of the meanings of the historic events. The authors address themselves to such questions as: the precipitating factors that trigger off a revolt; how many people have to participate—and in what fashion—in order that it be more than an encounter or a gathering; what portion of the people, and from what educational and occupational levels, are caught up in the action; how the ghetto residents who are non-participants view the occurrence and, finally, the permanent effects of such events on ghetto life. It is a large task, and it is done skillfully, resulting in a work indispensable for an understanding of American race relations.

What the authors have done is to organize, analyze, and synthesize the research findings of themselves and others. They pursue this task methodically and sometimes, I suggest, a bit uncritically. There were times when it appeared that people being interviewed were giving the answers that they thought were right—those that the interviewer wanted or that would put the respondent or ghetto residents generally in a desired light. But this is a minor flaw.

It required no work of this sort to convince social scientists that the revolts were not the result of any conspiracy, unless it be the two hundred year old conspiracy—now that we are approaching the great bicentennial—of these United States to commit atrocities against an oppressed group. It is indicative of the narrow vision of American political leaders that they entertained such thoughts; more likely they verbalized them without believing in them. For those who clung to such beliefs, this might be a good example of what Hofstadter called the paranoid theme in American political life.

What did the revolts accomplish? Primarily, it appears to me, they placed American society in a paradoxical position. Rioting and looting had to be not only suppressed, but also denounced, and part of this denunciation was to say that "violence will get you nowhere"—a peculiar statement from leaders of a government of super-violence. At the same time, the grievances of the ghetto residents—euphemistically called "legitimate grievances," as if there were others—had to be confronted, conditions ameliorated—not, however, because there had been violence, but despite it. To carry out this dual program, there had to be reprisals against the rioters —who were not to be rewarded—and massive social reform—but not as a result of the violence. Actually, there were meager steps in both directions.

Watts was the Bunker Hill of the black people. However, this, like all analogies, fails us, for the blacks wanted equality: freedom with, not from, the whites. Watts was our Warsaw ghetto uprising, but again not quite, for it would happen again; in Detroit, Newark and elsewhere, and—as I write—in New York. We are in a quiescent period after an era of turbulence, but if this is to be only after such an era, and not before another one, it will require massive commitment. There is no sign of such commitment in any seats of power in America today, and there is no evidence of it around the corner. But light travels in a straight line, and social scientists, like others, cannot see around corners.

Feagin and Hahn have produced such an excellent summary of these important events that I hesitate to make a minor point of criticism, but their book is too valuable to have such an inadequate index. Finally, it is a book that made me wonder whether the authors were white or black— or one of each. It is a compliment to this work that I could not decide. But it may also be an indication that there is such a thing as social and political science, that is itself neither black nor white; not neutral on human matters but scientific on all matters.

EDWARD SAGARIN
Department of Sociology
City College of New York

ANDREW GREELEY. *Unsecular Man: The Persistence of Religion.* Pp. 280. New York: Schocken, 1972. $7.95.

As Professor Andrew Greeley states on page 1: "The thesis of the book, bluntly, is that the basic human religious needs and the basic religious functions have not changed very notably since the late Ice Age; what changes have occurred make religious questions more critical rather than less critical in the contemporary world." He insists that this is a volume of dissent from the conventional wisdom about the contemporary religious situation. He bases his stand on the grounds of sociological research and theory, and opposes the views found in popular journals, divinity schools, the self-defined relevant clerics and laymen, and those who espouse the pop sociological-religious analysis which has become part of the American intellectual preconscious. His points are well taken and his arguments sane and sound.

Professor Greeley contends that religion is not in a state of collapse, and that liberalism, socialism, and historicism have been unsuccessful rivals to religion. To him, mankind has not changed and there is no real reason to contend that there is less belief in the supernatural today, than in earlier generations. Furthermore, he thinks that it is ridiculous to analyze contemporary religiousness by limiting oneself to the university campus. "It is the sheerest sort of snobbery to reject the religion of the majority of the population as irrelevant to the analysis of contemporary re-

ligion. . . . Such snobbery becomes even less justifiable when tribalism appears on the university campus with a vengeance" (p. 8). Some of the warped thinking he blames on the overriding preoccupation of the media with youth.

Professor Greeley closely links ideas of community with those of religion, and tries to focus the reader to the reality that there are other types of community besides the campus, the commune, and the urban slum. He deplores the fact that the "liberal" academic establishment tends to ignore middle-class America, and has established one set of standards for it and another set for its chosen groups. He is of the opinion that, contrary to ideas of a generation gap, children usually follow the cultural mores and life patterns of their parents and that likes prefer likes, in religion and community. As for the alienation of the American intellectual; it does not stem from McCarthy, but "is in part imaginary, in part self imposed" (p. 115).

Each section of the book is highly provocative. Especially valuable are the parts that treat myths, community and ecclesiastical leadership. To Professor Greeley, the exponents of technology and progress, somewhere along the way, overlooked the sinfulness of man. By using statistics, Professor Greeley puts to bed—or places in a bad position—the clichés without any true basis, mouthed by the academic community for the last thirty years. Being familiar with the entrenched group, I rather doubt, however, that it will allow Professor Greeley's facts to confuse its prejudices.

In modern religion, myths are no longer self evident, but while we still acquire religions from a community and generally live them out in a community, we still, relatively speaking, have considerably more freedom from the community in making our religious choices than did our ancestors.

Professor Greeley uses quotes that are much too long, and in some places his style falters. On the other hand, some passages are entertaining and contain delightful irony and humor. More important, however, is that this is a significant book that should be read by all those interested in modern theology and the sociology of religion.

JOHN J. MURRAY
Chairman, Department of History
Coe College
Cedar Rapids
Iowa

T. O. JACOBS. *Leadership and Exchange in Formal Organizations.* Pp. xiv, 352. Alexandria, Va.: Human Resources Research Organization, 1971. $8.00.

Although this book was published two years ago, knowledge of its availability is probably not widespread. More's the pity, because it constitutes an extremely valuable survey of information about, or relevant to, institutional leadership. Its relative obscurity may be due to the fact that the research and writing attendant on publication was funded by the Office of Naval Research, and there has been no special interest in achieving wide circulation in the larger society.

The focus of the survey was "on influence processes in formal organizations." To this end, over one thousand separate titles—apparently representative of the range of literature pertinent to the topic of leadership—were reviewed. In many respects, the survey touches on most research areas of what is usually identified as the behavioral school of management thought.

Noting that there "has been a striking lack of precision in the use of the term 'leadership,' " the author, in summary, defines it in terms of social exchange theory. This has the effect of focusing on interactions between leaders and followers. Fortunately, the author did not ignore institutional aspects of leader-follower relations in his review of the literature, although the interpretation of research data tends to emphasize social exchange. Perhaps this bias is inevitable, since, as the author notes, there is limited research data about leadership in functioning formal organizations that involves more than small work groups.

One of the outstanding characteristics of the survey is the cogent discussion of the limitations and interconnections of the research data reviewed. It is not difficult to become lost in the apparent contradictions, as well as the complementarities of different experimental designs and conclusions in behavioral studies. The author not only manages to stay on target, but he contributes generously to the state of the art by making clear the limitations of various studies, due to different conceptualizations, perspectives and methodologies. Simultaneously, he shows the relationships between apparently disparate approaches and findings, however strong or tenuous they are.

The survey of leadership begins with a review of the trait approach, analysis of which suggested a situational variable. Various follow up studies on context are cited and discussed. Next the author reviews contemporary views on leadership: the Ohio, Michigan and Illinois studies, and the organizational psychology approach. Finding these views deficient, the author looks at the transactional approach to leadership and finds it more appealing and useful. From here on, social exchange theory is the tool for reviewing various aspects of leadership phenomena: individual motivation in formal organizations, small group processes, the organizational context and organizational effectiveness. Finally, the author reiterates his belief that the social exchange interpretation is the most effective perspective on leadership.

STEPHEN R. MICHAEL
School of Business Administration
Department of Management
University of Massachusetts
Amherst

DAVID JENKINS. *Job Power. Blue and White Collar Democracy.* Pp. vii, 375. Garden City: Doubleday, 1973. $8.95.

Spurred by the disaffection of large groups of blue collar workers from traditional liberal Democratic party politics, a growing number of social critics have turned their attention to an analysis of the problems of working class people on the production line. In the last six months, at least six books have been published on this subject, in addition to the publication of a report of the Department of Health, Education and Welfare and the release of Congressional hearings pursuant to the introduction of legislation on worker alienation. Jenkins' *Job Power* is the latest to cross my desk and one of the best of this lot.

While most of the other authors are clearly talking about a very restricted form of work reform within the confines of the existing mode of capitalist production in the United States, Jenkins, in the early chapters of his book, seems to be saying that changes in job structures and work relations will, of necessity, require systemic changes, in order for the job and work changes to be meaningful. To him, industrial democracy involves more than just profit-sharing plans; trade unionism of the traditional variety; human relations illusions of more worker participation; sensitivity training for foremen; making jobs more interesting and so forth. Though Jenkins' formula for alterations in work relations would have all these effects, he seems to be saying that the crucial dimension is a redistribution of power at the point of production, as a prelude to a redistribution of power system-wide. Or at least to me, this is the only context in which work changes make sense.

After taking us through some general discussions of contemporary problems of work, Jenkins provides us with a description of systems of production which involve different relations of production from the traditional hierarchical structure of work relations of capitalism. He includes discussions of early utopian experiments in the United States; the Israeli kibbutz; Yugoslav workers' management; codetermination in Germany; worker participation in France; experiments in the United States and experiments in the social democratic Scandinavian countries.

Jenkins is strongest in his discussion of work reform experiments in the United States and Scandinavian countries and weakest in his discussion of socialism. His rendition of Marxian theory on this point, merely reiterates the usual cold-war stereotypes, derived from the anti-Marxist critics who have established a set of erroneous strawmen, which bear little or no relation to Marx's own writing. My advice to anyone trying to break out of our ideological heritage, is to start from scratch and read the original Marxian writings.

Beyond this point, Jenkins is weak on his understanding of the decisive importance of socialism for the type of fundamental changes he intimates in the early sections of the book. In the last few chapters he seems to back off from his commitment to serious systemic change. Because the basic production relations of capitalism as a system involves an appropriation of surplus by a minority, that system produces severe inequalities in economic and political power. No attempt to change these production relations will be meaningful, unless capitalism as a system is changed. The introduction of socialism, in all its forms, throughout the world has meant the redistribution of control of that society's surplus and therefore an equalizing of economic and political power. Though the introduction of socialism does not automatically bring with it the participatory socialist institutions of workers' control, it is the only basis upon which a system of full workers' control can be built. Put differently, socialism is a necessary, though perhaps not a sufficient, condition for the introduction of the type of work relations which Jenkins supports. Without such an analysis of the transition to socialism, Jenkins' book, for all its interest, has nothing but a moral imperative upon which to rely. Something may be morally imperative—for example, the abolition of slavery—but take centuries to accomplish.

HOWARD M. WACHTEL
Department of Economics
The American University
Washington, D.C.

IRWIN FLESCHER. *Children in the Learning Factory: The Search for a Humanizing Teacher.* Pp. ix, 180. Philadelphia: Chilton Book Company, 1973. $5.95.

HARRY L. GRACEY. *Curriculum or Craftsmanship: Elementary School Teachers in a Bureaucratic System.* Pp. 208. Chicago: The University of Chicago Press, 1972. $9.50.

These two books are about learning in schools and "though this be madness, yet there is method in't." Gracey examines the organizational structure of an east coast elementary school and its relationship to the teaching methods and pupil responses found there. Irwin Flescher extolls the strengths and virtues of the humanizing teacher, while condemning the system that makes teachers both culprit and victim.

Gracey's report of his two year study details two classroom approaches characterized as production oriented and craftsman oriented teaching. He notes that the vast majority of teachers are production oriented—curriculum centered—and supported by the school bureaucracy, while the few craftsman oriented instructors—child centered—are frustrated by the bureaucracy and eventually forced to change their approach, or leave their position.

Basing his study on an industrial analogy, Gracey observes that many school people see learning as synonomous with work, and children as raw materials to be processed through a series of grades into standardized finished products, suitable for distribution to the employment or higher education markets. He notes how organizational controls are exercised to achieve uniform and efficient bureaucratic administration and how this is reinforced by the understanding that the classroom and school building should be quiet, orderly, and clean. Teachers must function within these confines and the result serves to effectively negate the key craftsman goal of individual instruction, based on the needs and interests of each pupil. To survive, they teach the curriculum in the acceptable ways and, over a period of time, become convinced that their actions actually constitute a realization of their original goals.

There are three possible responses for pupils in the bureaucracy: identification, submission, or rebellion. The "good" pupils are prepared "for life in a society of large scale organizations" but the bureaucracy provides "children in general with little opportunity to develop as individuals."

Gracey's study was made between 1961 and 1962, so that the critical educational issues and larger social questions of the past decade are not explored. Recent efforts to develop educational alternatives offer interesting organizational variations and there is the possibility that a growing number of teachers and schools do not conform to the author's industrial model.

While one senses the author's dissatisfaction with production type teaching, the reader is never treated to the implications of widespread craftsman type teaching, nor to any insights for establishing other approaches for educating youngsters; nor to resolving conflicts over the purposes of public schools. Nonetheless, Gracey's analysis is a thoughtful and intelligent appraisal of commonly found school bureaucracies and its relationship to the people who work and learn there. One would hope to see more studies along related lines.

Children in the Learning Factory is a series of "psychological talks to parents and teachers" that analyzes and explains several educational evils and obstacles—from television to T-groups; from troubled children to IQ tests—and concludes that the schools efficiently and effectively dehumanize.

Much of what is written has already been expressed by Silberman, Glasser, Holt, and others and much of what is proposed is too elusive or ambiguous to hold much prospect of serious consideration. The solution to inhumane schools, for instance, is found in the humanizing teacher who is called "the priestess." But salvation is not just around the corner since "one cannot simply become a priestess—it is a born gift." Her mysterious way of dealing with students is through exceptional tolerance, intuitive understanding, and loyal devotion.

Much of the book offers sermons as solutions and, in this reviewer's opinion, its unsupported fervor and rather wispy doctrine is not likely to convert many infidels into faithful believers of humanism. There is no index or bibliography.

TEDD LEVY

Norwalk
Connecticut

ALBERT ROSE. *Governing Metropolitan Toronto: A Social and Political Analysis, 1953–1971.* Pp. 224. Berkely, Cal.:

Universiy of California Press, 1973. $8.95.

Professor Rose, dean of the Faculty of Social Work at the University of Toronto and an active participant in the creation of metropolitan Toronto, has written a book wih a message for American planners and reformers. In a history/analysis of Toronto's two-tier system, Professor Rose shows how Metro Toronto was created in 1953, giving control of part, or the whole, of eleven regional functions to a central council. Reorganized in 1967, the central council now consists of representatives from five surrounding boroughs, plus Toronto, and has whole or partial authority over housing, transportation, planning schools and so forth.

In a limited sense, the reorganization was a success. It allowed coordination of metropolitan-wide problems; it allowed Toronto and surrounding boroughs to grow from one million in 1953 to two million in 1970, with new people housed, largely, in high-rise apartments. Assessed value and commercial value of the city of Toronto, which slumped during the depression and world war, revived; a uniform tax rate for the Metro area provided the financial base for development of a certain kind of capital improvement; and "a housebuilding industry emerged during the first five years of metropolitan government" (p. 31). A new expressway system linked residential sectors to newly-built shopping centers. Thus, a kind of framework was created for population and economic expansion.

But the development of Metro has been no success for inner-city residents. The powerful thrust of Professor Rose's critique is that the metro system is good for capital improvements, but hard on the poor who, in Metro-sponsored urban renewal and highway programs, find themselves evicted or facing eviction, while public housing projects are far behind schedule. An official Metro Planning Board report for 1963 states: "In the first ten-year capital works program adopted by Metro in 1955, the projected expenditure of $585 million . . . was allocated on the basis of 76% to roads, sewers and water supply; 21% to education; and only 3% to all of the other services and facilities, such as housing, welfare (etc.)" (p. 125). A newly-formed citizen's group successfully stopped construction of the massive Spadina Expressway, and several strong tenants associations have grown for the first time.

This reader came away with the conclusion that Metro serves the needs of expanding urban capitalism and the housebuilding industry, but has done nothing to reorient the distorted priorities which put the middle class in good housing and the poor in the streets.

EDWARD HAYES
Department of Government
Ohio University
Athens

BETTY YORBURG. *The Changing Family.* Pp. vii, 230. New York: Columbia University Press, 1973. $9.00.

Dr. Yorburg, assistant professor of Sociology at The City College of The City University of New York, is author of *Utopia and Reality: A Collective Portrait of American Socialists* (Columbia University Press, 1969.) In *The Changing Family,* Dr. Yorburg sets herself the task of presenting "a broad synthesis of accumulated social scientific knowledge about family life," without burdening the book with detailed sources and copious footnotes. By stepping back and taking a wide-angled look at family life over time, through the lenses of sociological theory, she achieves her goal of reflecting a unified theoretical perspective.

The seven chapters stretch across sociological and biological bases for understanding family life, types of family life and varieties of families around the world. These are followed by a direct focus on ethnic variations in American families—Blacks, Mexican-Americans, Japanese Americans, and Jewish Americans—as well as on social class differences among families in America.

The section on "Merging Trends in Family Life," gives one a taste of the flavor of the whole book:

Societies with high levels of technological development change rapidly and require highly educated, psychologically flexible, and mobile populations. The higher levels of education and the breakdown of extended family and community controls characteristic of modern societies promote a greater tendency to think critically and to use rational means for achieving goals, a decrease in ethnocentrism and an increase in tolerance of human differences (p. 185).

The concluding chapter "The Future of the American Family", although brief, hits many of the high spots, over much of the same ground as does Jessie Bernard in her more detailed full-length book, *The Future of Marriage* (World Publishing Company, 1972). The Bernard book apparently came out while Dr. Yorburg's book was in press, since it is not cited in the chapter notes. Dr. Yorburg's view is,

Much of the misery in contemporary family life is a mixture of objective deprivation and rising expectations. Changing expectations promote feelings of discontent, but they can also encourage constructive change in societies, families, and individuals. The standard of constructive change is the realization of the eternal human need for the fulfilled life—however this is defined. Government will have to render much more help to the American nuclear family for the realization of this goal and it will have to do it soon. It will either plan more effectively, or both the nation and the family will perish—because their ultimate fates are inseparable (p. 204).

This book will serve well the beginning student in family sociology, as well as the well-oriented family scholar who will enjoy arguing the author's many unsupported generalizations, assumptions and predictions.

EVELYN M. DUVALL
Sarasota
Florida

OTHER BOOKS

ALBRECHT-CARRIÉ, RENÉ. *A Diplomatic History of Europe Since the Congress of Vienna*. Revised ed. Pp. xv, 764. New York: Harper & Row, 1973. $6.95. Paperbound.

ALLENSWORTH, DON. *Public Administration: The Execution of Public Policy*. Pp. vii, 213. Philadelphia: J. B. Lippincott, 1973. $3.95. Paperbound.

ALTBACH, PHILIP and NORMAN I. UPHOFF. *The Student Internationals*. Pp. 214. Metuchen, N.J.: Scarecrow Press, 1973. $6.00.

ANDERSSON, J. GUNNAR. *Children of the Yellow Earth: Studies in Prehistoric China*. Pp. vii, 345. Cambridge, Mass.: MIT Press, 1973. $3.95. Paperbound.

AVRICH, PAUL, ed. *The Anarchists in the Russian Revolution*. Documents of Revolution. Pp. 179. Ithaca, N.Y.: Cornell University Press, 1973. $6.95. Paperbound, $2.95.

BAIN, RICHARD C. and JUDITH H. PARRIS. *Convention Decisions and Voting Records*. 2nd ed. Studies in Presidential Selection. Pp. vii, 350. Washington, D.C.: The Brookings Institution, 1973. $14.95.

BARNES, J. A. *Three Styles in the Study of Kinship*. Pp. 334. Berkeley, Cal.: University of California Press, 1972. $8.75.

BARON, SALO WITTMAYER. *A Social and Religious History of the Jews: Late Middle Ages and Era of European Expansion (1200–1650)*. *Resettlement and Exploration*. Pp. 550. New York: Columbia University Press, 1973. $15.00.

BAKER, JEROME, ed. *Critical Incidents in Child Care: A Case Book*. Pp. xix, 375. New York: Behavioral Publications, 1973. $15.95. Paperbound, $7.95.

BEN-AMITTAY, JACOB. *The History of Political Thought: From Ancient to Modern Times*. Pp. ix, 318. New York: Philosophical Library, 1972. $20.00.

BENEDICT, MICHAEL LES. *The Impeachment and Trial of Andrew Jackson*. Pp. x, 212. New York: W. W. Norton, 1973. $6.95. Paperbound, $2.45.

BENEVOLO, LEONARDO. *History of Modern Architecture, vol. 1, The Tradition of Modern Architecture, vol. 2, The Modern Movement*. Pp. vii, 868. Cambridge, Mass.: MIT Press, 1971. $35.00.

BERLINER, JOSEPH S. *Economy, Society and Welfare: A Study in Social Economics*. Praeger Special Studies in International Economics and Development. Pp. v, 196. New York: Praeger, 1972. $13.50.

BEST, JAMES J. *Public Opinion: Micro and Macro*. Pp. viii, 270. Homewood, Ill.: Dorsey, 1973. $4.95. Paperbound.

BHUINYA, NIRANJAN. *Parliamentary Democracy in Japan*. Pp. vii, 121. New York: Barnes & Noble, 1973. $6.50.

BILLINGTON, RAY ALLEN, ed. *People of the Plains and Mountains: Essays in the History of the West Dedicated to Everett*

Dick. Contributions in American History, no. 25. Pp. 213. Westport, Conn.: Greenwood, 1973. $12.50.

BLACKSTONE, WILLIAM T. *Political Philosophy: An Introduction*. Pp. vii, 266. New York: Thomas Y. Crowell, 1973. No price. Paperbound.

BOARDMAN, ROBERT and A. J. R. GROOM, eds. *The Management of Britain's External Relations*. Pp. v, 362. New York: Barnes & Noble, 1973. $16.50.

BOLLENS, JOHN C. and DALE ROGERS MARSHALL. *A Guide to Participation Field Work, Role Playing Cases, and Other Forms*. Pp. v, 160. Englewood Cliffs, N.J.: Prentice-Hall, 1973. No price.

BORNSTEIN, MORRIS. *Plan and Market: Economic Reform in Eastern Europe*. Pp. vii, 415. New Haven: Yale University Press, 1973. $15.00.

BOYD, JULIAN P., ed. *The Papers of Thomas Jefferson: 18, November 1790 to March 1791*. Pp. vii, 688. Princeton, N.J.: Princeton University Press, 1972. $20.00.

BRADEN, WILLIAM. *The Family Game: Identities for Young & Old*. Pp. vii, 148. New York: Quadrangle Books, 1973. $5.95. Paperbound, $2.95.

BRADFORD, SARAH. *Portugal*. Nations and Peoples Library. Pp. 192. New York: Walker, 1973. $8.50.

BRYANT, CLIFTON D. and J. GIPSON WELLS, eds. *Deviancy and the Family*. Pp. v, 472. Philadelphia: F. A. Davis, 1973. $6.00. Paperbound.

BREDEMEIER, HARRY C. and JUDY GETIS. *Environments, People, and Inequalities: Some Current Problems*. Pp. 341. New York: John Wiley, 1973. $8.25. Paperbound, $5.25.

BRITT, STEUART and HARPER W. BOYD, JR. *Marketing Management and Administrative Action*. 3rd ed. Pp. v, 693. New York: McGraw-Hill, 1973. No price. Paperbound.

BRODINE, VIRGINIA and MARK SELDEN, eds. *Open Secret: The Kissinger-Nixon Doctrine in Asia*. Pp. 218. New York: Harper & Row, 1972. $10.00. Paperbound, $1.50.

BUDHRAI, V. S. *Soviet Russia and the Hindustan Subcontinent*. Pp. vii, 296. Bombay, India: Somaiya, 1973. Rs. 40.00.

BURKE, LEE H. *Ambassador at Large: Diplomat Extraordinary*. Pp. xvi, 176. The Hague, Netherlands: Martinus Nijhoff, 1972. 30 guilders. Paperbound.

BURMAN, IAN D. *Lobbying at the Illinois Constitutional Convention*. Studies in *Illinois Constitution Making*. Pp. vii, 119.

Urbana, Ill.: University of Illinois, 1973. $3.45. Paperbound.

BUTTS, R. FREEMAN. *The Education of the West: A Formative Chapter in the History of Civilization*. Pp. iii, 631. New York: McGraw-Hill, 1973. $10.95.

CAGAN, PHILIP. *The Channels of Monetary Effects on Interest Rates*. NBER General Series 97. Pp. xiv, 127. New York: National Bureau of Economic Research, 1972. $5.00.

THE CARNEGIE COMMISSION ON HIGHER EDUCATION. *The Purposes and the Performance of Higher Education in the United States: Approaching the Year 2000*. Pp. vii, 107. New York: McGraw-Hill, 1973. $2.45. Paperbound.

CARTER, GWENDOLEN M. and JOHN H. HERTZ. *Government and Politics in the Twentieth Century*. 3rd ed. Pp. vii, 278. New York: Praeger, 1973. $9.00. Paperbound, $2.95.

CHENG, RONALD YE-LIN, ed. *The Sociology of Revolution Readings on Political Upheaval and Popular Unrest*. Pp. vii, 334. Chicago: Henry Regnery, 1973. $4.95. Paperbound.

CHERMAYEFF, IVAN et al. *The Design Necessity: A Casebook of Federally Initiated Projects in Visual Communications, Interiors and Industrial Design, Architecture, Landscape Environment*. Pp. 80. Cambridge, Mass.: MIT Press, 1973. $6.00. Paperbound.

CHOMSKY, NOAM. *For Reasons of State*. Pp. vii, 440. New York: Pantheon, 1973. $3.45. Paperbound.

CHRISTENSON, REO M. *Heresies Right and Left: Some Political Assumptions Reexamined*. Pp. 185. New York: Harper & Row, 1973. $2.95. Paperbound.

CHRISTMAN, HENRY M., ed. *Neither East Nor West: The Basic Documents of Non-Alignment*. Pp. v, 206. New York: Sheed & Ward, 1973. $7.95. Paperbound, $3.45.

CHRISTOPHER, JOHN B. *The Islamic Tradition*. Major Traditions of World Civilization. Pp. viii, 185. New York: Harper & Row, 1972. $2.95. Paperbound.

CLARK, G. KITSON. *Churchmen and the Condition of England 1832–1885*. Pp. ix, 353. New York: Barnes & Noble, 1973. $15.75.

CLARK, ROBERT E. *Reference Group Theory & Delinquency*. Pp. 129. New York: Behavioral Publications, 1973. $9.95. Paperbound, $4.95.

CLARKE, WILLIAM C. *Place and People: An Ecology of a New Guinean Community*. Pp. vi, 265. Berkeley, Cal.: University of California Press, 1971. $9.00.

COBBLEDICK, JAMES R. *Choice in American Foreign Policy: Options for the Future.* Pp. vii, 282. New York: Thomas Y. Crowell, 1973. No price. Paperbound.

COCHARAN, THOMAS C. *Social Change in America: The Twentieth Century.* Pp. ix, 178. New York: Harper & Row, 1972. $9.00. Paperbound, $2.75.

COHN, RUBIN G. *To Judge With Justice: History and Politics of Illinois Judicial Reform.* Studies in Illinois Constitution Making. Pp. ix, 164. Urbana, Ill.: University of Illinois Press, 1973. $3.45. Paperbound.

COLE, G. D. *The World of Labour.* Pp. v, 443. New York: Barnes & Noble, 1973. $19.50.

COLE, GEORGE F. *Politics and the Administration of Justice.* Sage Series on Politics and the Legal Order, vol. 2. Pp. 234. Beverly Hills, Cal.: Sage, 1973. No price.

DAHL, ROBERT A., ed. *Regimes and Oppositions.* Pp. 411. New Haven, Conn.: Yale University Press, 1973. $15.00.

DAVIS, GARY. *Psychology of Problem Solving: Theory and Practice.* Pp. ix, 206. New York: Basic Books, 1973. $7.95.

DICKINSON, WILLIAM B., ed. *Editorial Research Reports on the American Work Ethic.* Pp. i, 180. Washington, D.C.: Congressional Quarterly, 1973. No price. Paperbound.

DORSON, RICHARD M., ed. *Folklore and Folklife: An Introduction.* Pp. ix, 561. Chicago: The University of Chicago Press, 1972. $12.50.

DVORIN, EUGENE P. and ROBERT H. SIMMONS. *From Amoral to Humane Bureaucracy.* Pp. vii, 88. San Francisco: Canfield Press, 1972. $1.95. Paperbound.

EBENSTEIN, WILLIAM. *Today's Isms: Communism, Fascism, Capitalism, Socialism.* 7th ed. Pp. vii, 266. Englewood Cliffs, N.J.: Prentice-Hall, 1973. $7.95. Paperbound, $4.00.

ECONOMIC PLANNING CENTRE HELSINKI. *Growth Prospects for the Finnish Economy Up to 1980.* Pp. v, 183. Helsinki, Finland: Government Printing Centre, 1972. No price. Paperbound.

EDWARDS, HARRY. *Sociology of Sport.* Pp. vii, 395. Homewood, Ill.: The Dorsey Press, 1973. $9.95.

EISENMANN, CHARLES. *The University Teaching of Social Sciences: Law.* Teaching in the Social Sciences. Pp. 182. New York: Unipub, 1973. $5.00. Paperbound.

EVANS, ROBERT L. *The Fall and Rise of Man, If . . .* Pp. 259. Minneapolis, Minn.: Lund Press, 1973. $6.95. Paperbound, $3.95.

EVERSON, DAVID H. and JOANN POPARAD PAINE. *An introduction to Systematic Political Science.* Pp. xii, 296. Homewood, Dorsey, 1973. $5.95. Paperbound.

EVCK, FRANK, ed. *The Revolutions of 1848–49.* Pp. vii, 202. New York: Barnes & Noble, 1973. $10.50. Paperbound, $5.50.

FAIRBANK, JOHN K., EDWIN D. REISCHAUER and ALBERT M. CRAIG. *East Asia.* Pp. xii, 969. Boston, Mass.: Houghton Mifflin, 1973. $24.00.

FARRELL, BRIAN, ed. *The Irish Parliamentary Tradition.* Pp. 286. New York: Barnes & Noble, 1973. $11.00.

FELD, RICHARD D. and CARL GRAFTON. *The Uneasy Partnership: The Dynamics of Federal, State, and Urban Relations.* Pp. vii, 322. Palo Alto, Cal.: The National Press, 1973. $6.95. Paperbound, $3.95.

FISHBURN, PETER C. *The Theory of Social Choice.* Pp. vii, 259. Princeton, N.J.: Princeton University Press, 1973. $13.50.

FLOUD, RODERICK. *An Introduction to Quantitative Methods for Historians.* Pp. xi, 220. Princeton, N.J.: Princeton University Press, 1973. $7.50.

FOLEY, ARCHIE R. *Challenge to Community Psychiatry: A Dialogue Between Two Faculties.* Pp. v, 203. New York: Behavioral Publications, 1973. $10.95.

FRANKEL, JOSEPH. *Contemporary International Theory and the Behaviour of States.* Pp. 134. New York: Oxford University Press, 1973. $4.00. Paperbound, $1.95.

FR.-CHIROVSKY, NICHOLAS. *A History of the Russian Empire, vol. 1.* Pp. xi, 449. New York: Philosophical Library, 1973. $15.00.

FREEMAN, ROGER A. *Tax Loopholes: The Legend and the Reality.* Pp. 91. AEI-Hoover Policy Studies. Washington, D.C.: American Enterprise Institute for Public Policy Research, 1973. $3.00. Paperbound.

FRIEDMANN, JOHN. *Urbanization, Planning and National Development.* Pp. 352. Beverly Hills, Cal.: Sage, 1973. $12.50.

GAY, PETER and R. K. WEBB. *Modern Europe to 1815.* Pp. xiii, 536. New York: Harper & Row, 1973. No price. Paperbound.

GITTINGER, J. PRICE. *Economic Analysis of Agricultural Projects.* Pp. viii, 221. Baltimore, Md.: Johns Hopkins University, 1972. $10.00. Paperbound.

GLEIG, G. R. *The Campaigns of the British Army at Washington & New Orleans.* Pp. x, 208. Totowa, N.J.: Rowman and Littlefield, 1973. $10.00.

GOLEMBIEWSKI, ROBERT T. and MICHAEL WHITE. *Cases in Public Management*. Pp. ix, 180. Chicago: Rand McNally, 1973. $3.95. Paperbound.

GOODHEART, EUGENE. *Culture and the Radical Conscience*. Pp. 179. Cambridge, Mass.: Harvard University Press, 1973. $7.95.

GRETLER, ARMIN. *The Training of Adult Middle-Level Personnel*. Pp. 164. New York: Unipub, 1972. $4.00. Paperbound.

GUTMAN, HERBERT G. and GREGORY S. KEALEY, eds. *Many Pasts: Readings in American Social History, 1600–1876*. Vol. 1. Pp. 469. Englewood Cliffs, N.J.: Prentice-Hall, 1973. No price. Paperbound.

HALL, JEROME. *Foundations of Jurisprudence*. Pp. v, 184. Indianapolis: Bobbs-Merrill, 1973. No price.

HAMSHER, J. HERBERT and HAROLD SIGALL. *Psychology & Social Issues*. Pp. 550. New York: Macmillan, 1973. $5.95. Paperbound.

HANDY, ROLLO and E. C. HARWOOD. *Useful Procedures of Inquiry*. Pp. iii, 232. Great Barrington, Mass.: Behavioral Research Council, 1973. $12.50.

HARDING, A. *The Law Courts of Medieval England*. Historical Problems Studies and Documents 18. Pp. 201. New York: Barnes & Noble, 1973. $10.50.

HARDY, G. *Society in Conflict*. Pp. 184. Melbourne, Australia: Reform, 1973. No price.

HART, GARY WARREN. *Right from the Start: A Chronicle of the McGovern Campaign*. Pp. ix, 334. New York: Quadrangle Books, 1973. $7.95.

HEAD, RICHARD G. and ERVIN J. ROKKE, eds. *American Defense Policy*. 3rd ed. Pp. vii, 696. Baltimore, Md.: The Johns Hopkins Press, 1973. $17.50. Paperbound, $6.50.

HEIMANN, FRITZ, ed. *The Future of Foundations*. Pp. v, 278. Englewood Cliffs, N.J.: Prentice-Hall, 1973. $2.45. Paperbound.

HELMER, JOHN and NEIL A. EDDINGTON, eds. *Urbanman: The Psychology of Urban Survival*. Pp. vii, 247. New York: The Free Press, 1973. $9.95.

HETZLER, STANLEY A. *Applied Measures for Promoting Technological Growth*. Pp. xiii, 337. Boston, Mass.: Routledge and Kegan Paul, 1973. $15.00.

HINTON, HAROLD C. *An Introduction to Chinese Politics*. Pp. vii, 322. New York: Praeger, 1973. $9.50. Paperbound, $3.95.

HIRSCH, W. Z. *Financing Public First-Level and Second-Level Education in the U.S.A.* Financing Educational Systems: Specific Case Studies 3. Pp. 49. Paris: Unesco International Institute for Educational Planning, 1973. $2.00. Paperbound.

HIRSCHFIELD, ROBERT S., ed. *The Power of the Presidency: Concepts and Controversy*. 2nd ed. Up. 387. Chicago: Aldine, 1973. $9.75.

HOBHOUSE, L. T. *Democracy and Reaction*. Pp. vii, 280. New York: Barnes & Noble, 1973. $14.50.

HODGES, HAROLD M., JR., ed. *Conflict and Consensus: Readings Toward a Sociological Perspective*. Pp. xi, 570. New York: Harper & Row, 1973. $5.00. Paperbound.

HOLLEB, DORIS. *Colleges and the Urban Poor*. Pp. v, 175. Lexington, Mass.: D. C. Heath, 1972. No price.

HOPKINS, RAYMOND F. and RICHARD W. MANSBACH. *Structure and Process in International Politics*. Pp. vii, 498. New York: Harper & Row, 1973. $10.95.

HOUGHTON, D. HOBART and JENIFER DAGUT. *Source Material on the South African Economy: 1860–1970*. Vol. 2 1899–1919. Pp. v, 247. New York: Oxford University Press, 1973. $11.75.

HUBER, JOAN, ed. *Changing Women in a Changing Society*. Pp. 295. Chicago: The University of Chicago Press, 1973. $7.95. Paperbound, $2.95.

HUTT, ALLEN. *The Post-War History of the British Working Class*. Pp. 320. New York: Barnes & Noble, 1973. $12.50.

IRVING, BRIAN, ed. *Guyana: A Composite Monograph*. Pp. 87. Hato Rey, Puerto Rico: Inter-American University Press, 1973. $10.00. Paperbound, $5.00.

JAFFA, HARRY V. *Crisis of the House Divided: An Interpretation of the Lincoln-Douglas Debates*. Pp. 451. Seattle: Washington: University of Washington Press, 1973. $4.95. Paperbound.

JOHNSON, D. GALE. *Farm Commodity Programs: An Opportunity for Change*. Evaluative Studies. Pp. 114. Washington, D.C.: American Enterprise Institute for Public Policy Research, 1973. No price. Paperbound.

JOHNSON, E. L. *An Introduction to the Soviet Legal System*. Pp. ix, 248. New York: Barnes & Noble, 1973. $10.50. Paperbound, $5.25.

JOUGHIN, JEAN TEMPLIN. *The Paris Commune in French Politics*. Reissue. Pp. 529. New York: Russell & Russell, 1973. $23.00.

KAPLAN, MORTON A. *On Freedom & Human Dignity: The Importance of the Sacred in Politics*. Pp. v, 120. Morristown, N.J.: General Learning Press, 1973. No price. Paperbound.

KASDAN, ALAN RICHARD. *The Third World: A New Focus for Development.* Pp. 144. Morristown, N.J.: General Learning Corporation, 1973. $3.95. Paperbound.

KEEN, M. H. *England in the Later Middle Ages.* Pp. ix, 581. New York: Barnes and Noble, 1973. $13.00.

KELLEY, DARWIN. *Milligan's Fight Against Lincoln.* Pp. 121. New York: Exposition Press, 1973. $5.50.

KENNEDY, DANIEL R. and AUGUST KERBER. *Resocialization: An American Experiment.* Pp. x, 191. New York: Behavioral Publications, 1973. $9.95. Paperbound, $4.95.

KENNEDY, WILLIAM PAUL McCLURE. *The Constitution of Canada 1534–1937.* Reissue. Pp. vii, 626. New York: Russell & Russell, 1973. $25.00.

KINCHEN, OSCAR A. *Women Who Spied for the Blue and the Gray.* Pp. 165. Philadelphia, Pa.: Dorrance, 1973. $5.95.

KLAPP, ORRIN E. *Models of Social Order: An Introduction to Sociological Theory.* Pp. xi, 334. Palo Alto, Cal.: The National Press, 1973. $8.50.

KLEIN, PHILIP A. *The Management of Market-Oriented Economies: A Comparative Perspective.* Pp. 238. Belmont, Cal.: Wadsworth, 1973. No price. Paperbound.

KUCZYNSKI, JÜRGEN. *A Short History of Labour Conditions Under Industrial Capitalism in Great Britain & the Empire 1750–1944.* Pp. 193. New York: Barnes & Noble, 1973. $8.00.

KURLAND, PHILIP B., ed. *The Supreme Court Review 1972.* Pp. 329. Chicago: The University of Chicago Press, 1973. $16.00.

LANGFORD, P. *The First Rockingham Administration 1765–1766.* Oxford Historical Monographs. Pp. xi, 318. New York: Oxford University Press, 1973. $14.50.

LARSON, J. CALVIN. *Major Themes in Sociological Theory.* Pp. vii, 254. New York: David McKay, 1973. $3.95. Paperbound.

LEWIS, RICHARD S. and PHILIP M. SMITH, eds. *Frozen Future: A Prophetic Report from Antarctica.* Pp. vii, 455. New York: Quadrangle, 1973. $12.50.

LEVIN, NORA. *The Holocaust: The Destruction of European Jewry 1933–1945.* Pp. v, 784. New York: Schocken, 1973. $6.95. Paperbound.

LISTOKEN, DAVID. *The Dynamics of Urban Rehabilitation: Macro and Micro Analyses.* Pp. 238. New Brunswick, N.J.: Rutgers University Center for Urban Policy Research, 1973. $10.00.

LUMLEY, ROGER. *White-Collar Unionism in Britain: A Survey of the Present Position.* Pp. 160. New York: Barnes & Noble, 1973. $7.50. Paperbound, $3.25.

MANGOLD, MARGARET M., ed. *La Causa Chicana: The Movement for Justice.* Pp. ix, 218. New York: Family Service Association of America, 1972. $7.50.

MAY, JOHN D. *What Should Be Done? Debates from "The Advocates."* American Problems. Pp. v, 330. *A Guide for Instructors.* Pp. v, 94. Palo Alto, Calif.: The National Press, 1973. $4.95. Paperbound.

MELANSON, PHILIP H. *Knowledge, Politics and Public Policy: Introductory Readings in American Politics.* Pp. x, 303. Cambridge, Mass.: Winthrop, 1973. No price. Paperbound.

McCLURE, LARRY and CAROLYN BUAN, eds. *Essays on Career Education.* Pp. iii, 265. Portland, Or.: Northwest Regional Educational Laboratory, 1973. No price. Paperbound.

McCONNELL, JOHN WILKINSON. *The Evaluation of Social Classes.* Reissue. Pp. vii, 228. New York: Russell & Russell, 1973. $15.00.

MacCORKLE, STUART A. *Austin's Three Forms of Government.* Pp. vii, 155. San Antonio, Texas: The Naylor Company, 1973. $8.95.

McKINNEY, FRED. *Psychology in Action: Basic Readings.* 2nd ed. Pp. v, 499. New York: Macmillan, 1973. $5.95. Paperbound.

MacMILLAN, DONALD L. *Behavior Modification in Education.* Pp. vii, 232. New York: Macmillan, 1973. $4.95. Paperbound.

McMURRY, DONALD LeCRONE. *The Great Burlington Strike of 1888.* Reissue. Pp. v, 377. New York: Russell & Russell, 1973. $20.00.

McNEILL, WILLIAM H. and MARILYN ROBINSON WALDMAN, eds. *The Islamic World.* Readings in World History vol. 6. Pp. xi, 468. New York: Oxford University Press, 1973. $3.95. Paperbound.

McPHERSON, WILLIAM. *Ideology & Change: Radicalism and Fundamentalism in America.* Pp. vii, 301. Palo Alto, Cal.: The National Press, 1973. $4.95. Paperbound.

MOXLEY, WARDEN, comp. *Congressional Districts in the 1970s: Political and Demographic Profiles of 435 Congressional Districts.* Pp. 236. Washington, D.C.: Congressional Quarterly, 1973. $10.00. Paperbound.

MUMFORD, LEWIS. *Interpretations and Forecasts: 1922–1972.* Studies in Literature,

History, Biography, Technics and Contemporary Society. Pp. vii, 522. New York: Harcourt Brace Jovanovich, 1973. $12.95.

MURRAY, MICHELE, ed. *A House of Good Proportion: Images of Women in Literature.* Pp. 379. New York: Simon and Schuster, 1973. $3.95. Paperbound.

NANDA, B. R., ed. *Socialism in India.* Pp. v, 299. New York: Barnes & Noble, 1973. $12.00.

NASH, HENRY T. *American Foreign Policy: Response to a Sense of Threat.* Pp. vii, 247. Homewood, Ill.: The Dorsey Press, 1973. $4.95.

NASH, RODERICK. *From These Beginnings: A Biographical Approach to American History.* Pp. x, 548. New York: Harper & Row, 1973. $6.95.

NEGANDHI, ANANT R., ed. *Modern Organizational Theory.* Pp. 404. Kent, Ohio: Kent State University, 1973. $10.00.

NELKIN, DOROTHY. *Methadone Maintenance: A Technological Fix.* Pp. 164. New York: George Braziller, 1973. $6.95. Paperbound, $1.95.

NEWMAN, WILLIAM M. *American Pluralism: A Study of Minority Groups and Social Theory.* Pp. vii, 307. New York: Harper & Row, 1973. $3.95. Paperbound.

NIXON, RICHARD. *U.S. Foreign Policy for the 1970's: Shaping a Durable Peace.* A Report to the Congress by the President of the United States. Pp. iii, 234. Washington, D.C.: U.S. Government Printing Office, 1973. $1.85. Paperbound.

NOVAK, MICHAEL. *.The Rise of the Unmeltable Ethnics.* Pp. xiii, 373. New York: Collier Books, 1973. $2.95. Paperbound.

NOVICK, DAVID. *Current Practice in Program Budgeting (PPBS): Analysis and Case Studies Covering Government and Business.* Pp. v, 242. New York: Crane, Russak, 1973. $12.50.

NOWLAN, KEVIN B., ed. *Travel and Transport in Ireland.* Pp. 178. New York: Barnes & Noble, 1973. $8.75.

OLSEN, V. NORSKOV. *John Foxe and the Elizabethan Church.* Pp. 276. Berkeley: University of California Press, 1973. $11.50.

OMINDE, S. H. and C. N. EJIOGU, eds. *Population Growth & Economic Development in Africa.* Pp. xi, 421. New York: Humanities Press, 1972. $25.50.

O'NEILL, JOHN. *Sociology as a Skin Trade: Essays towards a Reflexive Sociology.* Pp. xi, 274. New York: Harper & Row, 1973. $8.00. Paperbound, $2.95.

OSGOOD, ROBERT E., et al. *Retreat from Empire? The First Nixon Administration.*

America & the World, vol. 2. Pp. 360. Baltimore, Md.: The Johns Hopkins University Press, 1973. $14.50. Paperbound, $3.95.

OWEN, HENRY, ed. *The Next Phase in Foreign Policy.* Pp. viii, 345. Washington, D.C.: The Brookings Institute, 1973. $8.95. Paperbound, $3.50.

PAYNE, JAMES L. *Foundation of Empirical Political Analysis.* Pp. 150. Chicago: Markham, 1973. $8.50.

PERRY, JOHN and ERNA. *The Social Web: An Introduction to Sociology.* Pp. vii, 575. San Francisco, Cal.: Canfield Press, 1973. $7.95. Paperbound.

PERRY, JOHN A. and MURRAY, B. SEIDLER. *Patterns of Contemporary Society: An Introduction to Social Science.* Pp. 286. San Francisco, Cal.: Canfield, 1973. $4.50. Paperbound.

PERRY, P. J. *British Agriculture 1875–1914. Debates in Economic History.* Pp. vii, 180. New York: Barnes & Noble, 1973. $9.50. Paperbound, $4.75.

PESCATELLO, ANN, ed. *Female and Male in Latin America: Essays.* Pp. ix, 342. Pittsburgh, Pa.: University of Pittsburgh Press, 1973. $9.95.

PÉTONNET, COLETTE. *"Those" People: The Subculture of a Housing Project.* Contributions in Sociology, no. 10. Pp. xxiii, 293. Westport, Conn.: Greenwood, 1973. $11.50.

PHILLIPS, JOHN L. *Statistical Thinking: A Structural Approach.* Pp. xv, 124. San Francisco: W. H. Freeman, 1973. $5.95. Paperbound, $2.50.

PIERCE, ROY. *French Politics and Political Institutions.* 2nd ed. Pp. ix, 368. New York: Harper & Row, 1973. $3.50. Paperbound.

PIHL, MARSHALL R., ed. *Listening to Korea: A Korean Anthology.* Pp. vii, 249. New York: Praeger, 1973. $9.00.

PLANT, RAYMOND. *Hegel.* Pp. 214. Bloomington: Indiana University Press, 1973. $7.95.

POLLARD, STEWART M. L., ed. *Proudly Serving the Cause of Patriotism: An Anthology of Definitions of Patriotism.* Pp. 90. Washington, D.C.: Monumental Press, 1973. $2.00. Paperbound.

PORTER, JACK NUSAN. *Student Protest and the Technocratic Society: The Case of ROTC.* 2nd ed. Pp. x, 136. Milwaukee, Wis.: Zalonka Publications, 1973. $5.95. Paperbound, $2.95.

QUANBECK, ALTON H. and BARRY M. BLECHMAN. *Strategic Forces Issues for the Mid-*

Seventies. Studies in Defense Policy. Pp. vii, 94. Washington, D.C.: The Brookings Institution, 1973. $1.95. Paperbound.

RAMM, AGATHA. *Sir Robert Morier: Envoy and Ambassador in the Age of Imperialism 1876–1893.* Pp. 386. New York: Oxford University Press, 1973. $21.00.

RASMUSSEN, DAVID W. *Urban Economics.* Pp. vii, 196. New York: Harper & Row, 1973. $4.95. Paperbound.

RASMUSSEN, JOHN, ed. *Man in Isolation & Confinement.* Pp. vii, 330. Chicago: Aldine, 1973. $9.50.

REEDY, GEORGE E. *The Presidency in Flux.* Pp. 133. New York: Columbia University Press, 1973. $5.95.

REIMAN, JEFFREY H. *In Defense of Political Philosophy: A Reply to Robert Paul Wolff's In Defense of Anarchism.* Pp. xiii, 87. New York: Harper & Row, 1972. $6.00. Paperbound, $1.95.

REISSNER, WILL, ed. *Documents of the Fourth International: The Formative Years (1933–40).* Pp. 448. New York: Pathfinder Press, 1973. $10.00. Paperbound, $3.45.

REYNOLDS, LARRY T. and JAMES M. HENSLIN. *American Society: A Critical Analysis.* Pp. vii, 337. New York: David McKay, 1973. $3.95. Paperbound.

RICHARDS, PETER G. *The Backbenchers.* Pp. 248. London, England: Faber and Faber, 1973. $14.75.

RIESMAN, DAVID and VERNE A. STADTMAN, eds. *Academic Transformation: Seventeen Institutions under Pressure.* Pp. 489. New York: McGraw-Hill, 1973. $12.50.

ROBERTS, Albert R., ed. *Readings in Prison Education.* Pp. v, 415. Springfield, Ill.: Charles C Thomas, 1973. $15.95.

ROGERS, WILLIAM P. *United States Foreign Policy 1972.* Pp. 743. Washington, D.C.: Department of State, 1973. No price. Paperbound.

ROTH, PHILIP. *The Great American Novel.* Pp. 382. New York: Holt, Rinehart and Winston, 1973. $8.95.

RUBIN, LILLIAN B. *Busing & Backlash: White against White in an Urban School District.* Pp. 248. Berkeley, Cal.: University of California Press, 1972. $2.45. Paperbound.

RUSSETT, B. *No Clear and Present Danger.* Pp. 111. New York: Harper & Row, 1972. $6.00.

SATTERFIELD, ARCHIE. *Chilkoot Pass: Then and Now.* Pp. 183. Anchorage, Alaska: Alaska Northwest, 1973. $3.95. Paperbound.

SCHLESINGER, ARTHUR M., JR. ed. *History of U.S. Politics. Vol. 1: 1789–1860, vol. 2: 1860–1910, vol. 3: 1910–1945, vol. 4, 1945–1972.* Pp. 3,528. New York: R. R. Bowker, 1973. $135.00.

SCHNEIDER, LOUIS and CHARLES BONJEAN, eds. *The Idea of Culture in the Social Sciences.* Pp. vi, 149. Cambridge, England: At the University Press, 1973. $9.95. Paperbound, $2.95.

SCHUSTER, DEREK V. *Bad Blood Among Brothers: An Inside View Behind Today's Separatist Movements.* Pp. 253. New York: Vantage, 1972. $7.95.

SCHWARTZMAN, EDWARD. *Campaign Craftsmanship: A Professional's Guide to Campaigning for Elective Office.* Pp. 272. New York: Universe Books, 1973. $8.50. Paperbound, $3.95.

SCIENTIFIC AMERICAN. *Cities: Their Origin, Growth and Human Impact.* Pp. 297. San Francisco: W. H. Freeman, 1973. $12.00. Paperbound, $5.50.

SEAMAN, L. C. B. *Victorian England: Aspects og English and Imperial History 1837–1901.* Pp. vii, 484. New York: Barnes & Noble, 1973. $10.00. Paperbound, $5.00.

SILVERMAN, MARTIN G. *Disconcerting Issue: Meaning and Struggle in a Resettled Pacific Community.* Pp. ix, 362. Chicago: University of Chicago Press, 1971. No price.

SMITH, JAMES NOEL. *The Decline of Galveston Bay: A Profile of Government's Failure to Control Pollution in an Endangered American Estuary.* Pp. vii, 127. Washington, D.C.: The Conservation Foundation, 1972. $2.00. Paperbound.

SMITH, ROBERT FREEMAN. *The United States and Revolutionary Nationalism in Mexico, 1916–1932.* Pp. ix, 288. Chicago: The University of Chicago Press, 1972. $12.00.

SNYDER, LOUIS L. *The Dreyfus Case.* A Documentary History. Pp. vii, 414. New Brunswick, N.J.: Rutgers University Press, 1973. $17.50.

SPRAGENS, THOMAS A., JR. *The Politics of Motion: The World of Thomas Hobbes.* Pp. 234. Lexington: The University Press of Kentucky, 1973. $7.75.

STEIN, BRUNO and S. M. MILLER, eds. *Incentives and Planning in Social Policy.* Studies in Health, Education and Welfare. Pp. vii, 214. Chicago: Aldine, 1973. $6.00.

STERNLIEB, GEORGE. *The Urban Housing Dilemma: The Dynamics of New York City's Rent Controlled Housing.* Pp. 748. New Brunswick, N.J.: Rutgers University Center for Urban Policy Research, 1972. $20.00.

STEVENSON, T. H. *Politics and Government.* Pp. ix, 435. Totowa, N.J.: Littlefield, Adams, 1973. $2.95. Paperbound.

STONE, LAWRENCE. *The Causes of the English Revolution 1529–1642.* Pp. ix, 168. New York: Harper & Row, 1972. $2.95. Paperbound.

STORR, RICHARD J. *The Beginning of the Future: A Historical Approach to Graduate Education in the Arts and Science.* Pp. xiii, 99. New York: McGraw-Hill, 1973. $5.95.

SUMEK, LYLE, STEVEN CARTER and MARY ANN ALLARD, eds. *An Anthology for the National Conference on Managing the Environment..* Pp. v, 108. Washington, D.C.: International City Management Association, 1973. No price. Paperbound.

SWARTZBAUGH, RICHARD GREY. *The Mediator: His Strategy for Power.* Pp. viii, 133. Cape Canaveral, Florida: Howard Allen, 1973. $4.95.

SYLVESTER, SAWYER F., ed. *The Heritage of Modern Criminology.* Pp. vii, 184. Cambridge, Mass.: Schenkman, 1972. No price.

TILLEMA, HERBERT K. *Appeal to Force: American Military Intervention in the Era of Containment.* Pp. v, 269. New York: Thomas Y. Crowell, 1973. No price. Paperbound.

TOMLIN, E. W. F. *Japan.* Nations and Peoples Library. Pp. 288. New York: Walker, 1973. $8.50.

TUAN, KAILIN, ed. *Modern Insurance Theory and Education: Vol. 2, The Confused Period of Transition, 1950–1699.* Pp. vii, 621. Orange, N.J.: Varsity Press, 1972. No price. Paperbound.

TURNBULL, JOHN G., C. ARTHUR WILLIAMS, JR. and EARL F. CHEIT. Economic and Social Security. 4th ed. Pp. iii, 728. New York: The Ronald Press, 1973. No price.

TRIVERS, HOWARD. *Three Crises in American Foreign Affairs and a Continuing Revolution.* Pp. 220. Carbondale, Ill.: Southern Illinois University Press, 1972. $6.95.

TROTSKY, LEON. *Leon Trotsky on Britain.* Introduction by George Novak. Pp. 336. New York: Pathfinder, 1973. $8.95. Paper-bound, $3.45.

TRUDEAU, G. B. *But This War Had Such Promise: A Doonesbury Book.* Pp. 130. New York: Holt, Rinehart and Winston, 1973. $1.50. Paperbound.

ULLMAN, RICHARD H. *The Anglo-Soviet Accord.* Pp. vii, 509. Princeton, N.J.: Princeton University Press, 1973. $17.50.

ULMAN, LLOYD, ed. *Manpower Programs in the Policy Mix.* Pp. vii, 166. Baltimore, Md.: The Johns Hopkins Press, 1973. $8.50.

UNITED NATIONS ASSOCIATION OF THE UNITED STATES OF AMERICA. *Foreign Policy Decision Making: The New Dimensions.* Pp. 103. New York: UNA-USA, 1973. $1.00.

VON BECK, HAROLD. *We Are Right and They Are Wrong.* Pp. 186. New York: Vantage Press, 1966. $3.95.

WEINSTEIN, ALLEN and FRANK OTTO GATELL, eds. *American Negro Slavery: A Modern Reader.* 2nd ed. Pp. vii, 439. New York: Oxford University Press, 1973. $9.50.

WHEELER, HARVEY, ed. *Beyond the Punitive Society.* Pp. x, 274. San Francisco: W. H. Freeman, 1973. $8.95.

WILKIE, JAMES W. *Elitolore.* Latin American Studes vol. 22. Pp. 87. Los Angeles, Cal.: Latin American Center, University of California, 1973. No price. Paperbound.

WILLIAMS, T. DESMOND, ed. *Secret Societies in Ireland.* Pp. xi, 207. New York: Barnes and Noble, 1973. $7.50.

WILLIE, CHARLES V., BERNARD M. KRAMER and BERTRAM S. BROWN, eds. *Racism and Mental Health.* Pp. xi, 604. Pittsburgh: University of Pittsburgh Press, 1973. $12.95

WILSON, JOHN. *Introduction to Social Movements.* Pp. 384. New York: Basic Books, 1973. $10.00.

WINSTANLEY, GERRARD. *The Law of Freedom in a Platform: Or, True Magistracy Restored.* Studies in the Libertarian Utopian Traditions. Pp. 160. New York: Schocken Books, 1973. $12.00. Paperbound, $2.95.

WOGAMAN, J. PHILIP, ed. *The Population Crises and Moral Responsibility.* Pp. iii, 340. Washington, D.C.: Public Affairs Press, 1973. $7.50.

WOLFE, ALAN. *The Seamy Side of Democracy: Repression in America.* Pp. vii, 306. New York: David McKay, 1973. $7.95.

WORSLEY, PETER. *The Third World.* Nature of Human Series Society Series. Pp. ix, 373. Chicago: University of Chicago Press, 1973. $3.95. Paperbound.

YOUNG, DAYTON. *One More Chance: To End Nuclear Blackmail Without Holocaust.* Pp. 124. Jericho, N.Y.: Exposition Press, 1973. $4.50.

ZAMORA, MARIO D., J. MICHAEL MAHAR and HENRY ORENSTEIN, eds. *Themes in Culture.* Pp. iii, 424. Quezon City, Philippines: Kayumanggi, 1971. $10.00.

THE AAPSS

announces publication of

Language and Area Studies Review

by Richard D. Lambert

Monograph No. 17, October 1973

A study sponsored by the Social Science Research Council

Copies may be purchased from the Sales Department
of the American Academy at $4.00 each
3937 Chestnut Street, Phila., Pa. 19104

Kindly mention THE ANNALS *when writing to advertisers*

FEC

FACULTY EXCHANGE CENTER

BOX 1866 LANCASTER, PA. 17604

The FEC aims to make it possible for an interested faculty member to exchange position with a colleague from another institution either on this continent or overseas where instruction is in English. The Center will bring to the attention of its members the names of others interested in exchange through the publication of a catalog containing the names of the instructors and their institutions, their fields of specialization and the region where they would like to teach. The catalog will be made available to registered members only. The first F.E.C. Catalog, to be released this fall, will show a membership representing over 30 disciplines from over 100 colleges and universities from U.S., Canada, and seven countries overseas.

For more information write for FEC brochure and registration form; both appear on outer cover of the September '73 A.A.U.P. Bulletin. You may use the registration form appearing there or a copy of it.

The 4-Dollar, 5-Minute, Whole-Earth, Political Scientist's Computerized Dream:

An Individually Tailored Research Source List.

Preliminary bibliographies with enlightening speed: we've put on computer the author and title of every article ever printed in any of 183 political science journals published the world over, the obscure along with the well-known, since those journals began—more than 115,000 articles in all, going back to 1886. We'll search the file by computer for any topic you select, furnishing a bibliography individually tailored to your needs—up to 25 citations for only $4, or 50 for $5, and more at the same rate until the sources are exhausted. You can devote your time to the heart of the matter—the reading, thinking and writing involved in preparing your research paper, thesis, dissertation or monograph. Send for free details, or call us with an order. (Phone orders are filled at $6 for up to 25 citations, $7 for 50, plus C.O.D. postage.) Call toll free to place your order: **800-854-3379** (In California, call us collect at area code 714, 557-6308.)

Copyright September 1973, Nexus Corp.

NEXUS™
INFORMATION SERVICES
Department 603,
Bldg. 3, Suite 201, 3001 Red Hill Ave.,
Costa Mesa, California 92626

THE NEXUS CORPORATION

Rush details of computer reference service.

NAME

STREET ADDRESS

CITY   STATE   ZIP

INDEX

New

Justice in South Africa
Albie Sachs

This lucidly and concisely written book offers perhaps the best recent introduction to understanding the growth and present-day functioning of the South African legal system. Professor Sachs explores the role of the courts, traditional African adjudication, and leading lawyers and rebels such as Smuts, Gandhi, and Mandela.

Perspectives on Southern Africa, #12
LC: 72-97749   304 pages $9.00

Urbanization and Political Change
The Politics of Lagos, 1917–1967
Pauline H. Baker

This major study of the politics of tropical Africa's largest city examines the impact of urbanization on the distribution and exercise of influence within the Nigerian capital as it grew from a colonial town of 100,000 people to a metropolis with a population of over one and one quarter million.
LC: 70-162001   384 pages $15.00

The Politics of Labor Legislation in Japan
National-International Interaction
Ehud Harari

This first study of the interaction of labor policy at the local, national, and international levels examines a case of freedom of association within the International Labor Organization. Mr. Harari traces the issue against both the prewar and postwar backgrounds, explaining why union leaders appealed for ILO involvement at that particular time, why the ILO responded favorably, how it exerted pressure on the Japanese government, and what considerations affected the government.
LC: 72-78945   250 pages $10.00

The French Budgetary Process
Guy Lord

"The best new description of budgeting in any country. He tells you how the process works, and he convinces you it works the way he says it does."—*Aron Wildavsky*   LC: 70-186113   256 pages $12.50

Prophet of Community
The Romantic Socialism of Gustav Landauer
Eugene Lunn

Gustav Landauer—literary critic, mystical philosopher, and left-wing activist—was Germany's major anarchist thinker of the beginning of the 20th Century. In this full-scale intellectual biography, Mr. Lunn depicts the evolution of Landauer's social thought and provides a background for a fresh examination of the intellectual cross-currents of the Wilhelmian era.   LC: 70-186105   352 pages $13.75

from California

University of California Press • Berkeley 94720

Kindly mention THE ANNALS *when writing to advertisers*

New from Columbia

THE PRESIDENCY IN FLUX
GEORGE E. REEDY

An extraordinarily timely new book by the author of *The Twilight of the Presidency*.

"[*The Presidency in Flux*] is rich in relevance and right on target in its prognostications."—John Barkham, *Barkham Reviews*

"This thoughtful discussion of the modern presidency, its isolation, its arrogance, its designation of all but one as servants, could be a diagnosis of the malignancy that is Watergate. It should be 'must' reading for those truly concerned with the future of the nation—if it is to be one possessing integrity."—William Flynn, *San Francisco Examiner* $5.95

PEARL HARBOR AS HISTORY
Japanese-American Relations, 1931–1941
DOROTHY BORG AND SHUMPEI OKAMOTO, EDITORS

Papers prepared by Japanese and American scholars, examining the part played by government and non-governmental institutions in the making of foreign policy in Japan and the United States during a crucial decade.
Studies of the East Asian Institute $25.00

Now available in paperback:

THE LATIN AMERICAN TRADITION
Essays on the Unity and the Diversity of Latin American Culture
CHARLES WAGLEY

Aiming at the removal of barriers to understanding, the essays in this volume explain the Latin American culture and its regional/internal subcultures for Anglo-Americans.
                                                                       $3.95

AFRICAN ELITE
The Big Men of a Small Town
JOAN VINCENT

Based on field work in Teso, Uganda, this book is invaluable for its distinction of method in capturing processes of change in a rural community presently made up of 19 different ethnic groups. $4.00

 COLUMBIA UNIVERSITY PRESS

Address for orders: 136 South Broadway, Irvington, New York 10533

The American Academy of Political and Social Science

3937 Chestnut Street   Philadelphia, Pennsylvania 19104

Board of Directors

NORMAN D. PALMER
HOWARD C. PETERSEN
WALTER M. PHILLIPS
PAUL R. ANDERSON
KARL R. BOPP
ELMER B. STAATS

MARVIN E. WOLFGANG
LEE BENSON
A. LEON HIGGINBOTHAM, JR.
RICHARD D. LAMBERT
R. JEAN BROWNLEE
COVEY T. OLIVER

Officers

President
MARVIN E. WOLFGANG

JAMES C. CHARLESWORTH, *President Emeritus*

Vice-Presidents
RICHARD D. LAMBERT, *First Vice-President*

JOSEPH S. CLARK   CLARK KERR

STEPHEN B. SWEENEY, *First Vice-President Emeritus*

Secretary   Treasurer   Counsel
NORMAN D. PALMER   HOWARD C. PETERSEN   HENRY W. SAWYER, III

Editors, THE ANNALS
RICHARD D. LAMBERT, *Editor*   ALAN W. HESTON, *Assistant Editor*

THORSTEN SELLIN, *Editor Emeritus*

Business Manager
INGEBORG HESSLER

Origin and Purpose. The Academy was organized December 14, 1889, to promote the progress of political and social science, especially through publications and meetings. The Academy does not take sides in controverted questions, but seeks to gather and present reliable information to assist the public in forming an intelligent and accurate judgment.

Meetings. The Academy holds an annual meeting in the spring extending over two days.

Publications. THE ANNALS is the bimonthly publication of The Academy. Each issue contains articles on some prominent social or political problem, written at the invitation of the editors. Also, monographs are published from time to time, numbers of which are distributed to pertinent professional organizations. These volumes constitute important reference works on the topics with which they deal, and they are extensively cited by authorities throughout the United States and abroad. The papers presented at the meetings of The Academy are included in THE ANNALS.

Membership. Each member of The Academy receives THE ANNALS and may attend the meetings of The Academy. Annual dues for individuals are $12.00 (for clothbound copies $16.00 per year). A life membership is $500. All payments are to be made in United States dollars.

Libraries and other institutions may receive THE ANNALS paperbound at a cost of $15.00 per year, or clothbound at $20.00 per year. Add $1.00 to above rates for membership outside U.S.A.

Single copies of THE ANNALS may be obtained by nonmembers of The Academy for $3.00 ($4.00 clothbound) and by members for $2.50 ($3.50 clothbound). A discount to members of 5 per cent is allowed on orders for 10 to 24 copies of any one issue, and of 10 per cent on orders for 25 or more copies. These discounts apply only when orders are placed directly with The Academy and not through agencies. The price to all bookstores and to all dealers is $3.00 per copy less 20 per cent, with no quantity discount. It is urged that payment be sent with each order. This will save the buyer the shipping charge and save The Academy the cost of carrying accounts and sending statements. Monographs may be purchased for $4.00 by individuals and $5.00 by institutions, with proportionate discounts.

All correspondence concerning The Academy or THE ANNALS should be addressed to the Academy offices, 3937 Chestnut Street, Philadelphia, Pa. 19104.